RAGNAROK

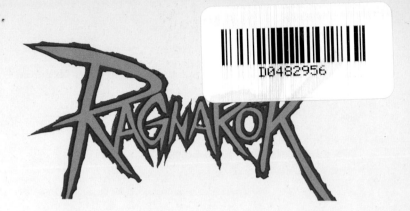

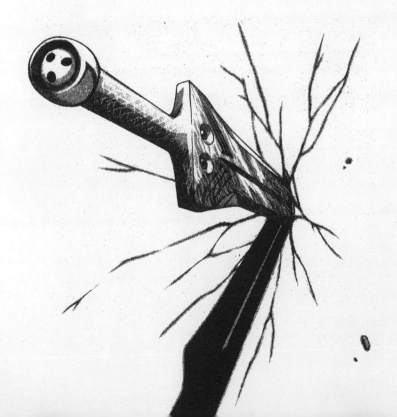

100% Authentic Manga Available from TOKYOPOP®:

COWBOY BEBOP
All-new adventures of interstellar bounty hunting, based on the hit anime seen on Cartoon Network.

MARMALADE BOY
A tangled teen romance for the new millennium.

REAL BOUT HIGH SCHOOL
At Daimon High, teachers don't break up fights...they grade them.

MARS
Biker Rei and artist Kira are as different as night and day, but fate binds them in this angst-filled romance.

GTO
Biker gang member Onizuka is going back to school...as a teacher!

CHOBITS
In the future, boys will be boys and girls will be...robots? The newest hit series from CLAMP!

SKULL MAN
They took his family. They took his face. They took his soul. Now, he's going to take his revenge.

DRAGON KNIGHTS
Part dragon, part knight, ALL glam. The most inept knights on the block are out to kick some demon butt.

INITIAL D
Delivery boy Tak has a gift for driving, but can he compete in the high-stakes world of street racing?

PARADISE KISS
High fashion and deep passion collide in this hot new shojo series!

KODOCHA: Sana's Stage
There's a rumble in the jungle gym when child star Sana Kurata and bully Akito Hayama collide.

ANGELIC LAYER
In the future, the most popular game is Angelic Layer, where hand-raised robots battle for supremacy.

LOVE HINA
Can Keitaro handle living in a dorm with five cute girls...and still make it through school?

Also Available from TOKYOPOP®:

PRIEST
The quick and the undead in one macabre manga.

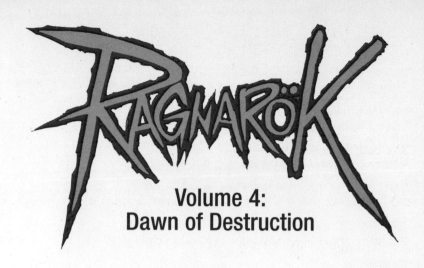

Volume 4:
Dawn of Destruction

By
Myung-Jin Lee

English Version
by
Richard A. Knaak

Los Angeles • Tokyo

Senior Editor - Jake Forbes
Copy Editors - Bryce Coleman, Paul Morrissey
Graphic Designer - Anna Kernbaum
Retouch & Lettering - Monalisa J.de Asis

Production Manager - Mario Rodriguez
Art Director - Matt Alford
VP Production - Ron Klamert
Publisher - Stuart Levy

email: editor@TOKYOPOP.com
Come visit us online at www.TOKYOPOP.com

A  Manga

TOKYOPOP® is an imprint of Mixx Entertainment, Inc.
5900 Wilshire Blvd., Ste. 2000, Los Angeles, CA 90036

ISBN: 1-931514-76-3

First TOKYOPOP Printing: November 2002

10 9 8 7 6 5 4 3 2

Manufactured in the USA.

Bonus Supplement

Ragnarök

Players Handbook

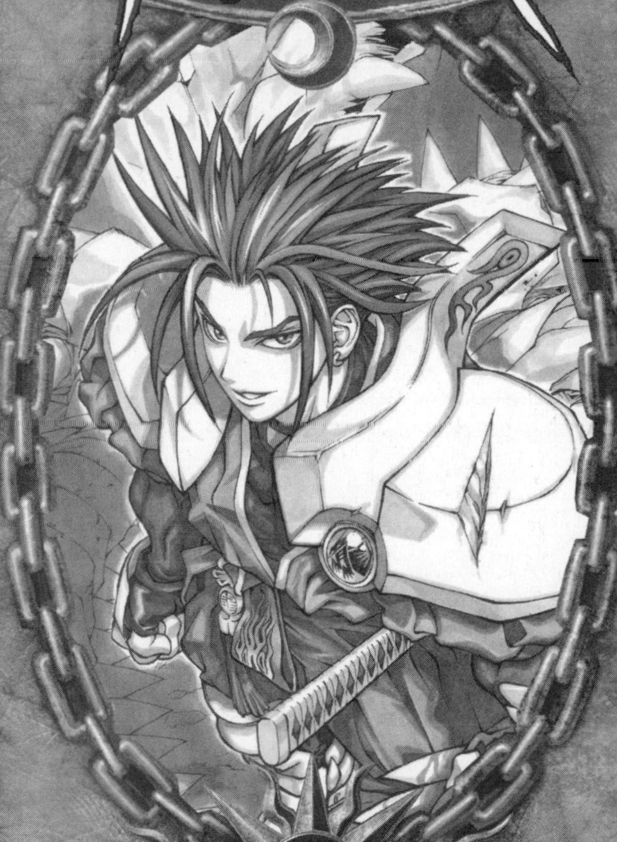

A complete guide to the characters
and story for novice adventurers.

HEROES

NOTE: THE FOLLOWING STATISTICS ARE INSPIRED BY THE MANGA, BUT DO NOT REFLECT ANY OFFICIAL RAGNAROK RPG. - EDITOR

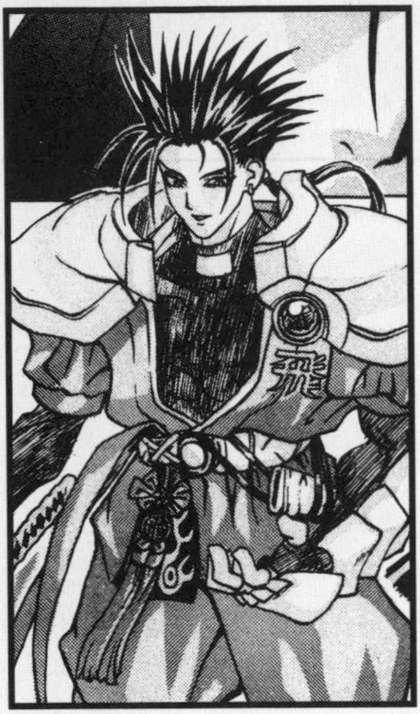

NAME: Chaos
Class: Rune Knight
Level: 9 (level up!)
Alignment: Chaotic Good
STR: 17
DEX: 10
CON: 15
INT: 12
WIS: 14
CHR: 16

Equipment:
Vision- Enchanted sword- STR +2

Rune Armor- AC -4, 20% bonus saving throw vs. magical attacks.

Notes:
The reincarnation of the fallen god Balder, Chaos has been told by his divine mother Frigg that the fate of the world rests in his hands. He now seeks "He who is both human and not."

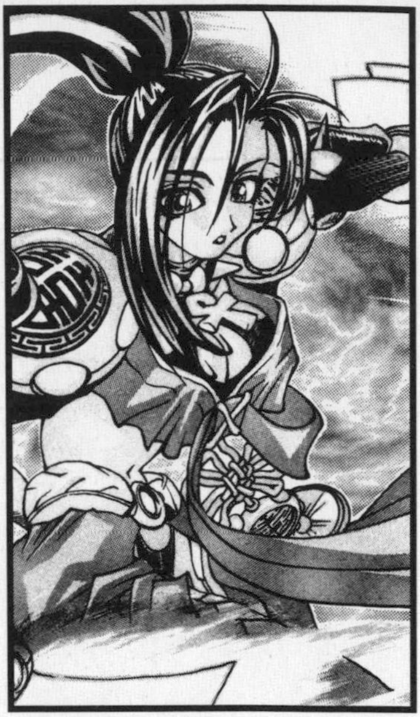

NAME: Iris Irine
Class: Cleric
Level: 5 (level up!)
Alignment: Lawful Good
STR: 7
DEX: 12
CON: 9
INT: 13
WIS: 16
CHR: 16

Equipment:
Chernryongdo- Enchanted dagger- STR +1, DEX +1, 1D4 damage if anyone but her touches it.

Irine Family Armor- AC -5, WIS +1

Notes:
Iris would have become the new leader of the city of Fayon... that is if it weren't destroyed by her sister, the Valkyrie Sara Irine. She now follows her close friend Chaos.

HEROES

NAME: Fenris Fenrir
Class: Warlock
Level: 9
Alignment: Neutral Good
STR: 14
DEX: 15
CON: 13
INT: 16
WIS: 12
CHR: 14

Equipment:
Psychic Medallion: Magic compass which leads its bearer to whatever his or her heart most desires.

Laevatein, Rod of Destruction- STR+1, extends to staff on command.

Notes:
The reincarnation of the Wolf God, Fenris helped Chaos to realize his identity. She now follows him on his quest.

NAME: Loki
Class: Assassin
Level: 9 (level up!)
Alignment: Lawful Neutral
STR: 14
DEX: 18
CON: 12
INT: 12
WIS: 14
CHR: 10

Equipment:
Sword of Shadows: + 4 to hit, damage +2

Bone Armor: AC -5, STR +2

Notes:
Greatest of the Assassins, Loki's anonymity is a testament to his skill at going unseen. His ability to keep a level head under stress makes him ideal for leading assault teams.

ENEMIES

NAME: Sara Irine
Class: Valkyrie
Level: 7
Alignment: Chaotic Neutral
STR: 14
DEX: 12
CON: 13
INT: 14
WIS: 15
CHR: 17

Equipment:
Haeryongdo, Sword of Retribution-
STR+2

Enchanted Parchments x 24

Notes:
One of the 12 Valkyries of Valhalla,
Sara Irine was sent to prevent Fenris
from completing her quest. After the
beholders spared her life at Fayon,
she was transported to a place yet
unkonwn.

NAME: Skurai
Class: Cursed Prosecutor
Level: 13 (level up!)
Alignment: Chaotic Evil
STR: 17
DEX: 16
CON: 19
INT: 15
WIS: 8
CHR: 12

Equipment:
Talatusu- Cursed sword- STR+2, HP
+12- cannot be discarded unless it
tastes the blood it is looking for.

Notes:
Skurai follows the will of his sword,
Talatsu, who seeks the one blood that
will quench his thirst. After meeting
Chaos at Fayon, he now seeks the
Rune Knight's blood.

NPC'S

Muninn and Huginn

Assassins

Odin's Beholders, these messengers can take the form of crows. They seem to be manipulating events, but to what end remains a mystery.

The ancient order of Assassins have maintained the balance of power in Midgard for centuries. A truly neutral organization, when any one group tips the scales with bloodshed, the Assassins repay in kind.

The story so far...

As days become short and the chill of winter sets upon our land, let us gather round and hear a tale of heroes and villains from an ancient land. Perhaps the flames of battle and the burning hearts of the vengeful can provide you some warmth in these cold times. This being the fourth installment of an epic story, let me remind you of what events have landed our players in their current situations.

1,000 years ago a war was waged between men, gods and demons for the fate of the world—the battle was called Ragnarok. Asgard did not fall and the fates of the mortal races are still in the hands of the god. As our story begins, Balder and Fenris, who died fighting to end the age of the gods, have been reborn in human form. Fenris is now a beautiful warlock and Balder resides in the body of the rune knight, Chaos, who has no knowledge of his divine past. The goddess Freya, who now rules Asgard, has sent her Valkyries to eliminate the two.

Another warrior hunts Balder – Skurai, the Cursed Prosecutor. He tracked the scent of a powerful blood to Chaos's hometown, Fayon, just as the city was under attack by the Valkyrie, Sara Irine. Chaos summoned the great dragon Nidhogg, proving his divine heritage, and defeating Sara and Skurai. Balder's mother, Frigg, visits Chaos and his companions, telling him that he is the only one capable of saving the world. His first task is to seek out "He who is both human and not."

Unbeknownst to Chaos, Skurai and Sara Irene were spared from death by agents of the gods. Skurai made his way to the Assassins' Guild, the sacred home of the ancient order of Assassins, in search of more powerful blood to quench his cursed swords thirst. The elite members of the order were on assignment, executing a corrupt follower of the demon Surt, when Skurai attacked. With its defenses lowered, the town was reduced to rubble and every Assassin slain. As the sun rises on our next chapter, the blood will flow once more in Ragnarok Vol. 4: Dawn of Destruction.

TOKYOPOP®

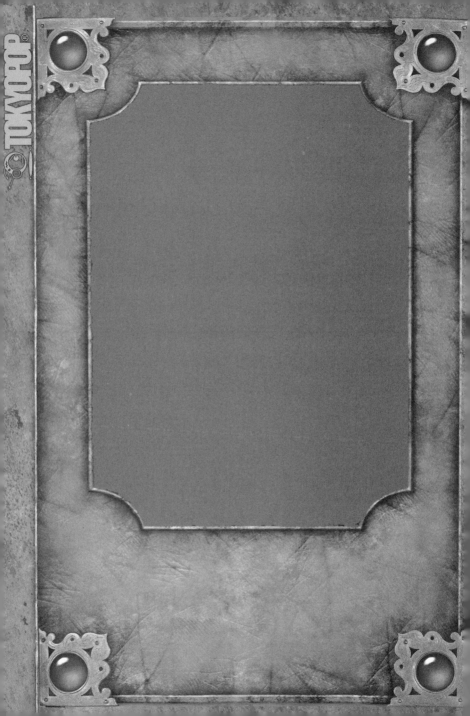

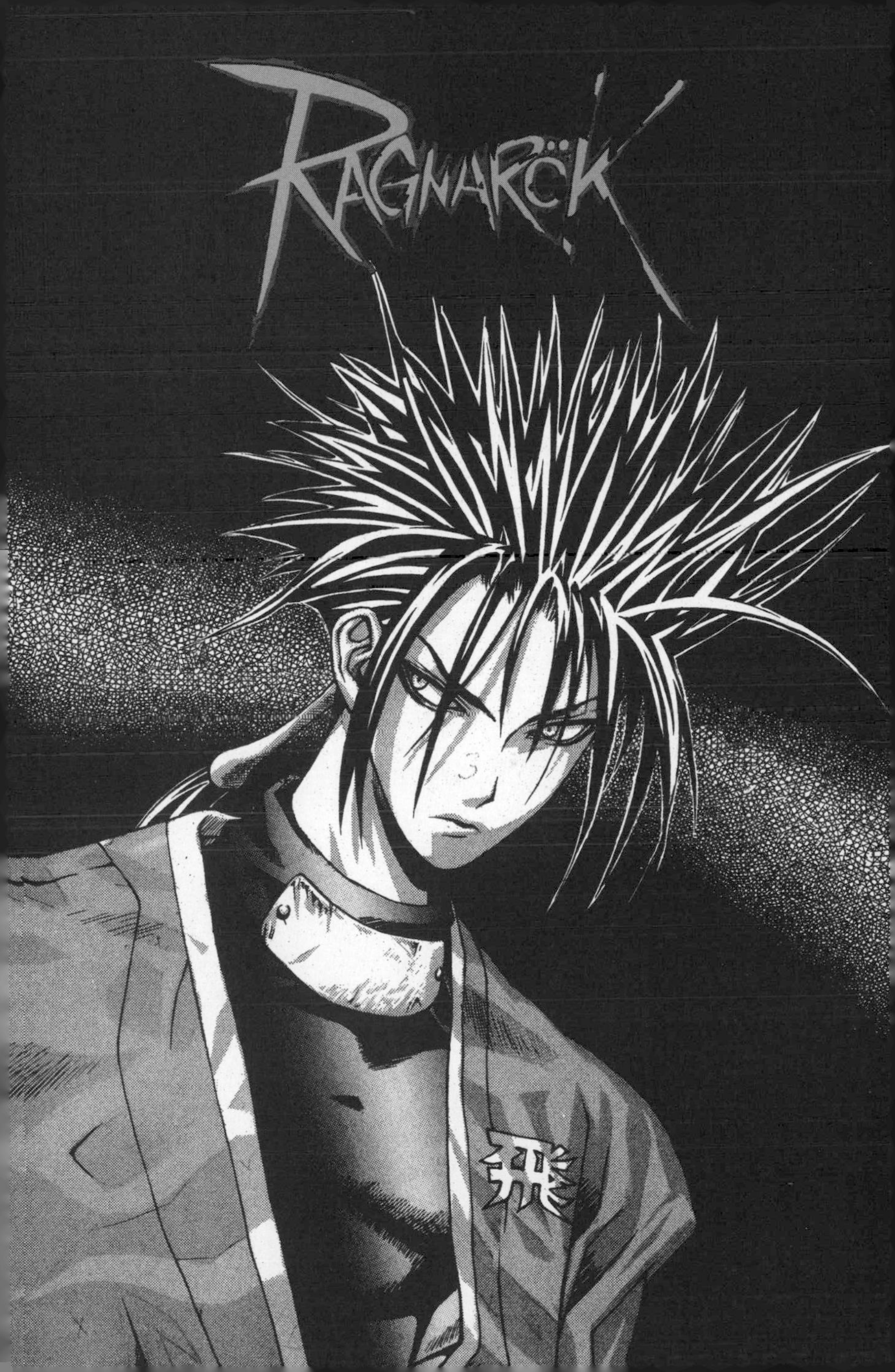
RAGNARÖK
飛

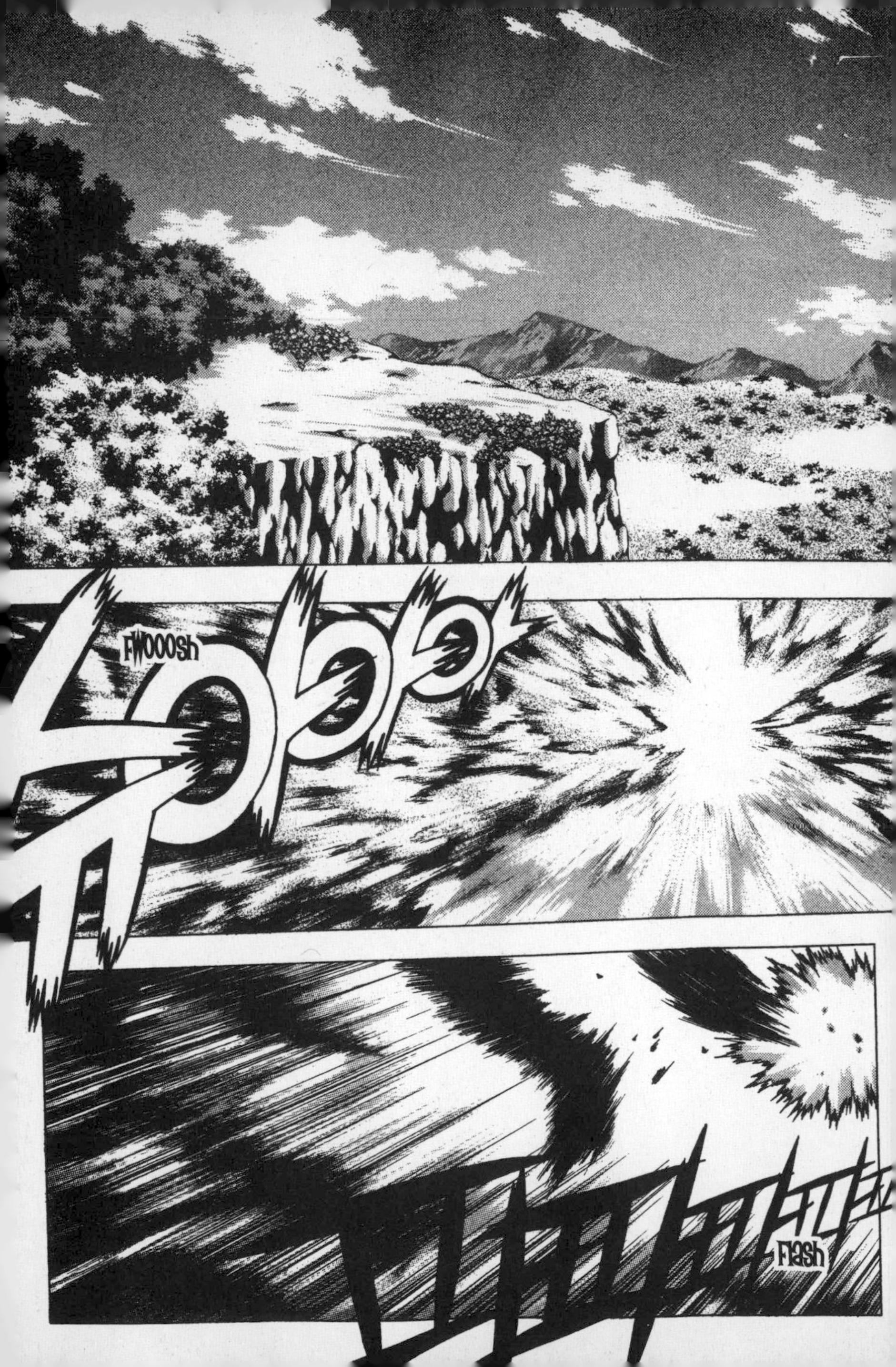
FWOOOSH
FLASH

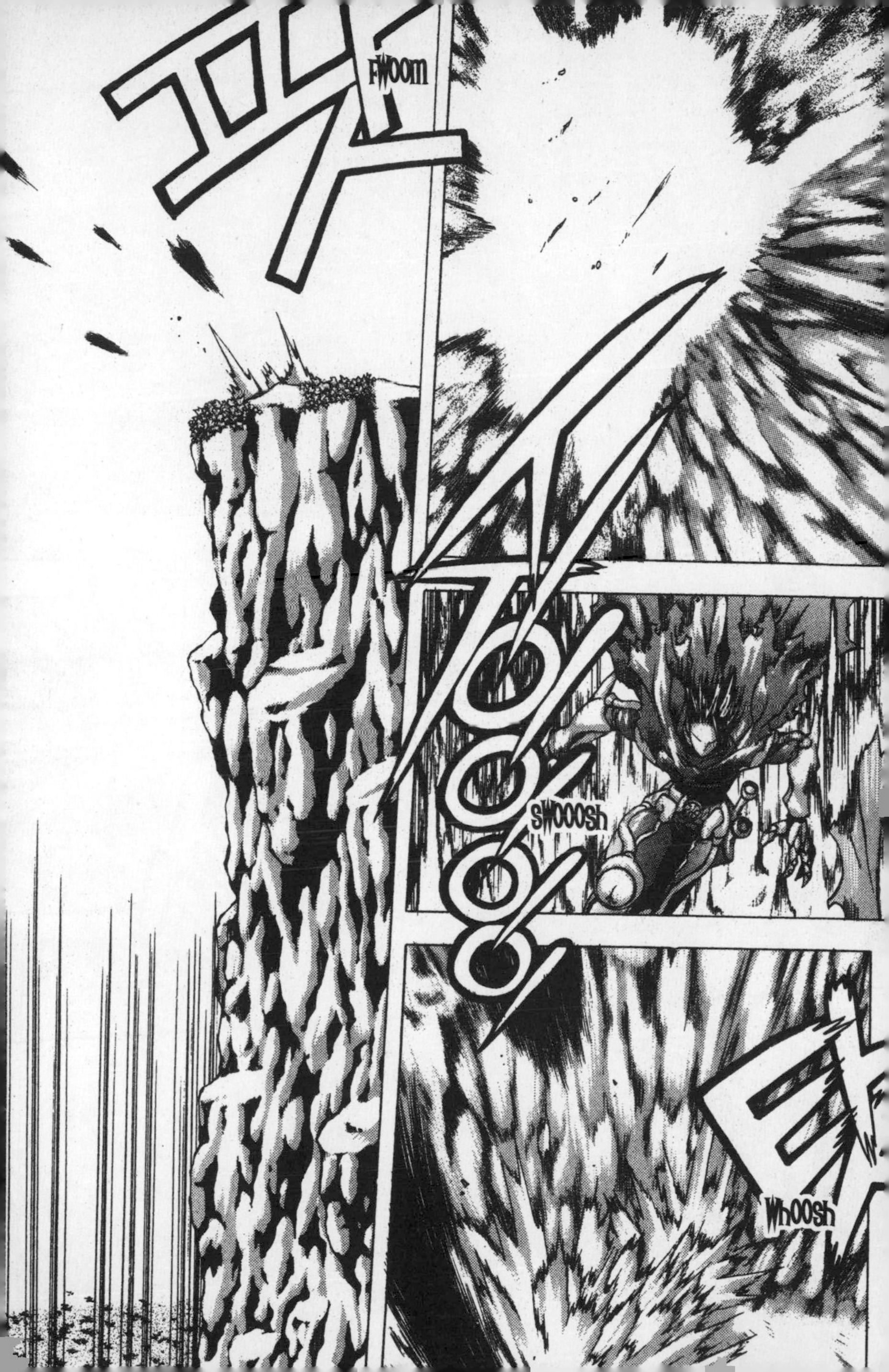
FWOOM
SWOOOSH
WHOOSH

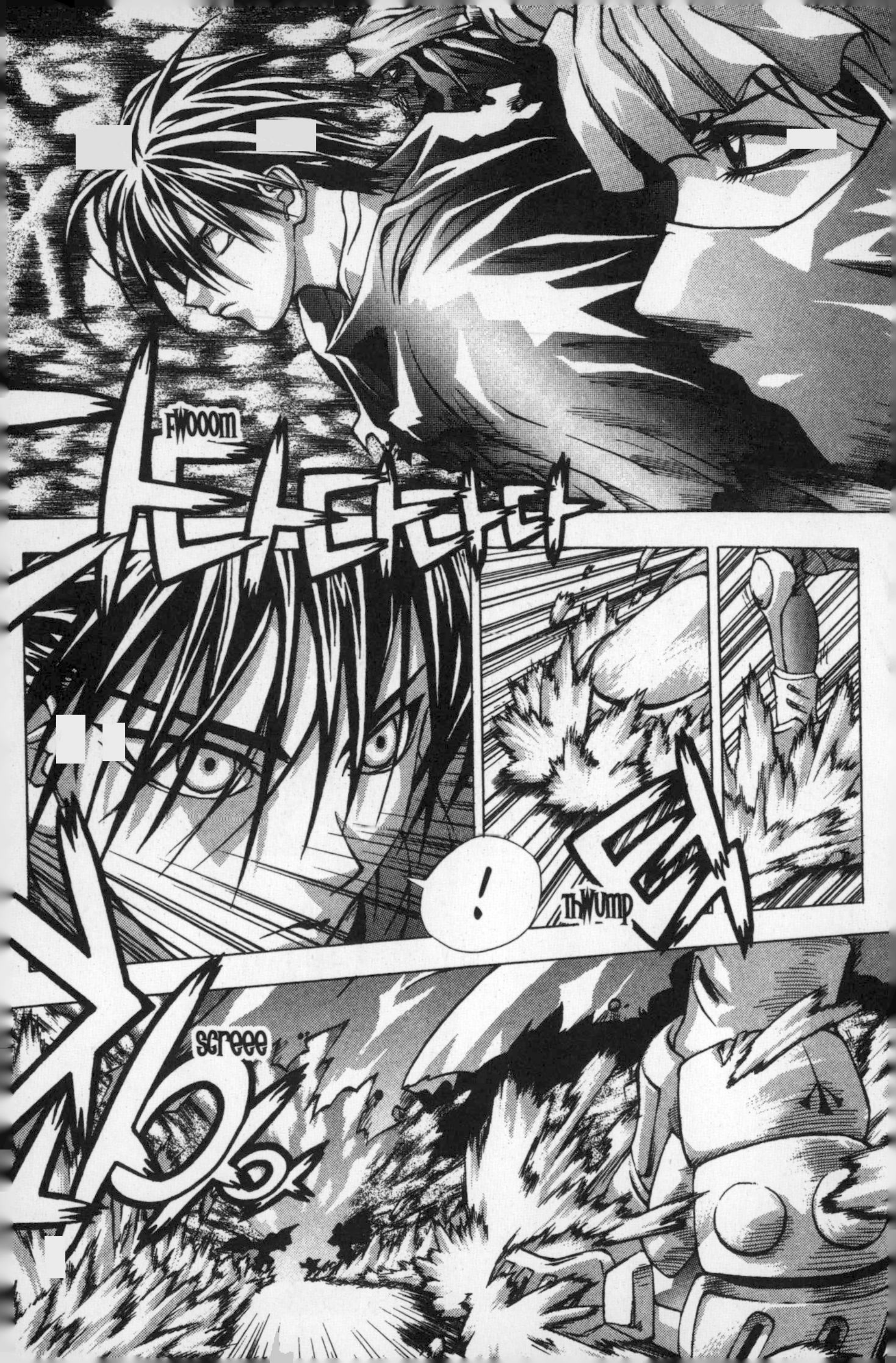
FWOOOM
!
ThWUMP
screee

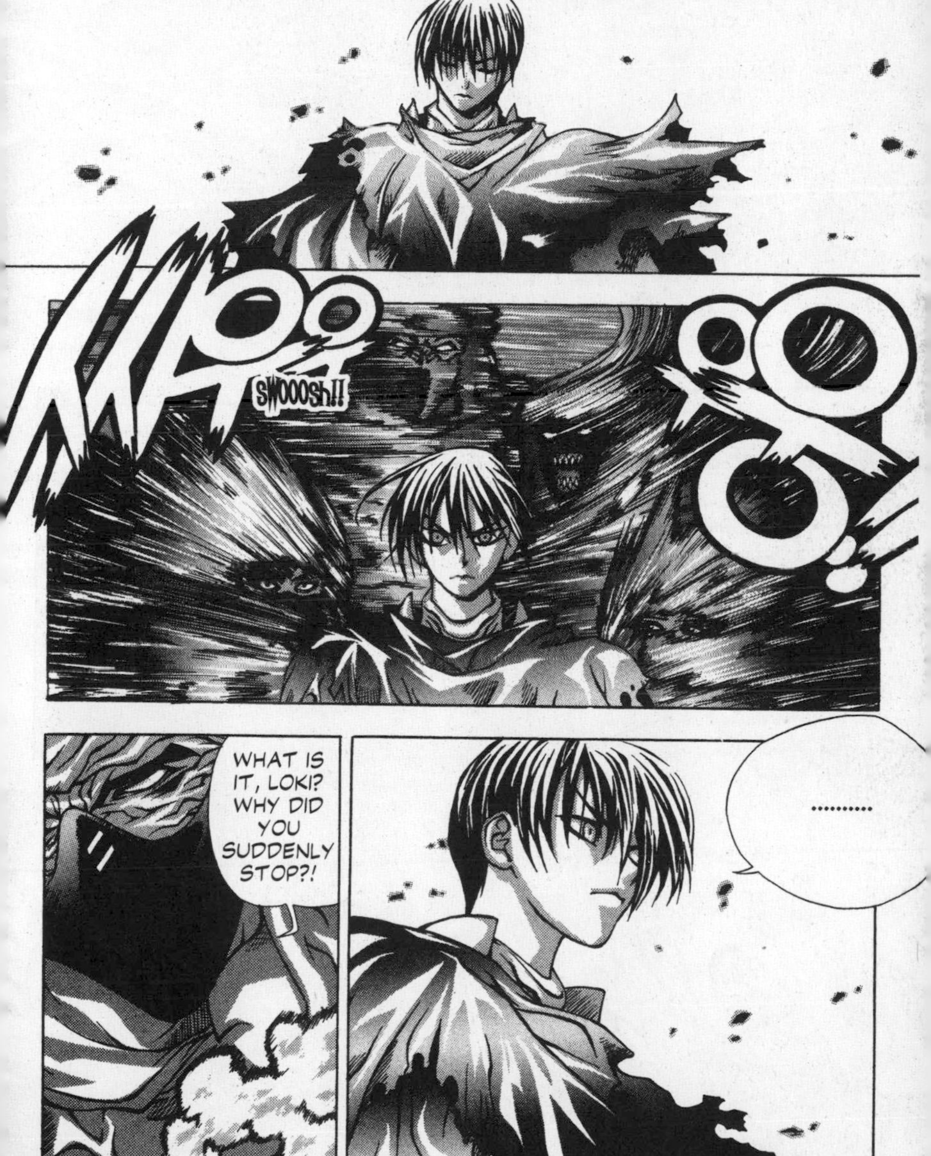
SWOOOSH!!
WHAT IS IT, LOKI? WHY DID YOU SUDDENLY STOP?!
....

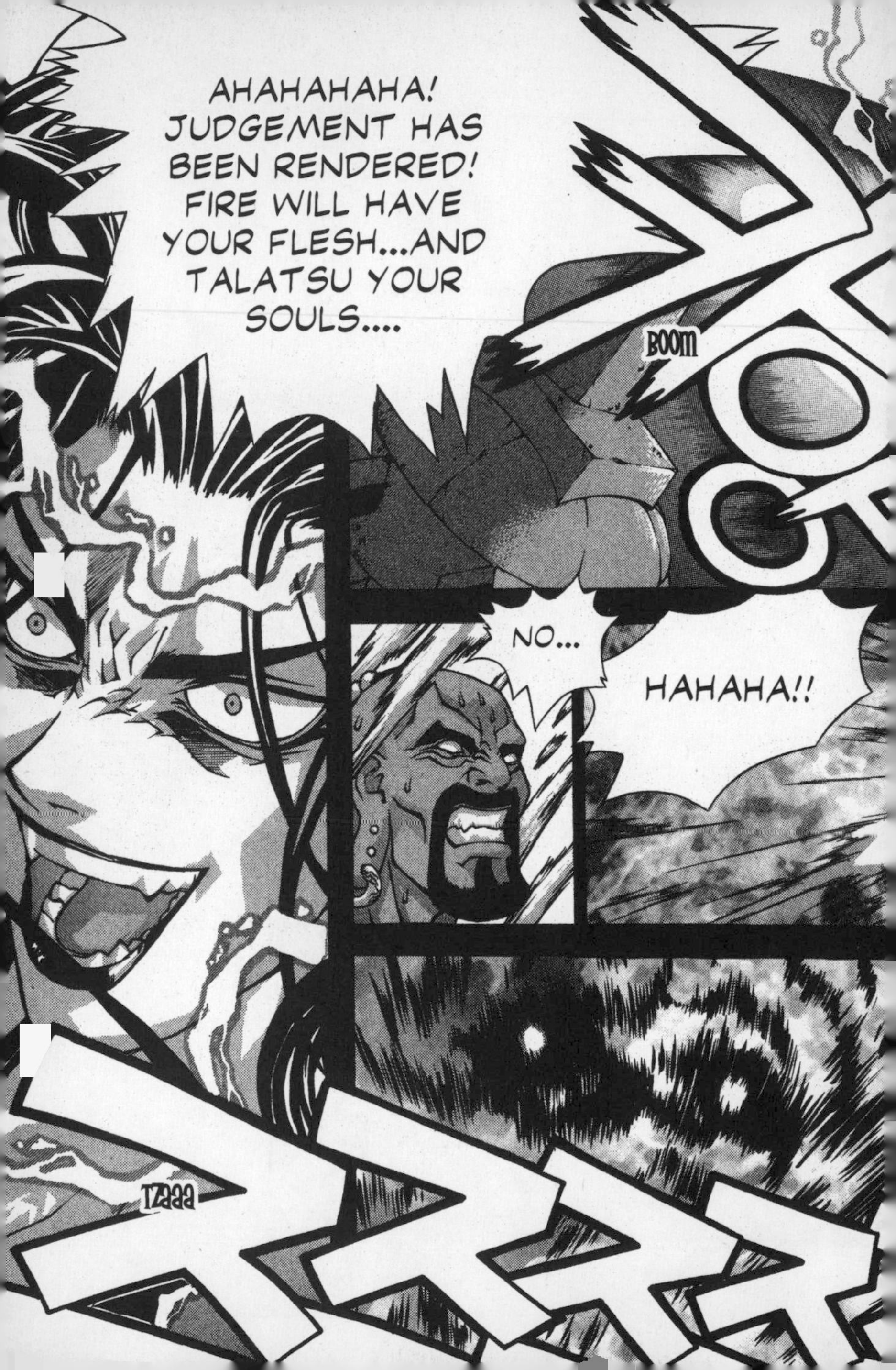
AHAHAHAHA! JUDGEMENT HAS BEEN RENDERED! FIRE WILL HAVE YOUR FLESH...AND TALATSU YOUR SOULS....
BOOM
NO...
HAHAHA!!
TZAAA

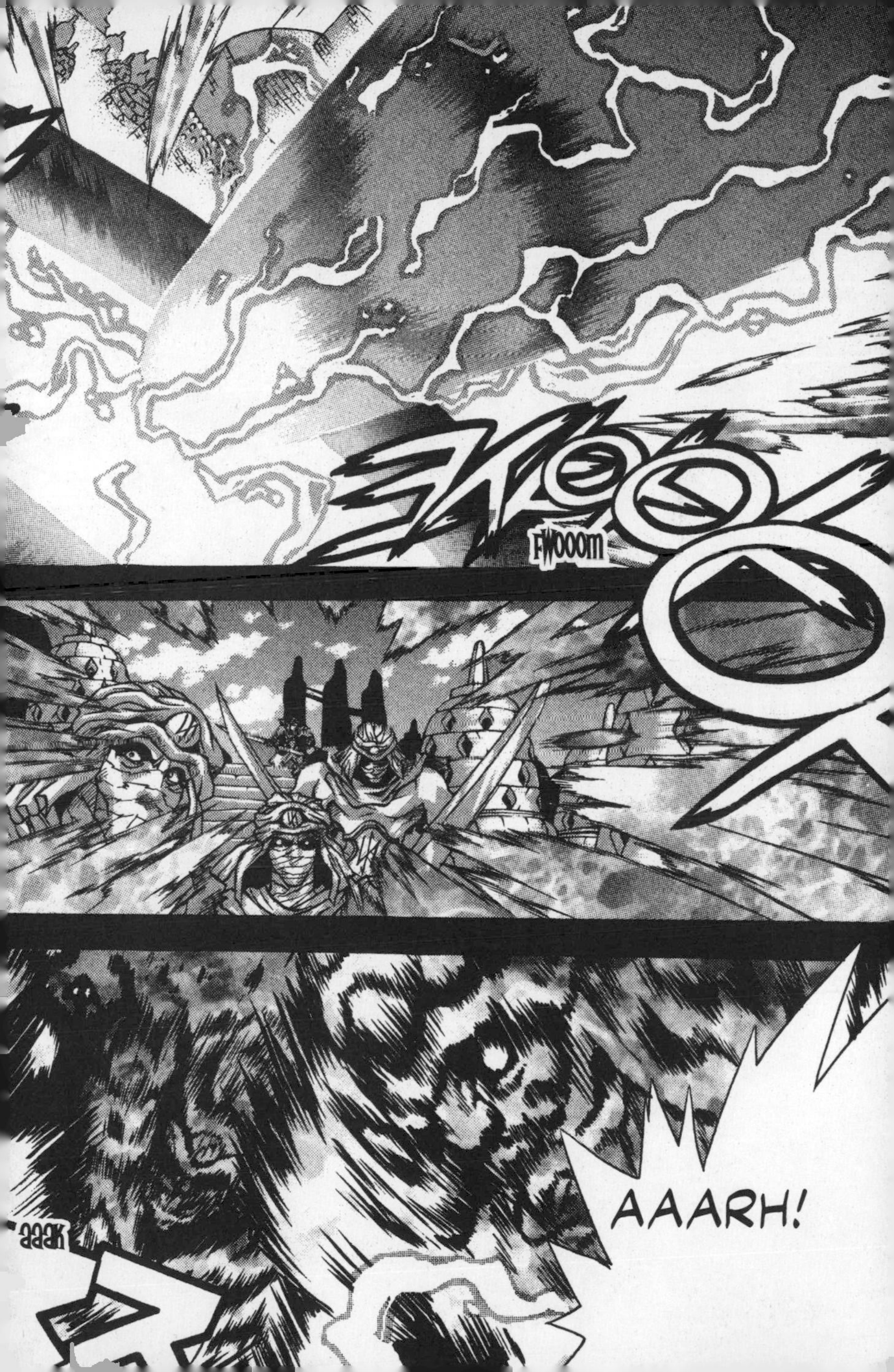
FWOOOM
AAARH!
aaak

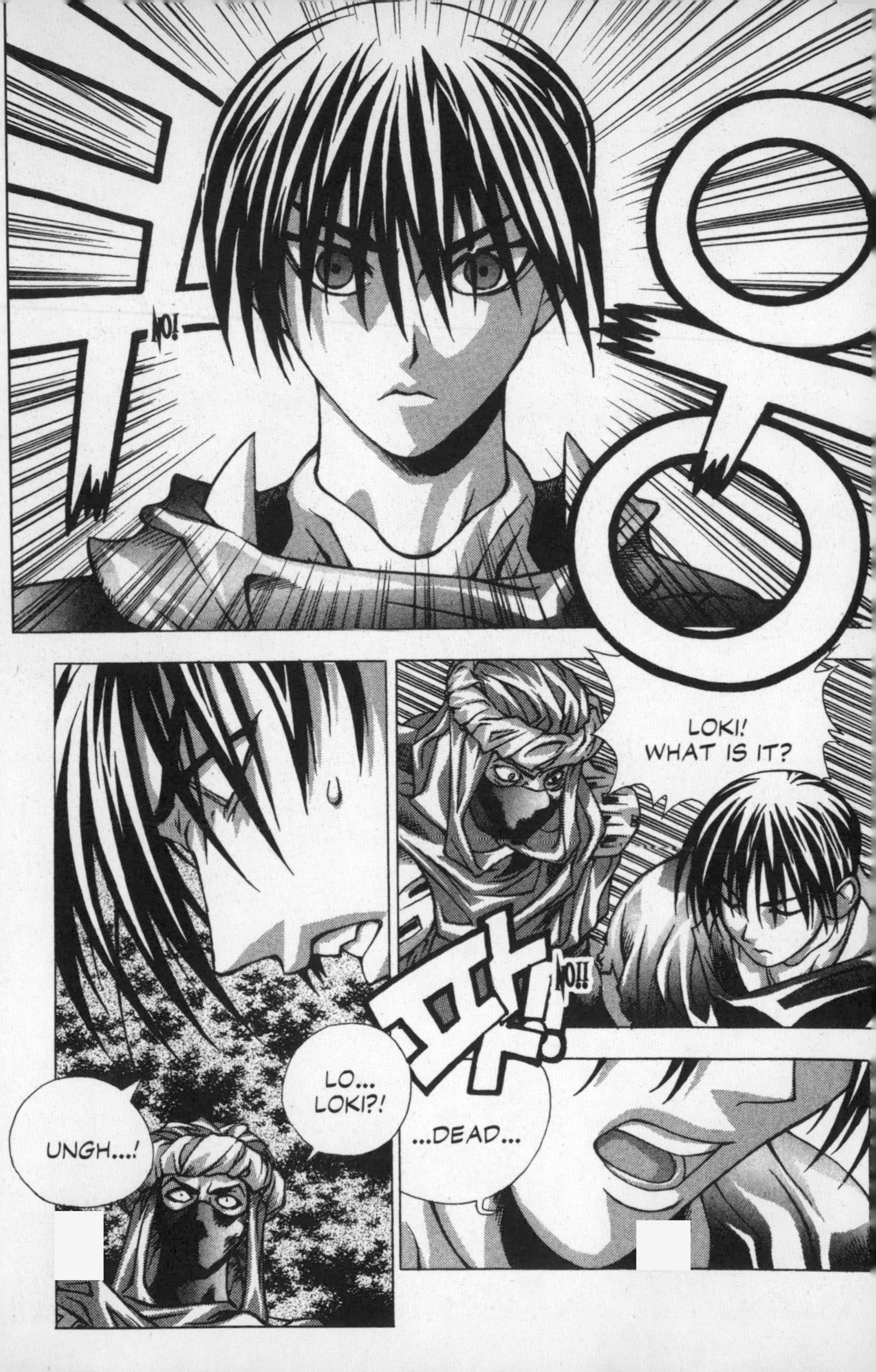
NO!
UNGH...!
LO... LOKI?!
LOKI! WHAT IS IT?
NO!!
...DEAD...

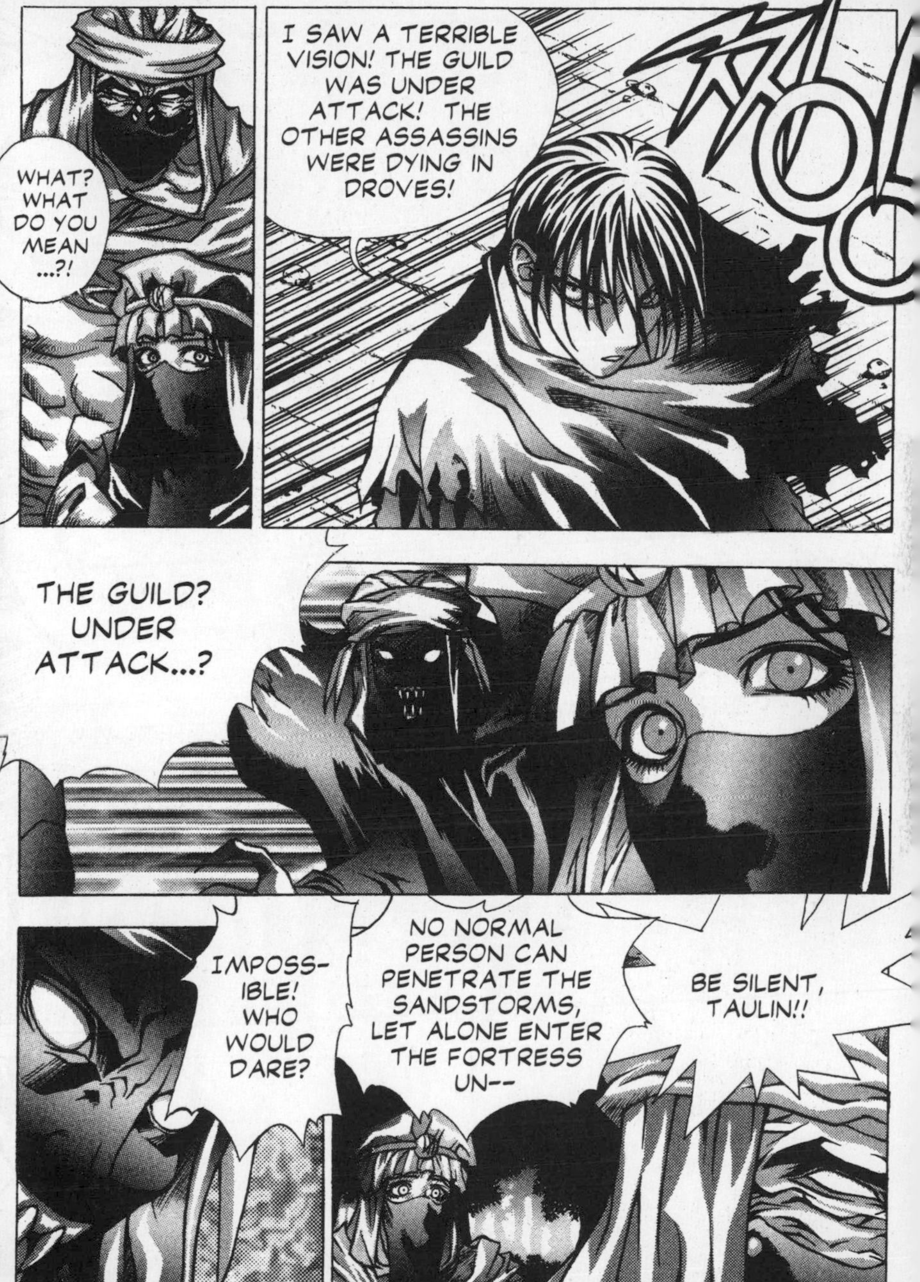
WHAT? WHAT DO YOU MEAN ...?!
I SAW A TERRIBLE VISION! THE GUILD WAS UNDER ATTACK! THE OTHER ASSASSINS WERE DYING IN DROVES!
THE GUILD? UNDER ATTACK...?
IMPOSS-IBLE! WHO WOULD DARE?
NO NORMAL PERSON CAN PENETRATE THE SANDSTORMS, LET ALONE ENTER THE FORTRESS UN--
BE SILENT, TAULIN!!

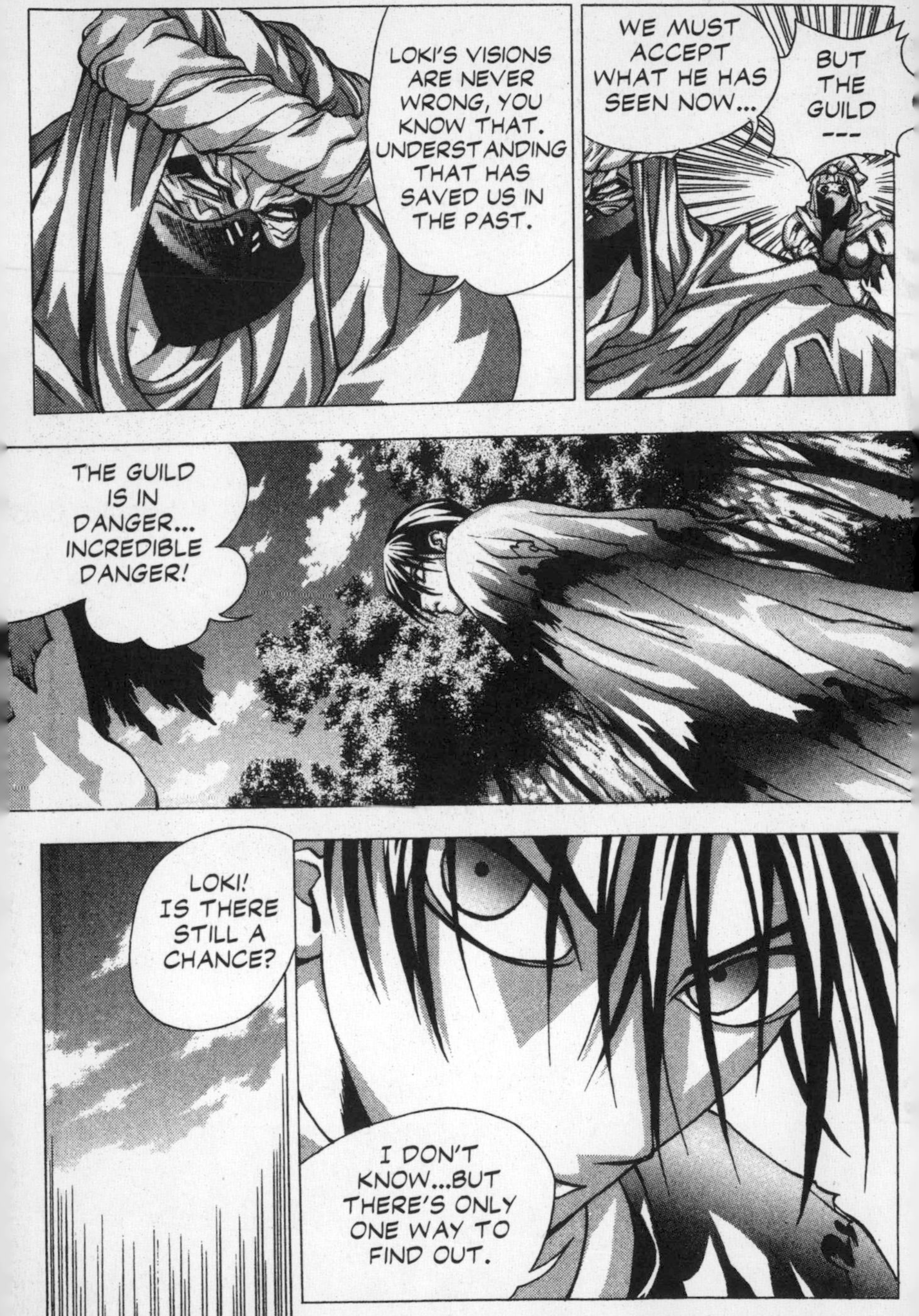
LOKI'S VISIONS ARE NEVER WRONG, YOU KNOW THAT. UNDERSTANDING THAT HAS SAVED US IN THE PAST.
WE MUST ACCEPT WHAT HE HAS SEEN NOW...
BUT THE GUILD ---
THE GUILD IS IN DANGER... INCREDIBLE DANGER!
LOKI! IS THERE STILL A CHANCE?
I DON'T KNOW...BUT THERE'S ONLY ONE WAY TO FIND OUT.

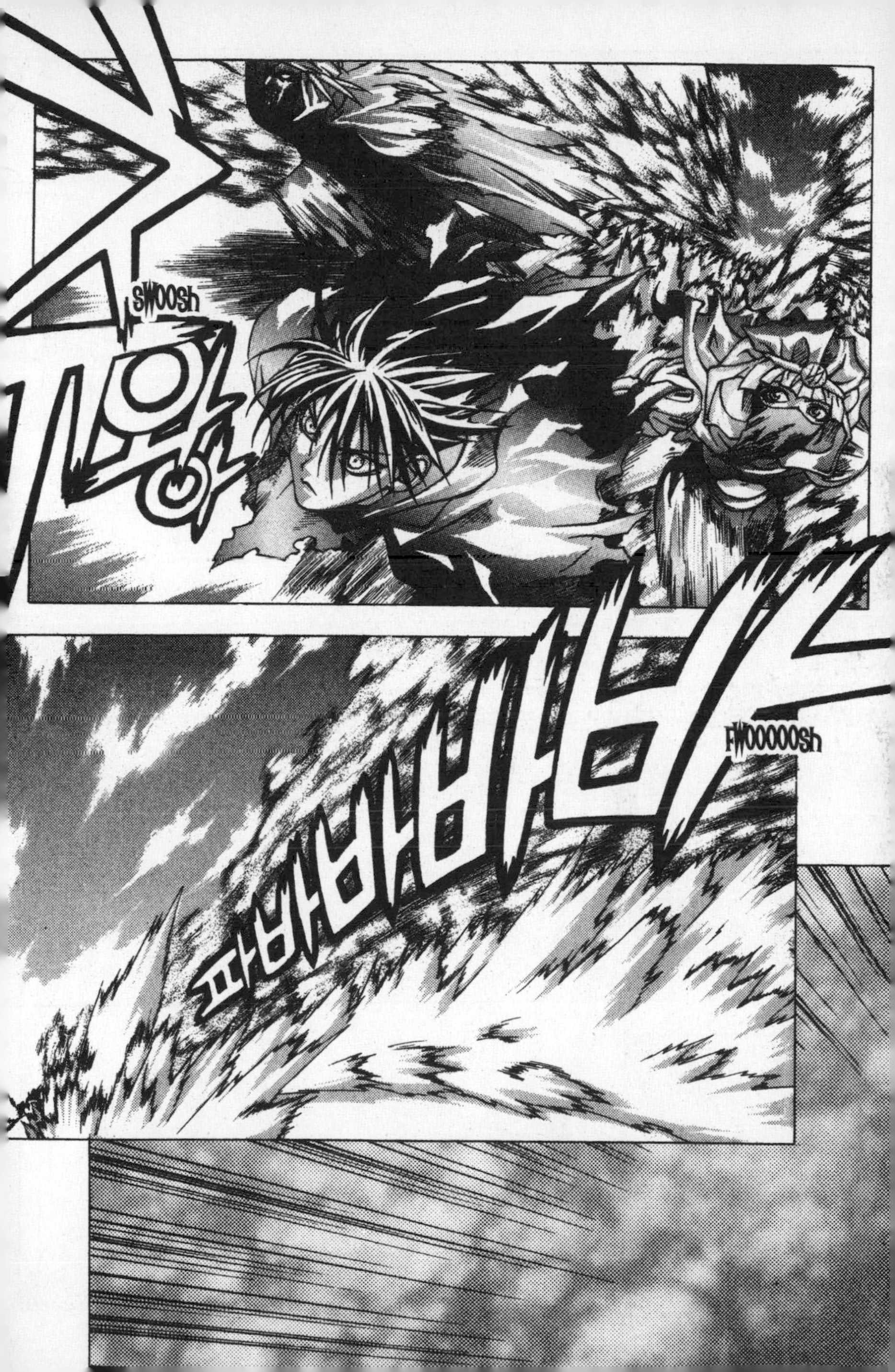
SWOOSH
FWOOOOOSH

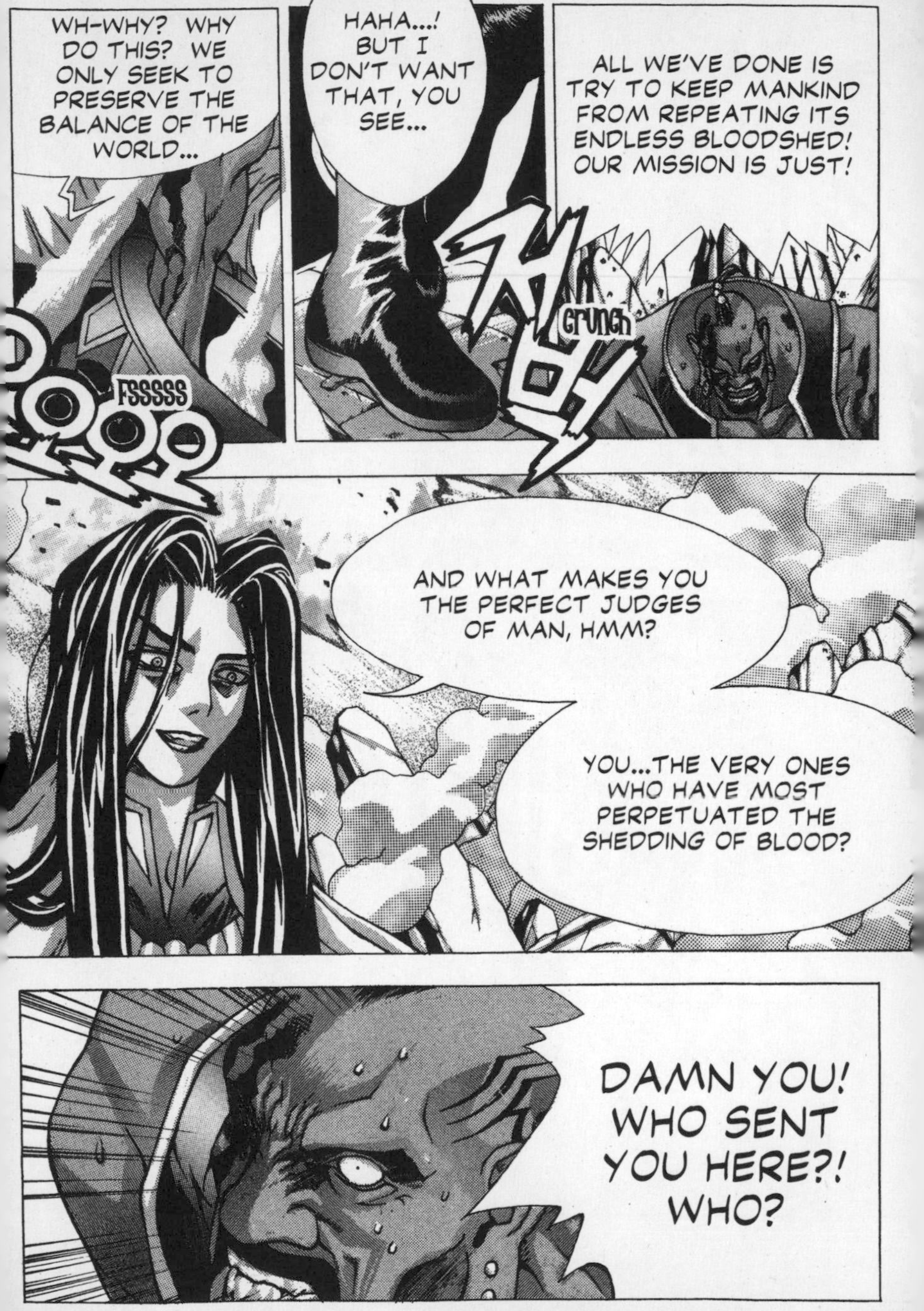
WH-WHY? WHY DO THIS? WE ONLY SEEK TO PRESERVE THE BALANCE OF THE WORLD...
FSSSSS
HAHA...! BUT I DON'T WANT THAT, YOU SEE...
ALL WE'VE DONE IS TRY TO KEEP MANKIND FROM REPEATING ITS ENDLESS BLOODSHED! OUR MISSION IS JUST!
crunch
AND WHAT MAKES YOU THE PERFECT JUDGES OF MAN, HMM?
YOU...THE VERY ONES WHO HAVE MOST PERPETUATED THE SHEDDING OF BLOOD?
DAMN YOU! WHO SENT YOU HERE?! WHO?

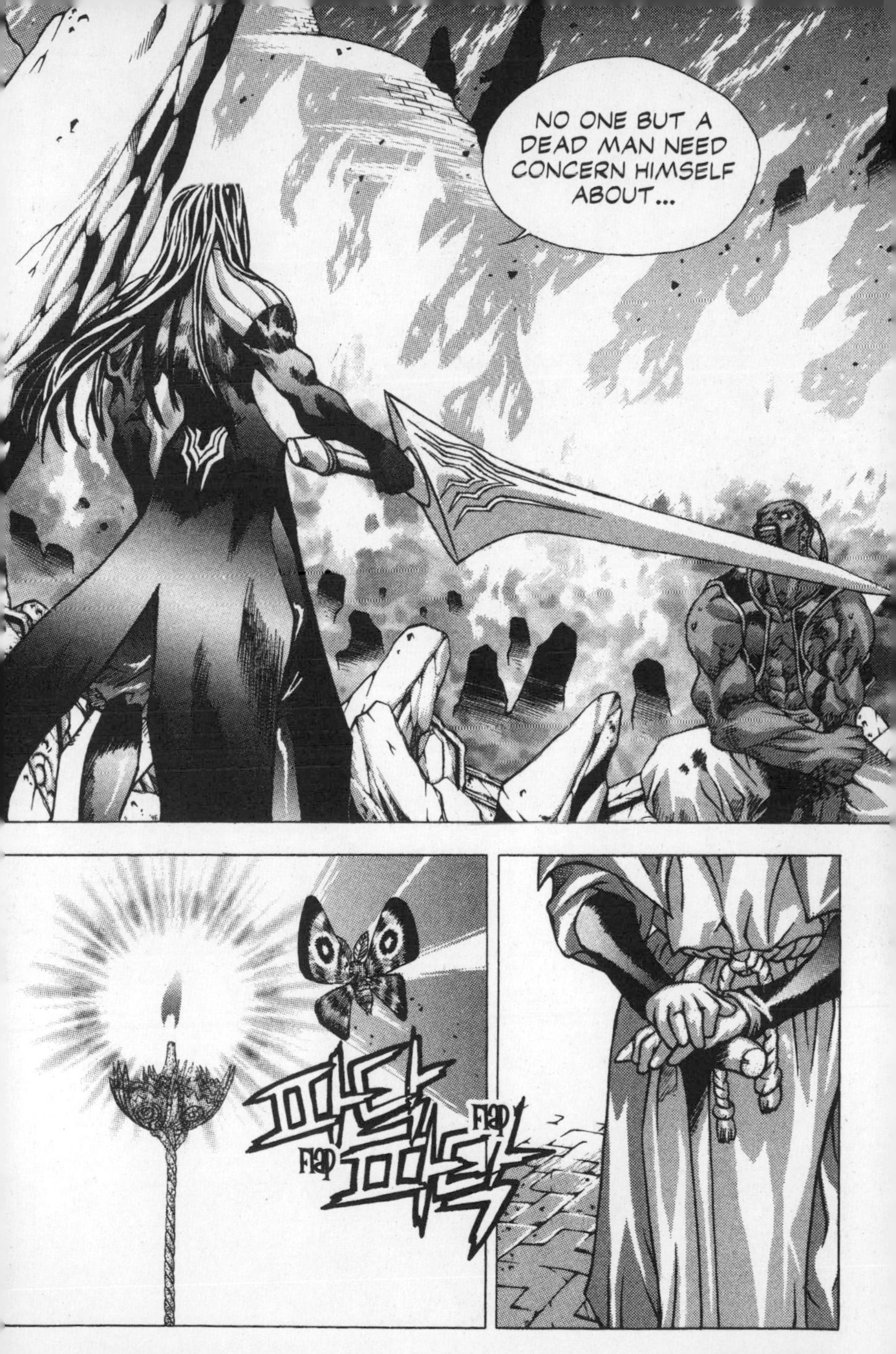
NO ONE BUT A DEAD MAN NEED CONCERN HIMSELF ABOUT...
FLAP
FLAP

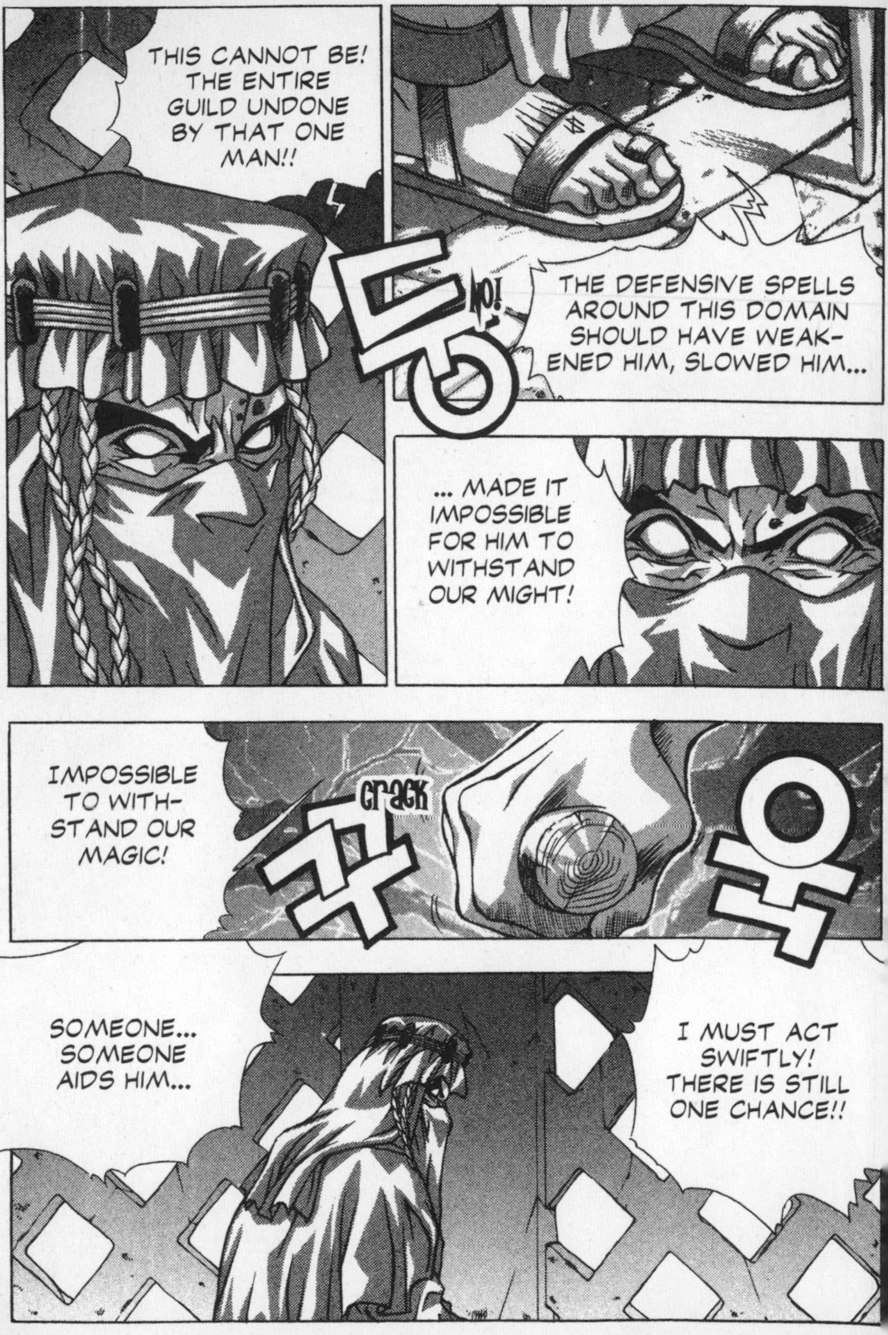
THIS CANNOT BE! THE ENTIRE GUILD UNDONE BY THAT ONE MAN!!
NO!
THE DEFENSIVE SPELLS AROUND THIS DOMAIN SHOULD HAVE WEAK-ENED HIM, SLOWED HIM...
... MADE IT IMPOSSIBLE FOR HIM TO WITHSTAND OUR MIGHT!
IMPOSSIBLE TO WITH-STAND OUR MAGIC!
crack
SOMEONE... SOMEONE AIDS HIM...
I MUST ACT SWIFTLY! THERE IS STILL ONE CHANCE!!

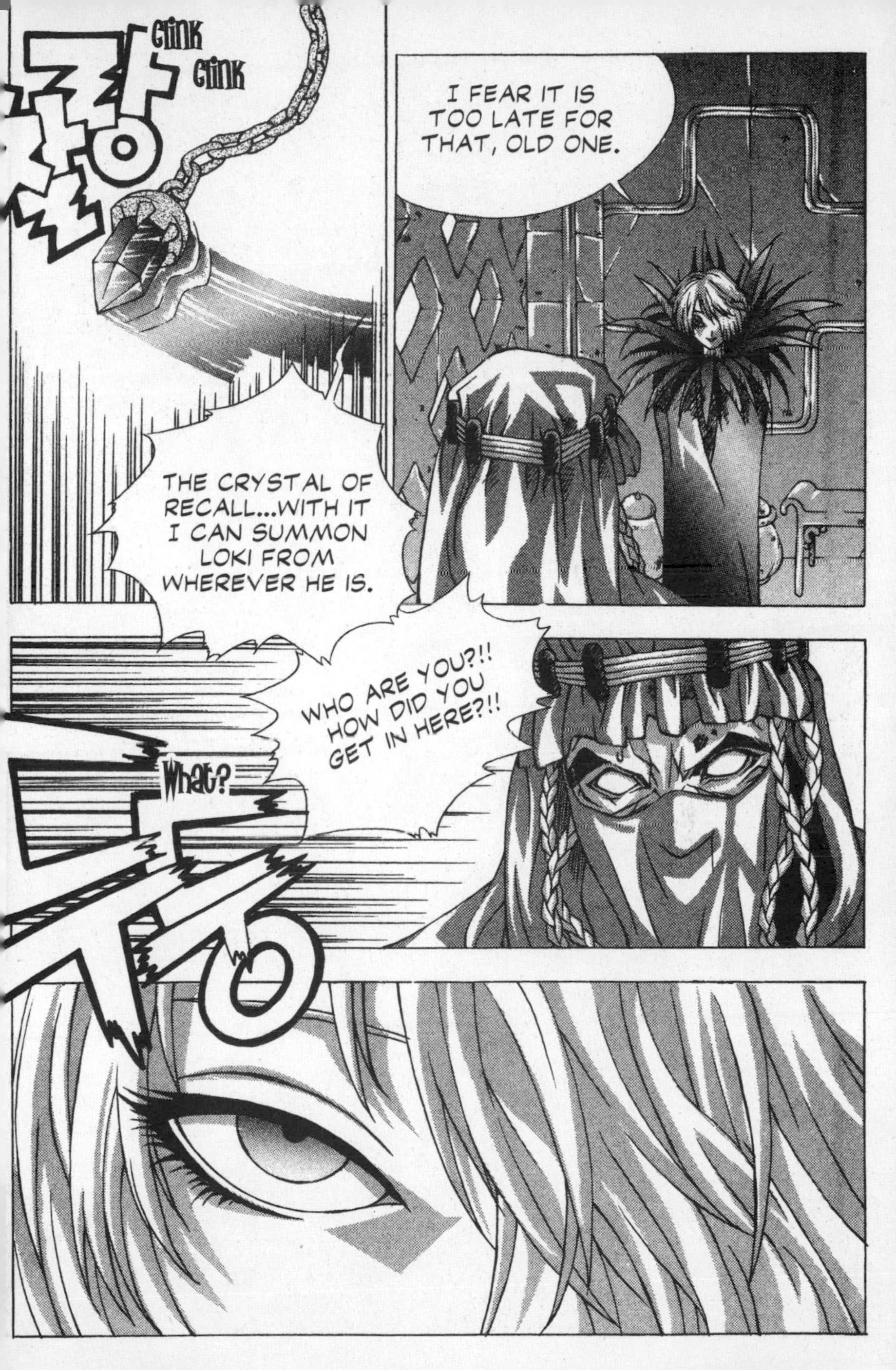

CLINK
CLINK
THE CRYSTAL OF RECALL...WITH IT I CAN SUMMON LOKI FROM WHEREVER HE IS.
I FEAR IT IS TOO LATE FOR THAT, OLD ONE.
What?
WHO ARE YOU?!! HOW DID YOU GET IN HERE?!!

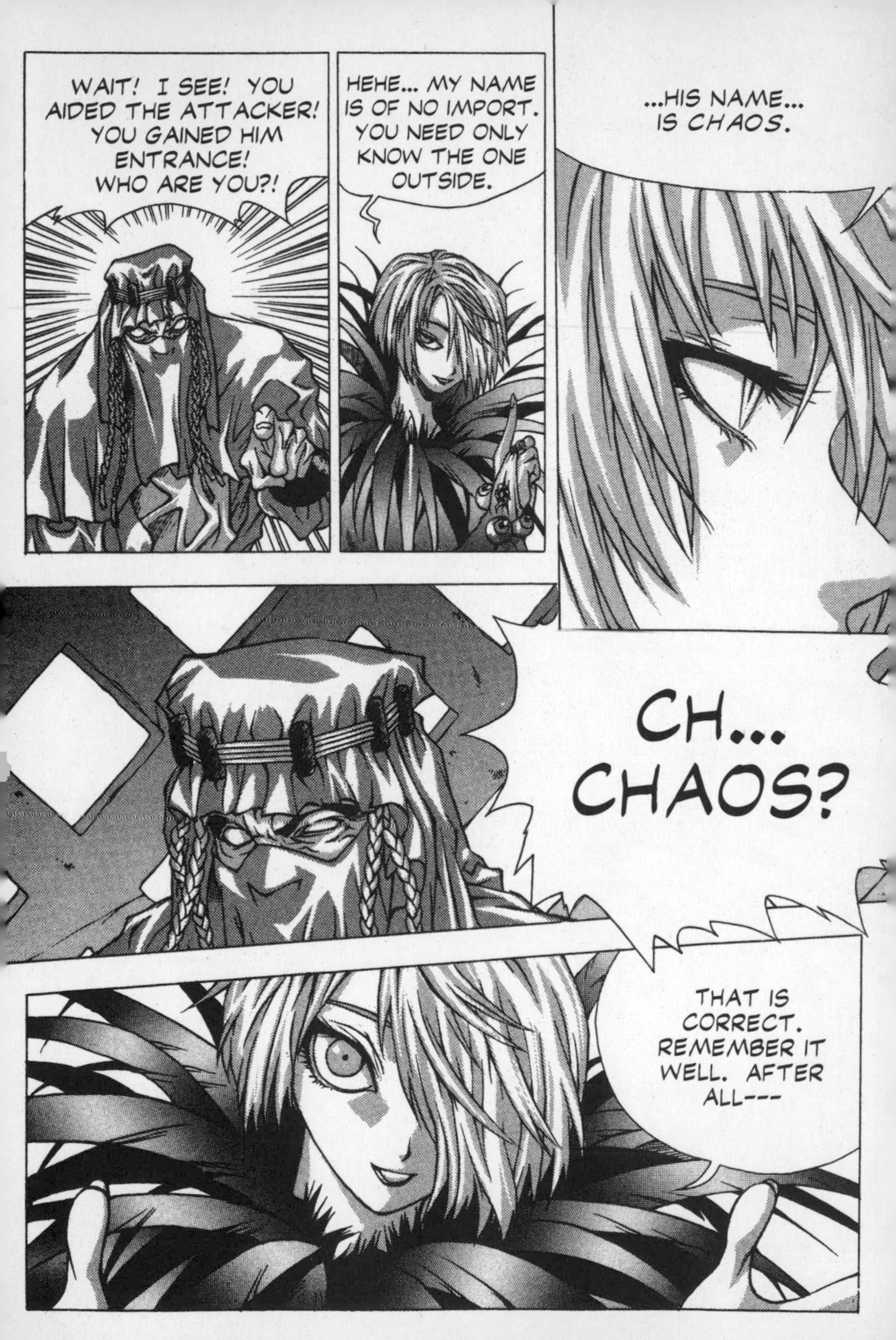
WAIT! I SEE! YOU AIDED THE ATTACKER! YOU GAINED HIM ENTRANCE! WHO ARE YOU?!
HEHE... MY NAME IS OF NO IMPORT. YOU NEED ONLY KNOW THE ONE OUTSIDE.
...HIS NAME... IS *CHAOS*.
CH... CHAOS?
THAT IS CORRECT. REMEMBER IT WELL. AFTER ALL---

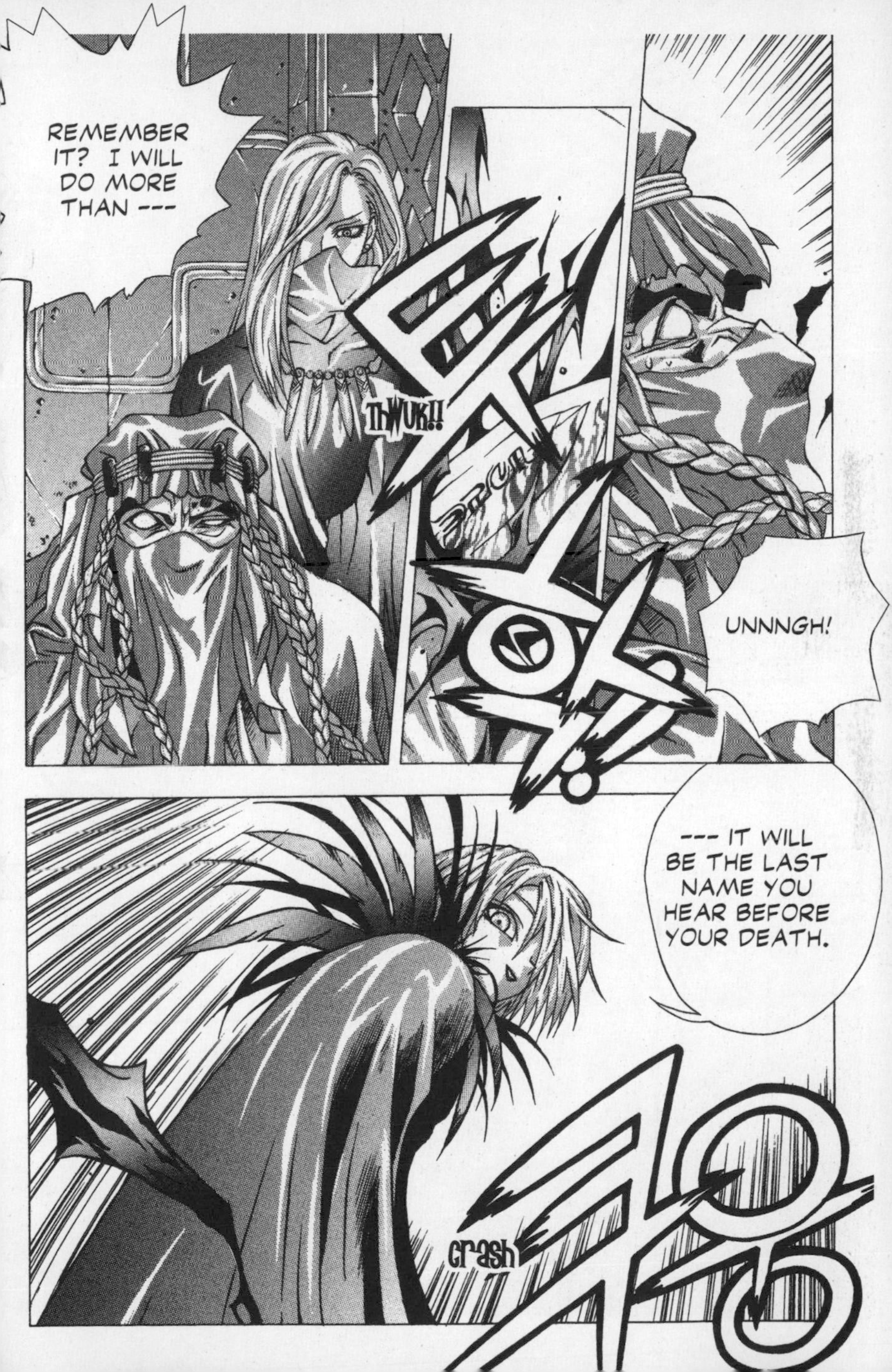
REMEMBER IT? I WILL DO MORE THAN ---
ThWUK!!
UNNNGH!
--- IT WILL BE THE LAST NAME YOU HEAR BEFORE YOUR DEATH.
crash

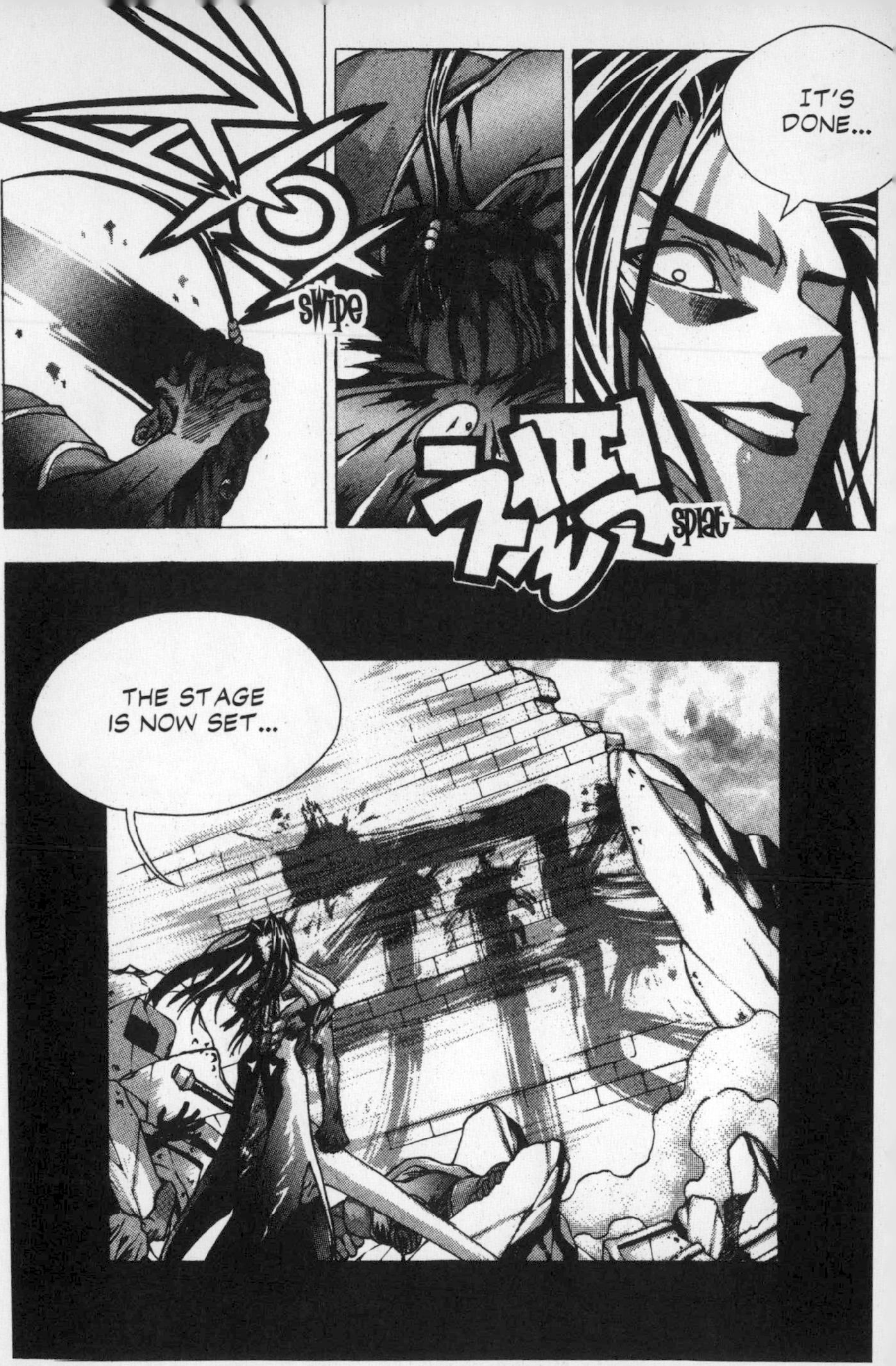
swipe
IT'S DONE...
splat
THE STAGE IS NOW SET...

RAGNAROK
라그나로크
IN TO THE ABYSS

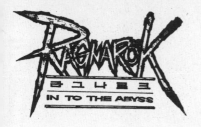

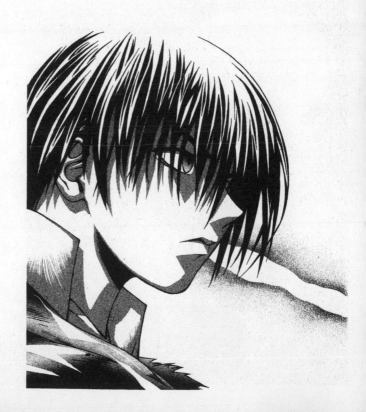

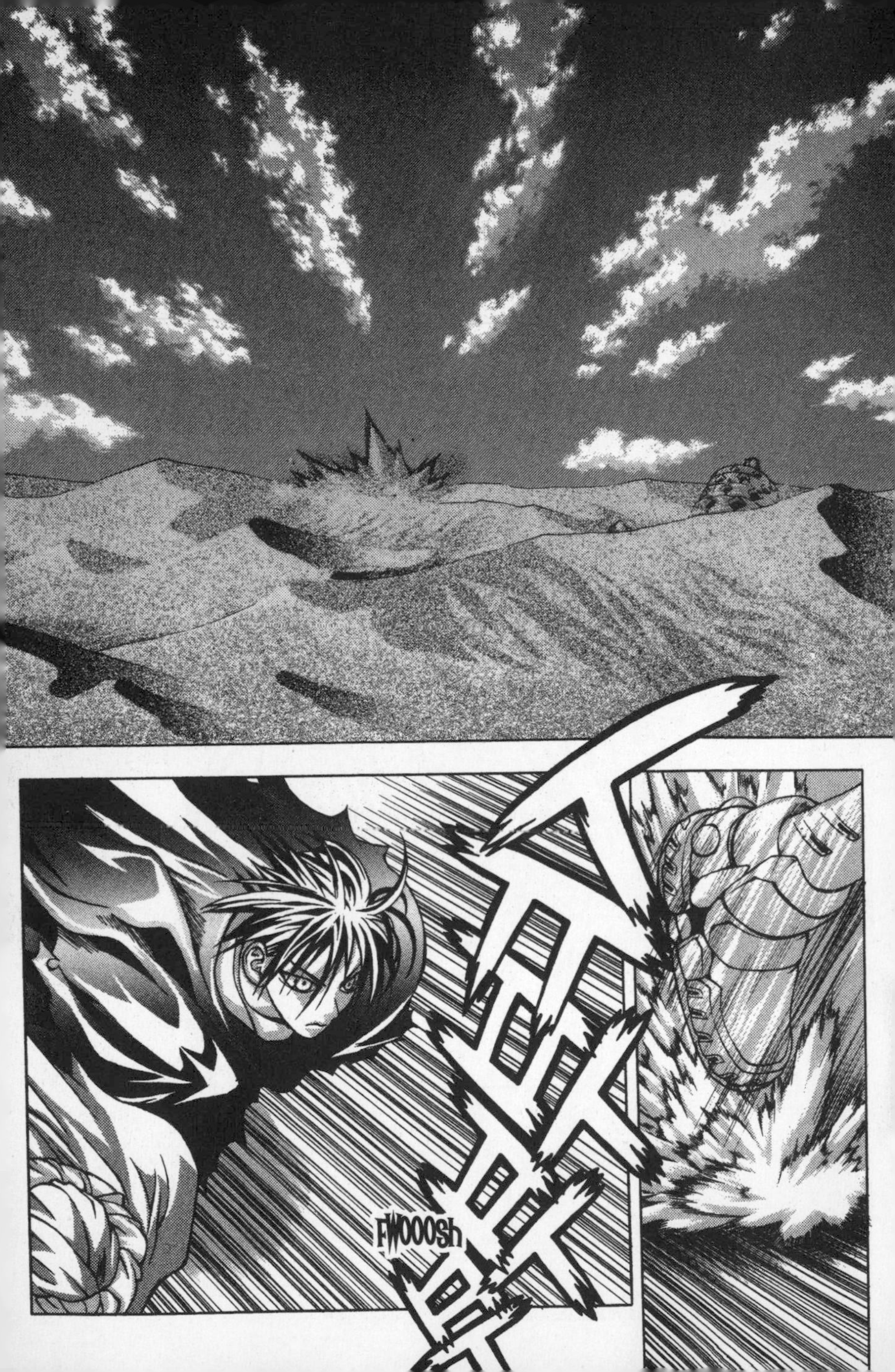
FWOOOSh

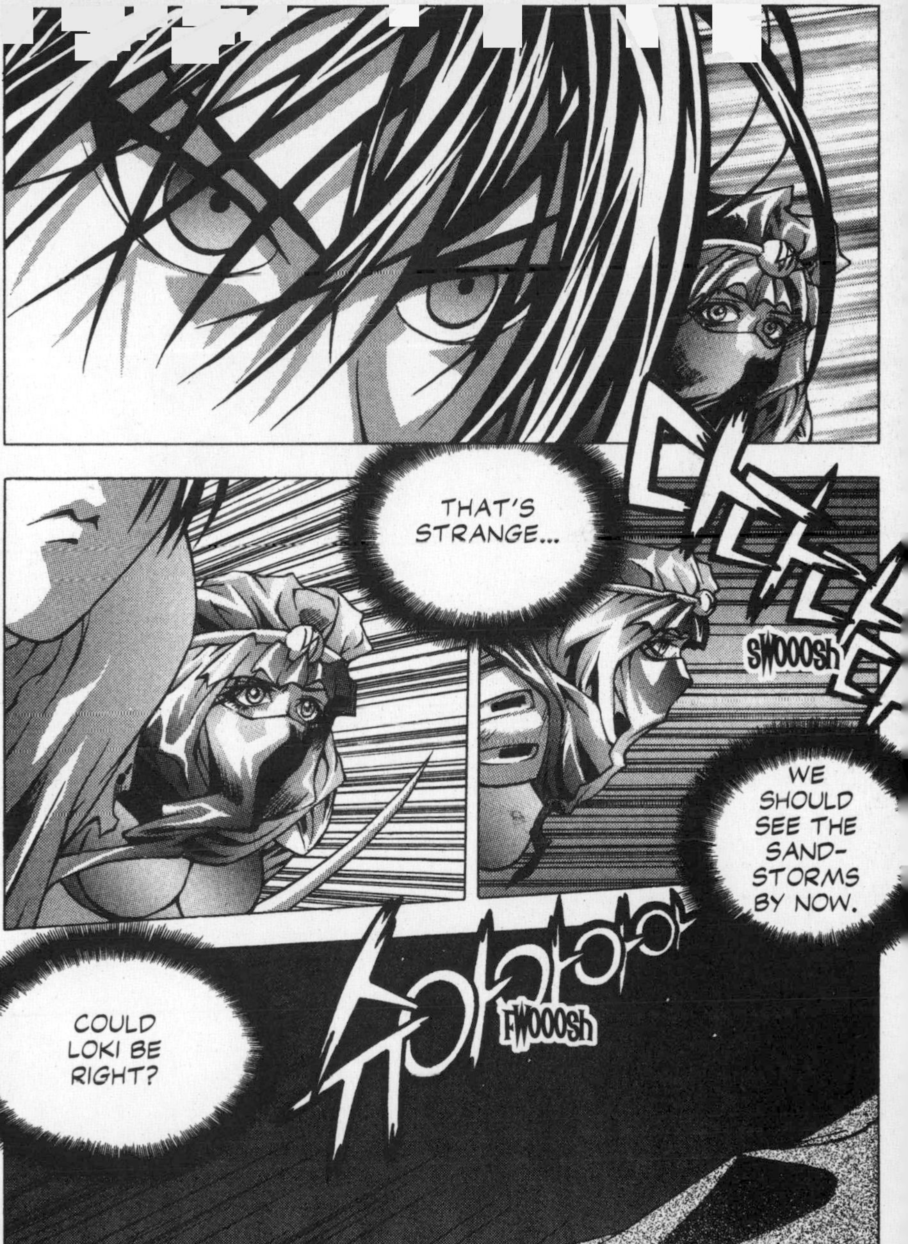
THAT'S STRANGE...
SWOOOSH
WE SHOULD SEE THE SAND-STORMS BY NOW.
COULD LOKI BE RIGHT?
FWOOOSH

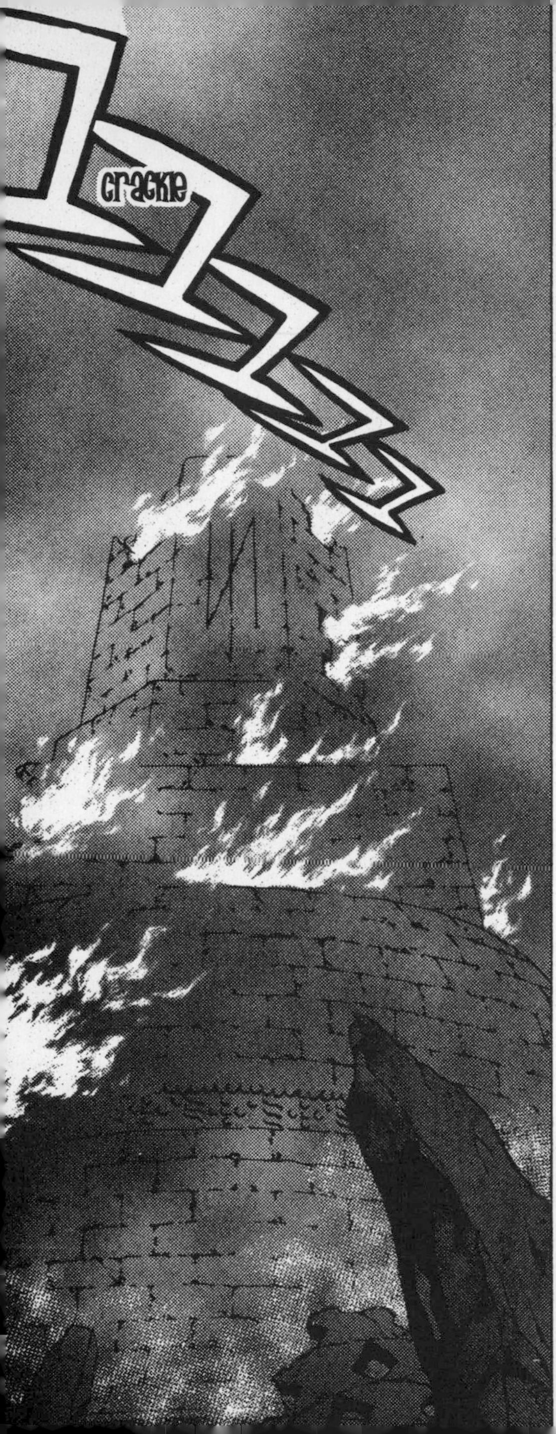
CRACKLE
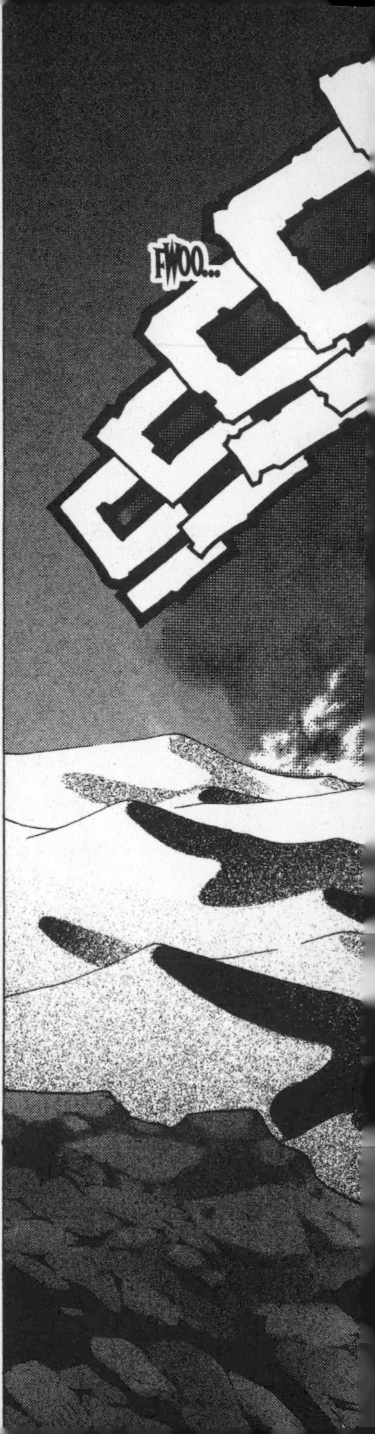
FWOO...

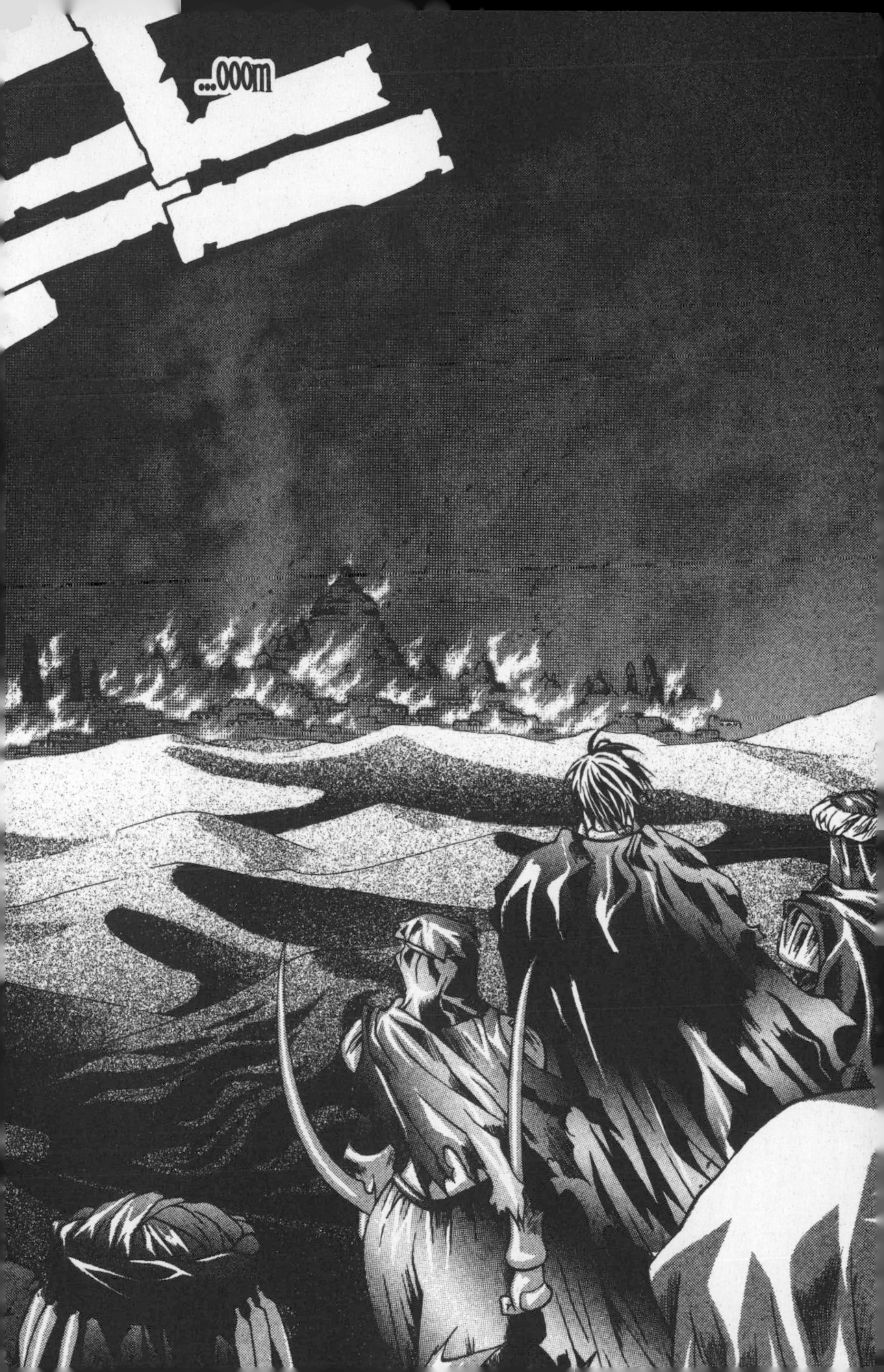
...OOOM

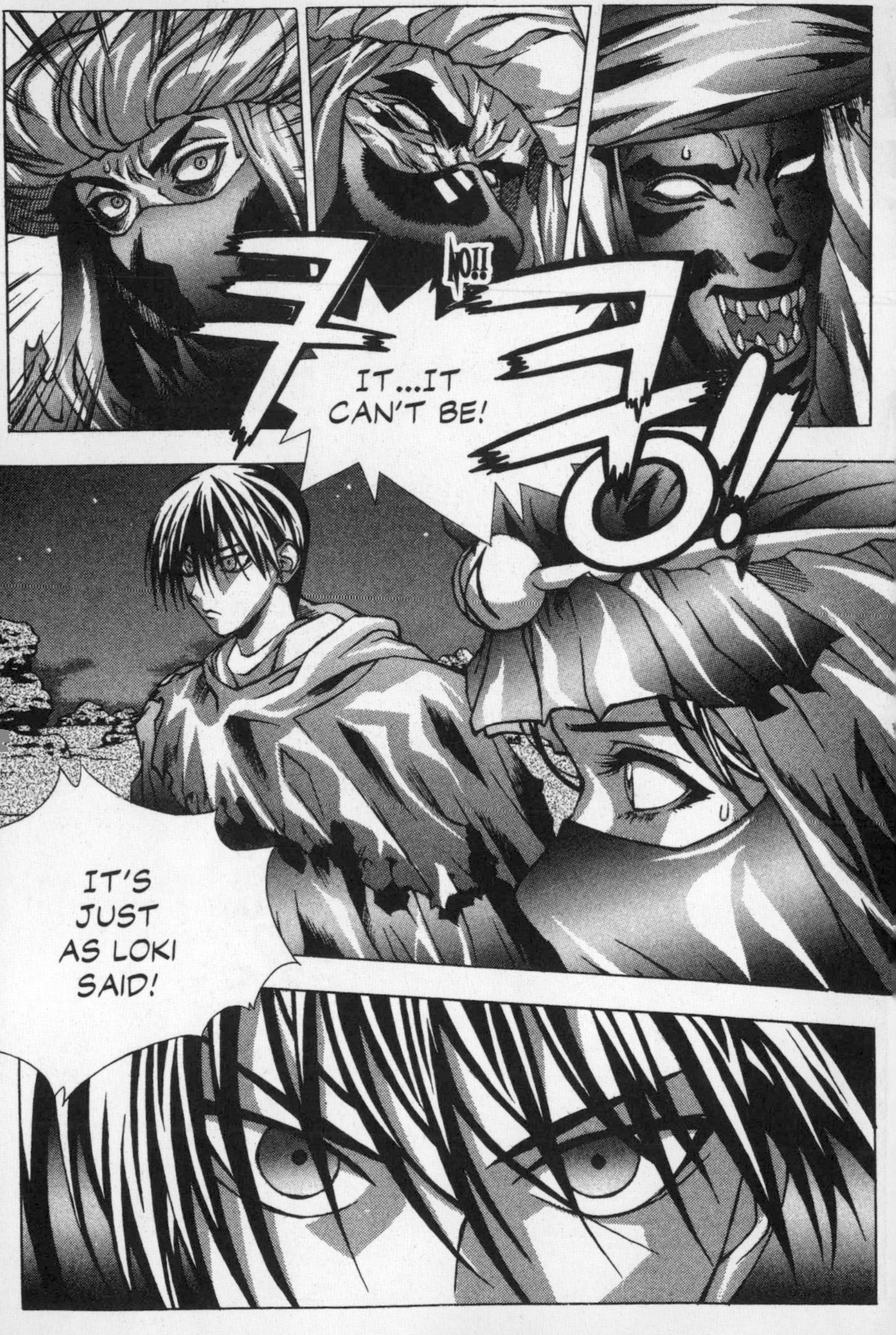
NO!!
IT...IT CAN'T BE!
IT'S JUST AS LOKI SAID!

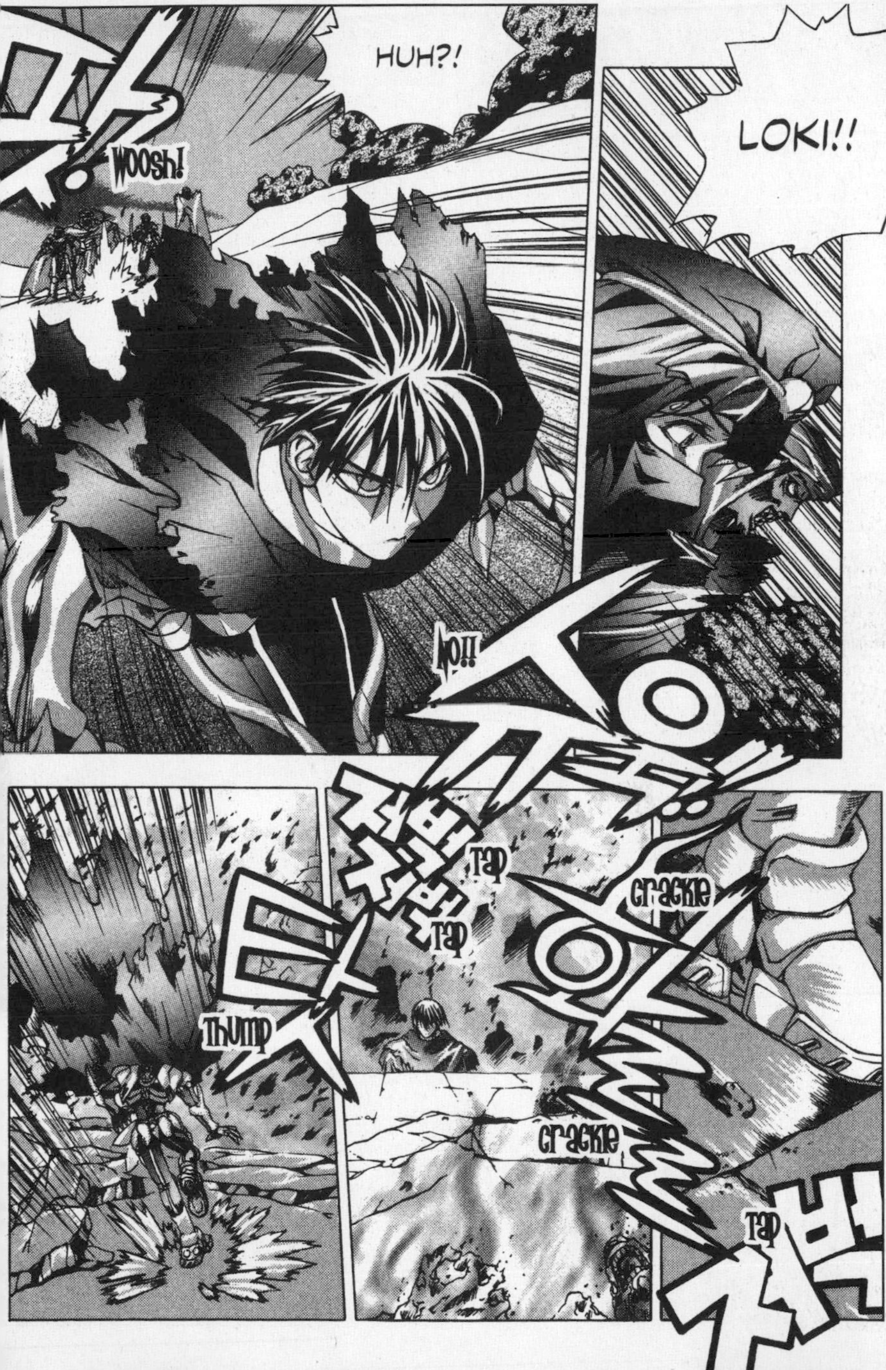
WOOSH!
HUH?!
LOKI!!
NO!!
TAP
TAP
THUMP
CRACKLE
CRACKLE
TAP

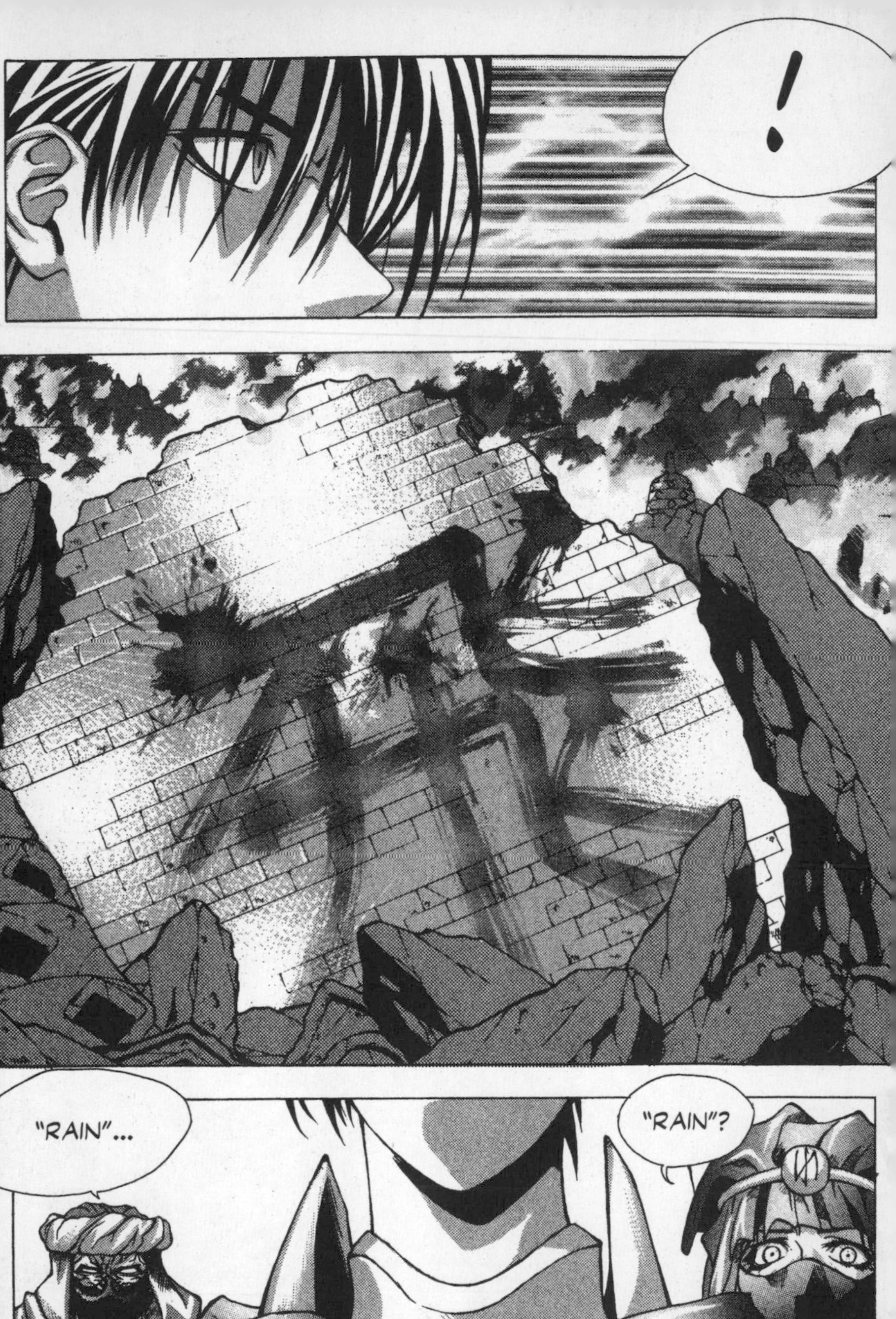
!
"RAIN"...
"RAIN"?

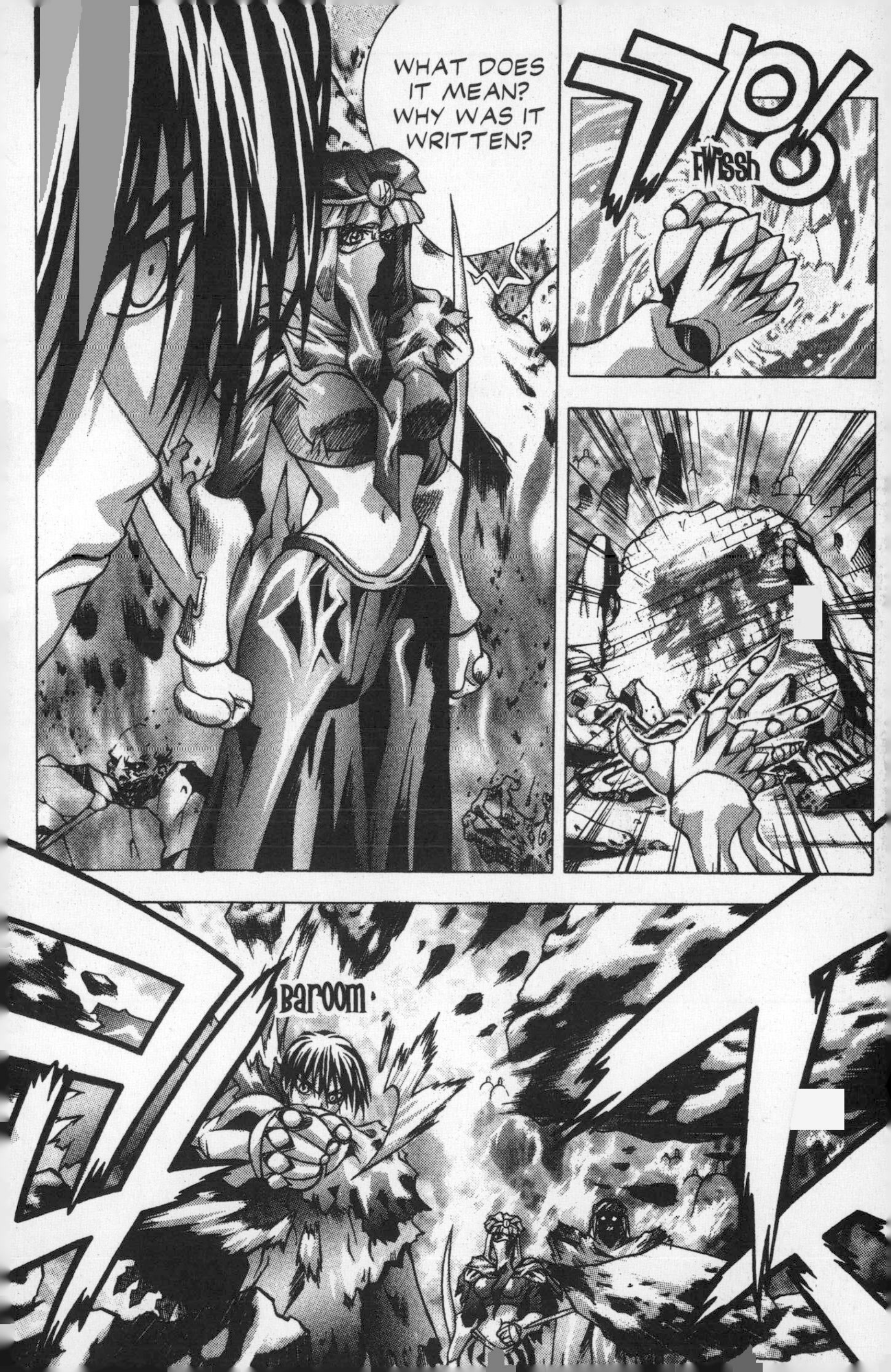
WHAT DOES IT MEAN? WHY WAS IT WRITTEN?
FWISSH
BAROOM

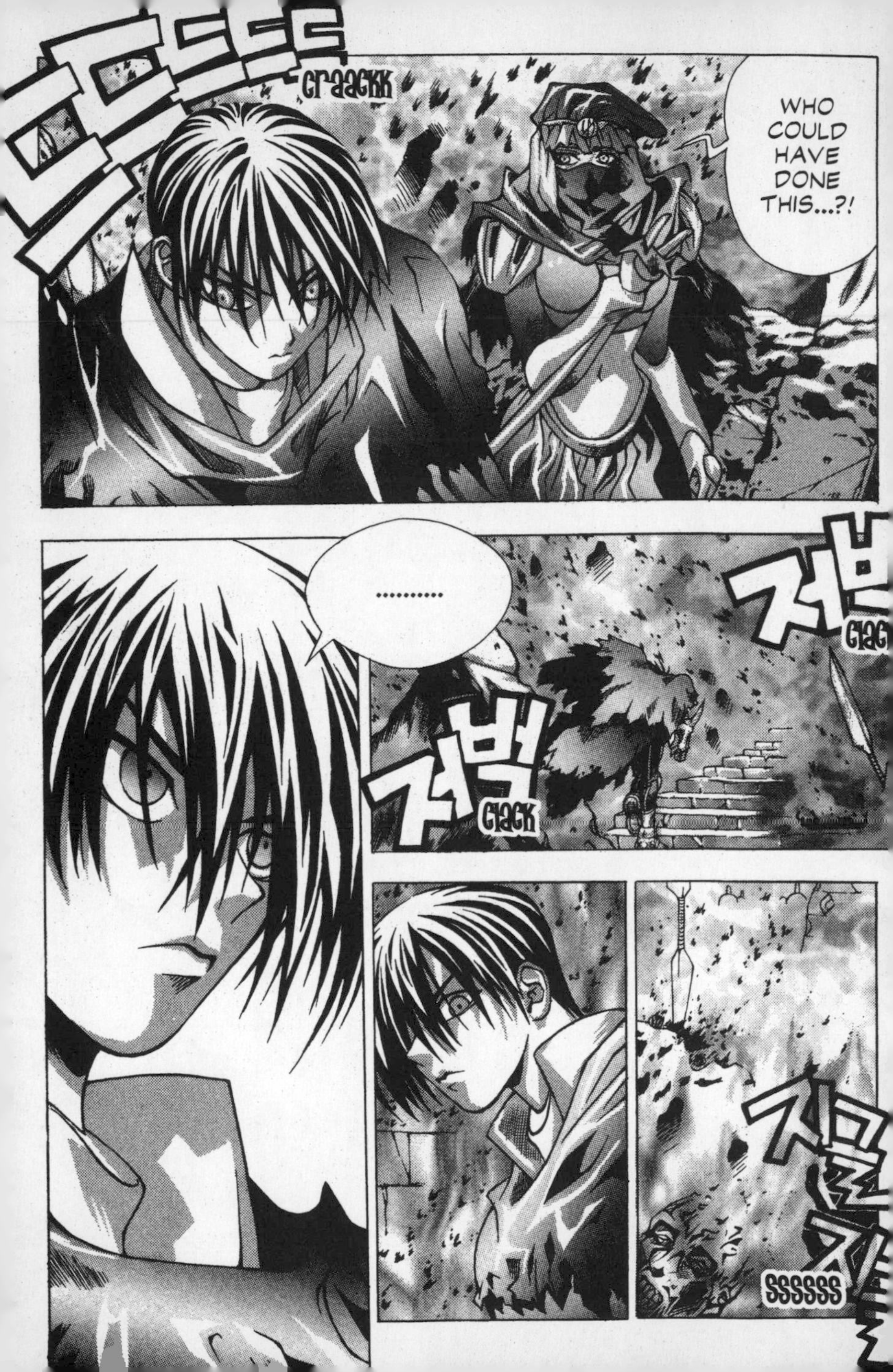

CRAACKK
WHO COULD HAVE DONE THIS...?!
....
CLACK
CLACK
SSSSSS

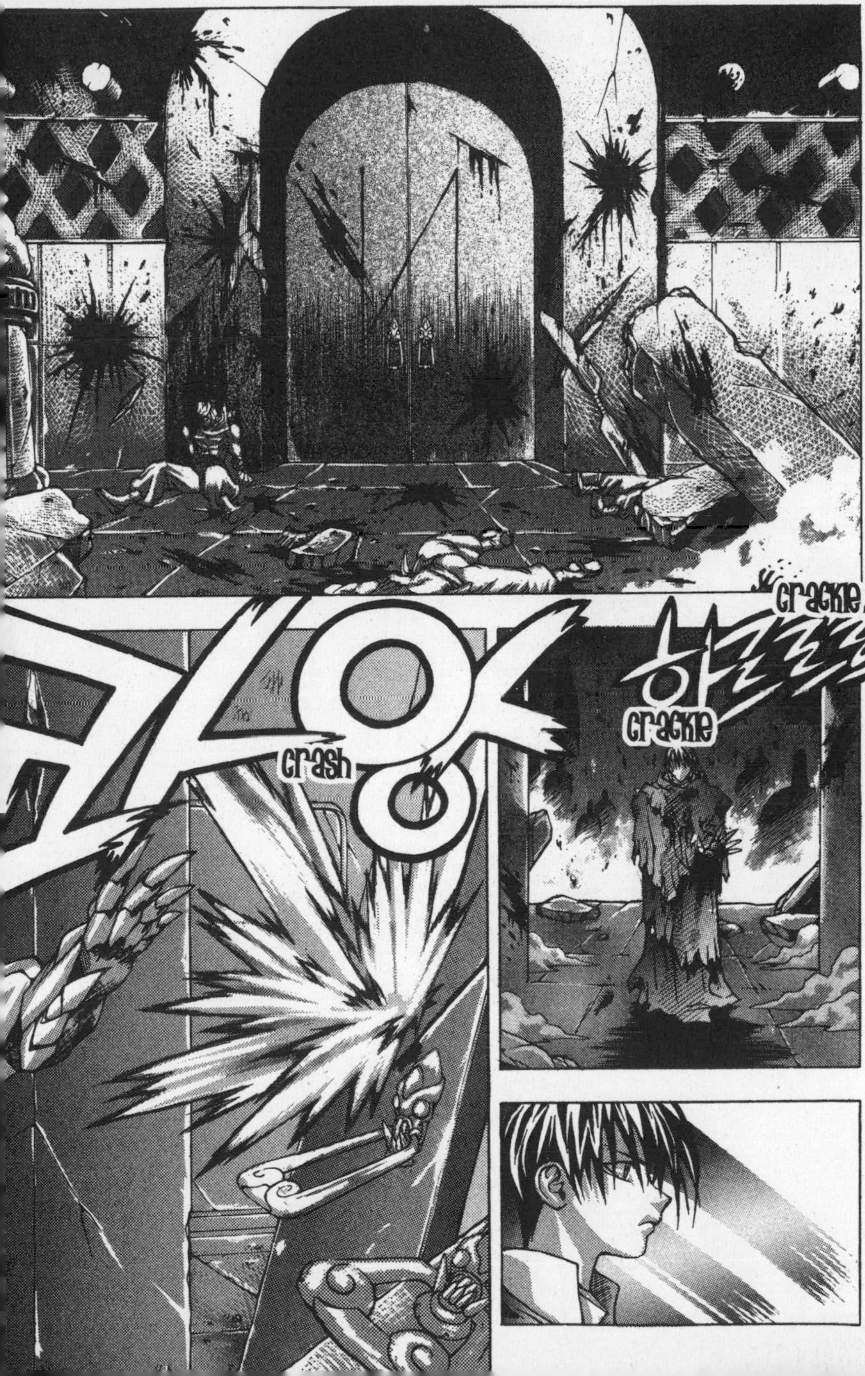
crash
crackle
crackle

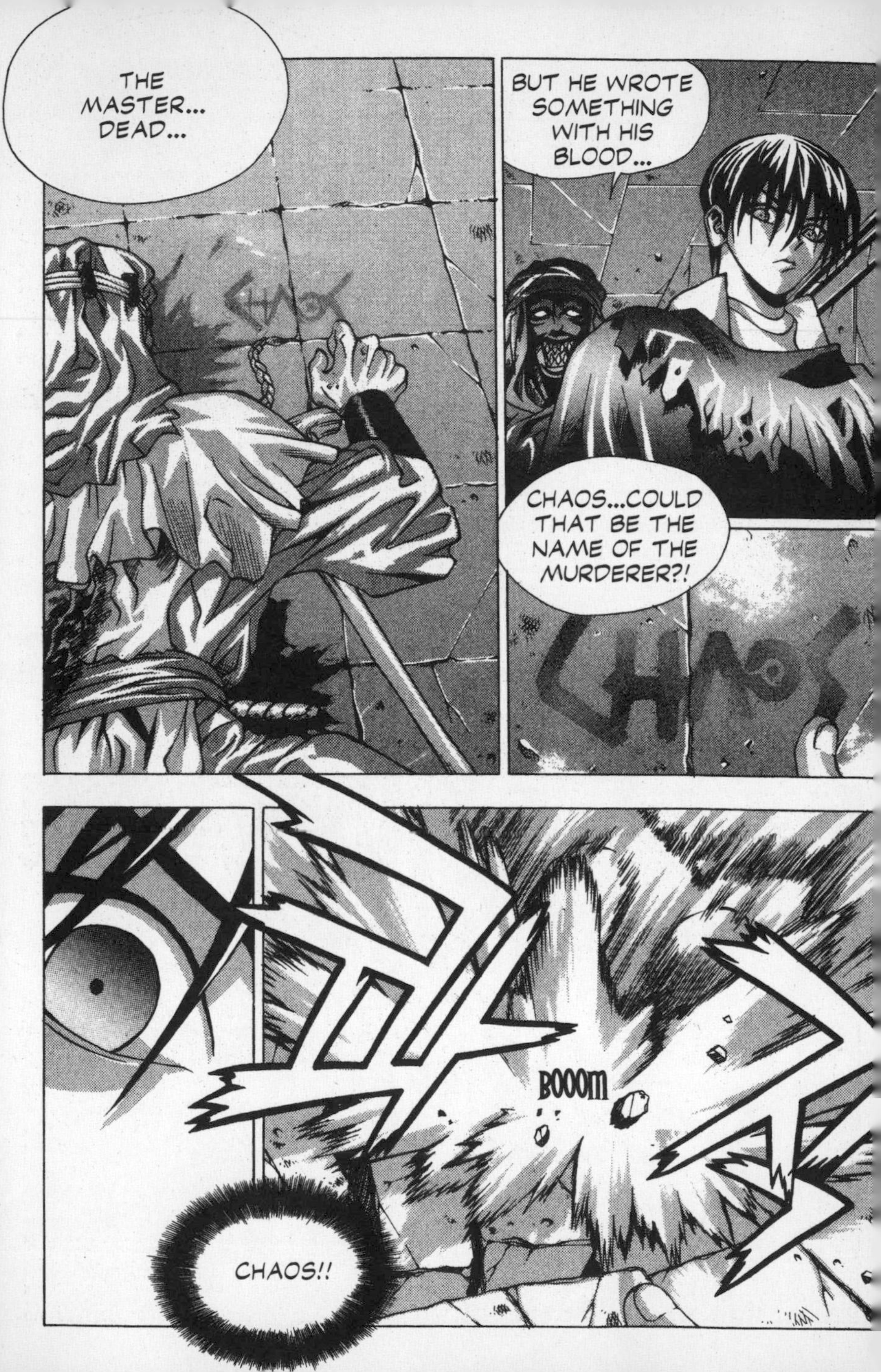
THE MASTER... DEAD...
BUT HE WROTE SOMETHING WITH HIS BLOOD...
CHAOS...COULD THAT BE THE NAME OF THE MURDERER?!
BOOOM
CHAOS!!

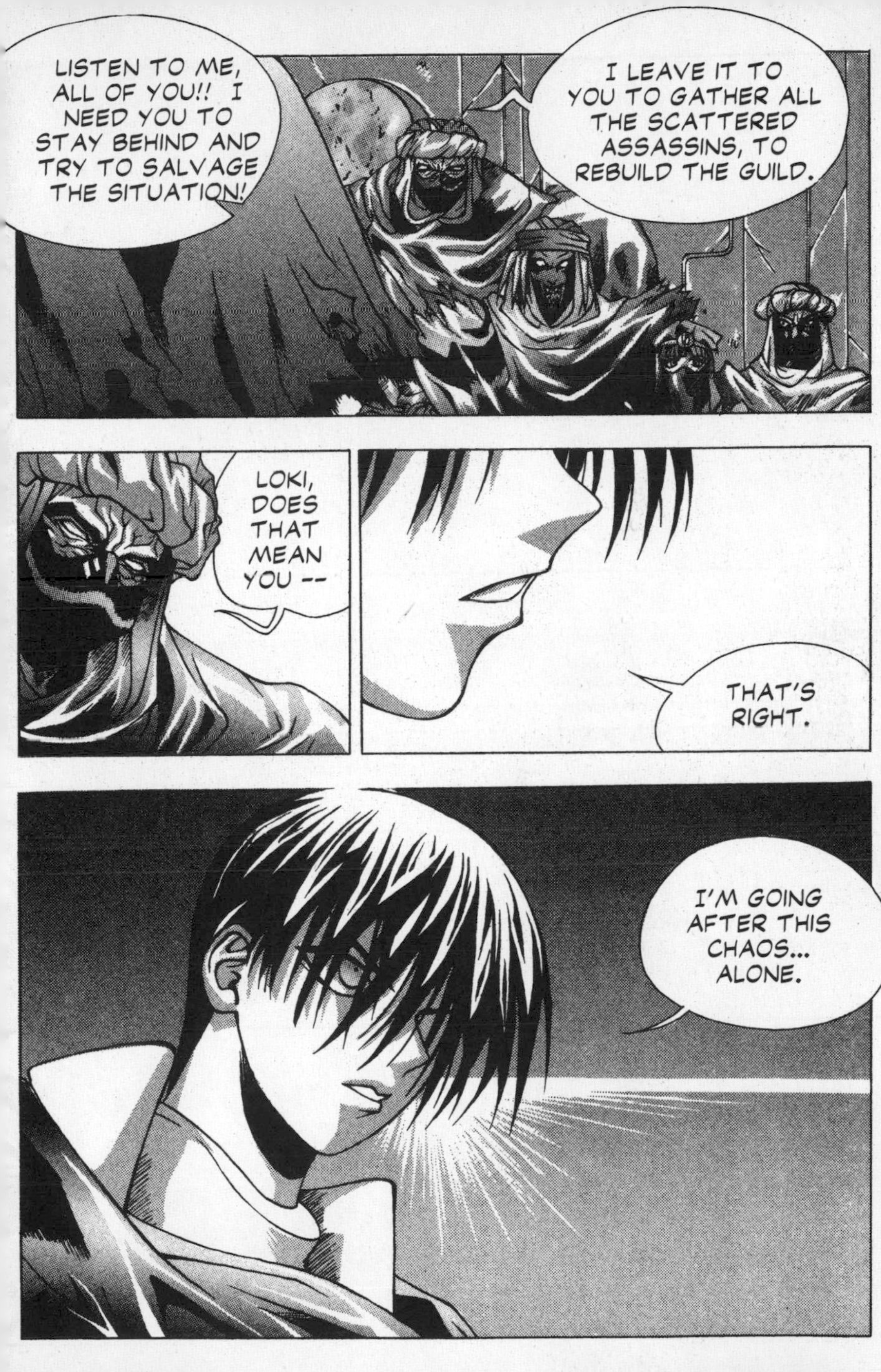
LISTEN TO ME, ALL OF YOU!! I NEED YOU TO STAY BEHIND AND TRY TO SALVAGE THE SITUATION!
I LEAVE IT TO YOU TO GATHER ALL THE SCATTERED ASSASSINS, TO REBUILD THE GUILD.
LOKI, DOES THAT MEAN YOU --
THAT'S RIGHT.
I'M GOING AFTER THIS CHAOS... ALONE.

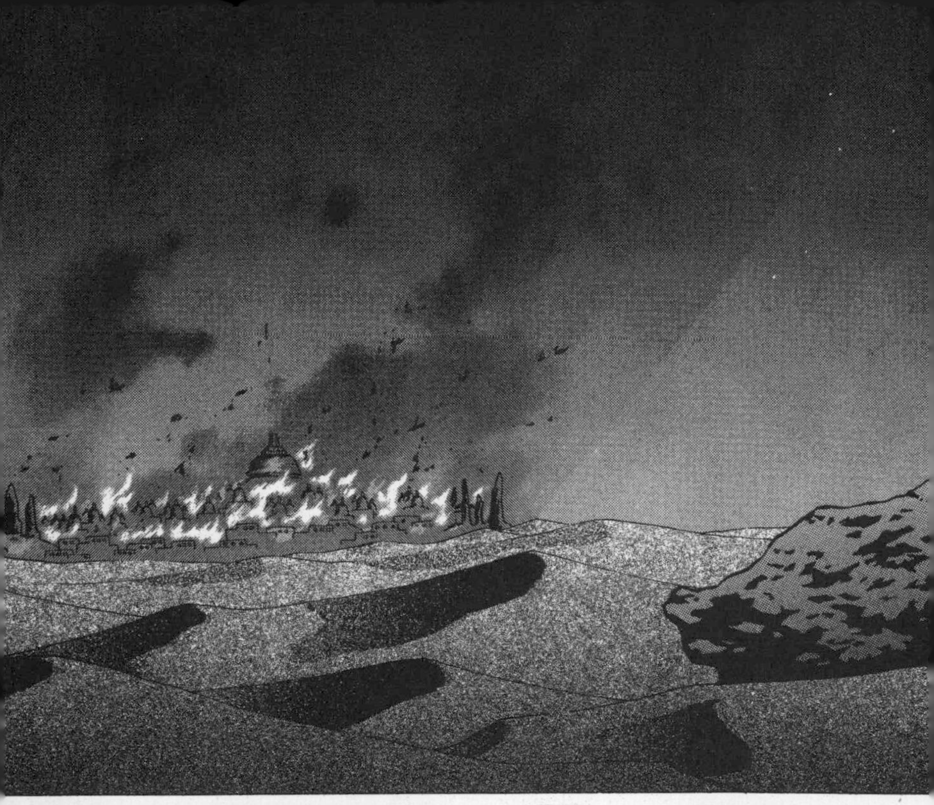

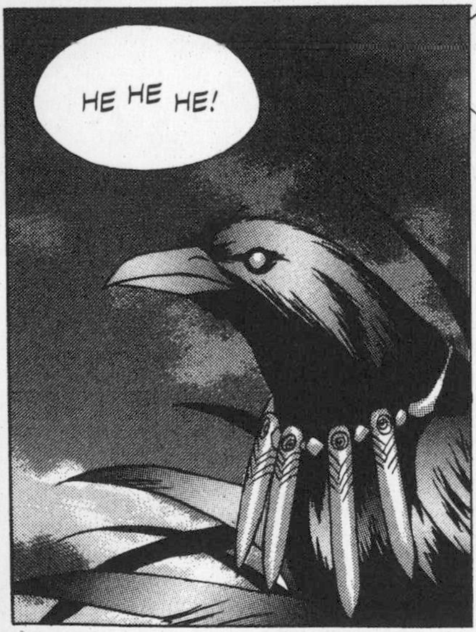
HE HE HE!

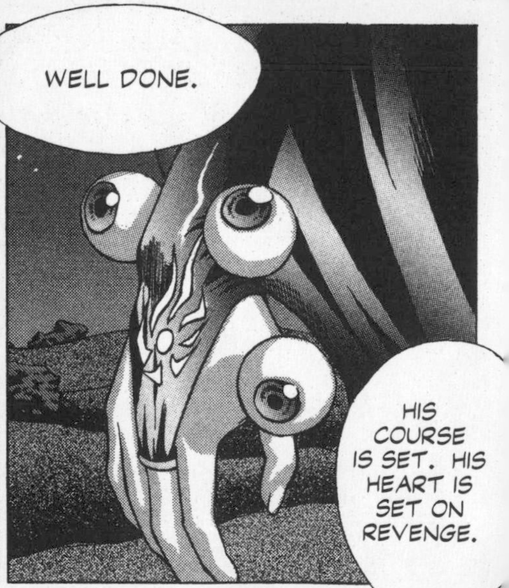
WELL DONE.
HIS COURSE IS SET. HIS HEART IS SET ON REVENGE.

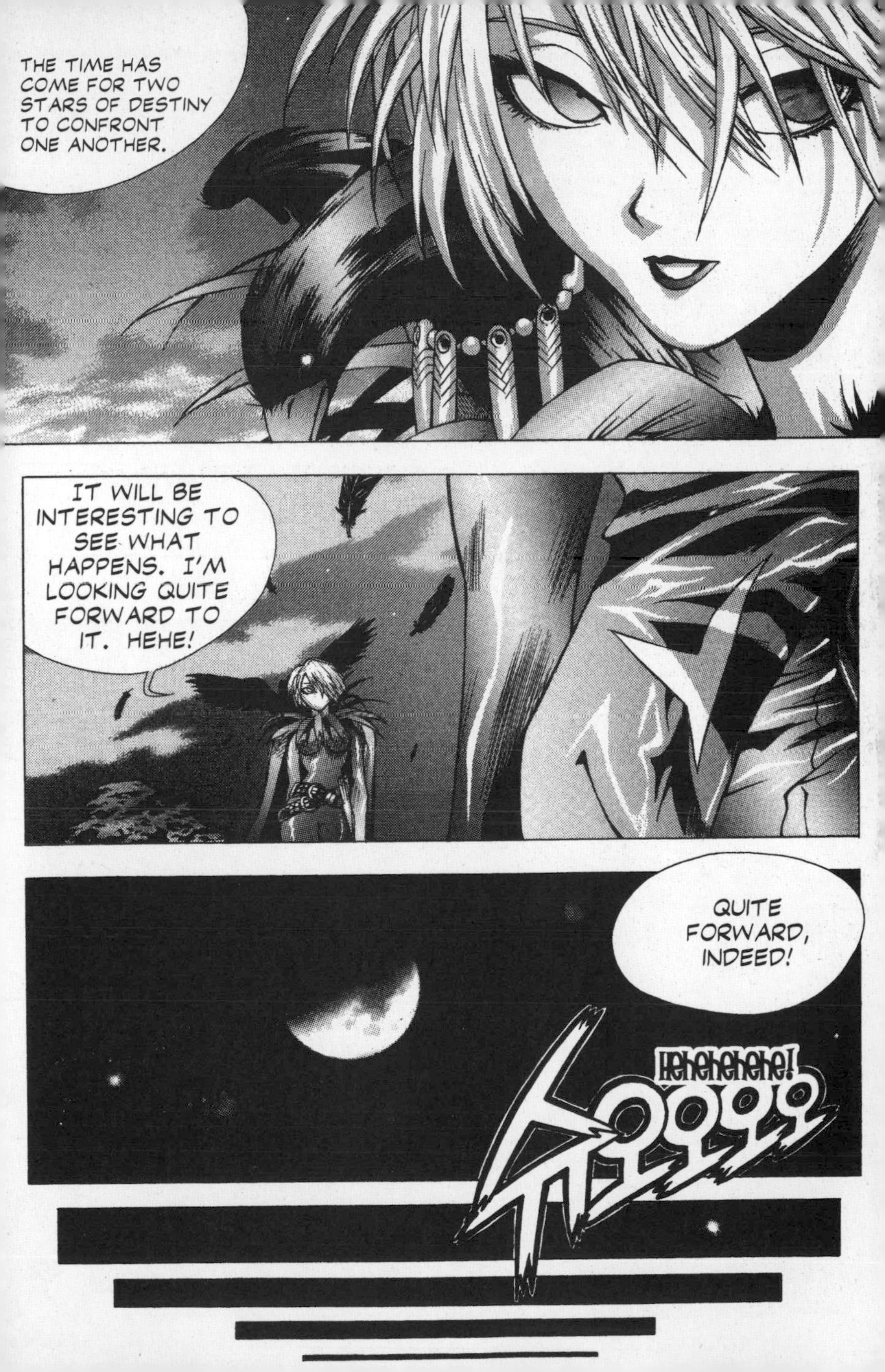
THE TIME HAS COME FOR TWO STARS OF DESTINY TO CONFRONT ONE ANOTHER.
IT WILL BE INTERESTING TO SEE WHAT HAPPENS. I'M LOOKING QUITE FORWARD TO IT. HEHE!
QUITE FORWARD, INDEED!
HEHEHEHEHE!

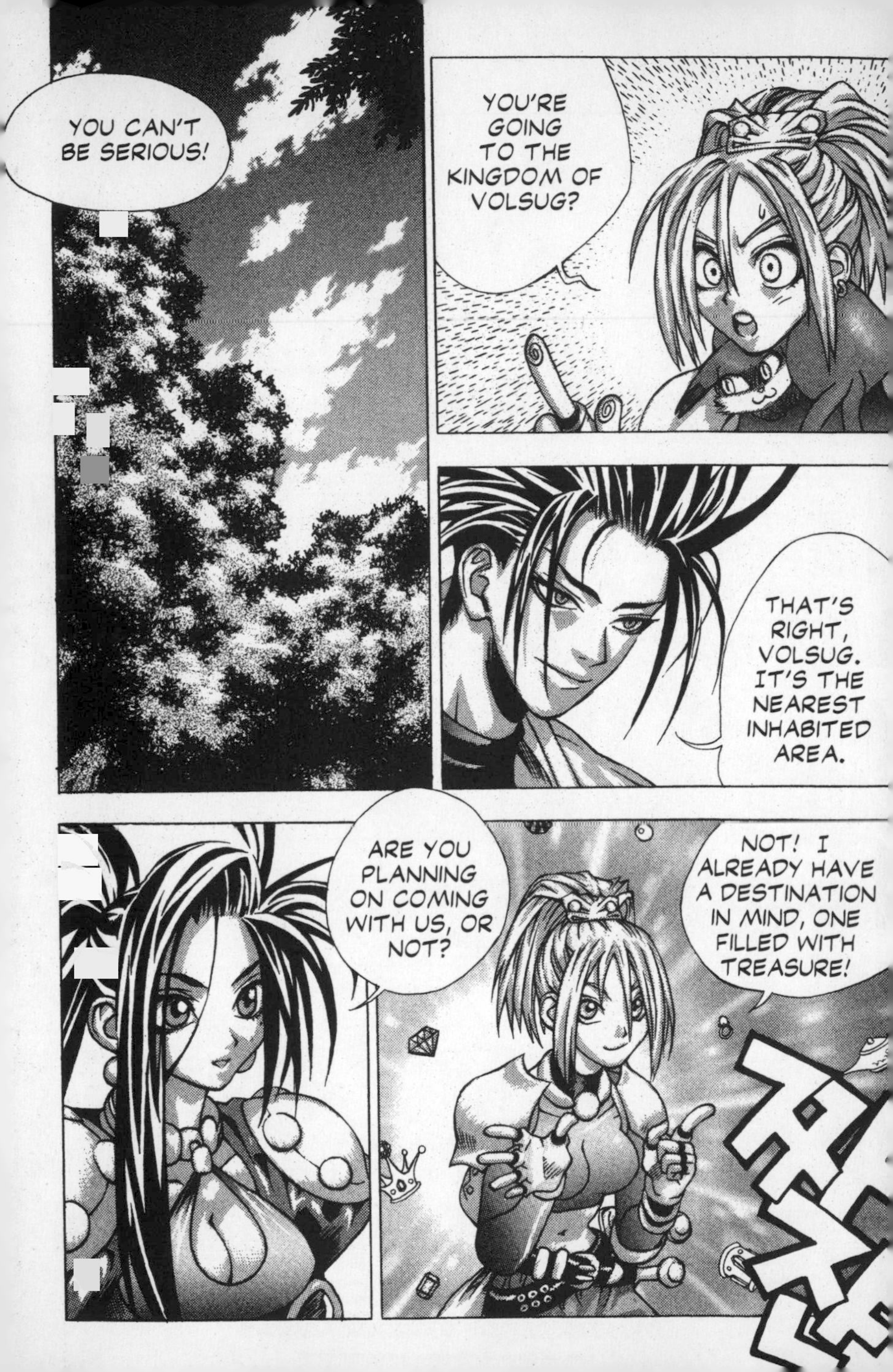
YOU CAN'T BE SERIOUS!
YOU'RE GOING TO THE KINGDOM OF VOLSUG?
THAT'S RIGHT, VOLSUG. IT'S THE NEAREST INHABITED AREA.
ARE YOU PLANNING ON COMING WITH US, OR NOT?
NOT! I ALREADY HAVE A DESTINATION IN MIND, ONE FILLED WITH TREASURE!

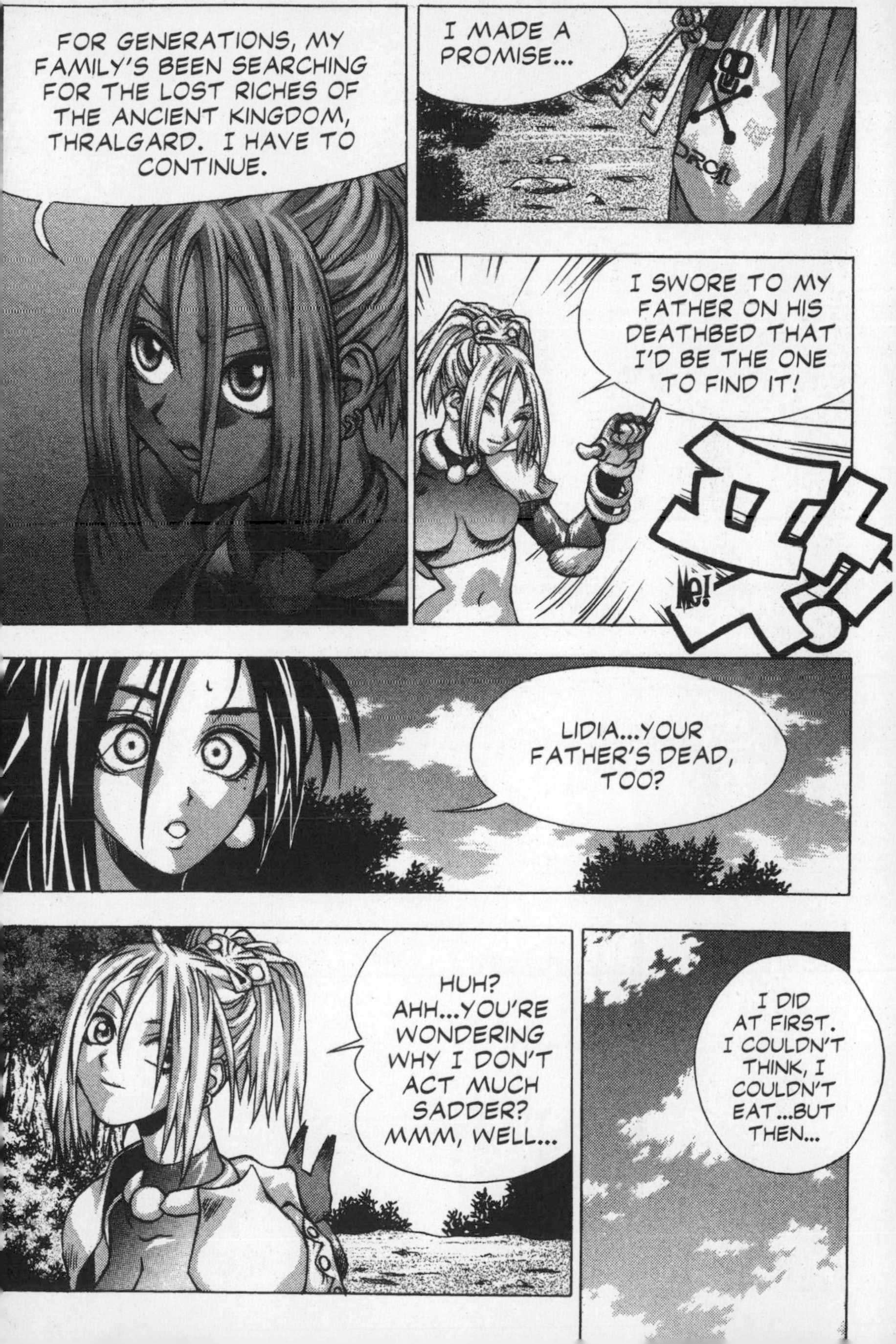

FOR GENERATIONS, MY FAMILY'S BEEN SEARCHING FOR THE LOST RICHES OF THE ANCIENT KINGDOM, THRALGARD. I HAVE TO CONTINUE.
I MADE A PROMISE...
I SWORE TO MY FATHER ON HIS DEATHBED THAT I'D BE THE ONE TO FIND IT!
Me!
LIDIA...YOUR FATHER'S DEAD, TOO?
HUH? AHH...YOU'RE WONDERING WHY I DON'T ACT MUCH SADDER? MMM, WELL...
I DID AT FIRST. I COULDN'T THINK, I COULDN'T EAT...BUT THEN...

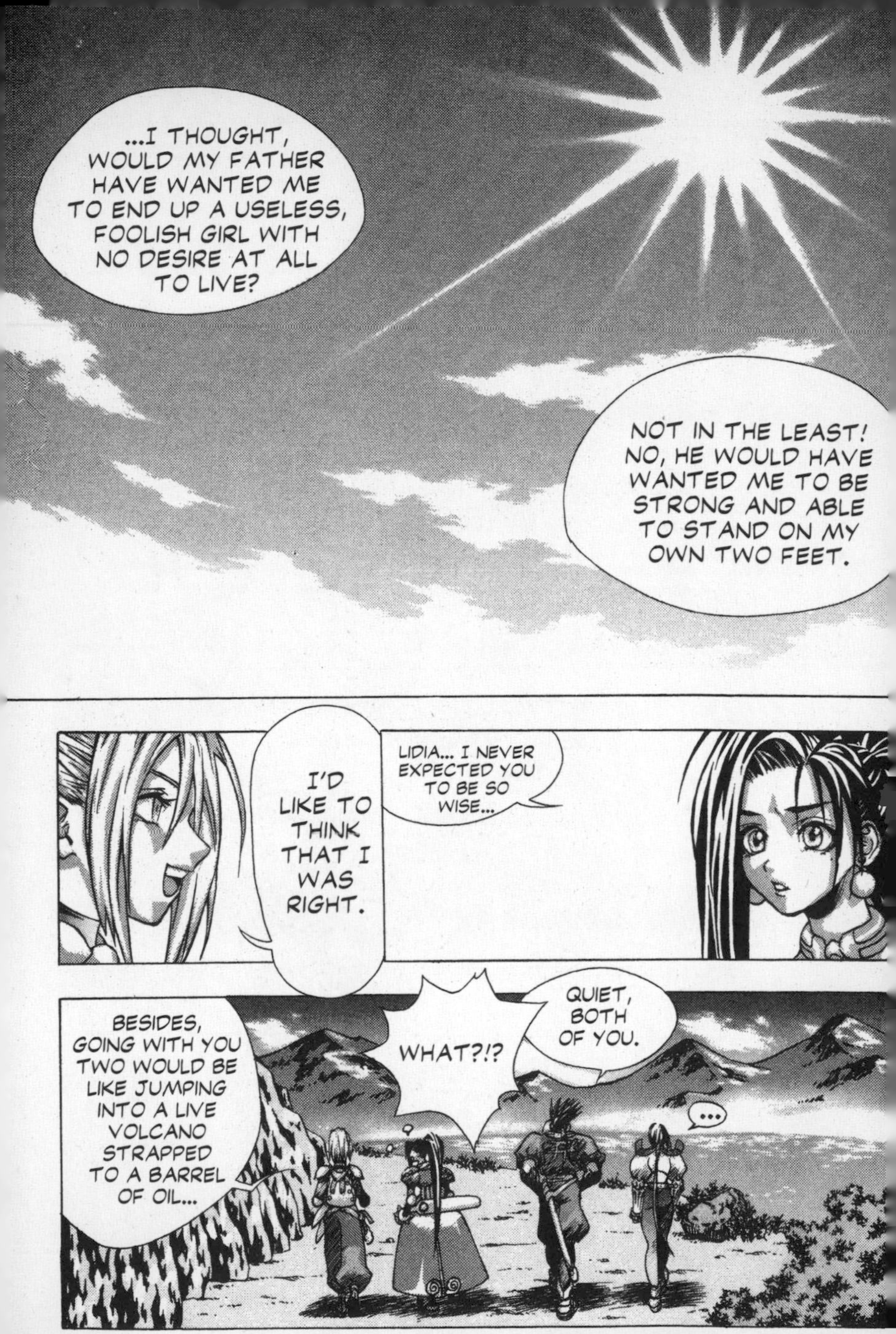
...I THOUGHT, WOULD MY FATHER HAVE WANTED ME TO END UP A USELESS, FOOLISH GIRL WITH NO DESIRE AT ALL TO LIVE?
NOT IN THE LEAST! NO, HE WOULD HAVE WANTED ME TO BE STRONG AND ABLE TO STAND ON MY OWN TWO FEET.
I'D LIKE TO THINK THAT I WAS RIGHT.
LIDIA... I NEVER EXPECTED YOU TO BE SO WISE...
BESIDES, GOING WITH YOU TWO WOULD BE LIKE JUMPING INTO A LIVE VOLCANO STRAPPED TO A BARREL OF OIL...
WHAT?!?
QUIET, BOTH OF YOU.
...

RAGNAROK
라그나로크
IN TO THE ABYSS

Thief - Treasure Hunter

How are you? There wasn't much going on for me around the region of Fayon, so I'll be heading off to Thralgard...an adventure which should prove very, very interesting! Don't worry, though, Chaos and the others haven't seen the last of me.... Until we meet again!

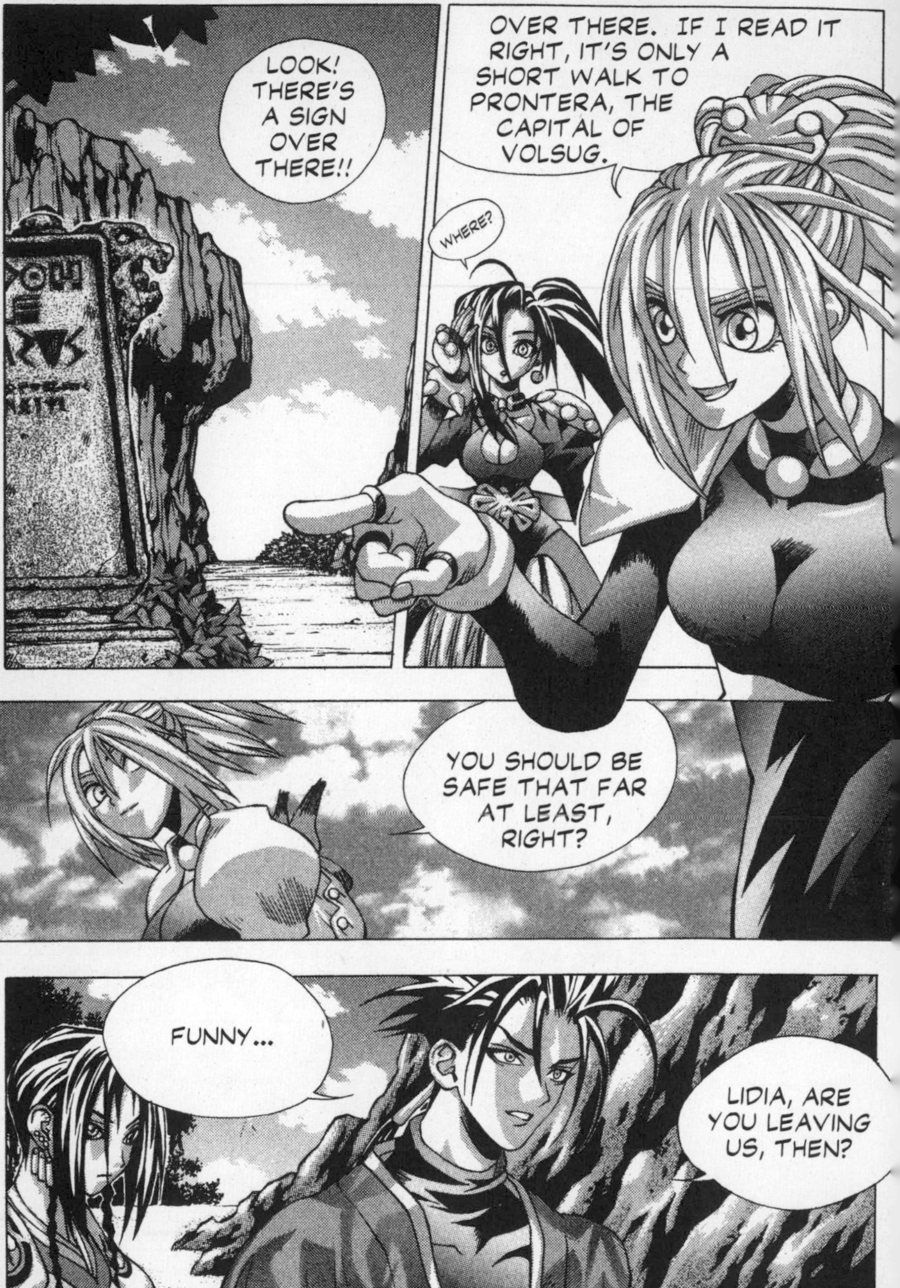
LOOK! THERE'S A SIGN OVER THERE!!
OVER THERE. IF I READ IT RIGHT, IT'S ONLY A SHORT WALK TO PRONTERA, THE CAPITAL OF VOLSUG.
WHERE?
YOU SHOULD BE SAFE THAT FAR AT LEAST, RIGHT?
FUNNY...
LIDIA, ARE YOU LEAVING US, THEN?

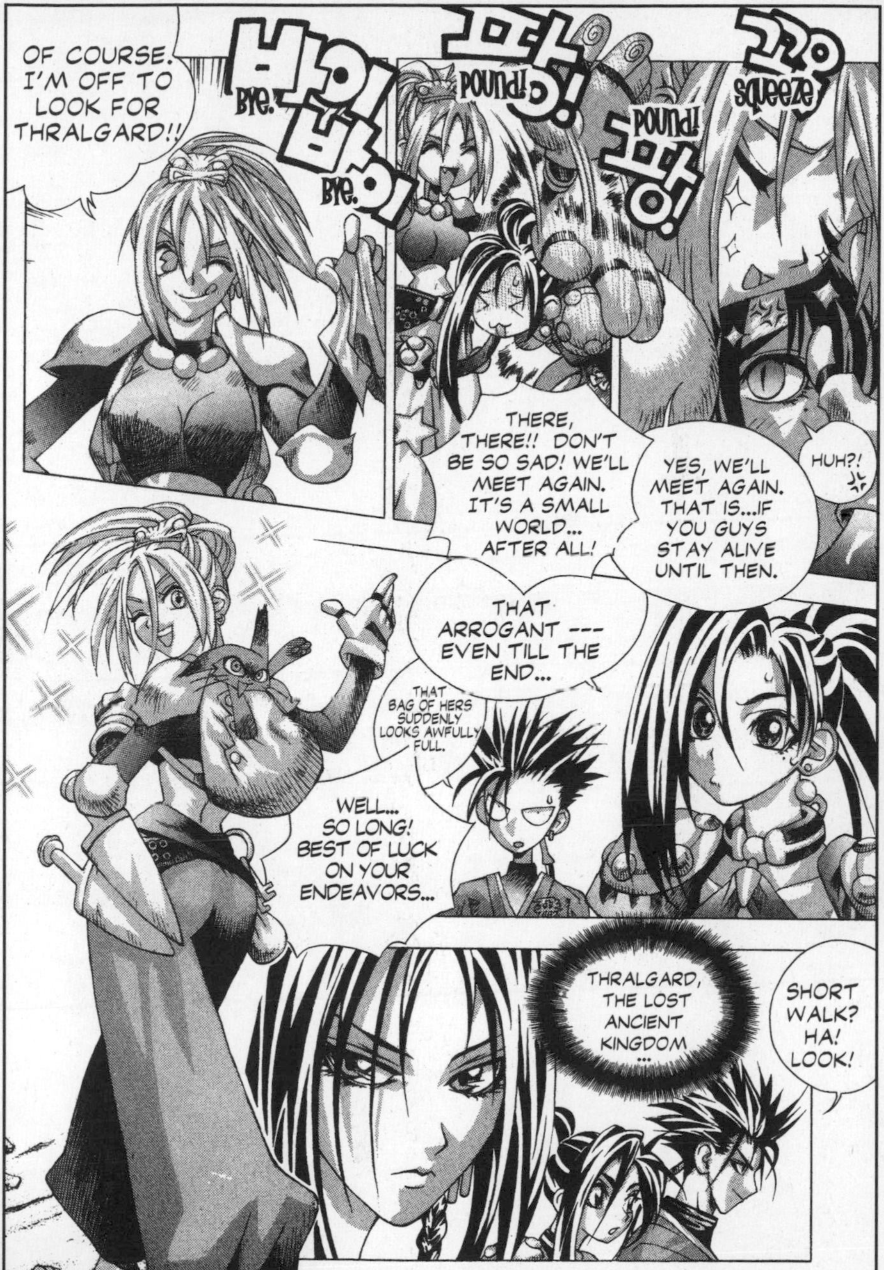
OF COURSE. I'M OFF TO LOOK FOR THRALGARD!!
바이!
BYE.
바이!
BYE.
콩!
POUND!
콩!
POUND!
SQUEEZE
HUH?!
THERE, THERE!! DON'T BE SO SAD! WE'LL MEET AGAIN. IT'S A SMALL WORLD... AFTER ALL!
YES, WE'LL MEET AGAIN. THAT IS...IF YOU GUYS STAY ALIVE UNTIL THEN.
THAT ARROGANT --- EVEN TILL THE END...
THAT BAG OF HERS SUDDENLY LOOKS AWFULLY FULL.
WELL... SO LONG! BEST OF LUCK ON YOUR ENDEAVORS...
THRALGARD, THE LOST ANCIENT KINGDOM ...
SHORT WALK? HA! LOOK!

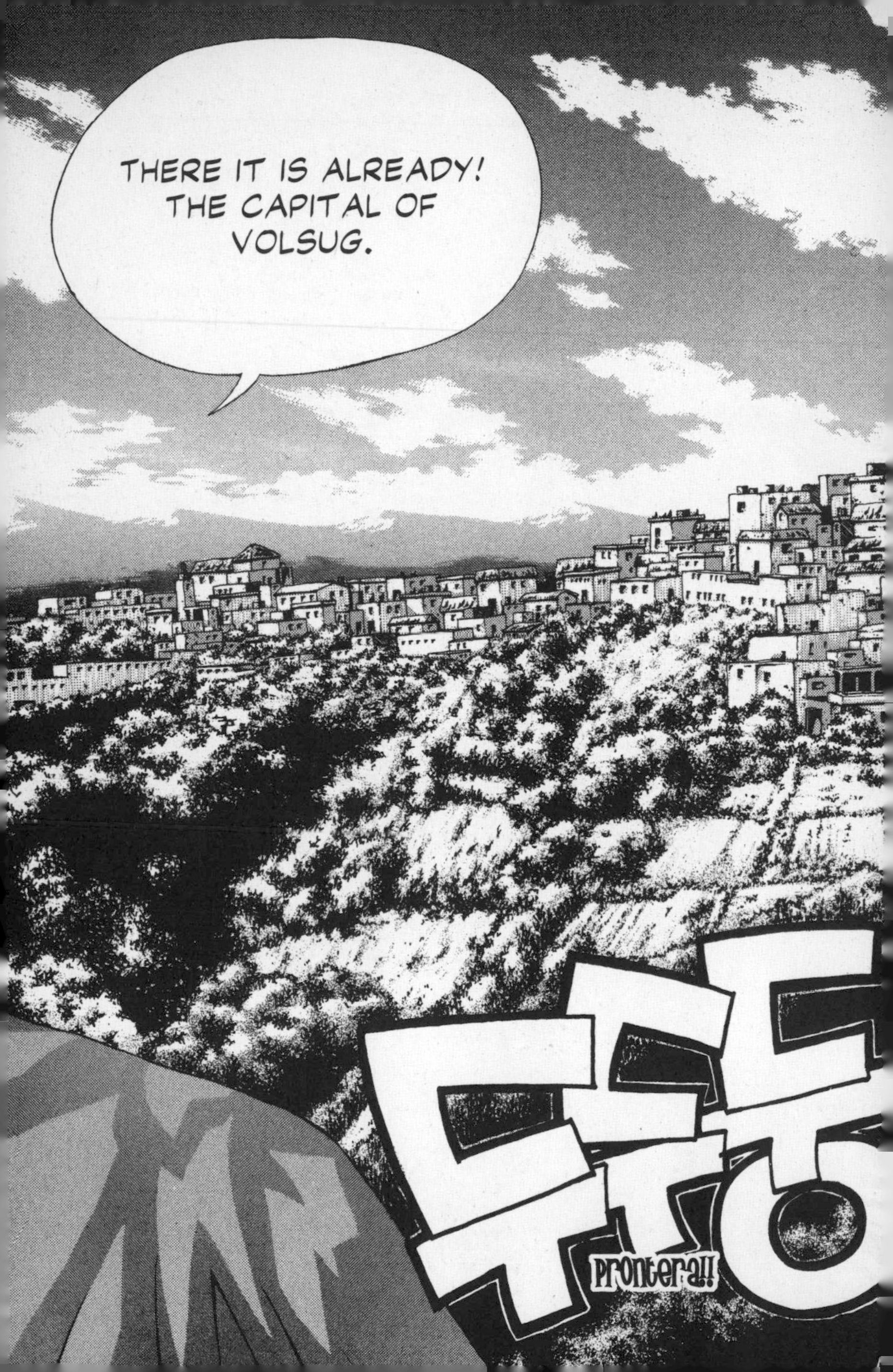
THERE IT IS ALREADY! THE CAPITAL OF VOLSUG.
Prontera!!

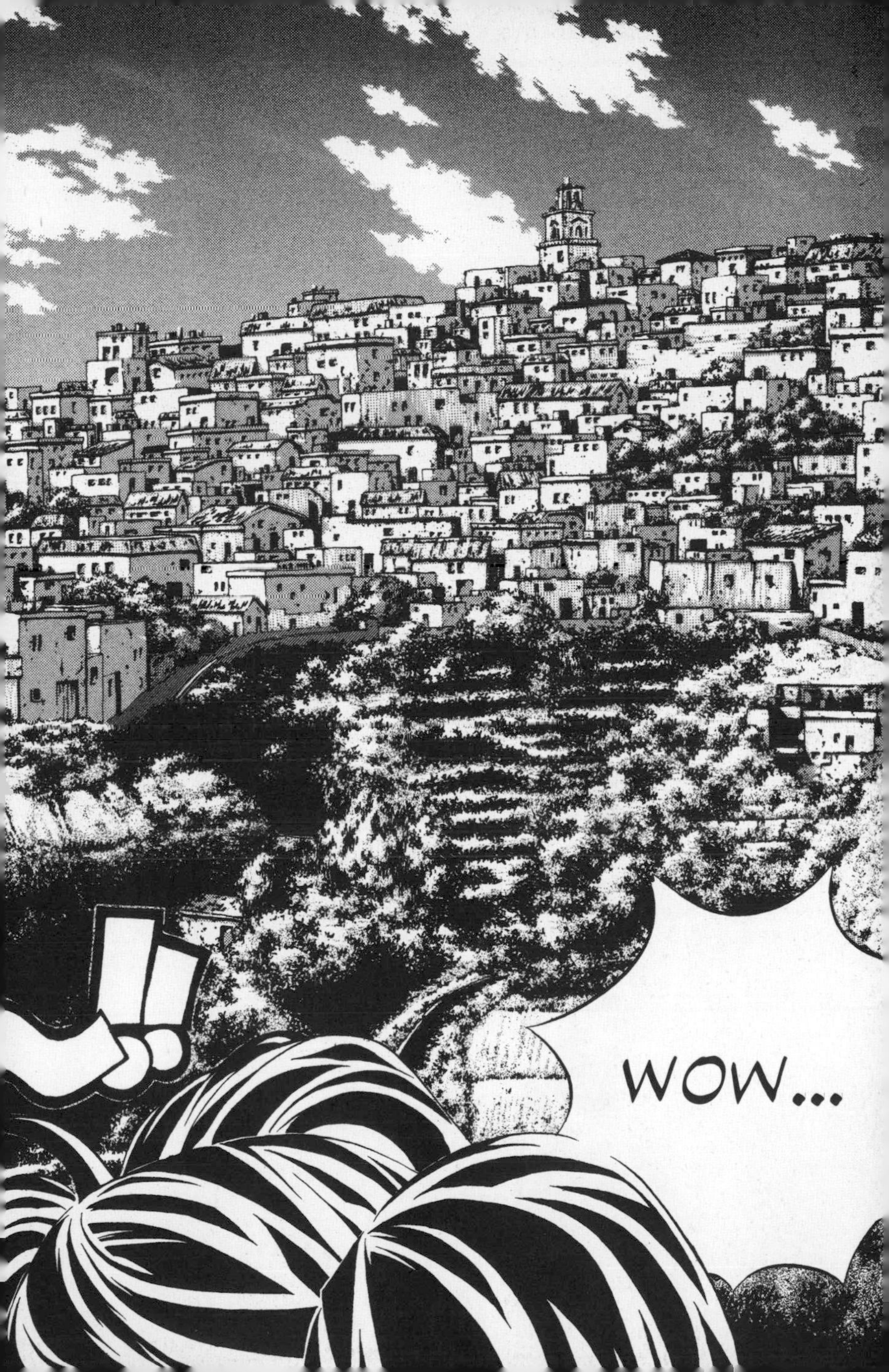
WOW...

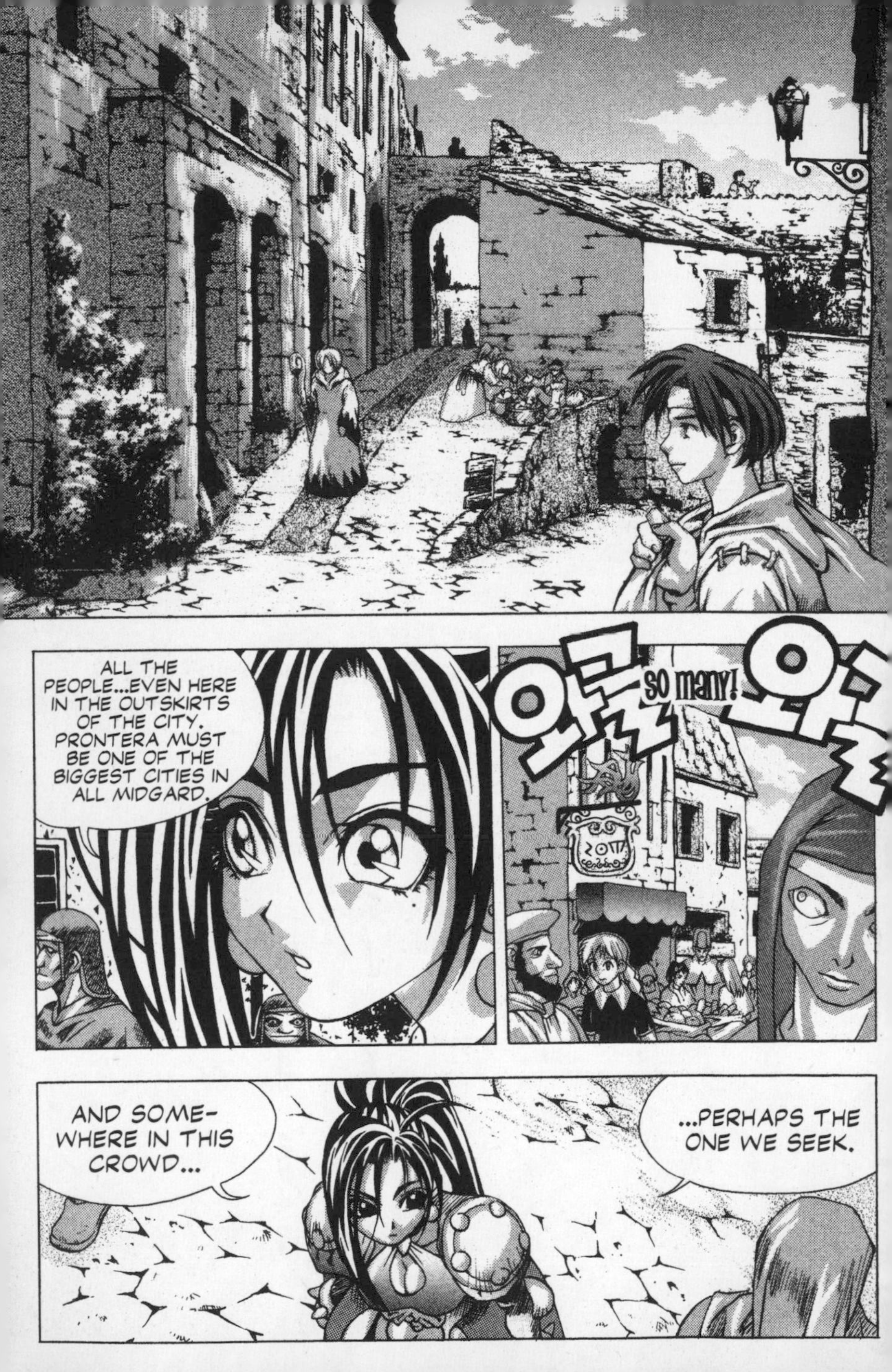
ALL THE PEOPLE...EVEN HERE IN THE OUTSKIRTS OF THE CITY. PRONTERA MUST BE ONE OF THE BIGGEST CITIES IN ALL MIDGARD.
so many!
AND SOME-WHERE IN THIS CROWD...
...PERHAPS THE ONE WE SEEK.

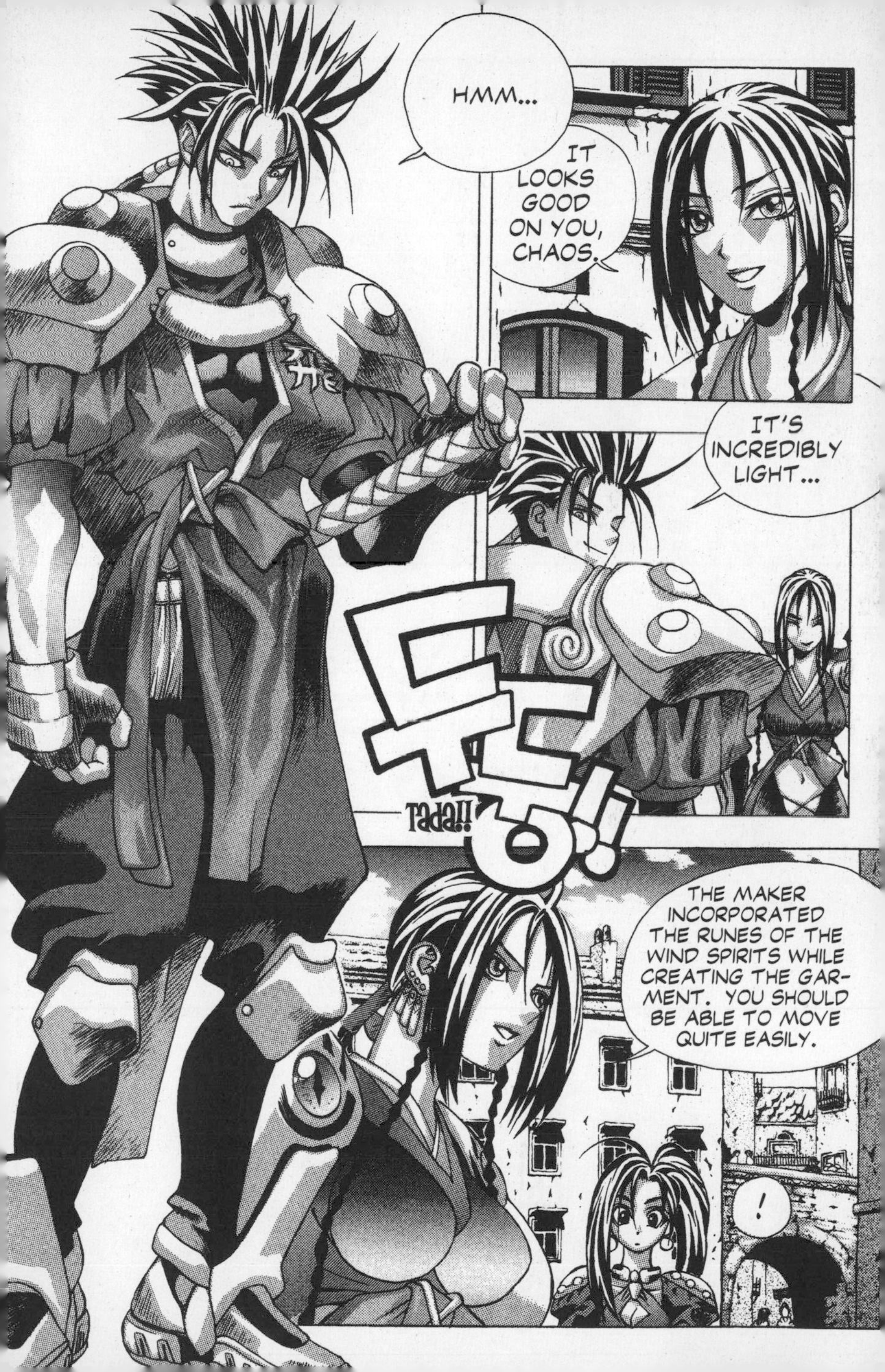
HMM...
IT LOOKS GOOD ON YOU, CHAOS.
IT'S INCREDIBLY LIGHT...
TADA!!
THE MAKER INCORPORATED THE RUNES OF THE WIND SPIRITS WHILE CREATING THE GAR- MENT. YOU SHOULD BE ABLE TO MOVE QUITE EASILY.
!

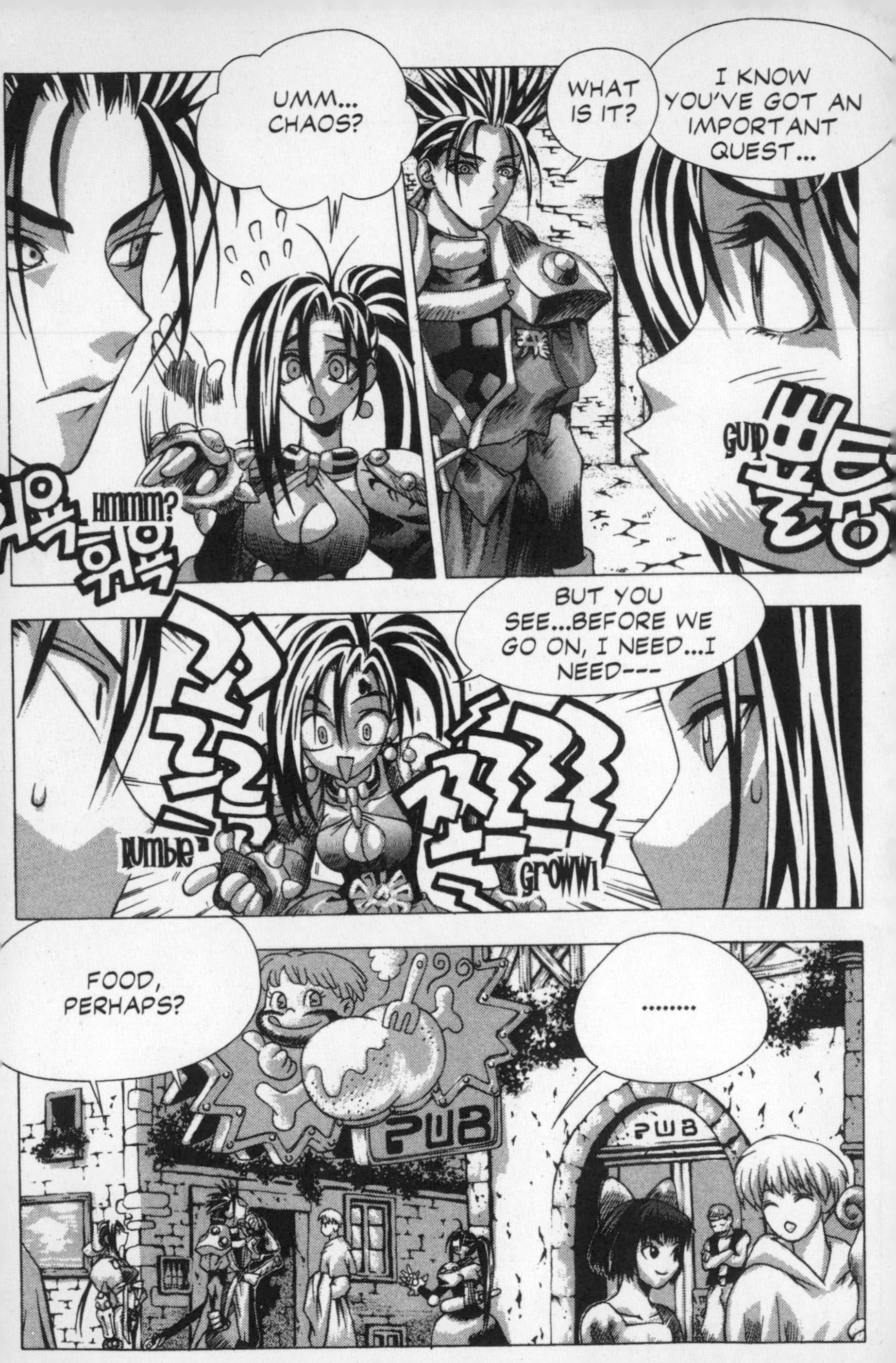
UMM... CHAOS?
HMMMM?
WHAT IS IT?
I KNOW YOU'VE GOT AN IMPORTANT QUEST...
GULP
BUT YOU SEE...BEFORE WE GO ON, I NEED...I NEED---
RUMBLE
GROWWL
FOOD, PERHAPS?
PUB
....
PUB

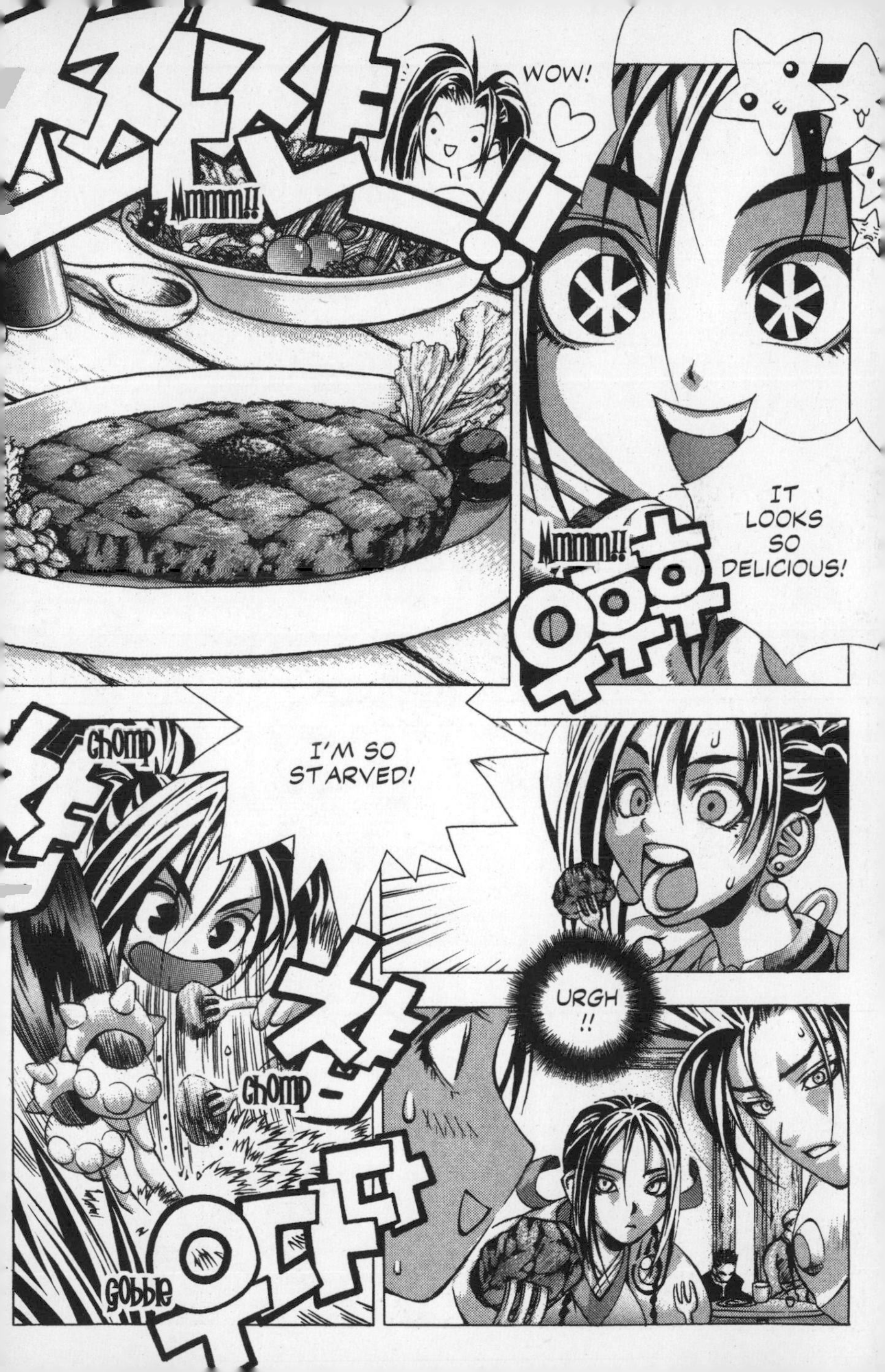
IT LOOKS SO DELICIOUS!
Mmmm!!
WOW!
Mmmm!!
URGH !!
I'M SO STARVED!
Chomp
Chomp
Gobble

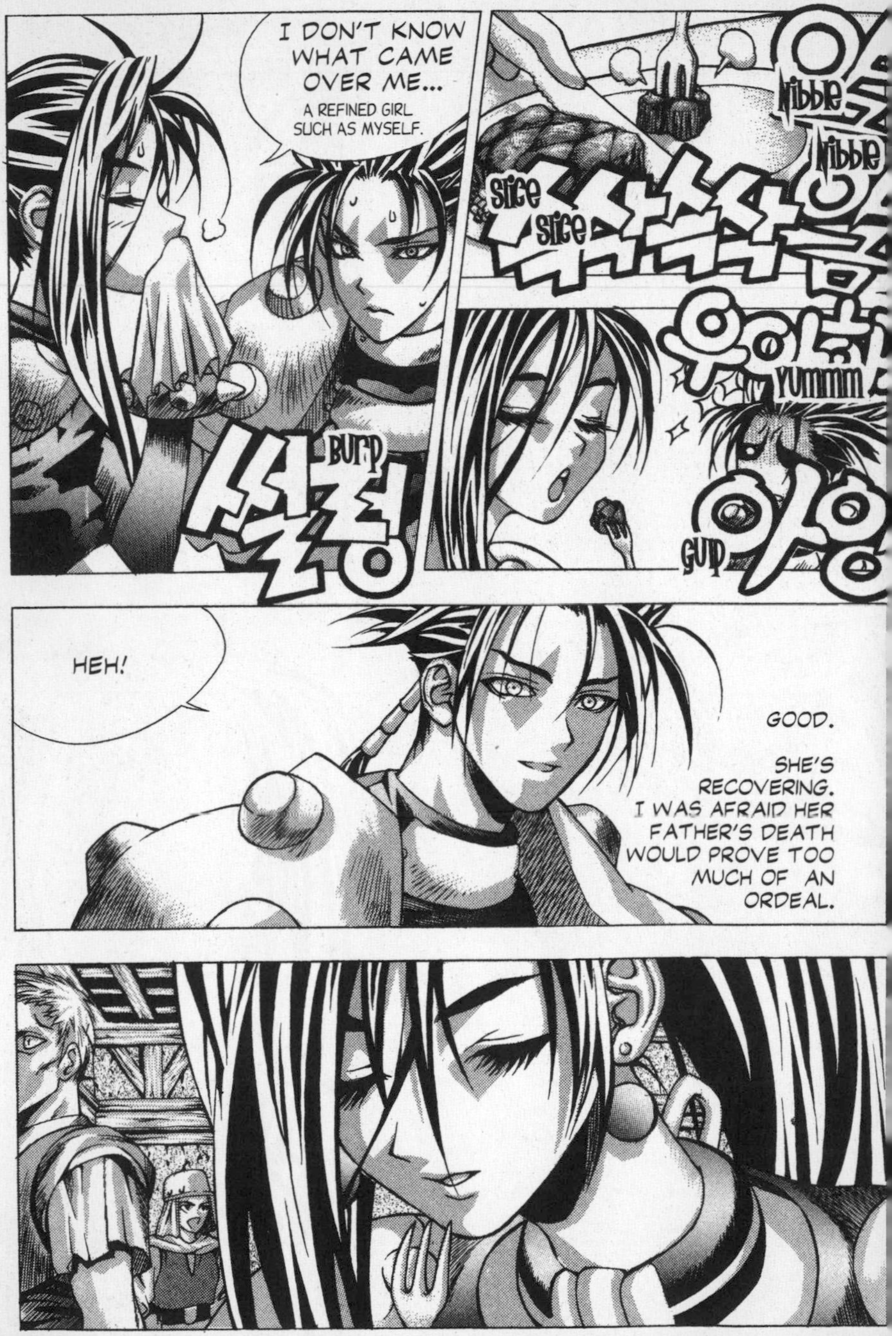
I DON'T KNOW WHAT CAME OVER ME...
A REFINED GIRL SUCH AS MYSELF.
BURP
SLICE
SLICE
NIBBLE
NIBBLE
YUMMM
GULP
HEH!
GOOD.
SHE'S RECOVERING.
I WAS AFRAID HER FATHER'S DEATH WOULD PROVE TOO MUCH OF AN ORDEAL.

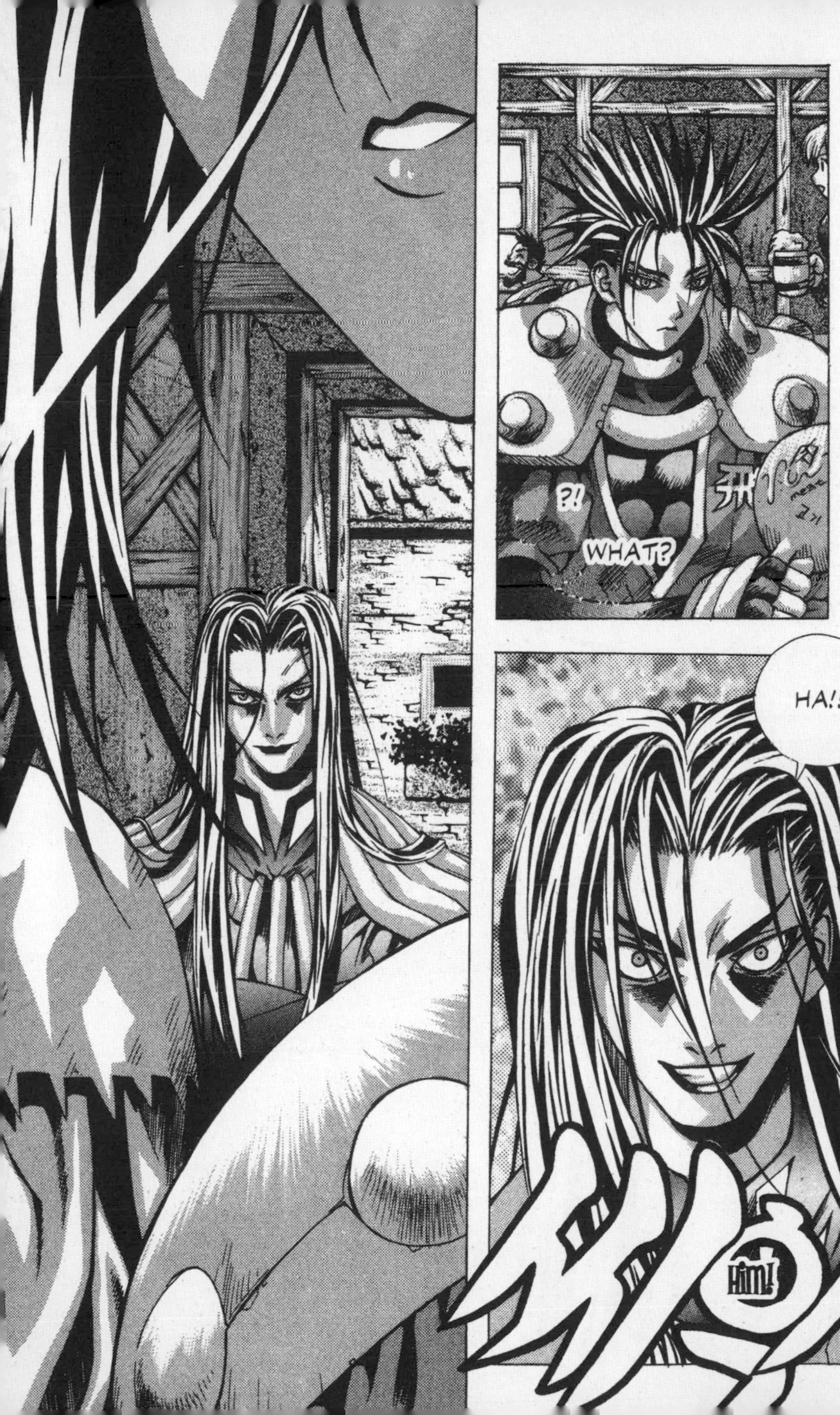
?!
WHAT?
HA!!
HiM!

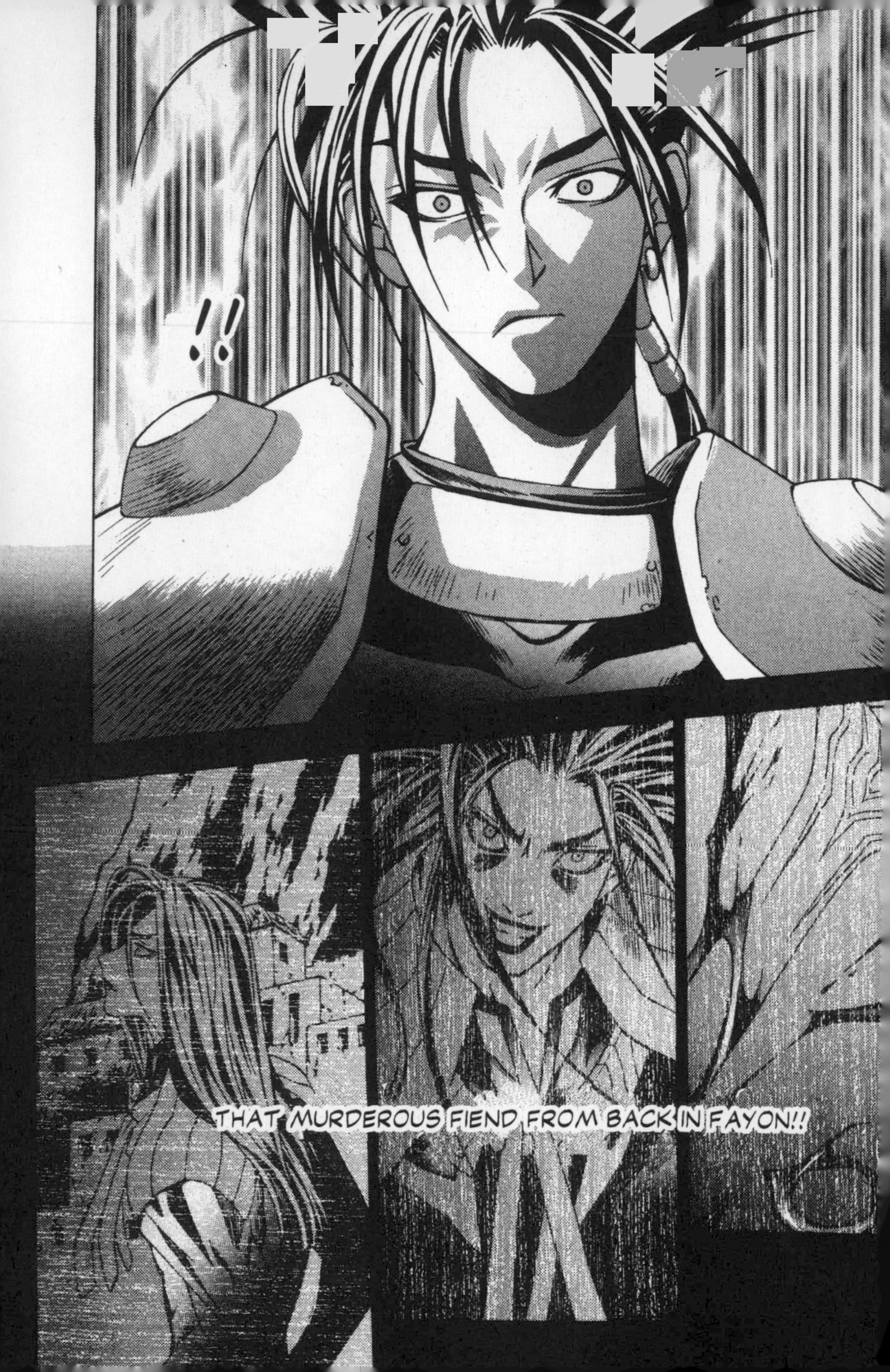
!!
THAT MURDEROUS FIEND FROM BACK IN FAYON!!

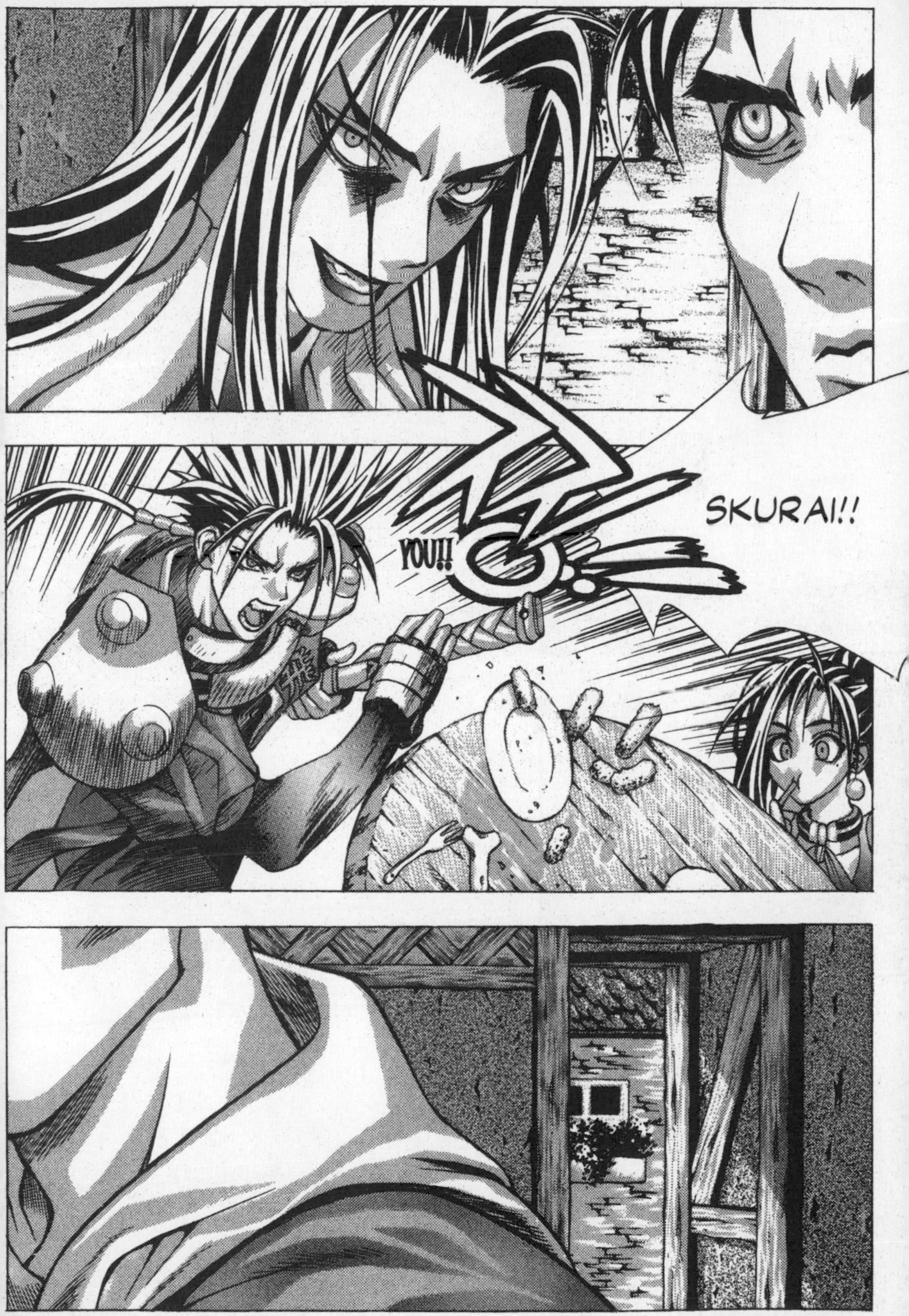
YOU!!
SKURAI!!

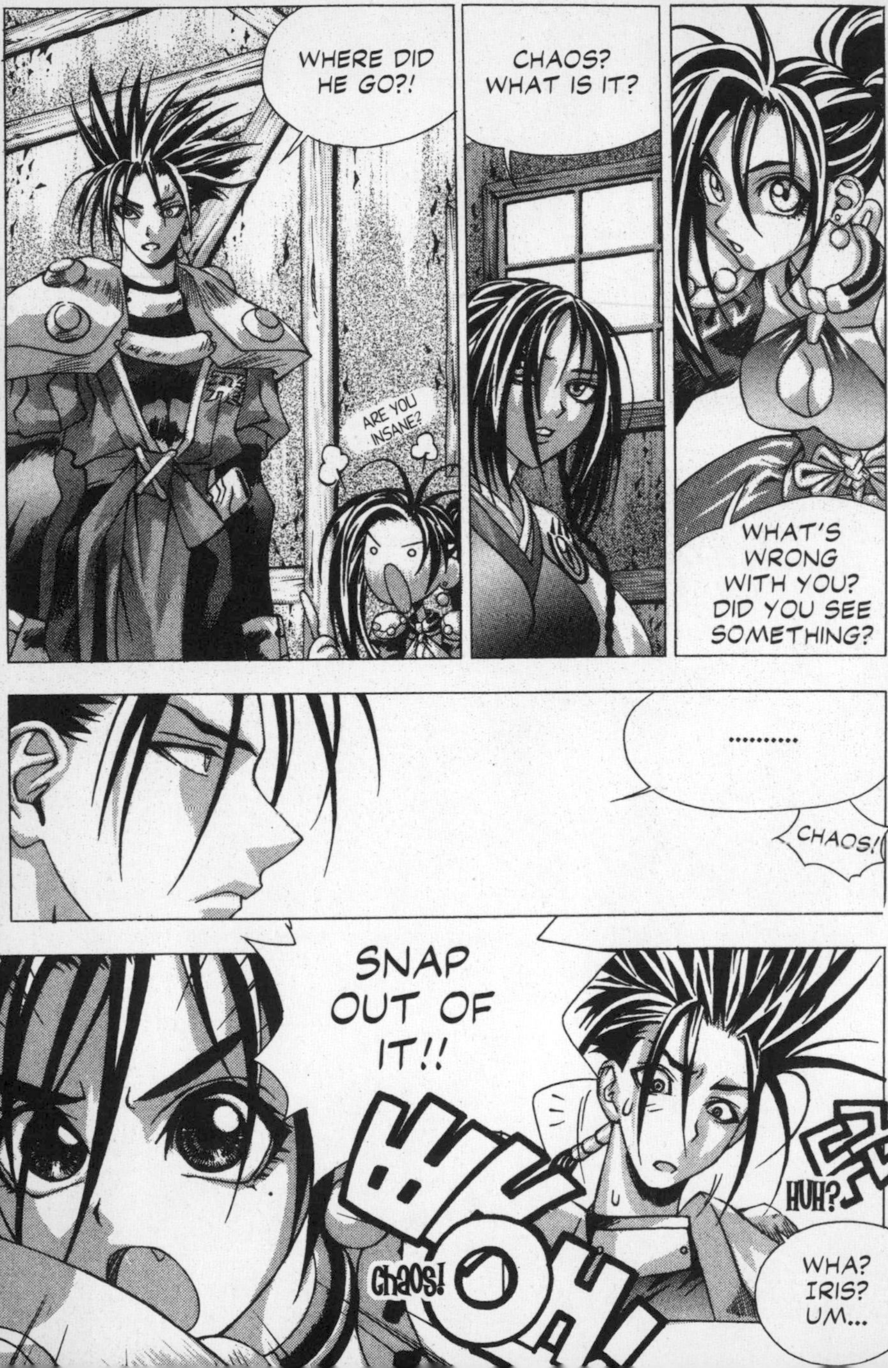
WHERE DID HE GO?!
ARE YOU INSANE?
CHAOS? WHAT IS IT?
WHAT'S WRONG WITH YOU? DID YOU SEE SOMETHING?
....
CHAOS!
SNAP OUT OF IT!!
WHOA!!
CHAOS!
HUH?
WHA? IRIS? UM...

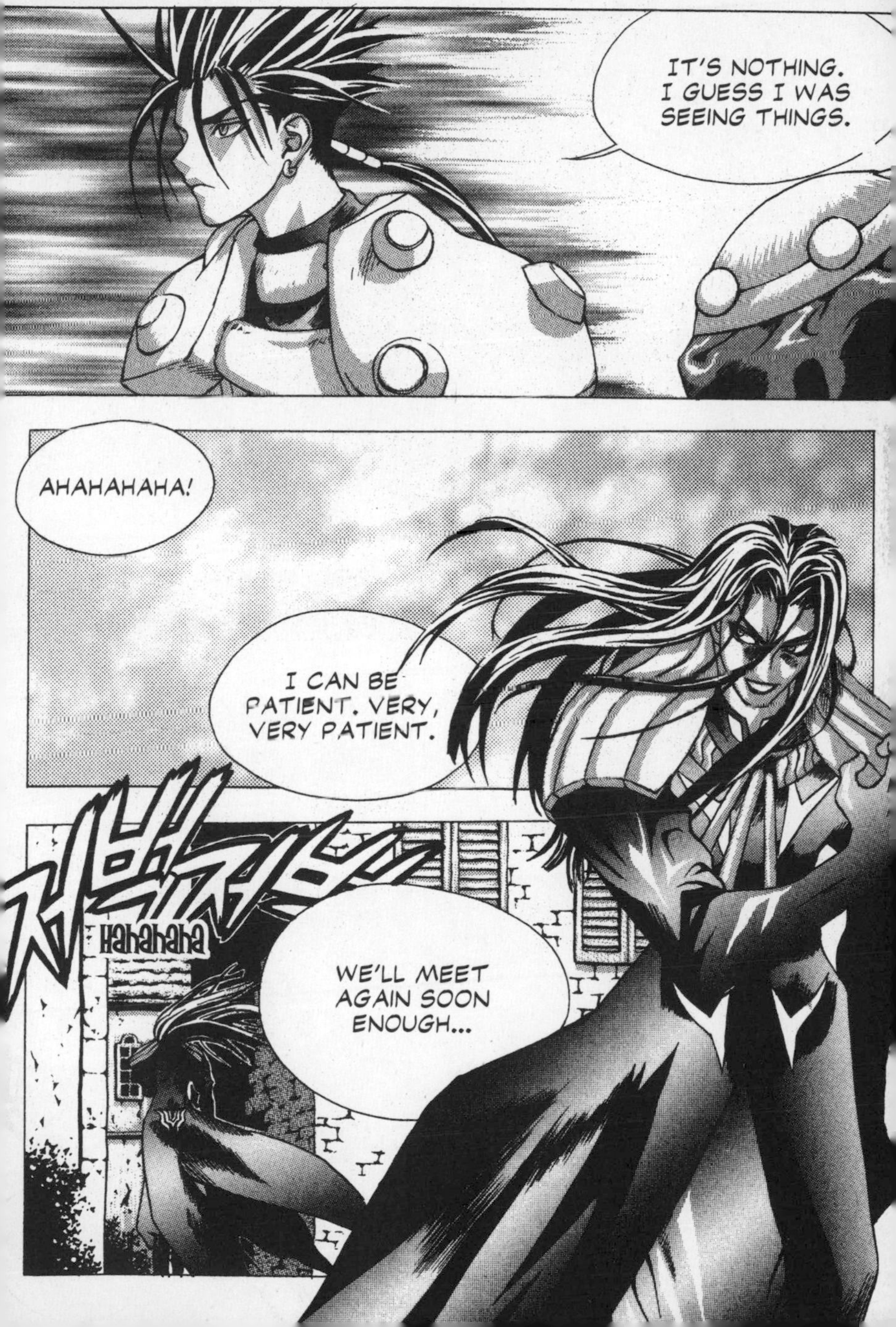
IT'S NOTHING. I GUESS I WAS SEEING THINGS.
AHAHAHAHA!
I CAN BE PATIENT. VERY, VERY PATIENT.
Hahahaha
WE'LL MEET AGAIN SOON ENOUGH...

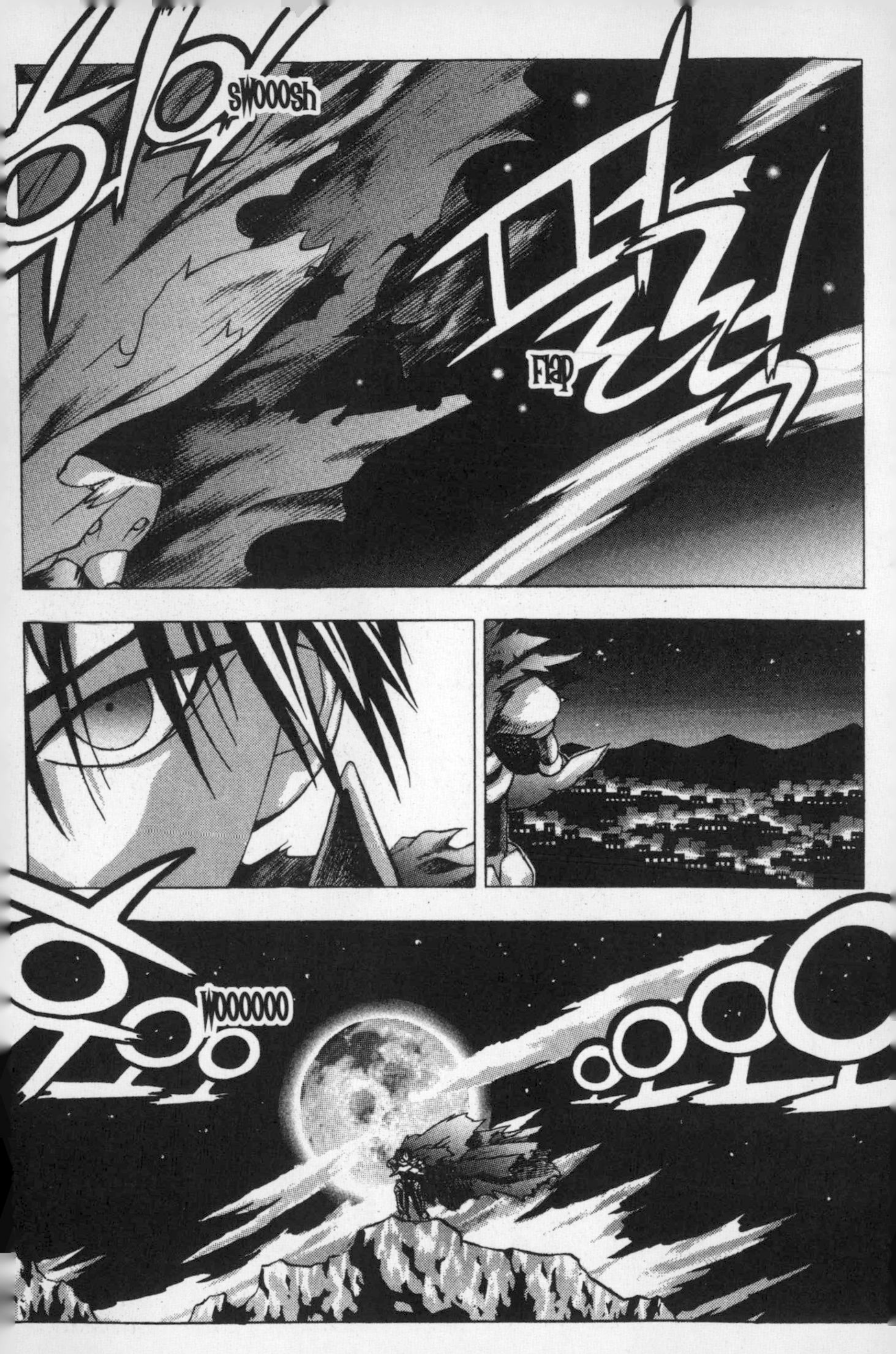
swooosh
Flap
WOOOOOO

RAGNAROK
라그나로크
IN TO THE ABYSS

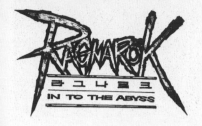

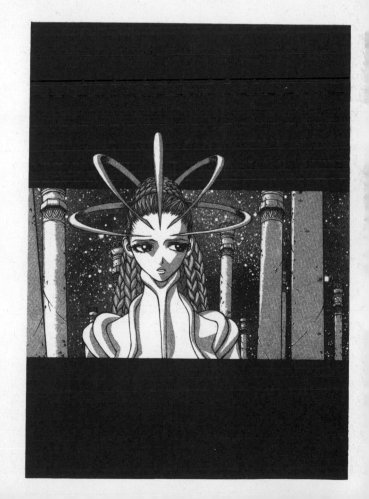

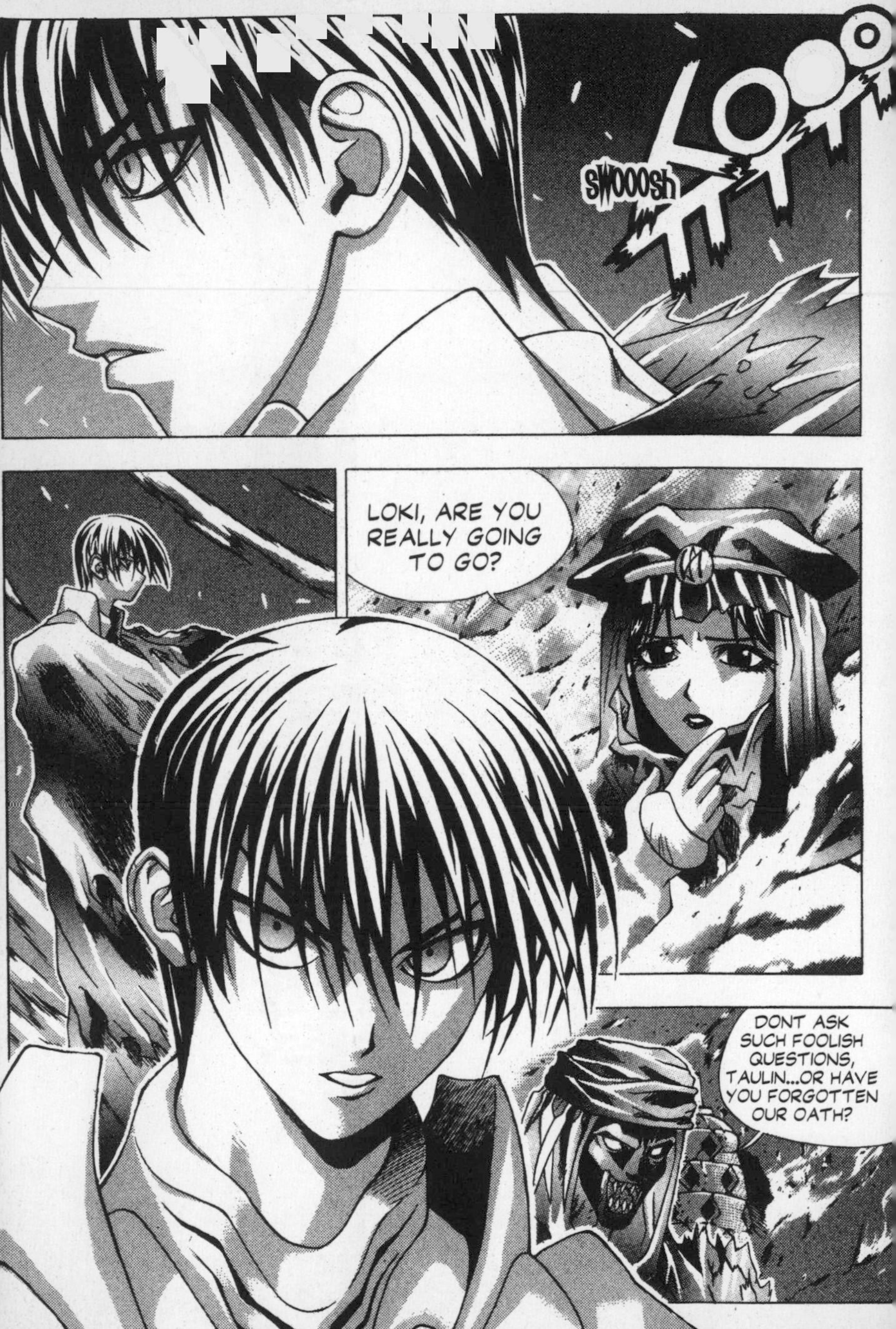
SWOOOSH
LOKI, ARE YOU REALLY GOING TO GO?
DONT ASK SUCH FOOLISH QUESTIONS, TAULIN...OR HAVE YOU FORGOTTEN OUR OATH?

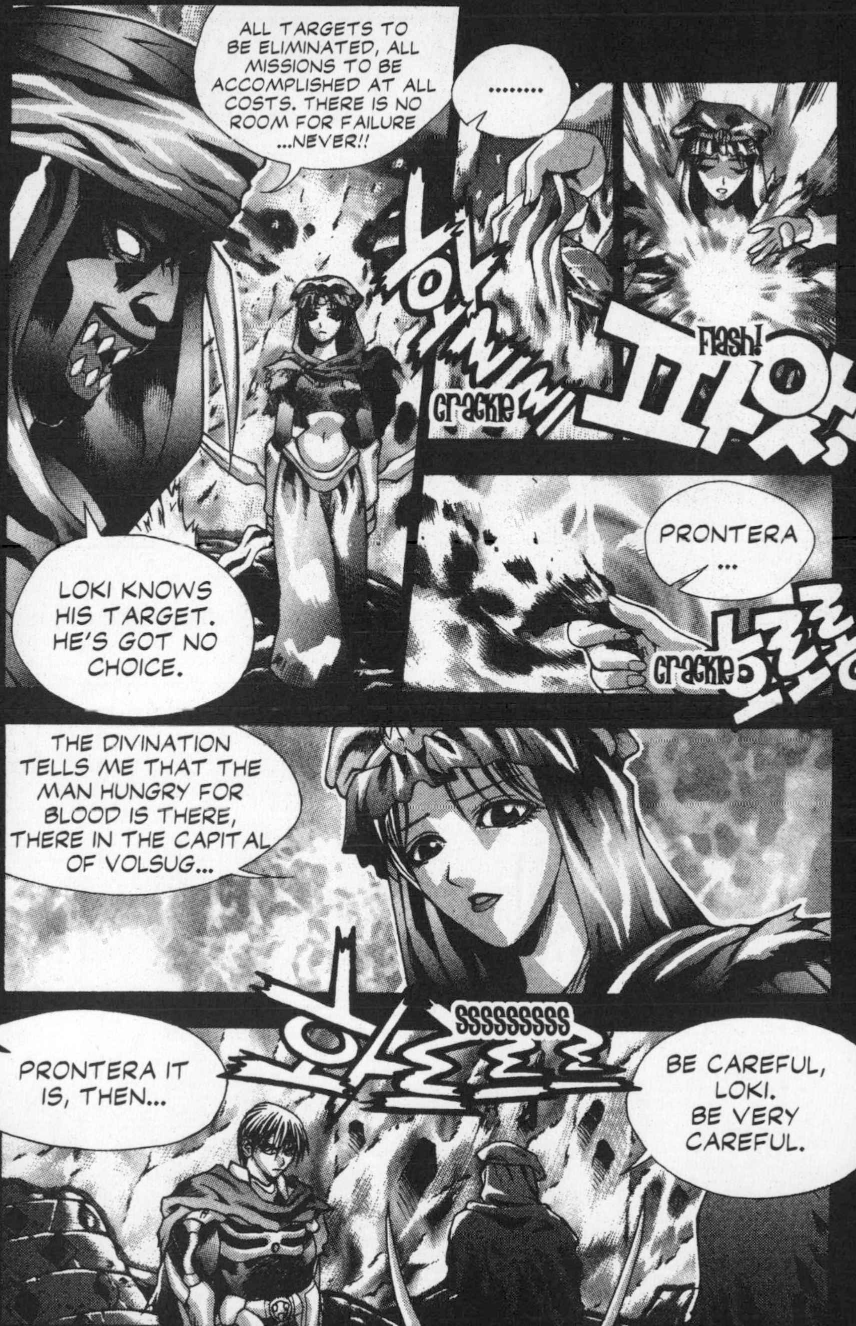
ALL TARGETS TO BE ELIMINATED, ALL MISSIONS TO BE ACCOMPLISHED AT ALL COSTS. THERE IS NO ROOM FOR FAILURE ...NEVER!!
LOKI KNOWS HIS TARGET. HE'S GOT NO CHOICE.
....
CRACKLE
FLASH!
파앗!
PRONTERA ...
CRACKLE
THE DIVINATION TELLS ME THAT THE MAN HUNGRY FOR BLOOD IS THERE, THERE IN THE CAPITAL OF VOLSUG...
PRONTERA IT IS, THEN...
SSSSSSSSS
BE CAREFUL, LOKI. BE VERY CAREFUL.

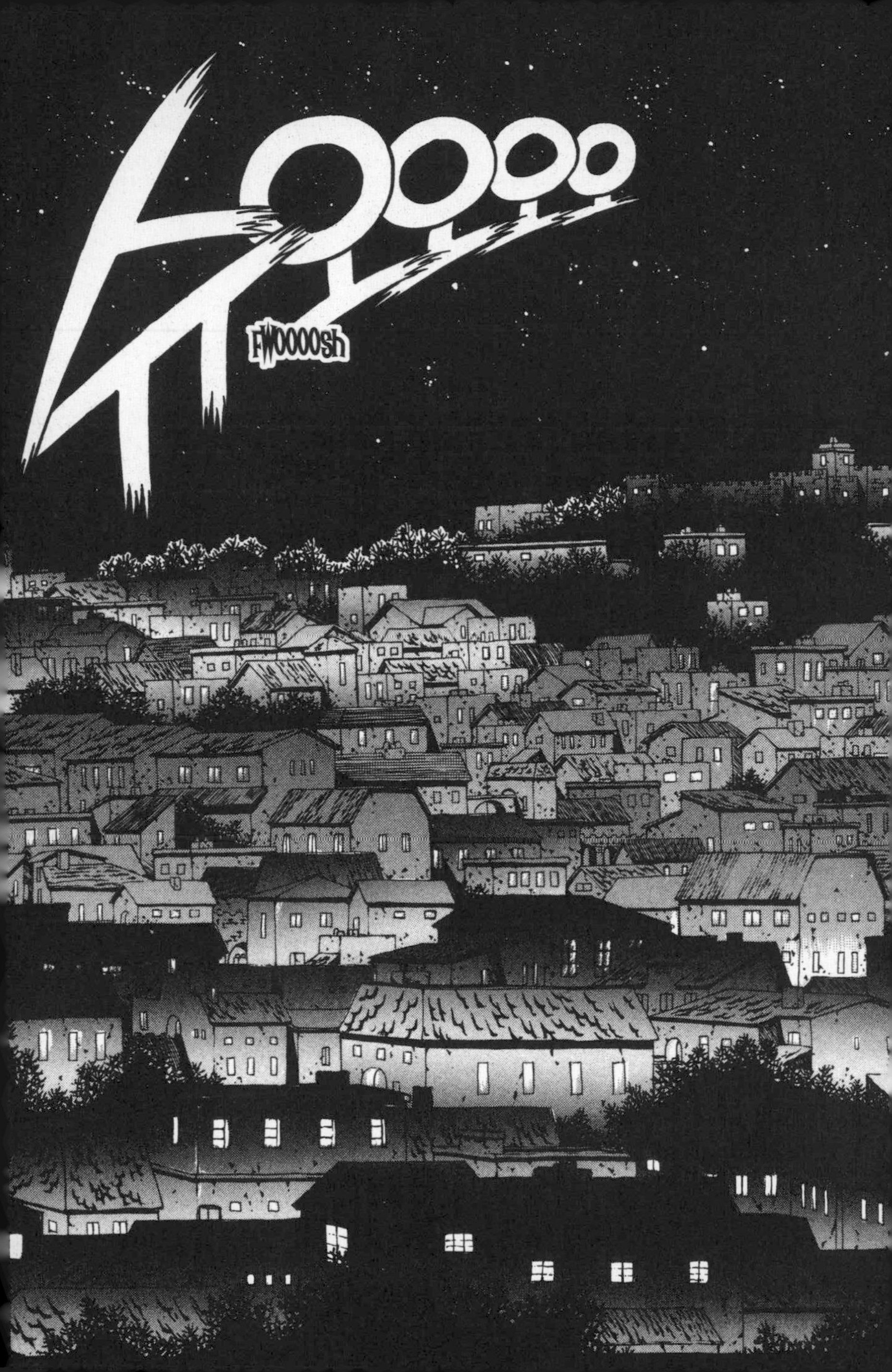
AOOOO
FWOOOOSh

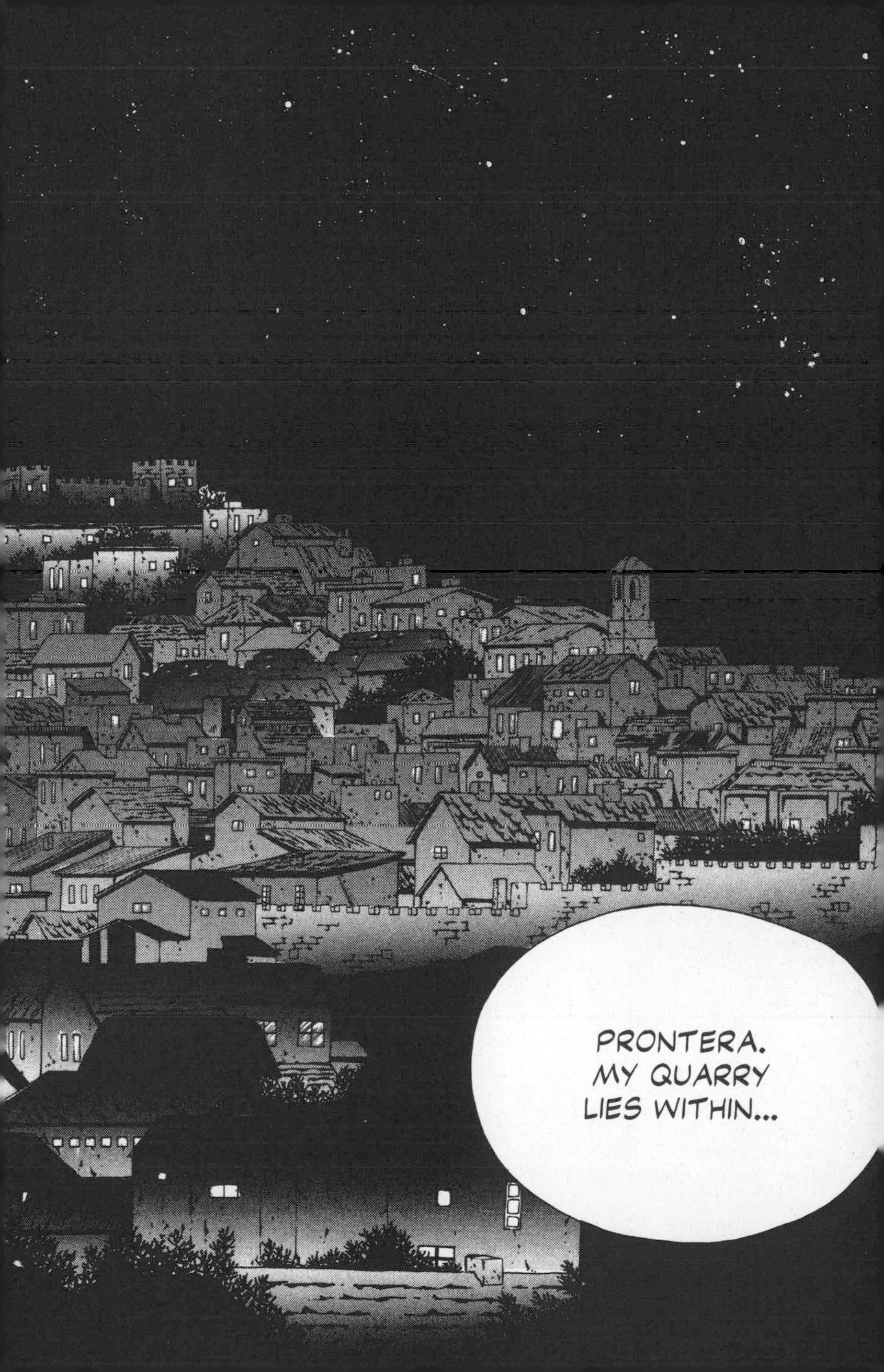
PRONTERA. MY QUARRY LIES WITHIN...

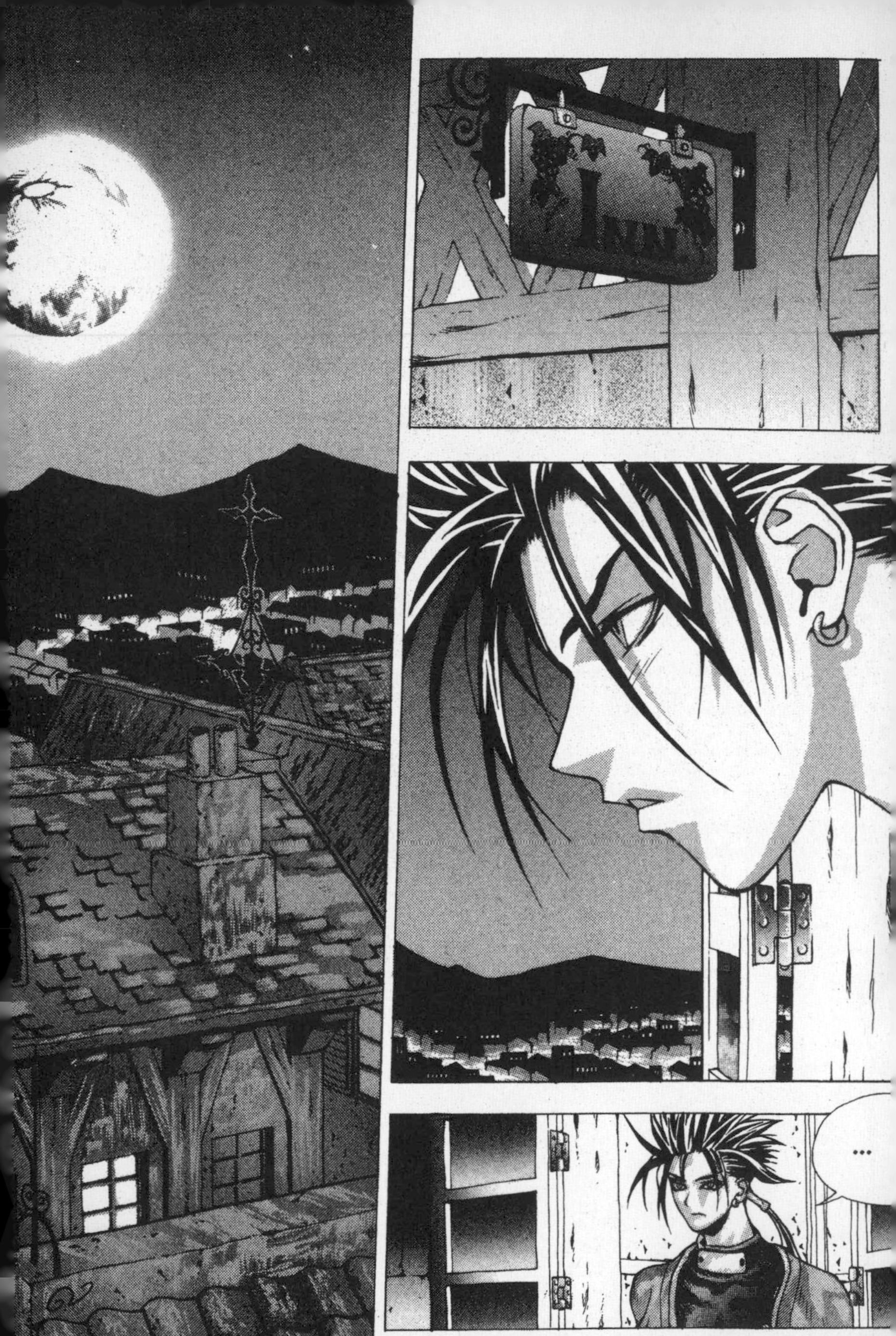
INN
...

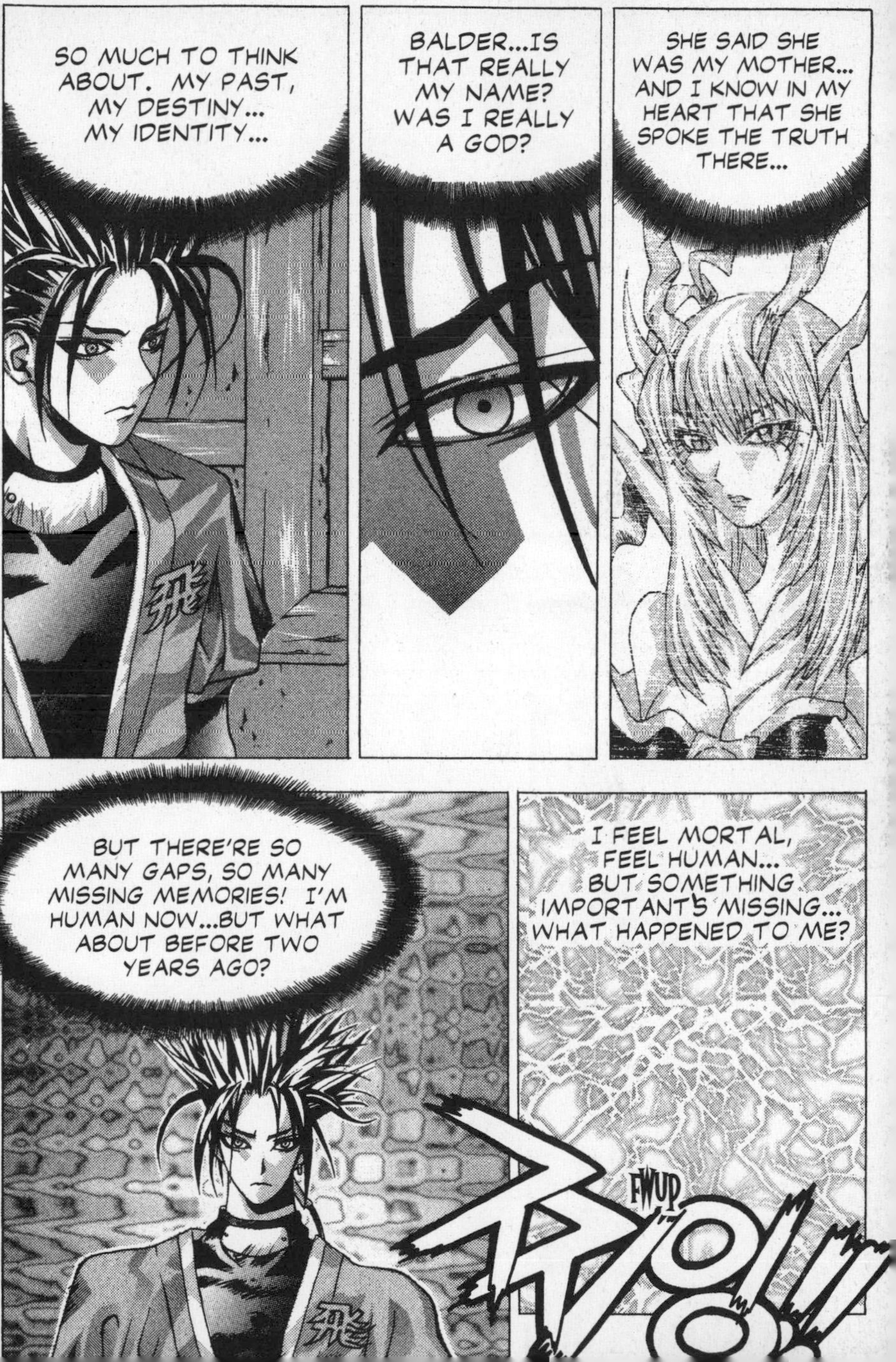

SO MUCH TO THINK ABOUT. MY PAST, MY DESTINY... MY IDENTITY...
BALDER...IS THAT REALLY MY NAME? WAS I REALLY A GOD?
SHE SAID SHE WAS MY MOTHER... AND I KNOW IN MY HEART THAT SHE SPOKE THE TRUTH THERE...
BUT THERE'RE SO MANY GAPS, SO MANY MISSING MEMORIES! I'M HUMAN NOW...BUT WHAT ABOUT BEFORE TWO YEARS AGO?
I FEEL MORTAL, FEEL HUMAN... BUT SOMETHING IMPORTANT'S MISSING... WHAT HAPPENED TO ME?
FWUP

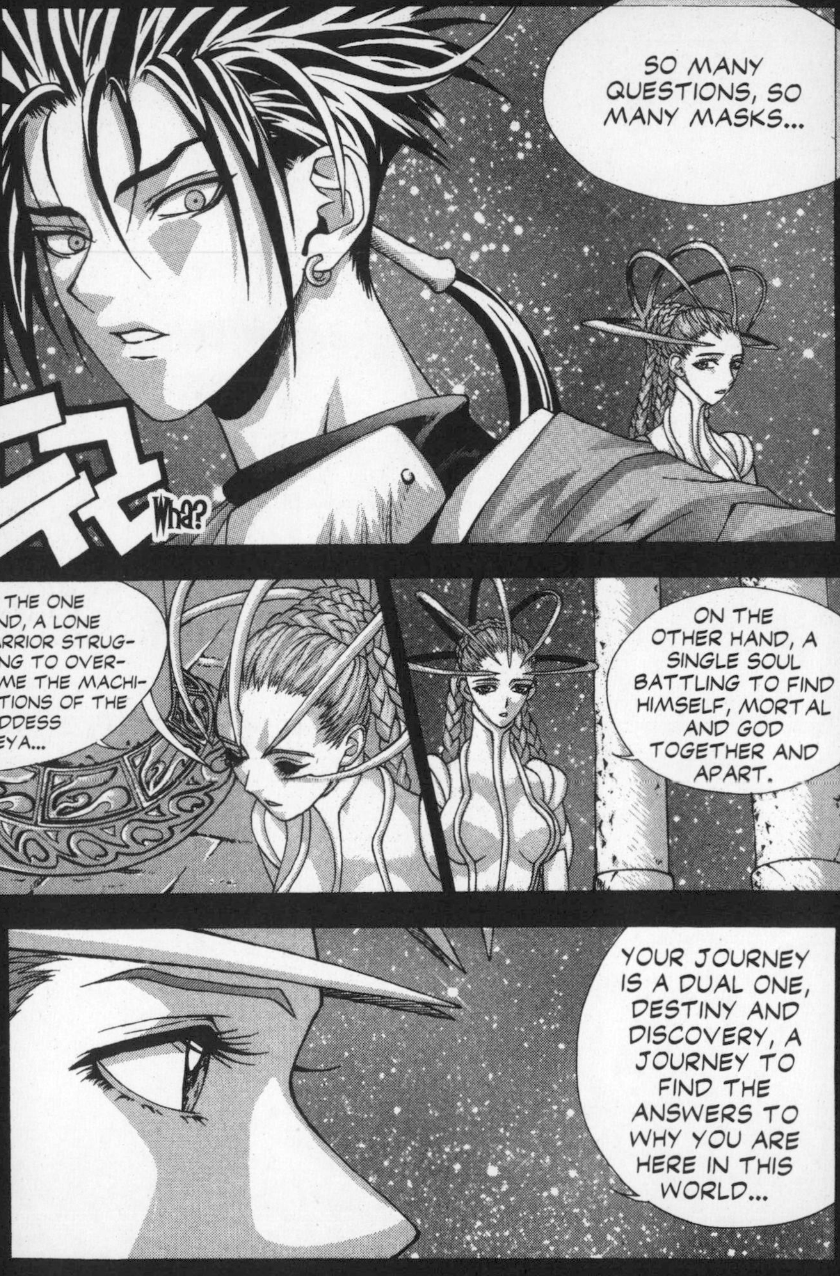
SO MANY QUESTIONS, SO MANY MASKS...
Wha?
ON THE ONE HAND, A LONE WARRIOR STRUG-GLING TO OVER-COME THE MACHI-NATIONS OF THE GODDESS FREYA...
ON THE OTHER HAND, A SINGLE SOUL BATTLING TO FIND HIMSELF, MORTAL AND GOD TOGETHER AND APART.
YOUR JOURNEY IS A DUAL ONE, DESTINY AND DISCOVERY, A JOURNEY TO FIND THE ANSWERS TO WHY YOU ARE HERE IN THIS WORLD...

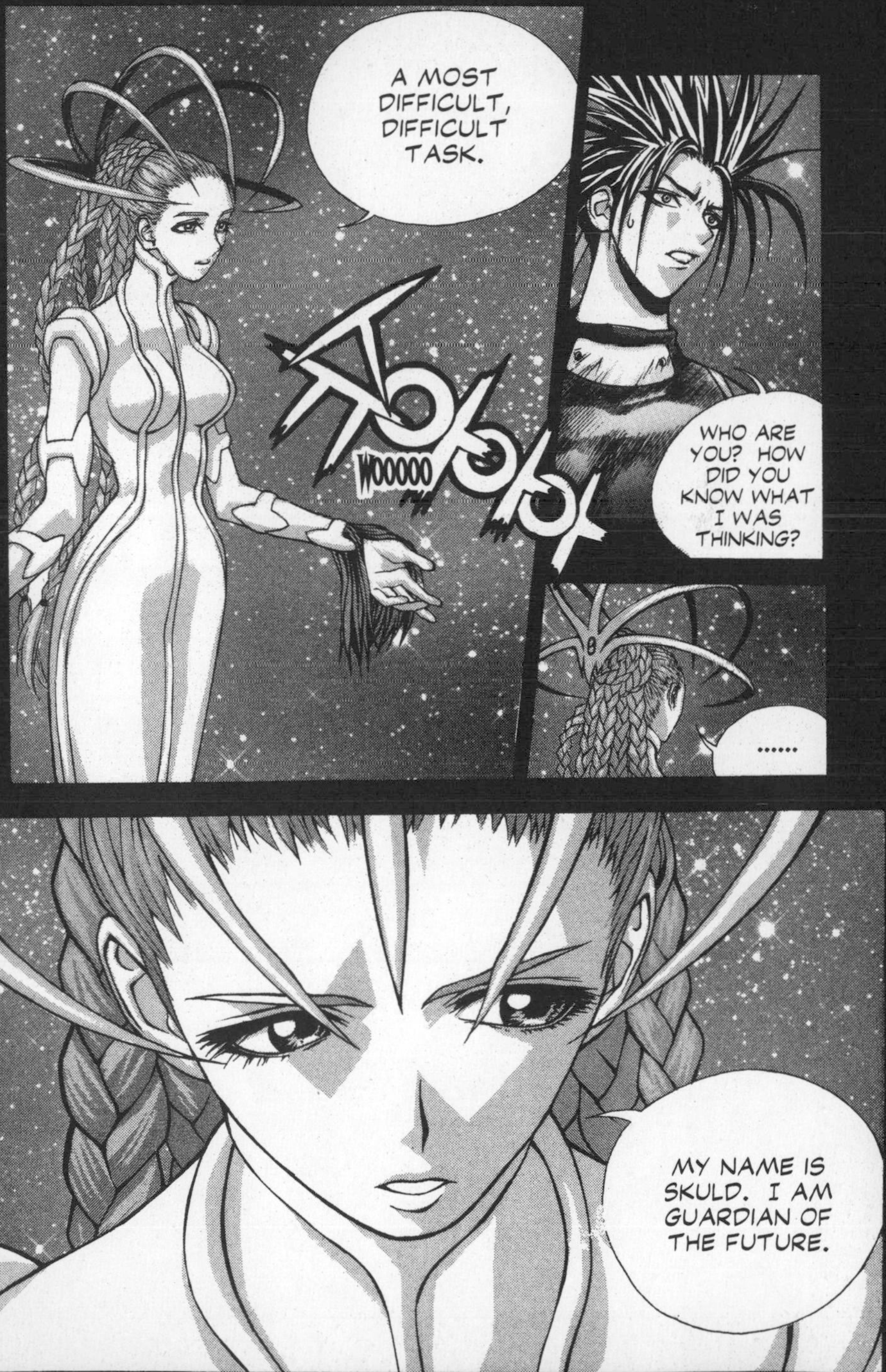
A MOST DIFFICULT, DIFFICULT TASK.
WOOOOO
WHO ARE YOU? HOW DID YOU KNOW WHAT I WAS THINKING?
......
MY NAME IS SKULD. I AM GUARDIAN OF THE FUTURE.

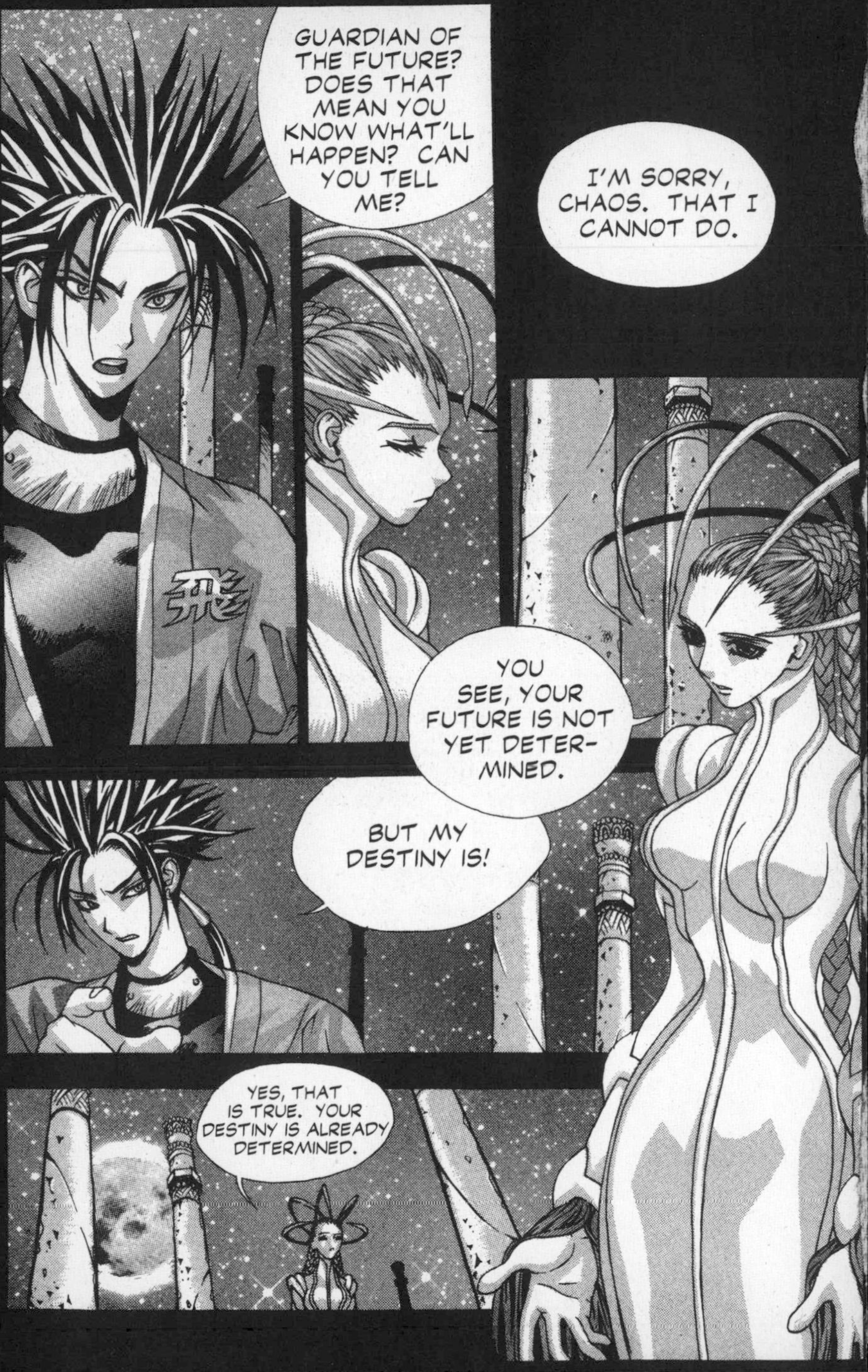
GUARDIAN OF THE FUTURE? DOES THAT MEAN YOU KNOW WHAT'LL HAPPEN? CAN YOU TELL ME?
I'M SORRY, CHAOS. THAT I CANNOT DO.
YOU SEE, YOUR FUTURE IS NOT YET DETER-MINED.
BUT MY DESTINY IS!
YES, THAT IS TRUE. YOUR DESTINY IS ALREADY DETERMINED.

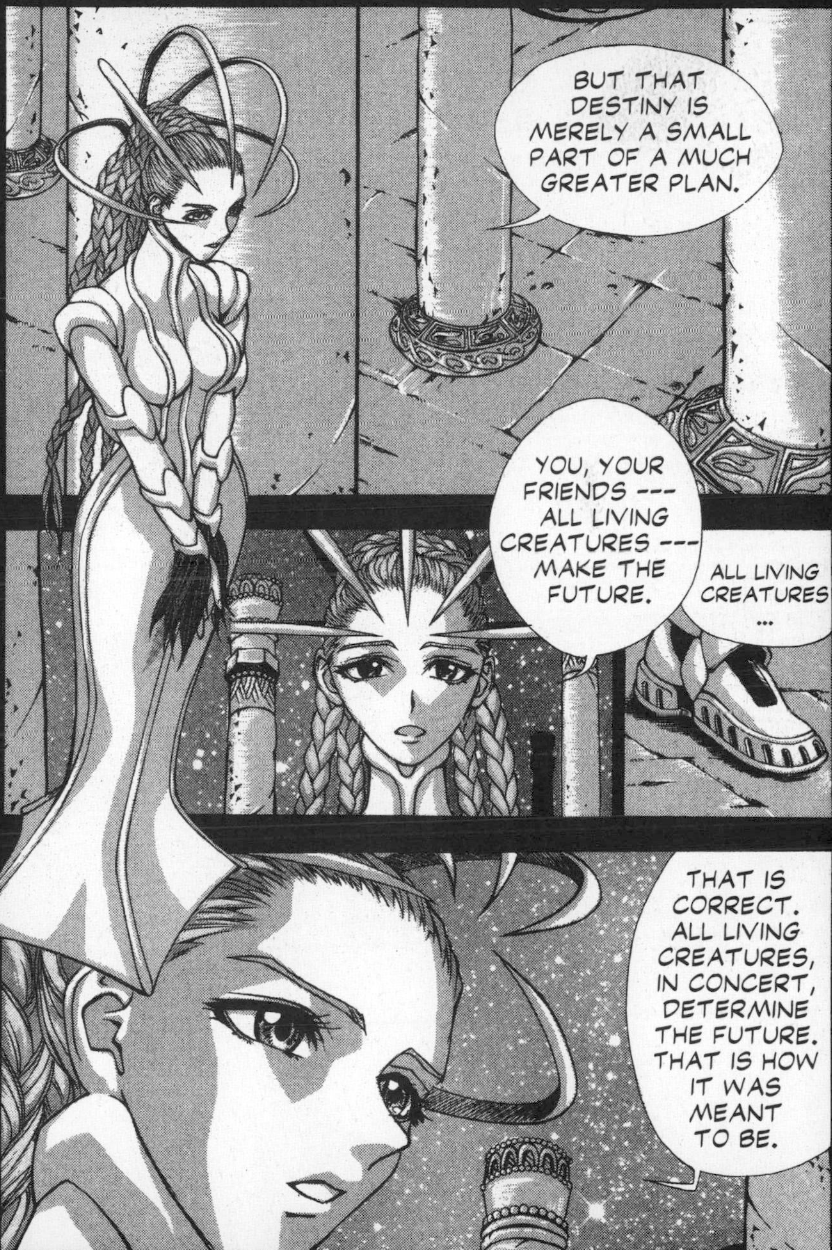
BUT THAT DESTINY IS MERELY A SMALL PART OF A MUCH GREATER PLAN.
YOU, YOUR FRIENDS --- ALL LIVING CREATURES --- MAKE THE FUTURE.
ALL LIVING CREATURES ...
THAT IS CORRECT. ALL LIVING CREATURES, IN CONCERT, DETERMINE THE FUTURE. THAT IS HOW IT WAS MEANT TO BE.

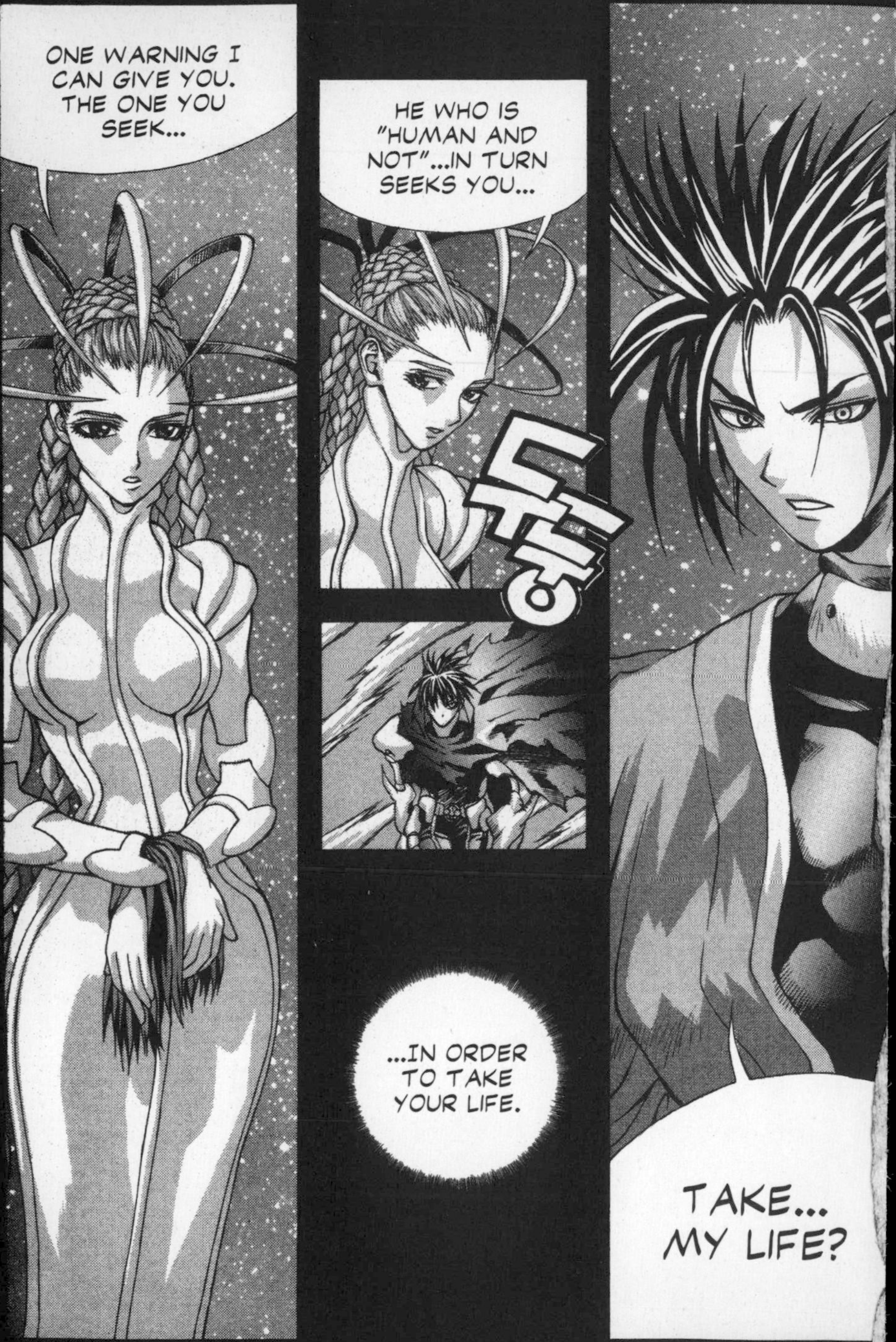
ONE WARNING I CAN GIVE YOU. THE ONE YOU SEEK...
HE WHO IS "HUMAN AND NOT"...IN TURN SEEKS YOU...
...IN ORDER TO TAKE YOUR LIFE.
TAKE... MY LIFE?

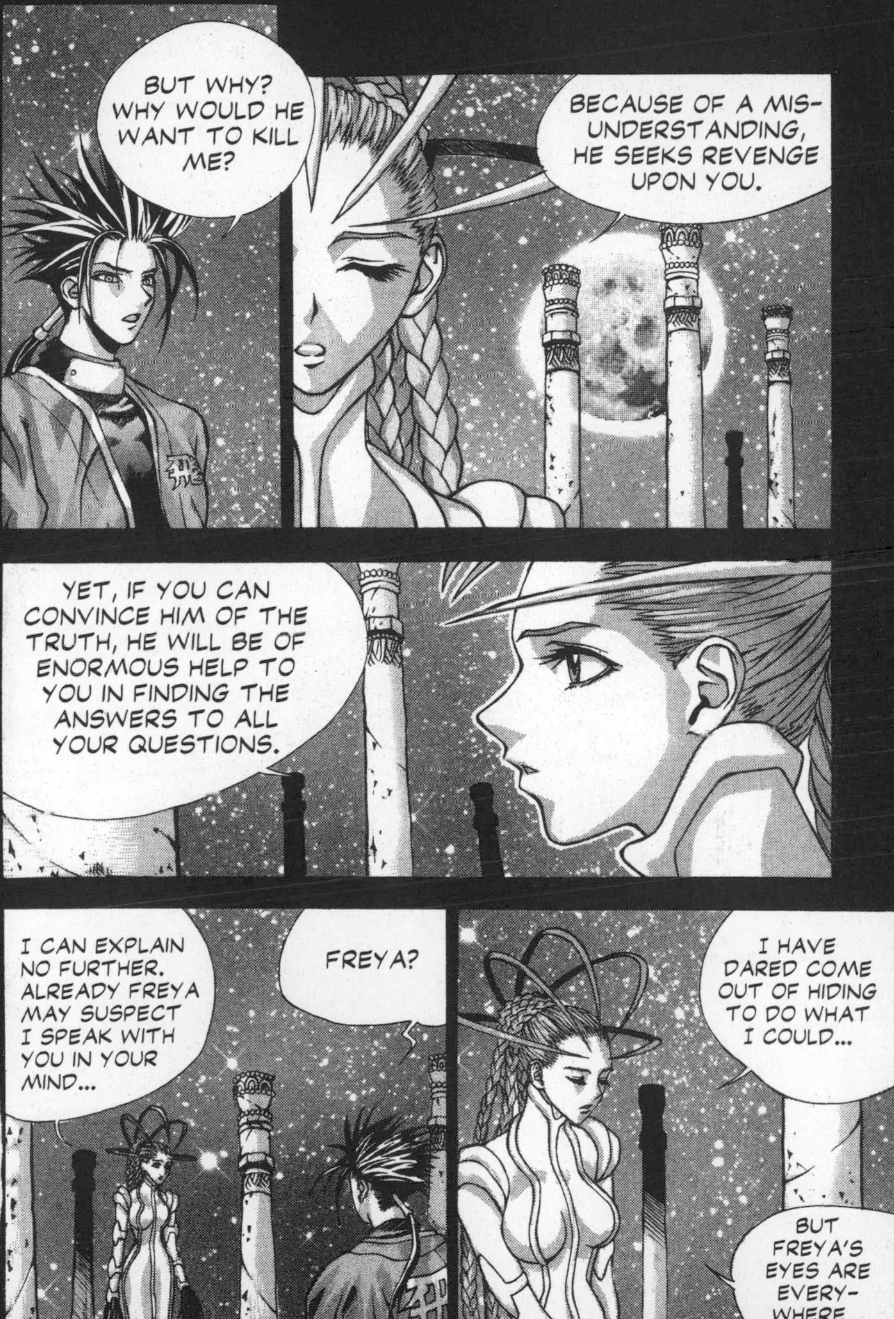
BUT WHY? WHY WOULD HE WANT TO KILL ME?
BECAUSE OF A MIS-UNDERSTANDING, HE SEEKS REVENGE UPON YOU.
YET, IF YOU CAN CONVINCE HIM OF THE TRUTH, HE WILL BE OF ENORMOUS HELP TO YOU IN FINDING THE ANSWERS TO ALL YOUR QUESTIONS.
I CAN EXPLAIN NO FURTHER. ALREADY FREYA MAY SUSPECT I SPEAK WITH YOU IN YOUR MIND...
FREYA?
I HAVE DARED COME OUT OF HIDING TO DO WHAT I COULD...
BUT FREYA'S EYES ARE EVERY-WHERE...

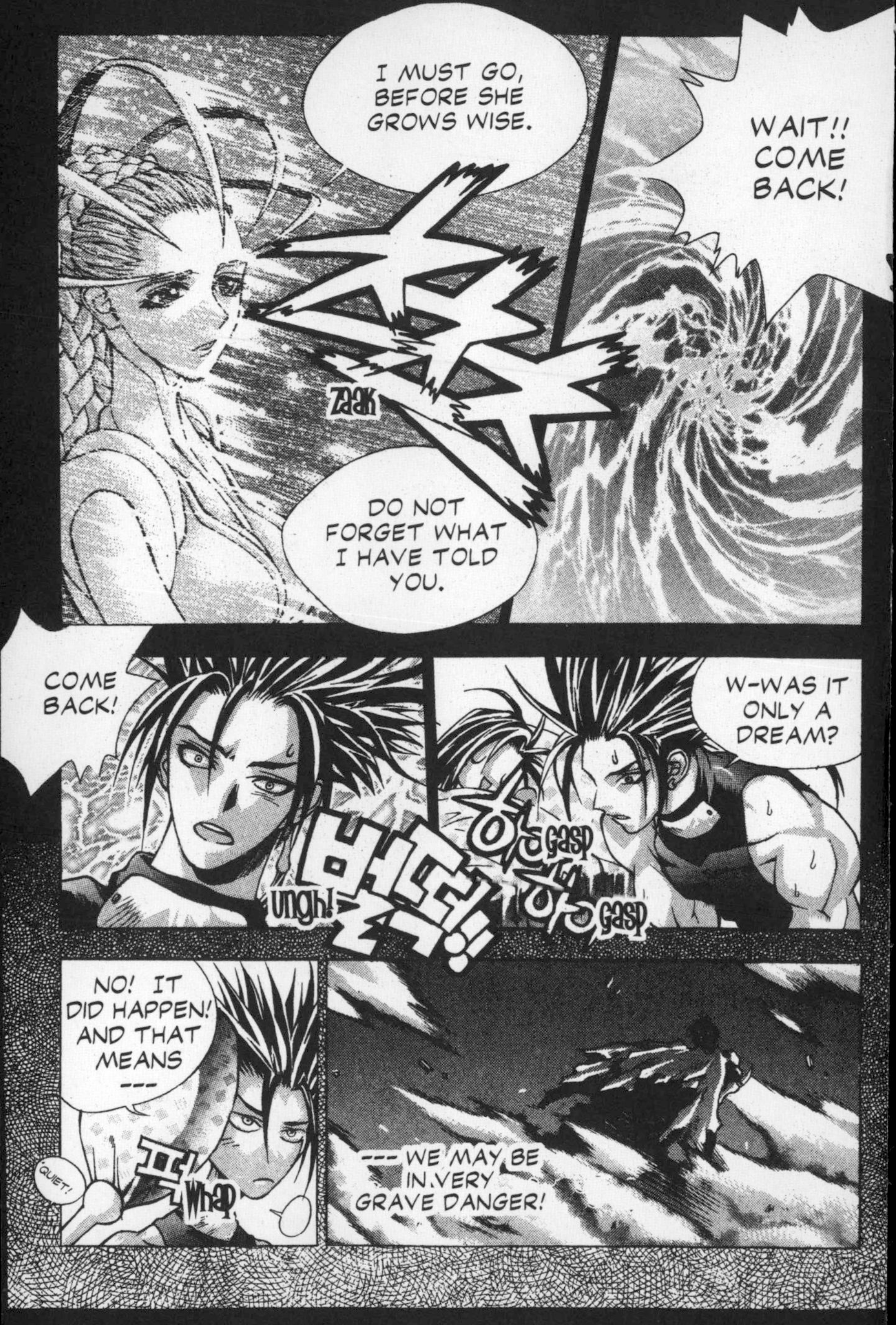
I MUST GO, BEFORE SHE GROWS WISE.
ZAAK
DO NOT FORGET WHAT I HAVE TOLD YOU.
WAIT!! COME BACK!
COME BACK!
UNGH!
W-WAS IT ONLY A DREAM?
GASP
GASP
NO! IT DID HAPPEN! AND THAT MEANS ---
QUIET!
WHAP
--- WE MAY BE IN VERY GRAVE DANGER!

RAGNAROK

라그나로크

IN TO THE ABYSS

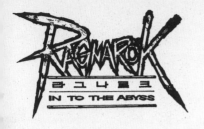

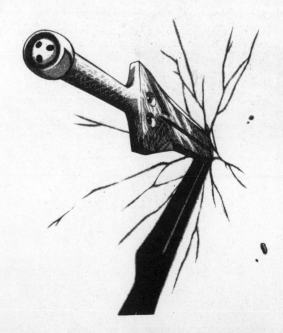

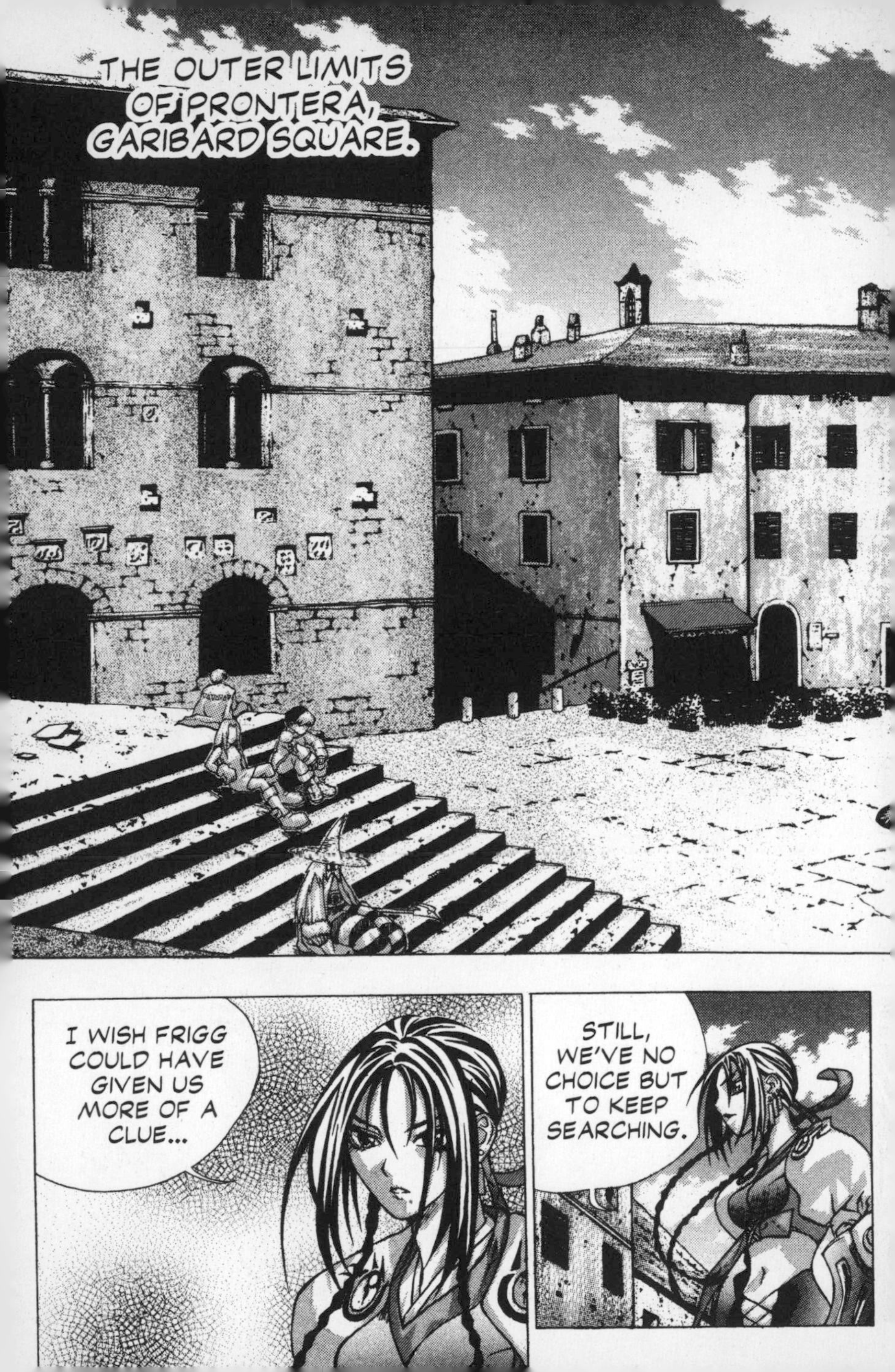
THE OUTER LIMITS OF PRONTERA, GARIBARD SQUARE.
I WISH FRIGG COULD HAVE GIVEN US MORE OF A CLUE...
STILL, WE'VE NO CHOICE BUT TO KEEP SEARCHING.

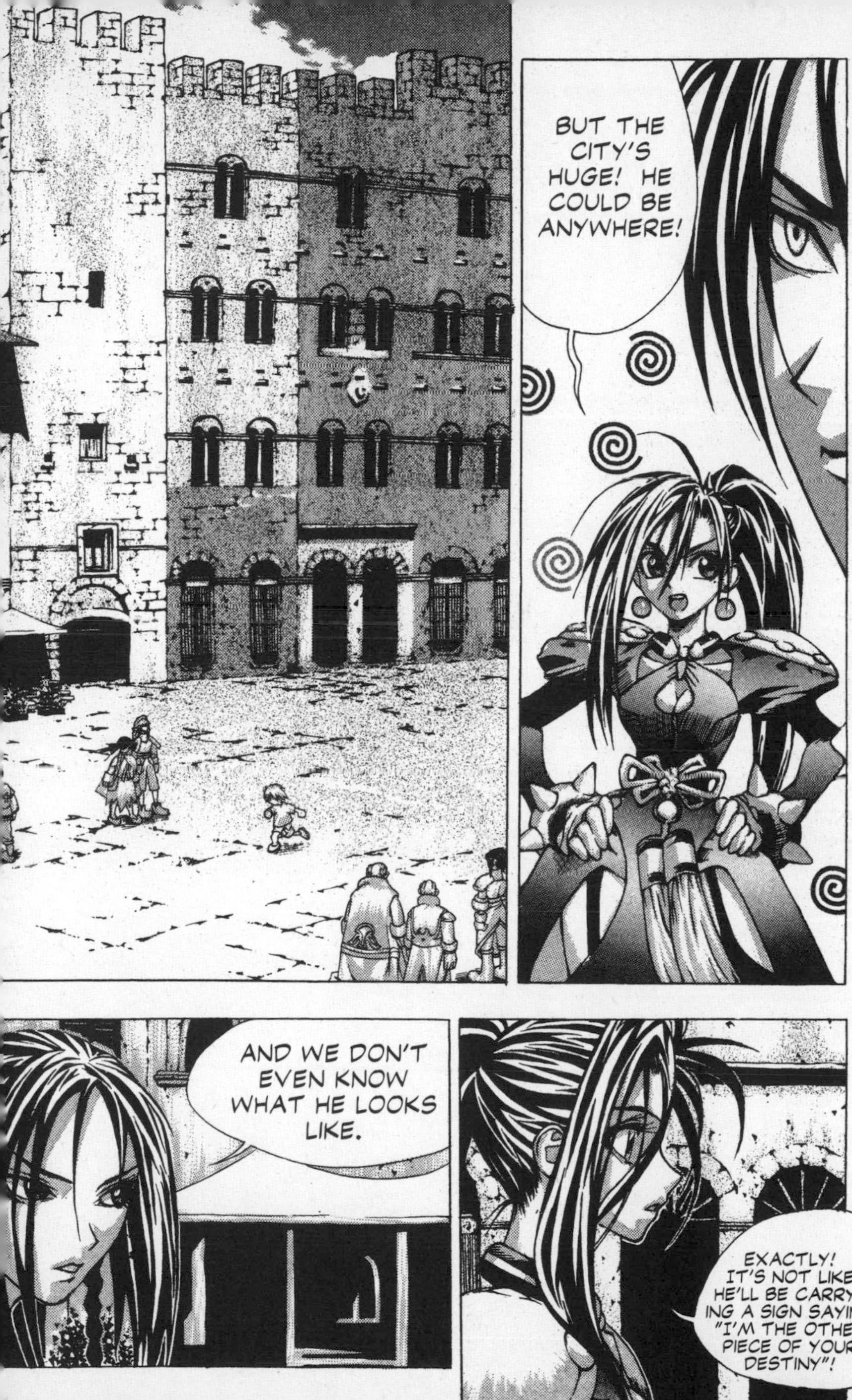

BUT THE CITY'S HUGE! HE COULD BE ANYWHERE!
AND WE DON'T EVEN KNOW WHAT HE LOOKS LIKE.
EXACTLY! IT'S NOT LIKE HE'LL BE CARRY-ING A SIGN SAYING "I'M THE OTHER PIECE OF YOUR DESTINY"!

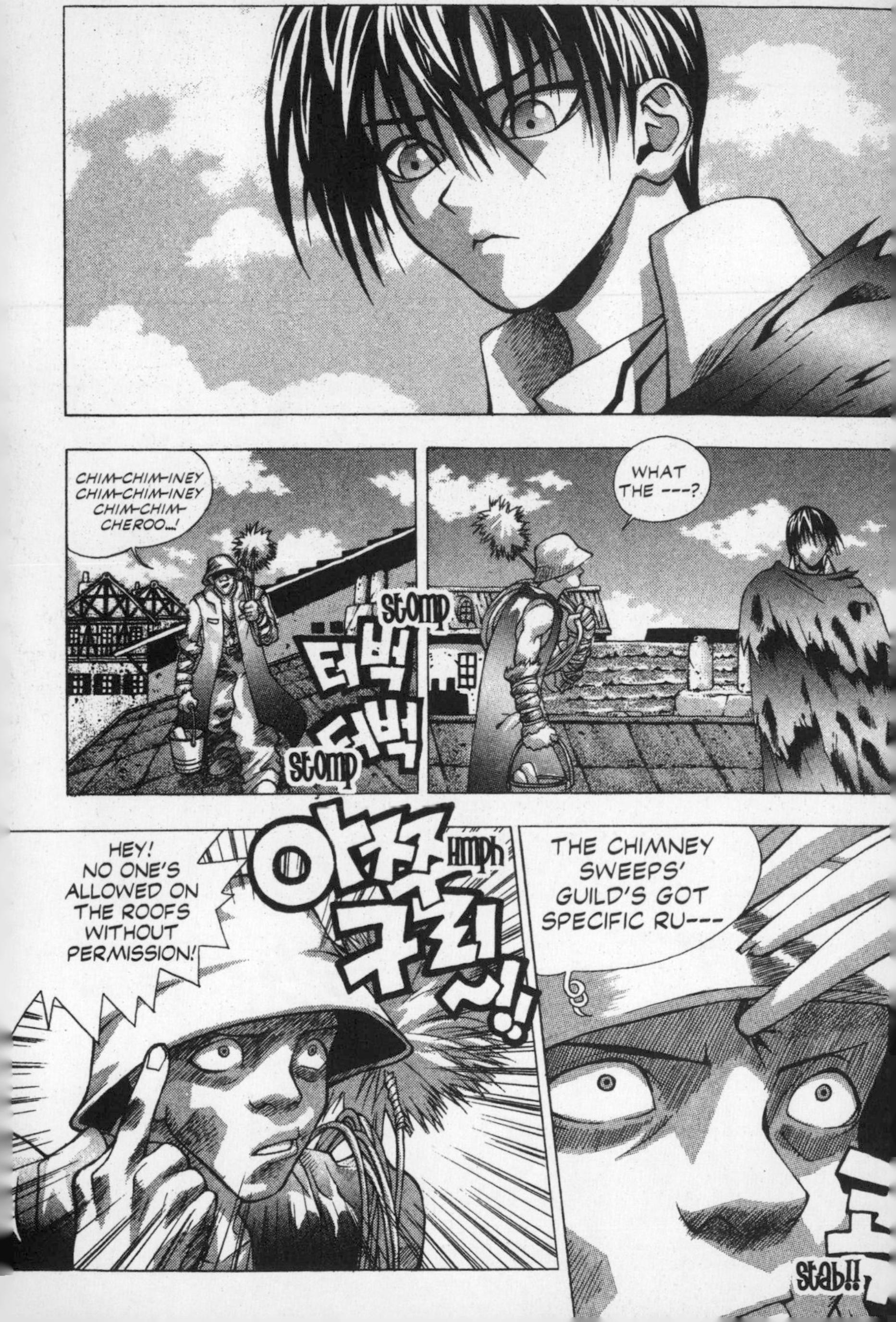
CHIM-CHIM-INEY CHIM-CHIM-INEY CHIM-CHIM-CHEROO...!
stomp
터벅
터벅
stomp
WHAT THE ---?
HEY! NO ONE'S ALLOWED ON THE ROOFS WITHOUT PERMISSION!
HMPH
THE CHIMNEY SWEEPS' GUILD'S GOT SPECIFIC RU---
stab!!

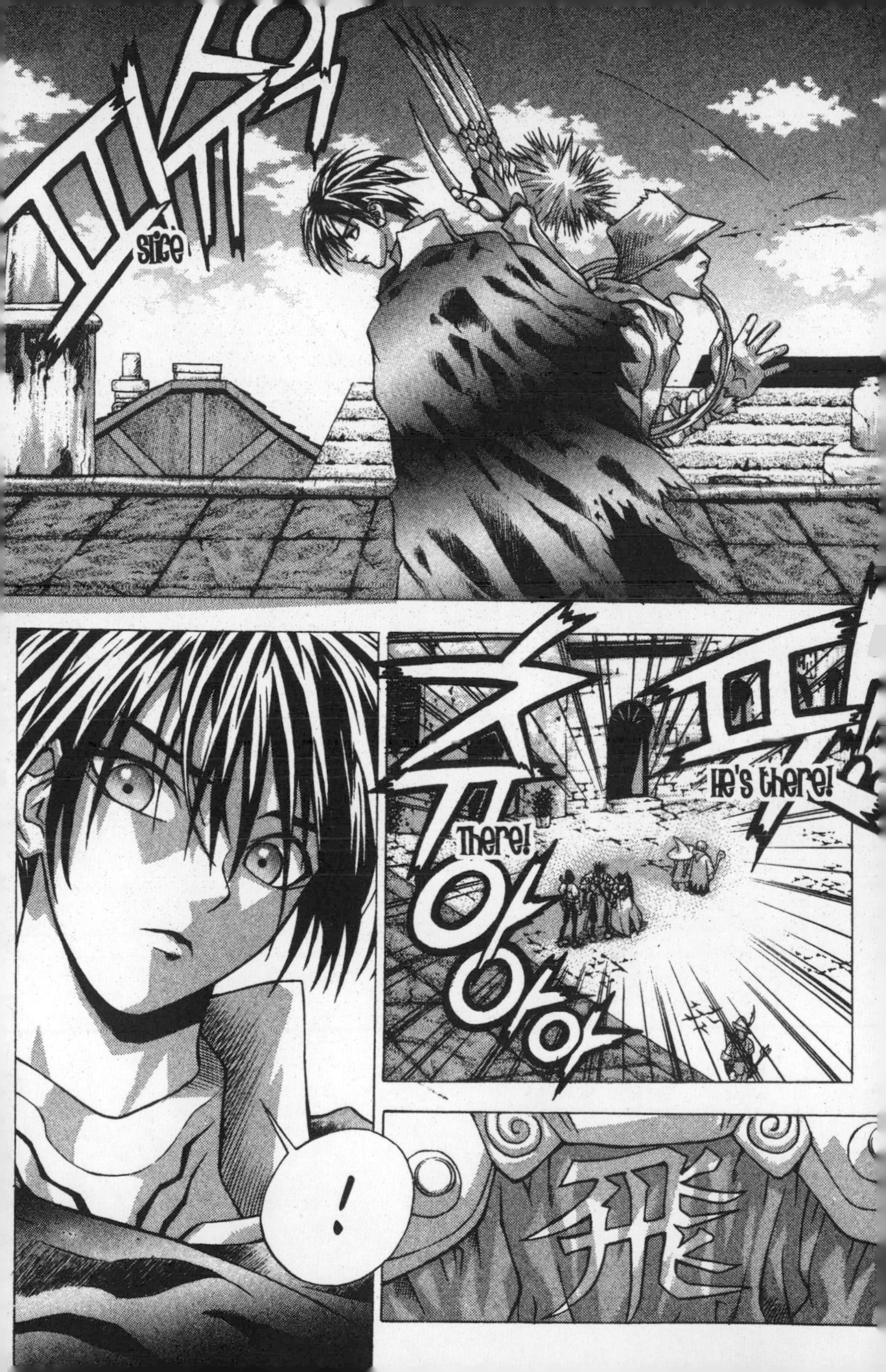
slice
!
There!
He's there!

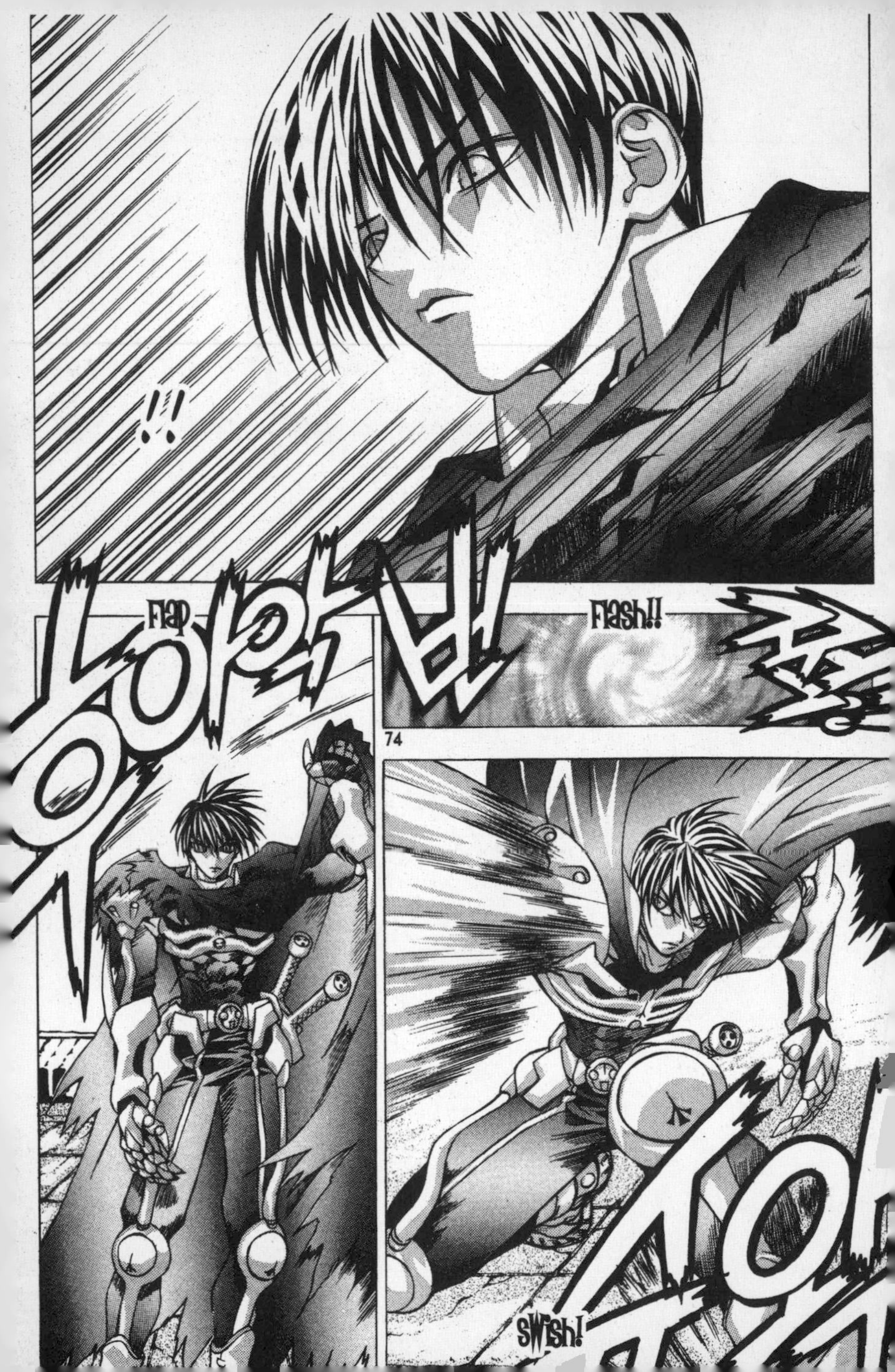
!!
Flap
Flash!!
Swish!

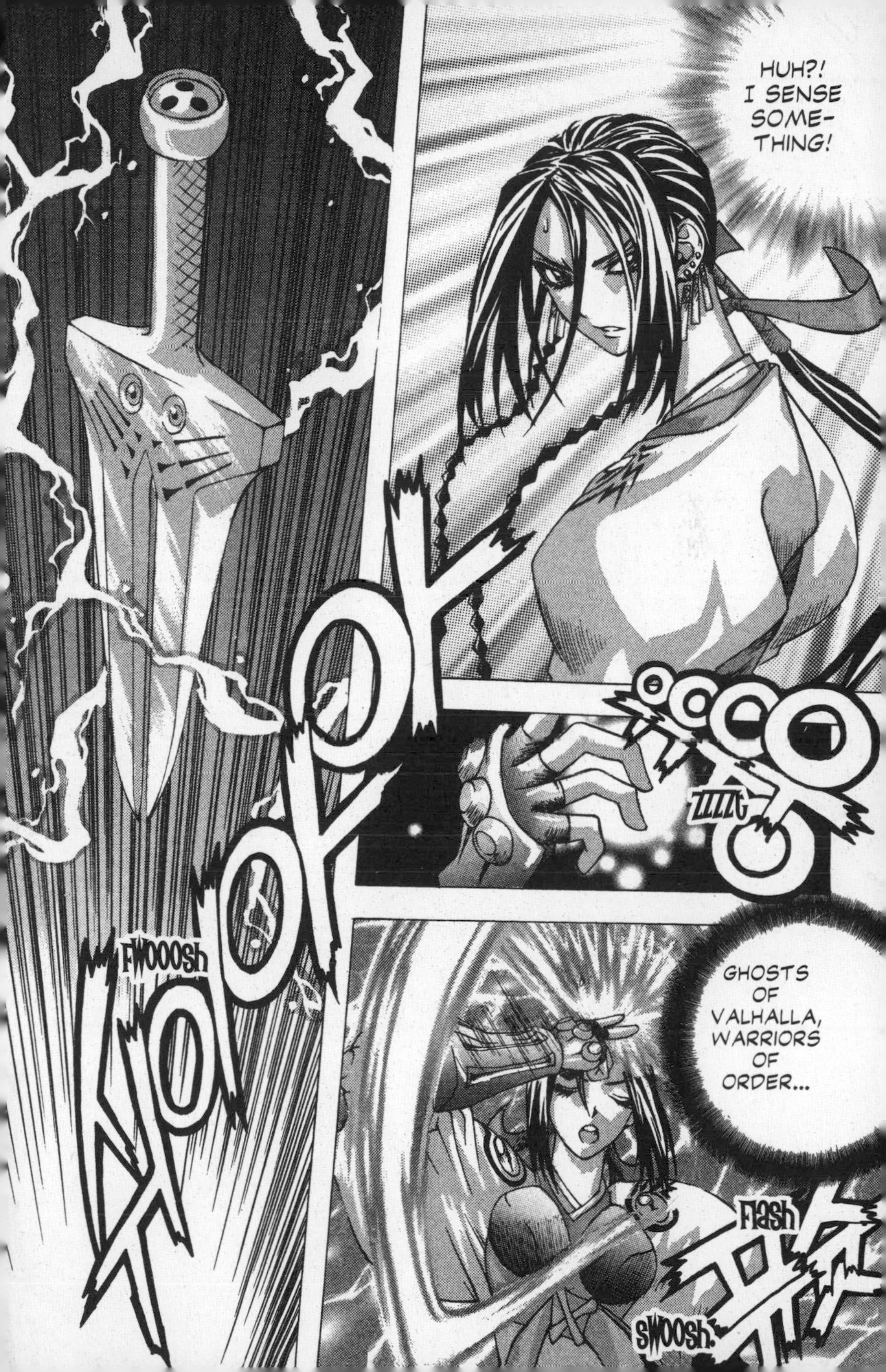
FWOOOSH
HUH?! I SENSE SOME-THING!
ZZZZG
GHOSTS OF VALHALLA, WARRIORS OF ORDER...
FLASH
SWOOSH

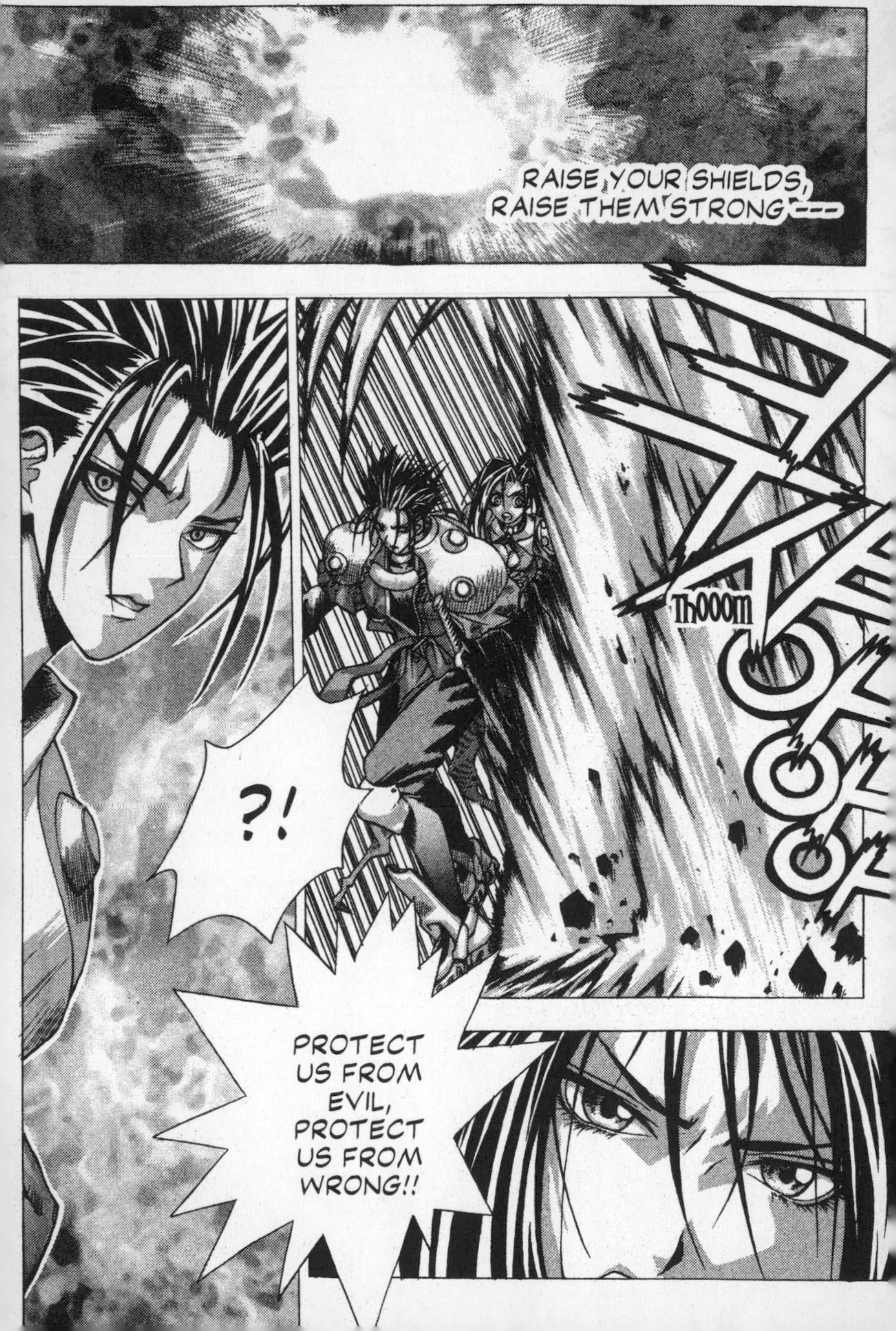
RAISE YOUR SHIELDS, RAISE THEM STRONG---
?!
ThOOOM
PROTECT US FROM EVIL, PROTECT US FROM WRONG!!

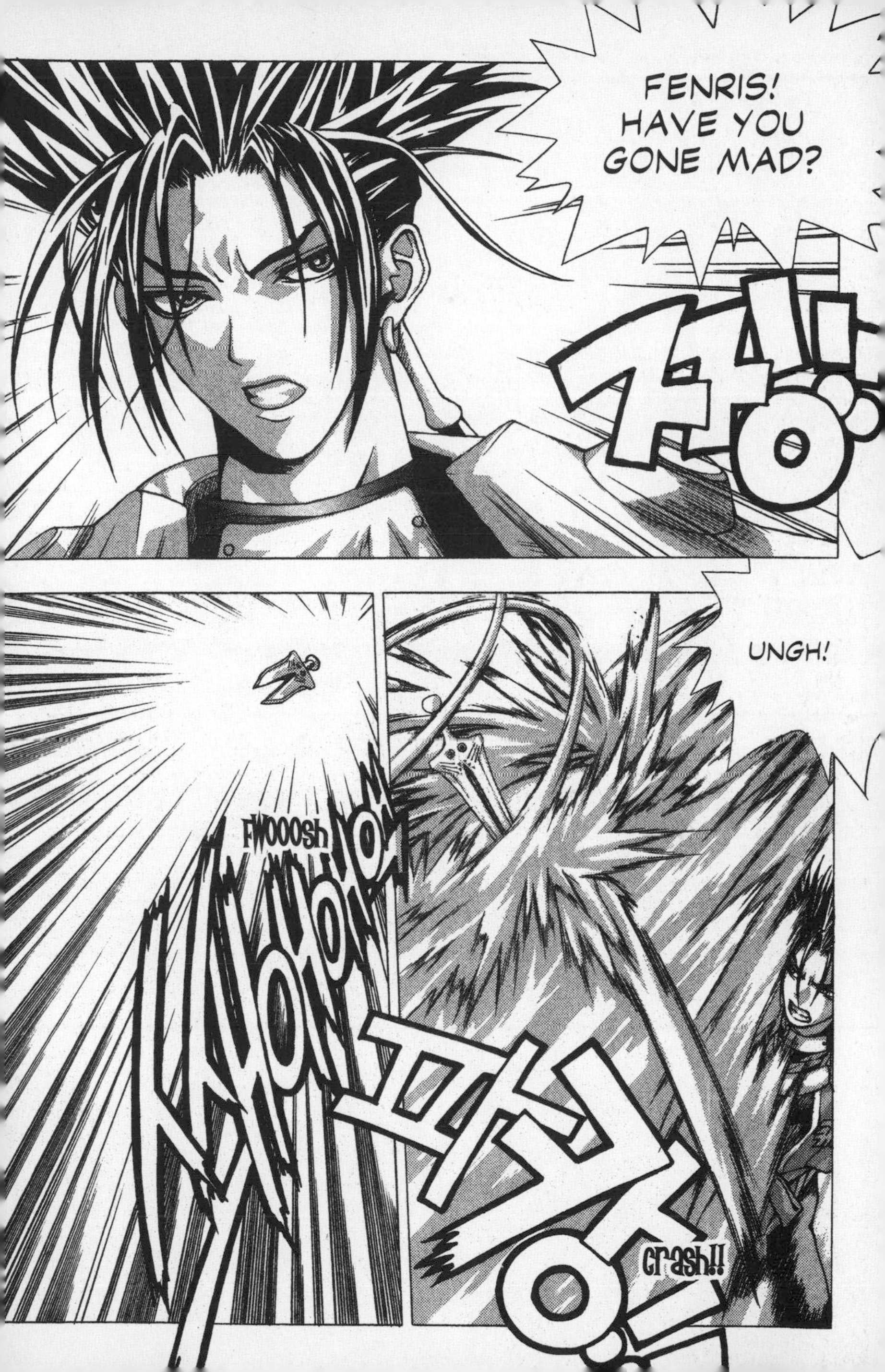
FENRIS! HAVE YOU GONE MAD?
FWOOOsh
UNGH!
crash!!

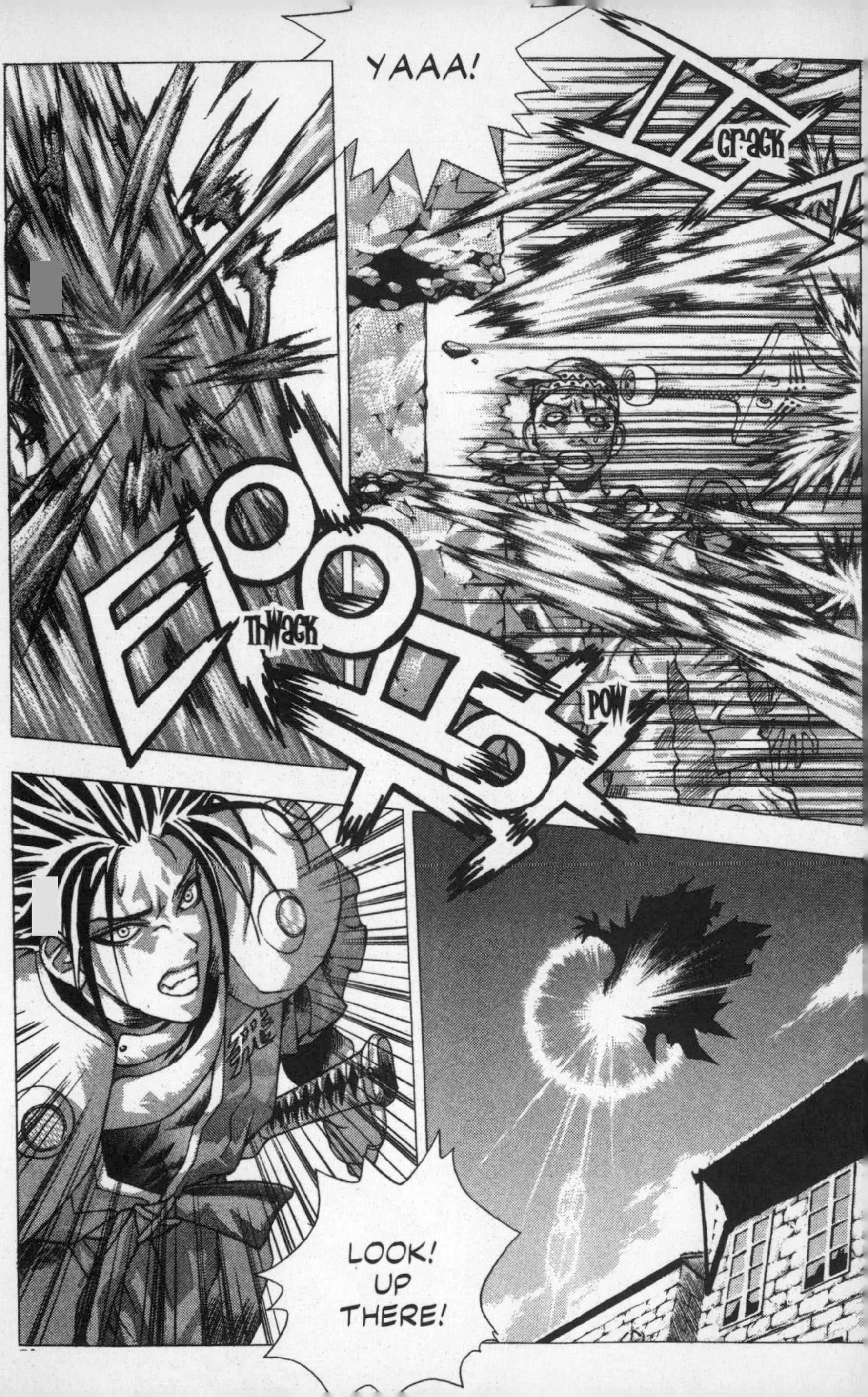
YAAA!
crack
THWACK
POW
LOOK! UP THERE!

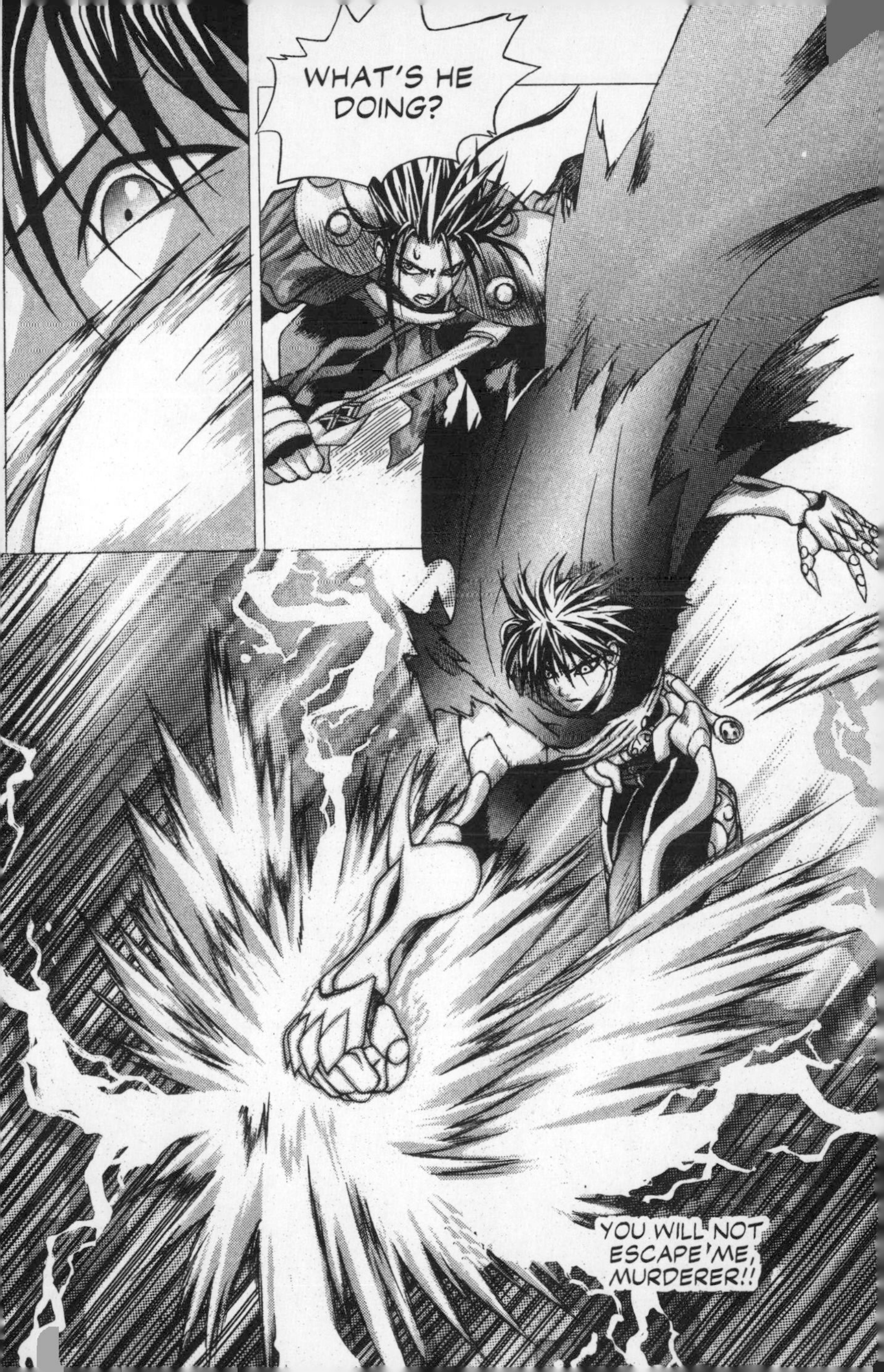
WHAT'S HE DOING?
YOU WILL NOT ESCAPE ME, MURDERER!!

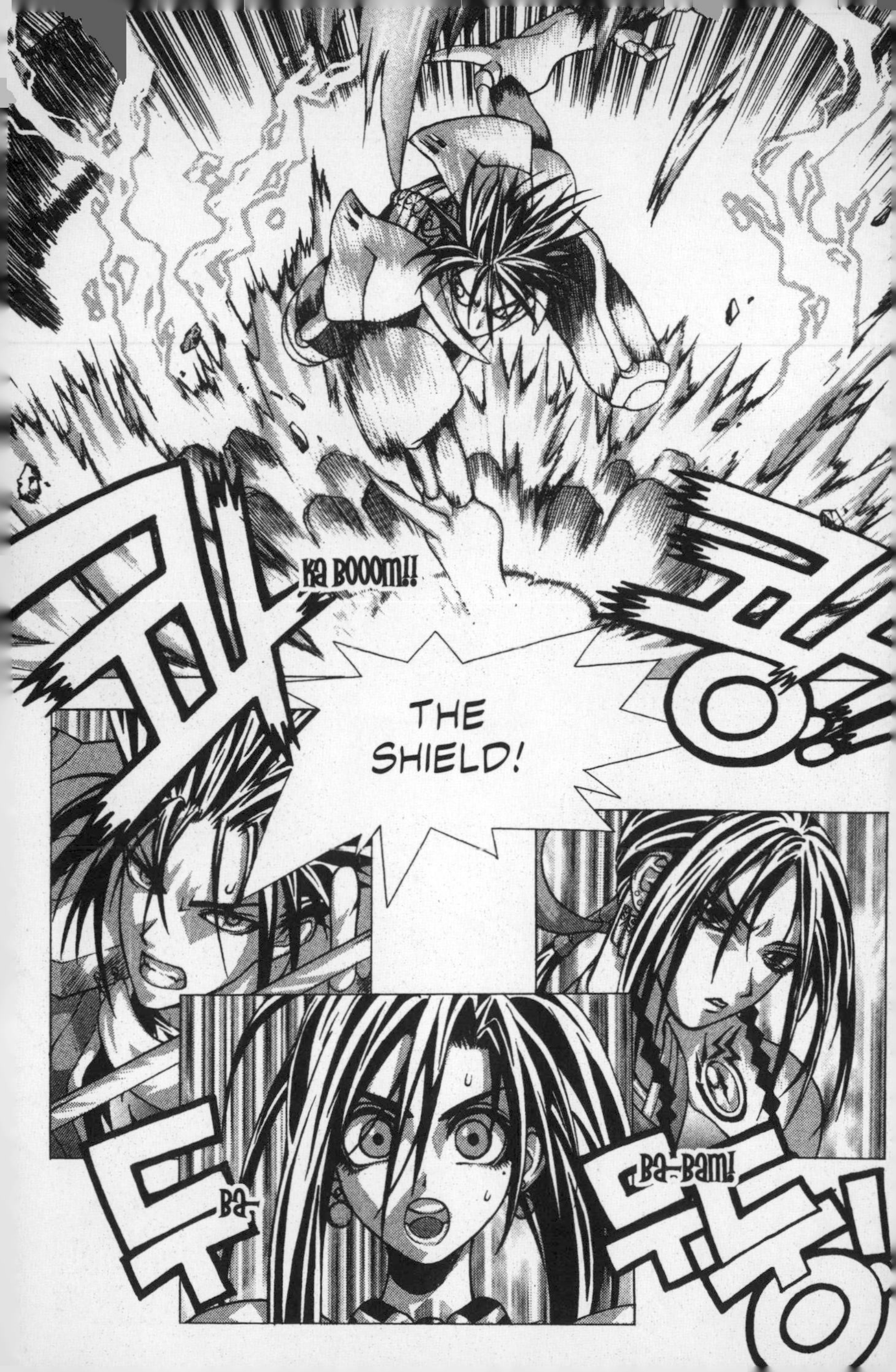
KA BOOOM!!
THE SHIELD!
BA-
BA-BAM!

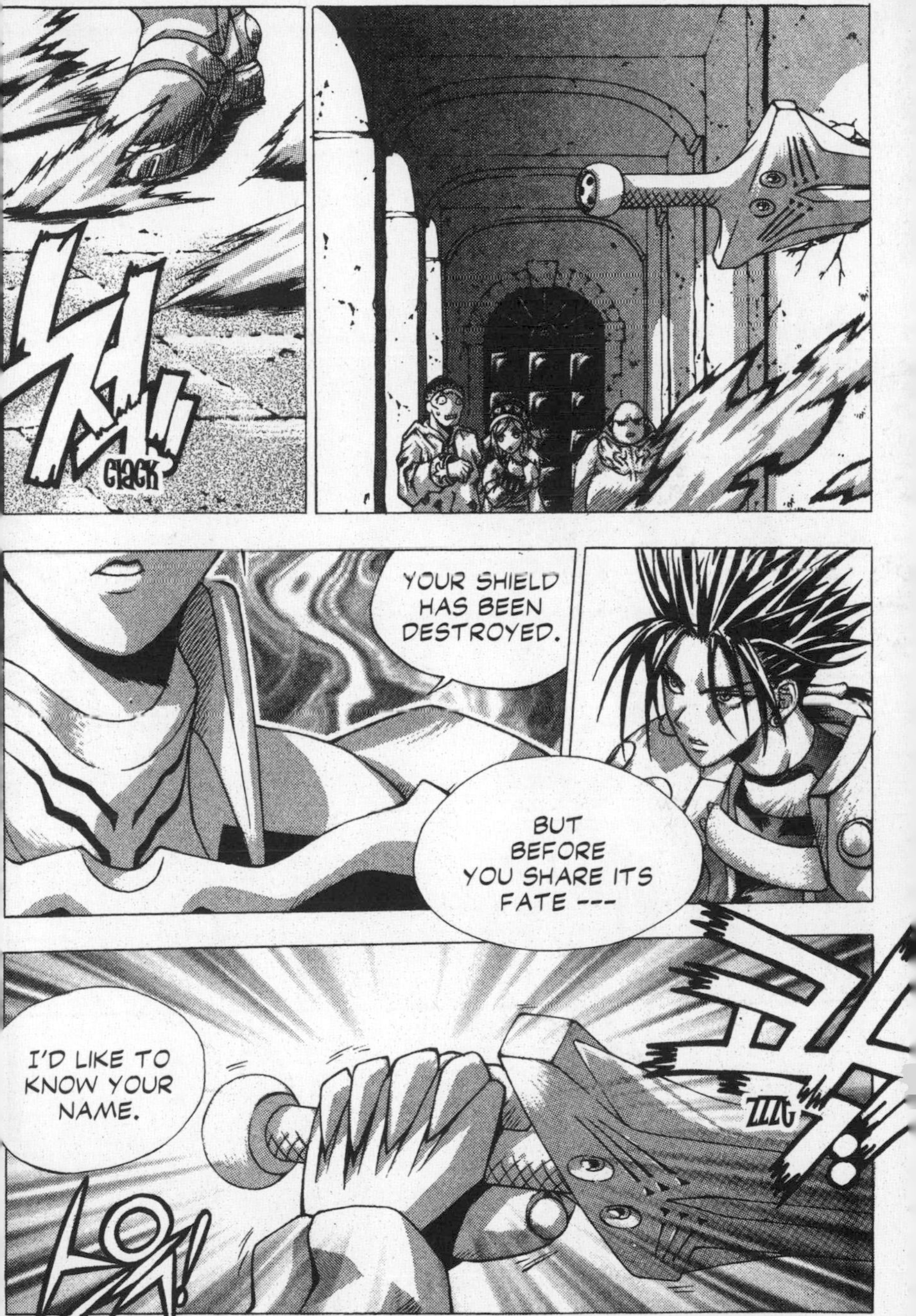
CLACK
YOUR SHIELD HAS BEEN DESTROYED.
BUT BEFORE YOU SHARE ITS FATE ---
I'D LIKE TO KNOW YOUR NAME.

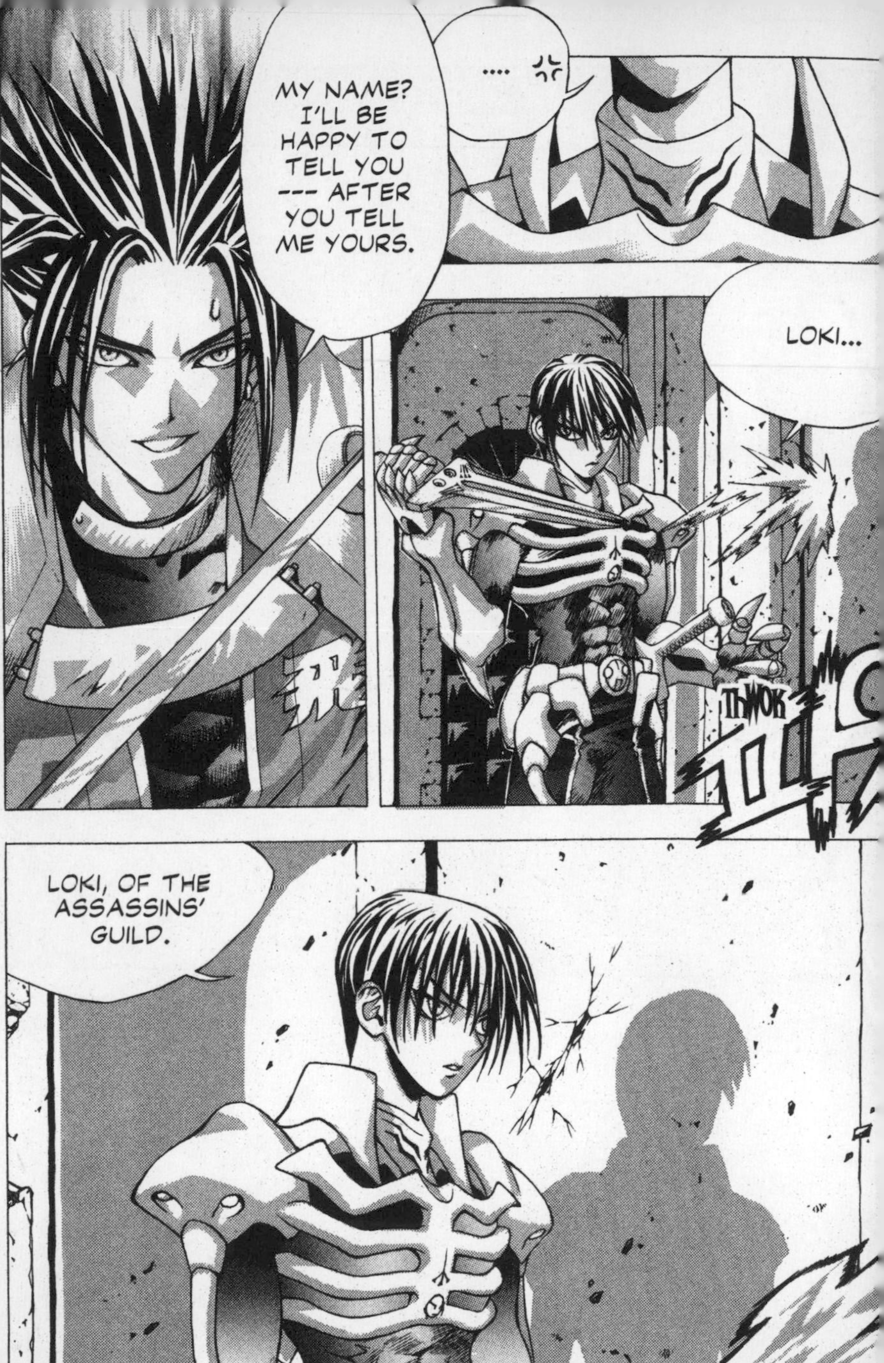
MY NAME? I'LL BE HAPPY TO TELL YOU --- AFTER YOU TELL ME YOURS.
....
LOKI...
ThWOK
LOKI, OF THE ASSASSINS' GUILD.

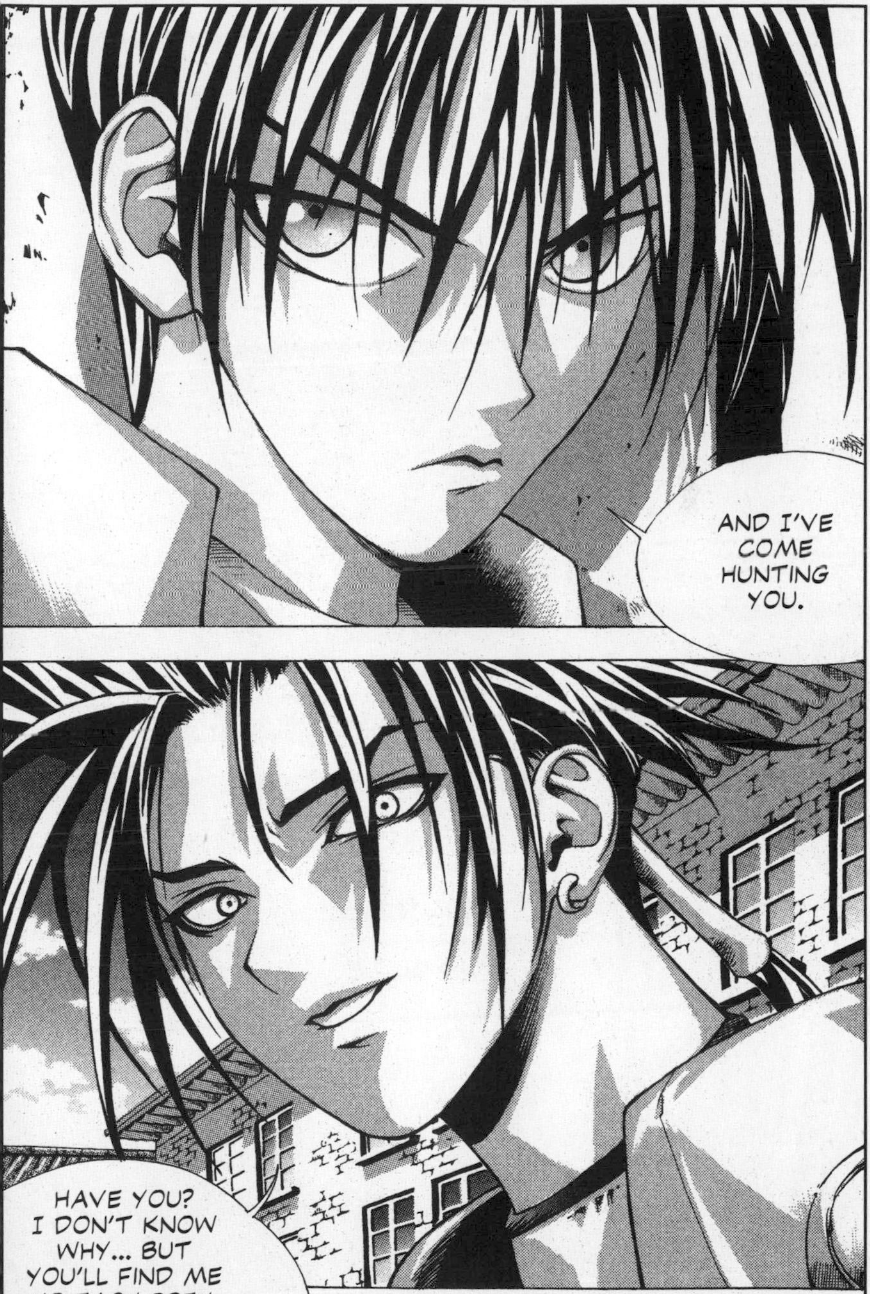
AND I'VE COME HUNTING YOU.
HAVE YOU? I DON'T KNOW WHY... BUT YOU'LL FIND ME NO EASY PREY.

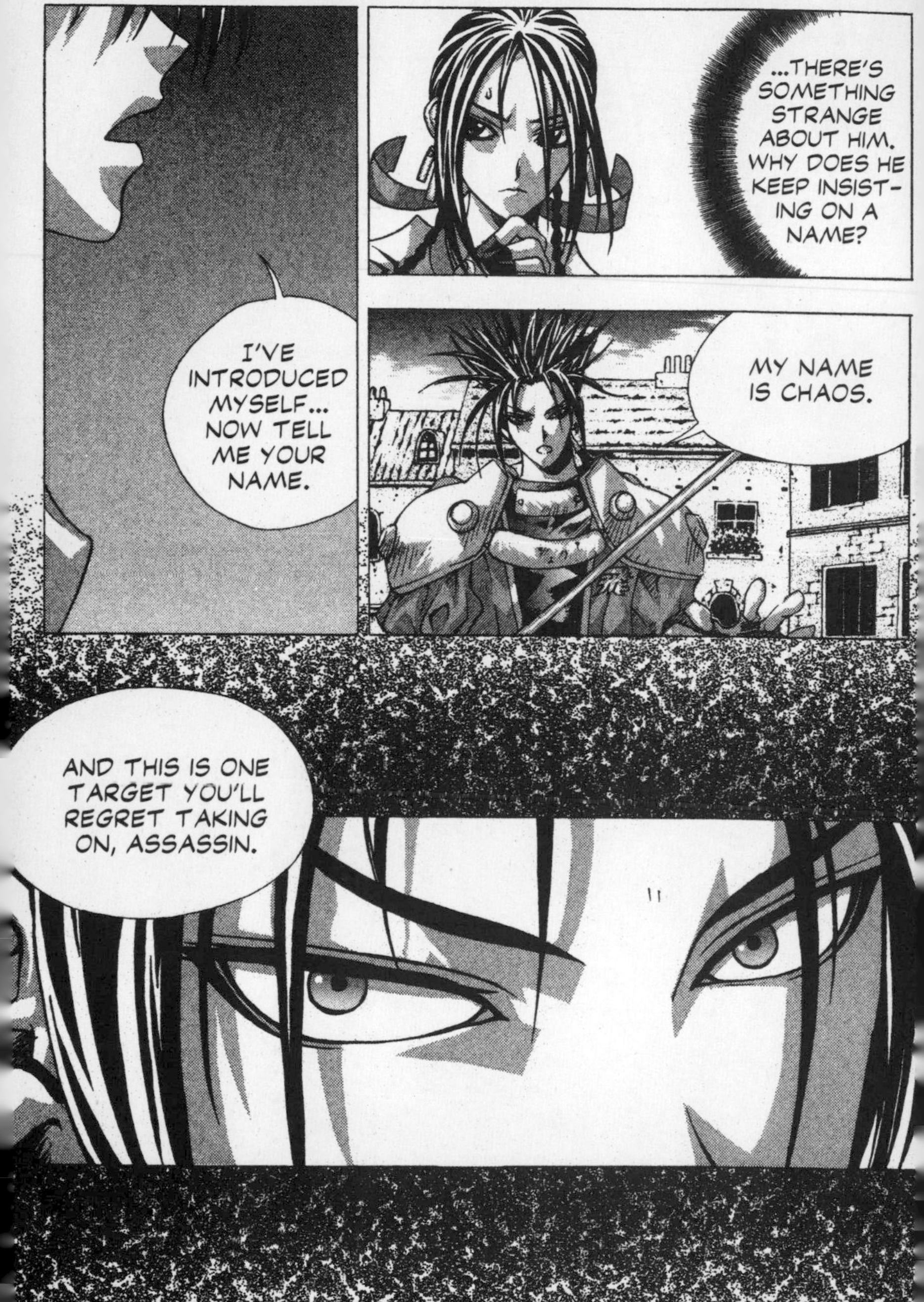
I'VE INTRODUCED MYSELF... NOW TELL ME YOUR NAME.
...THERE'S SOMETHING STRANGE ABOUT HIM. WHY DOES HE KEEP INSIST-ING ON A NAME?
MY NAME IS CHAOS.
AND THIS IS ONE TARGET YOU'LL REGRET TAKING ON, ASSASSIN.

RAGNAROK

라그나로크

IN TO THE ABYSS

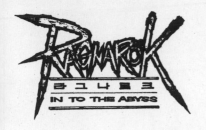

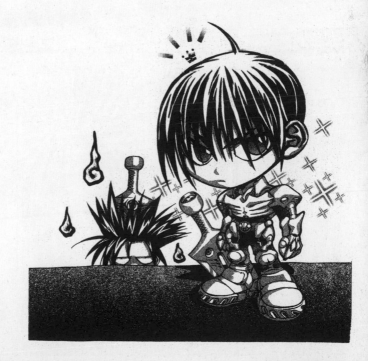

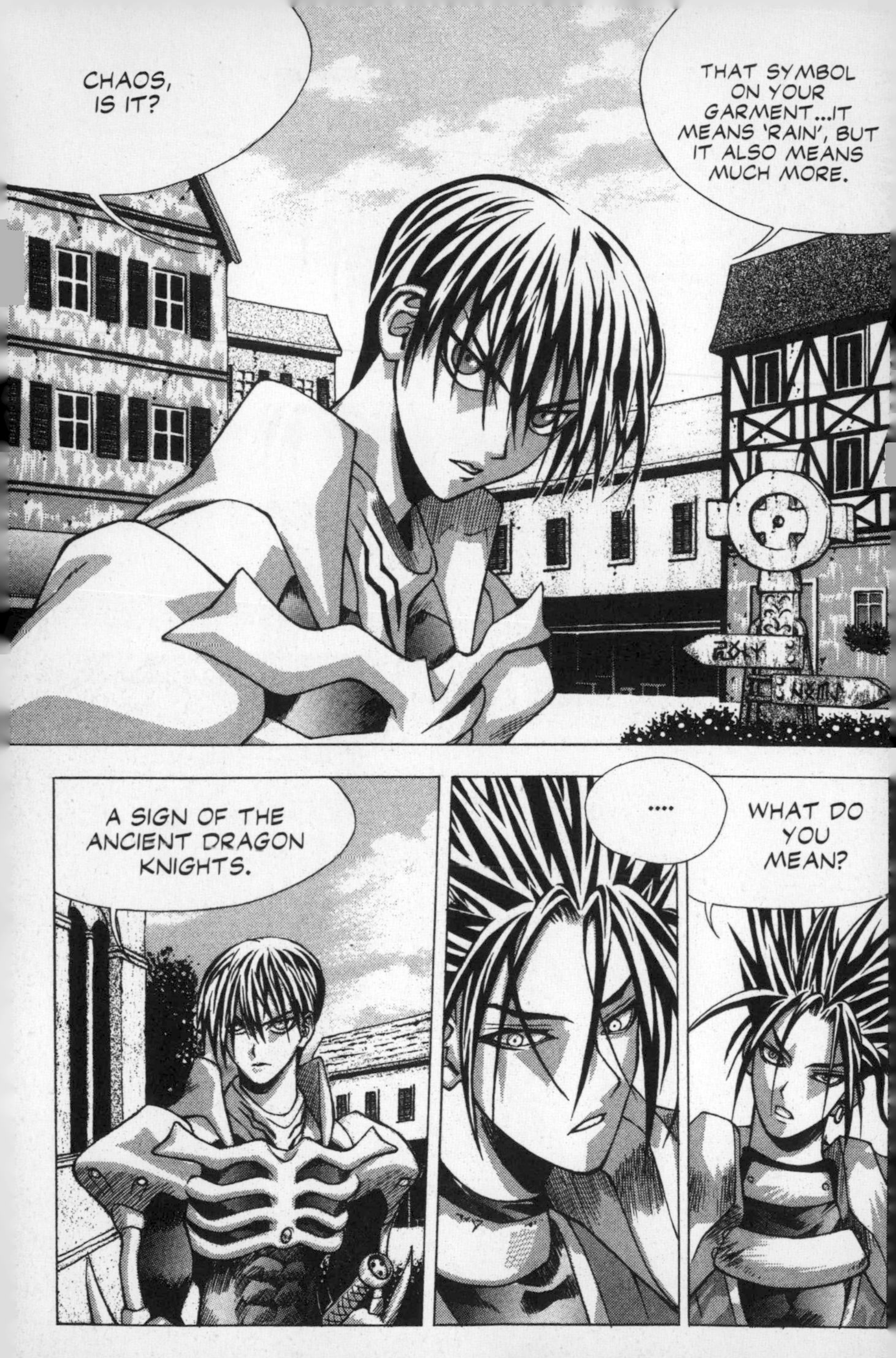
CHAOS, IS IT?
THAT SYMBOL ON YOUR GARMENT...IT MEANS 'RAIN', BUT IT ALSO MEANS MUCH MORE.
A SIGN OF THE ANCIENT DRAGON KNIGHTS.
....
WHAT DO YOU MEAN?

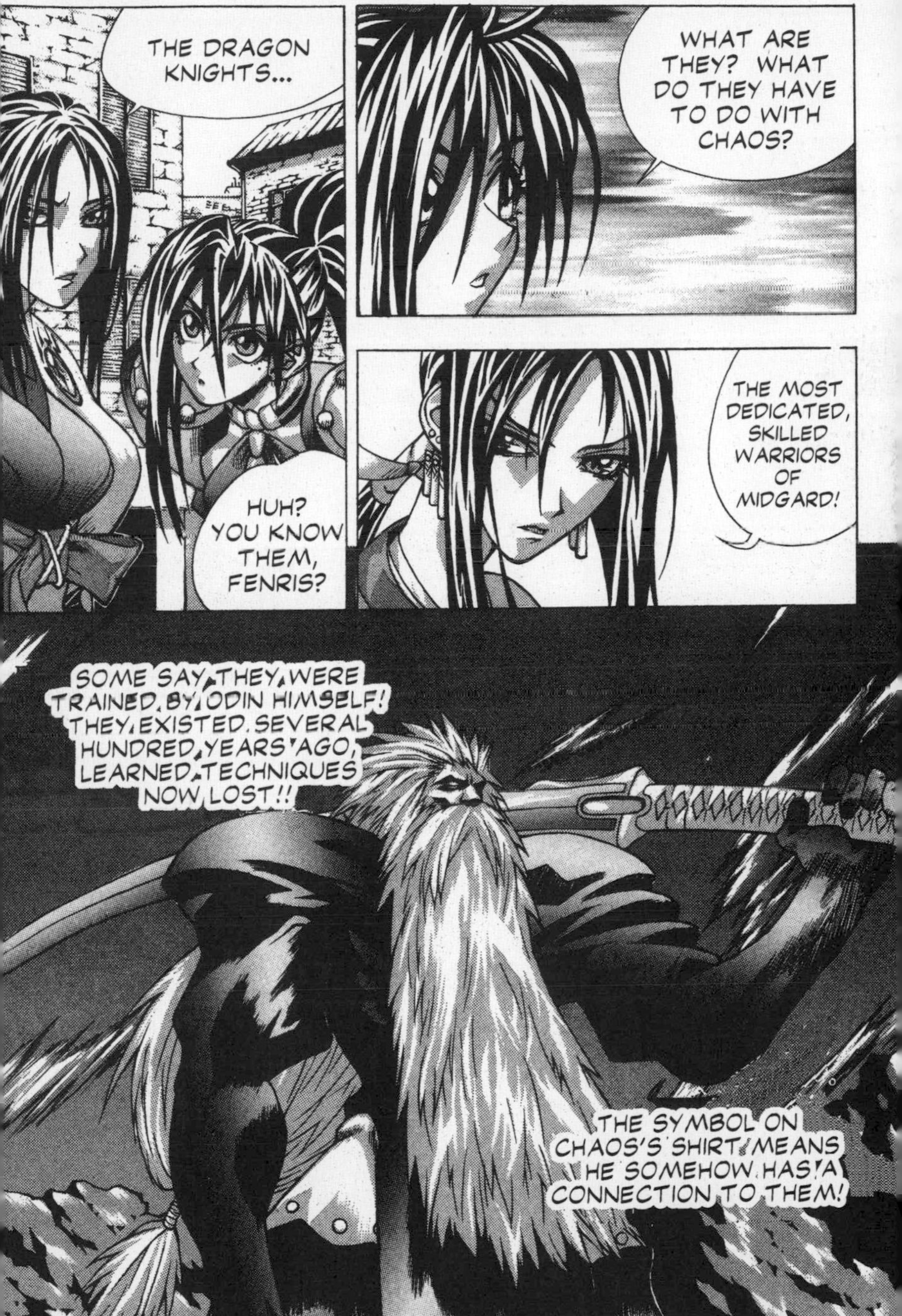
THE DRAGON KNIGHTS...
HUH? YOU KNOW THEM, FENRIS?
WHAT ARE THEY? WHAT DO THEY HAVE TO DO WITH CHAOS?
THE MOST DEDICATED, SKILLED WARRIORS OF MIDGARD!
SOME SAY THEY WERE TRAINED BY ODIN HIMSELF! THEY EXISTED SEVERAL HUNDRED YEARS AGO, LEARNED TECHNIQUES NOW LOST!!
THE SYMBOL ON CHAOS'S SHIRT MEANS HE SOMEHOW HAS A CONNECTION TO THEM!

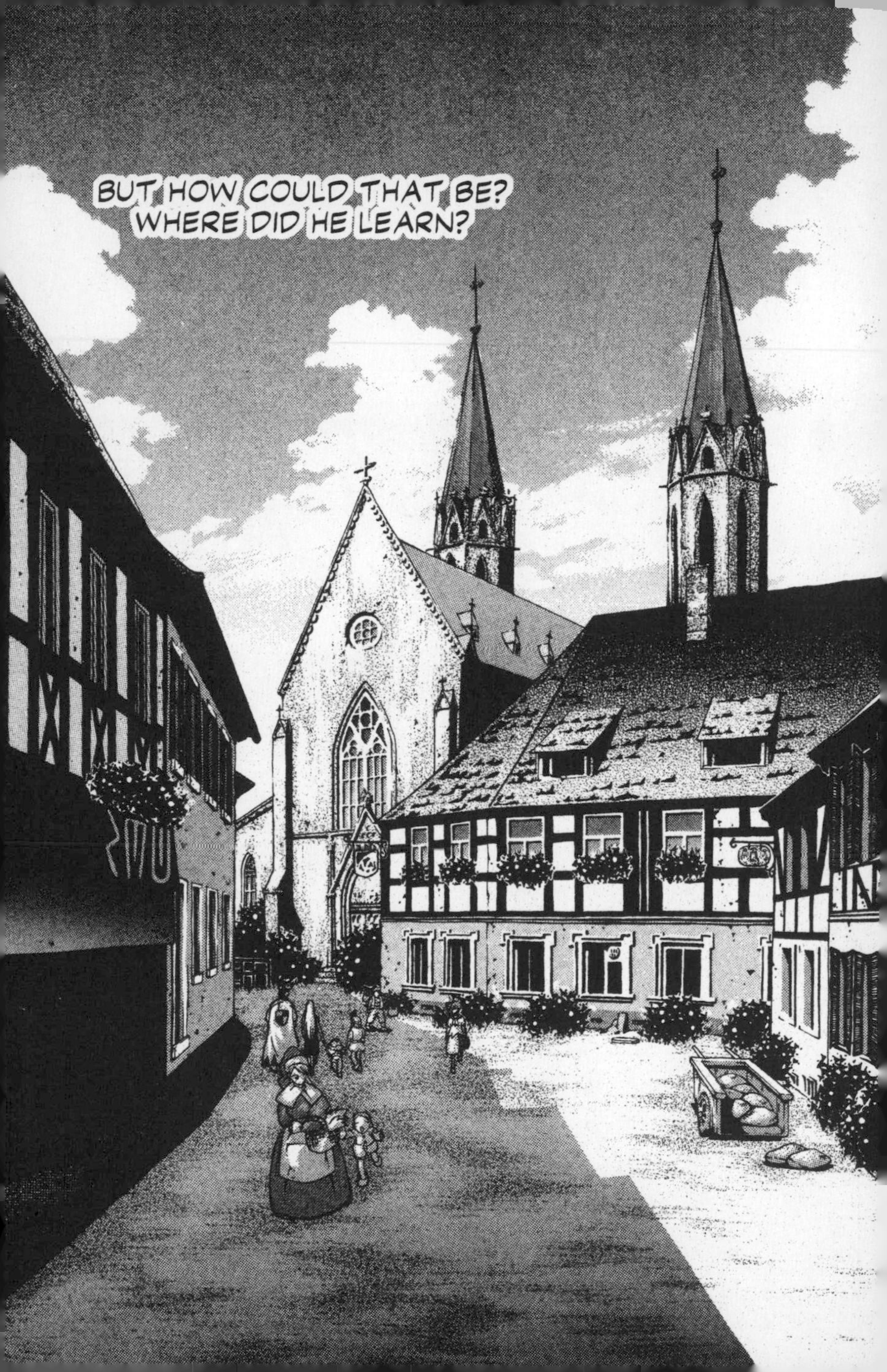
BUT HOW COULD THAT BE? WHERE DID HE LEARN?

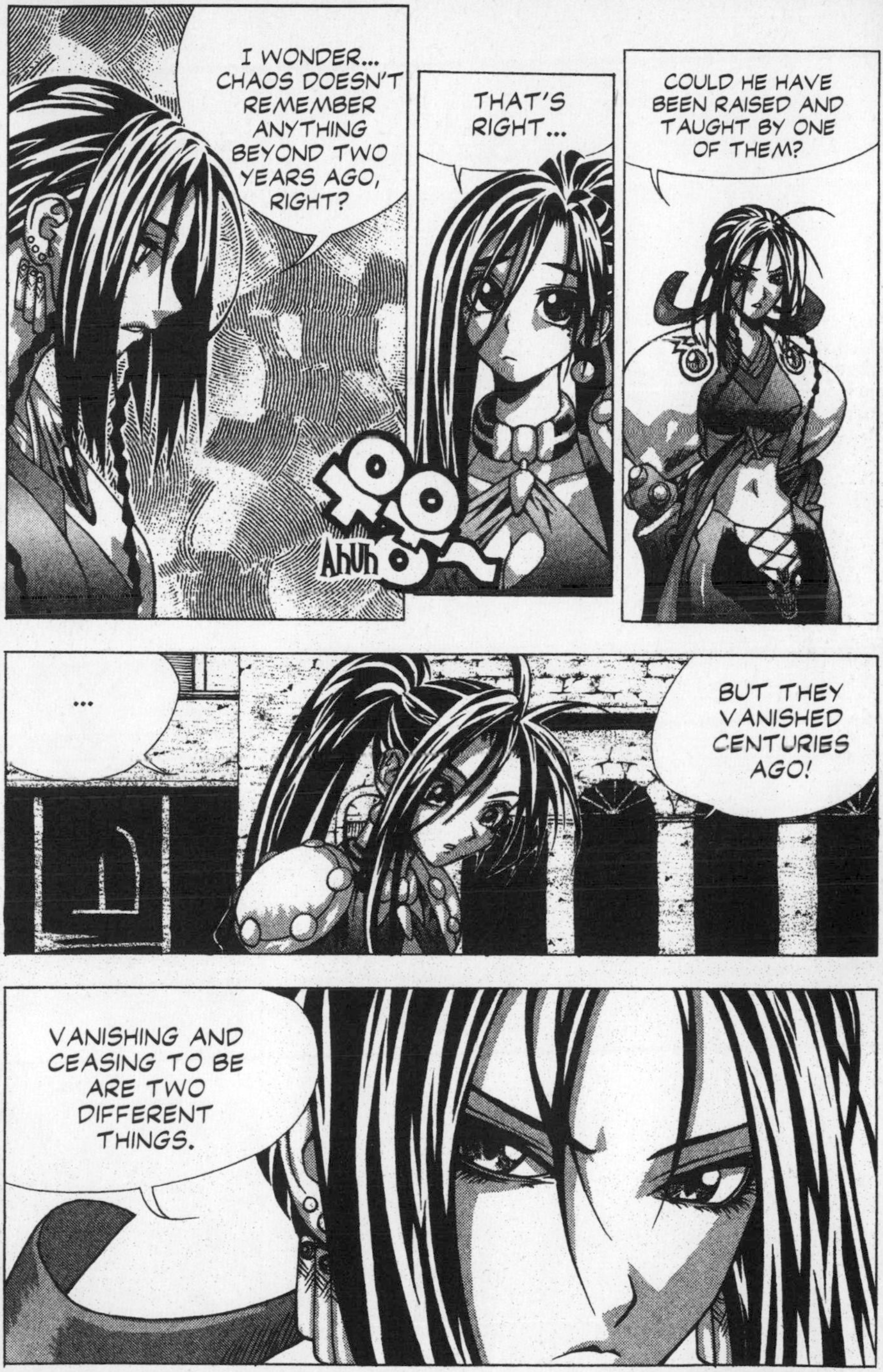
I WONDER... CHAOS DOESN'T REMEMBER ANYTHING BEYOND TWO YEARS AGO, RIGHT?
THAT'S RIGHT...
AhUh
COULD HE HAVE BEEN RAISED AND TAUGHT BY ONE OF THEM?
...
BUT THEY VANISHED CENTURIES AGO!
VANISHING AND CEASING TO BE ARE TWO DIFFERENT THINGS.

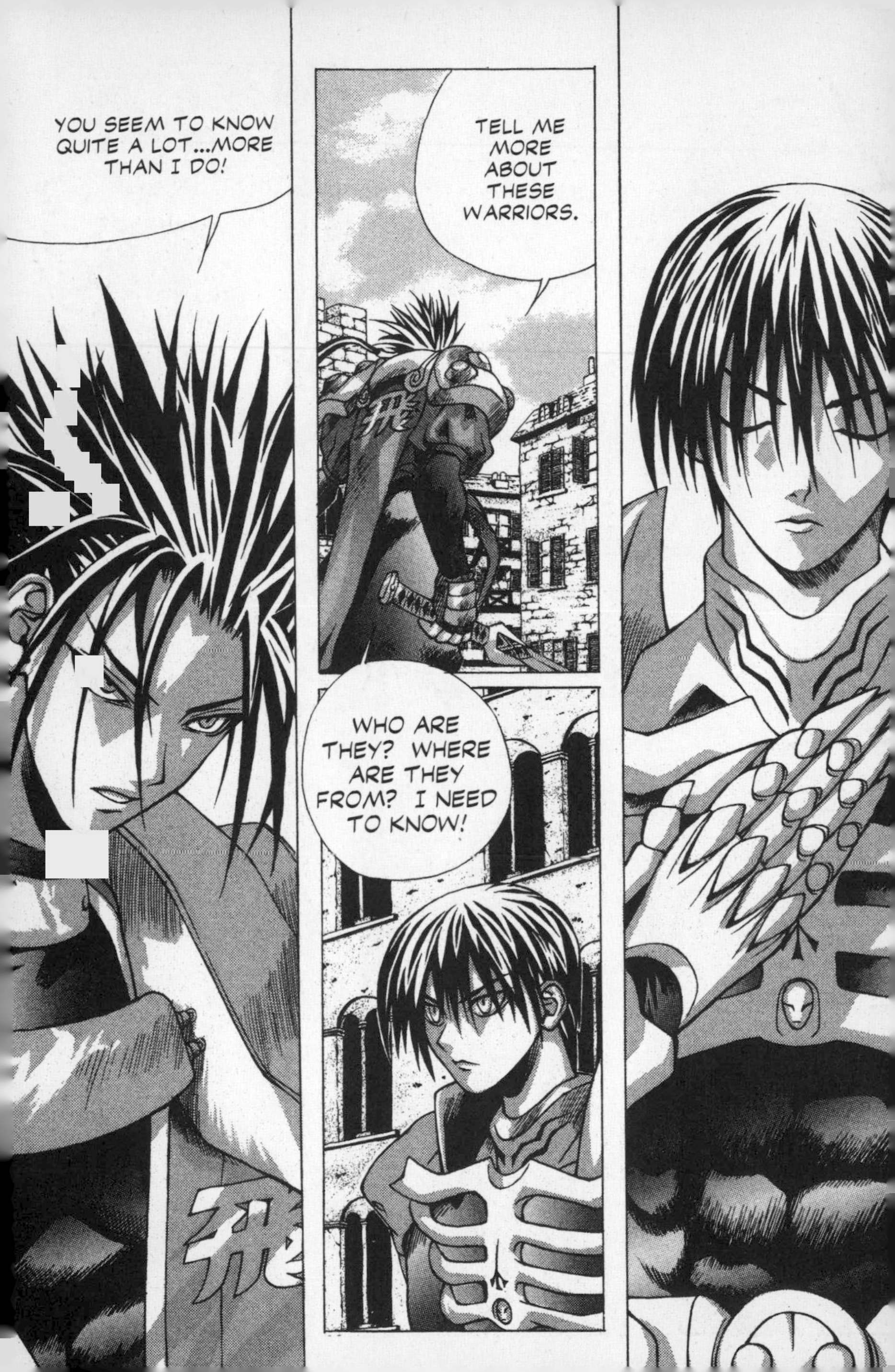
YOU SEEM TO KNOW QUITE A LOT...MORE THAN I DO!
TELL ME MORE ABOUT THESE WARRIORS.
WHO ARE THEY? WHERE ARE THEY FROM? I NEED TO KNOW!

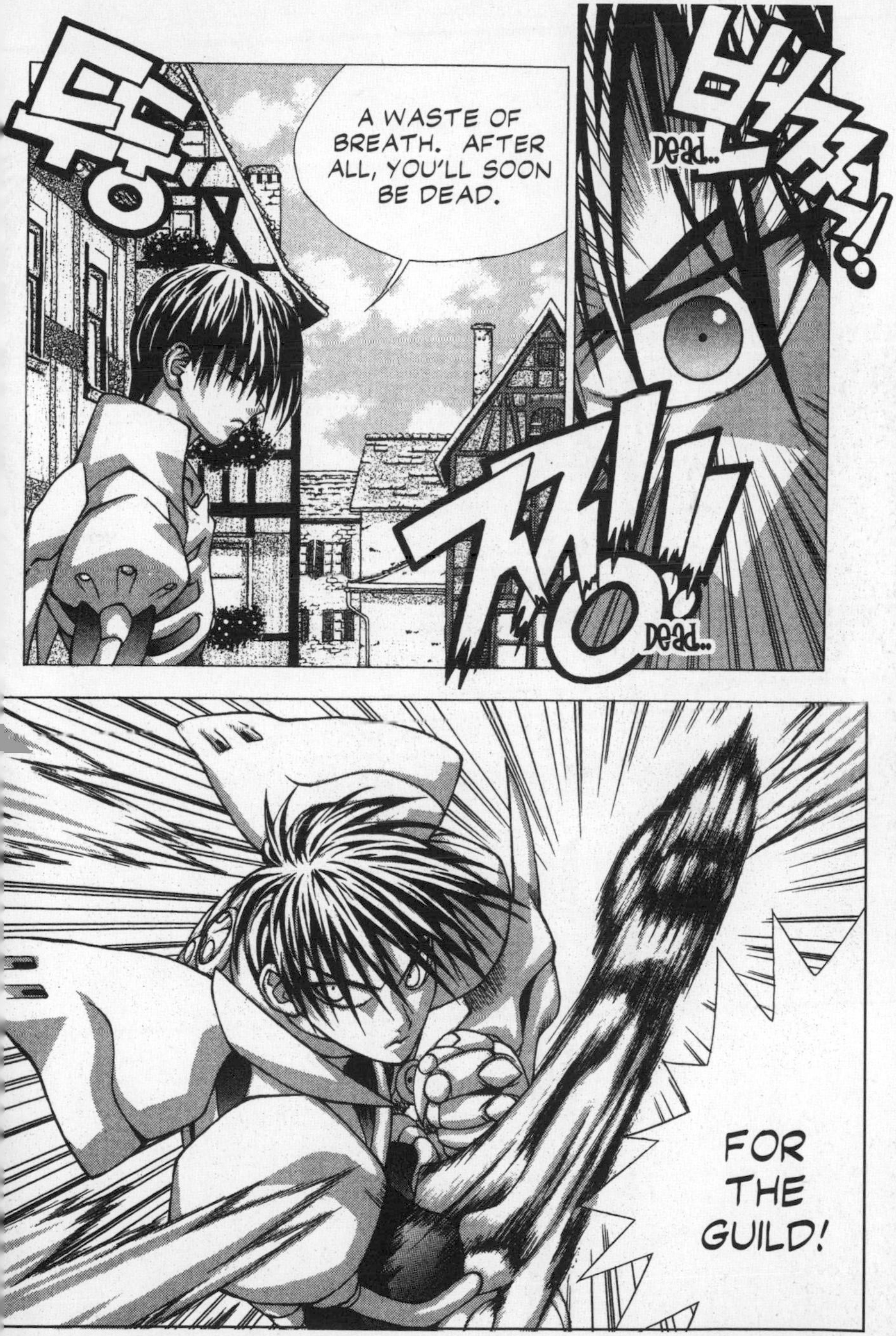
A WASTE OF BREATH. AFTER ALL, YOU'LL SOON BE DEAD.
Dead...
Dead...
FOR THE GUILD!

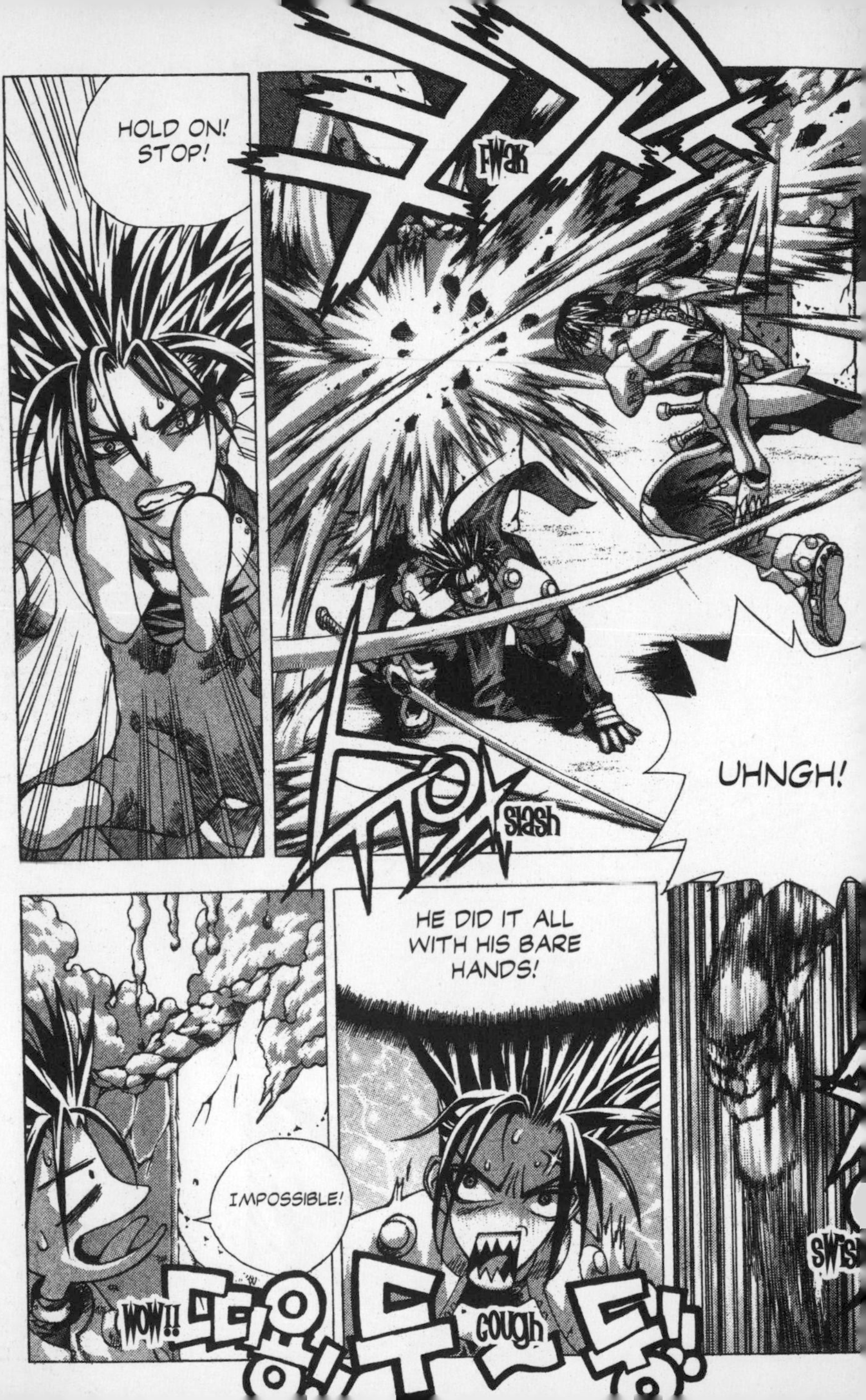
HOLD ON! STOP!
FWAK
slash
UHNGH!
IMPOSSIBLE!
WOW!!
HE DID IT ALL WITH HIS BARE HANDS!
cough
swis

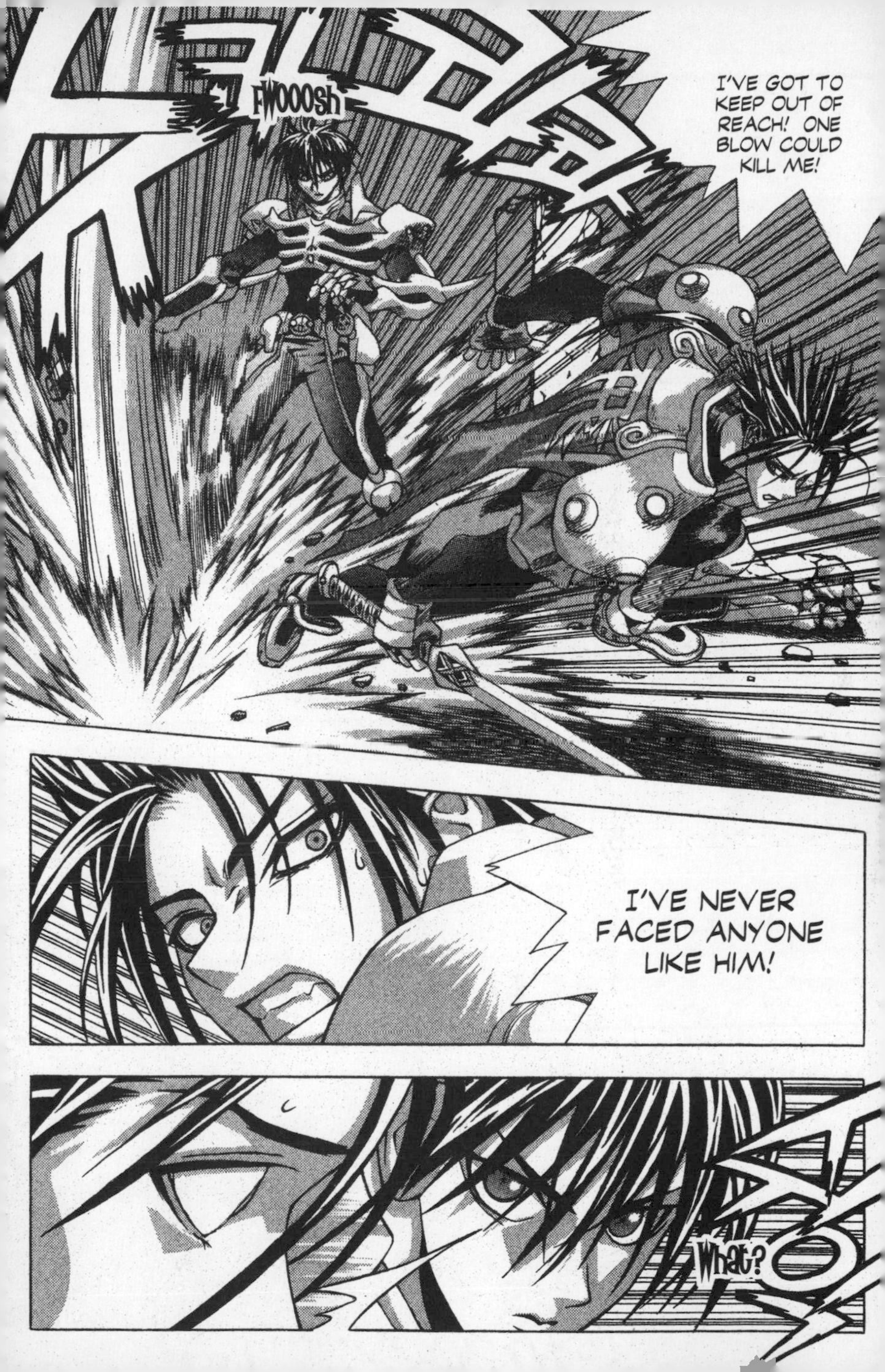
FWOOOSH
I'VE GOT TO KEEP OUT OF REACH! ONE BLOW COULD KILL ME!
I'VE NEVER FACED ANYONE LIKE HIM!
What?

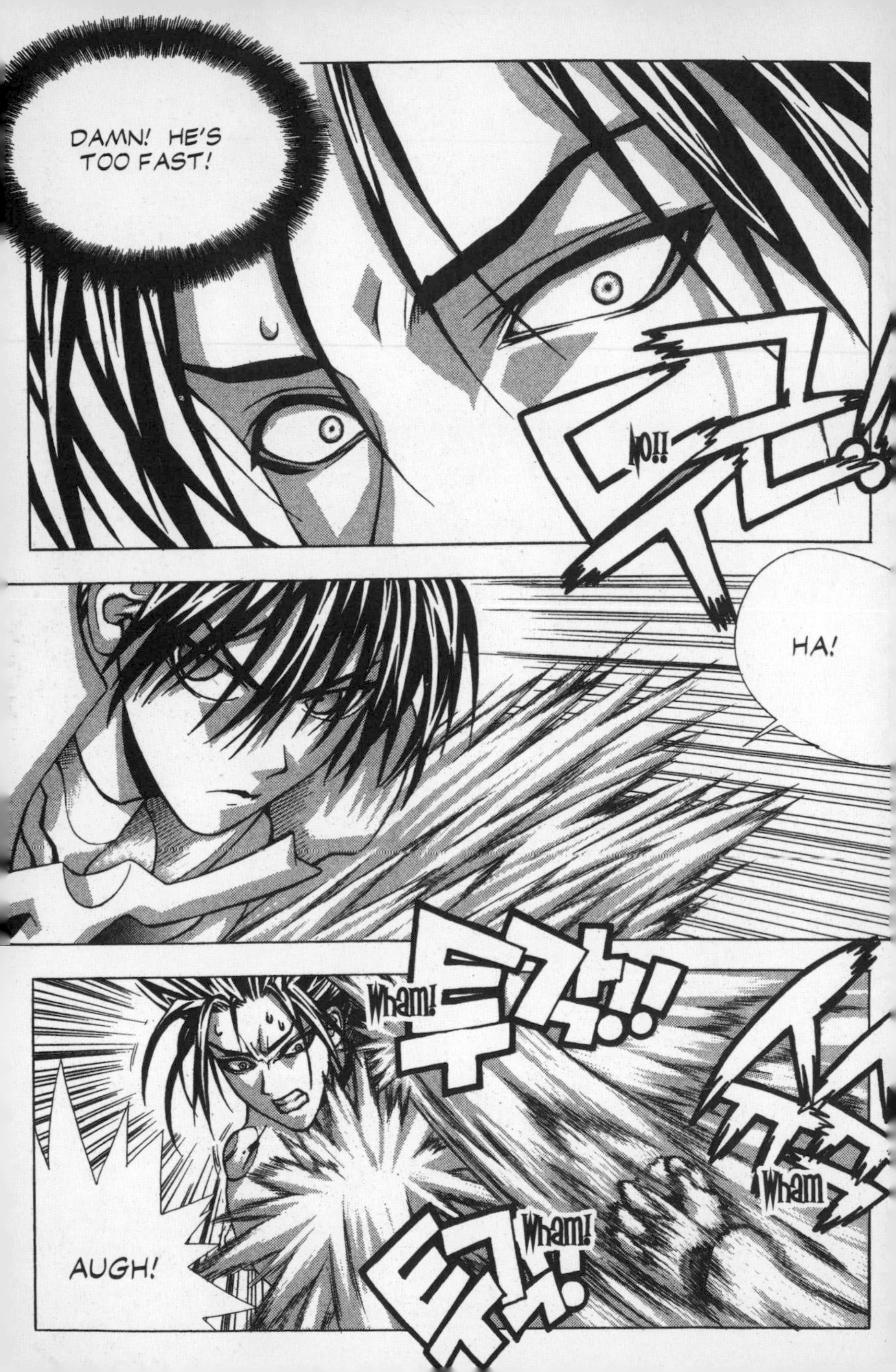
DAMN! HE'S TOO FAST!
NO!!
HA!
Wham!
AUGH!
Wham!
Wham

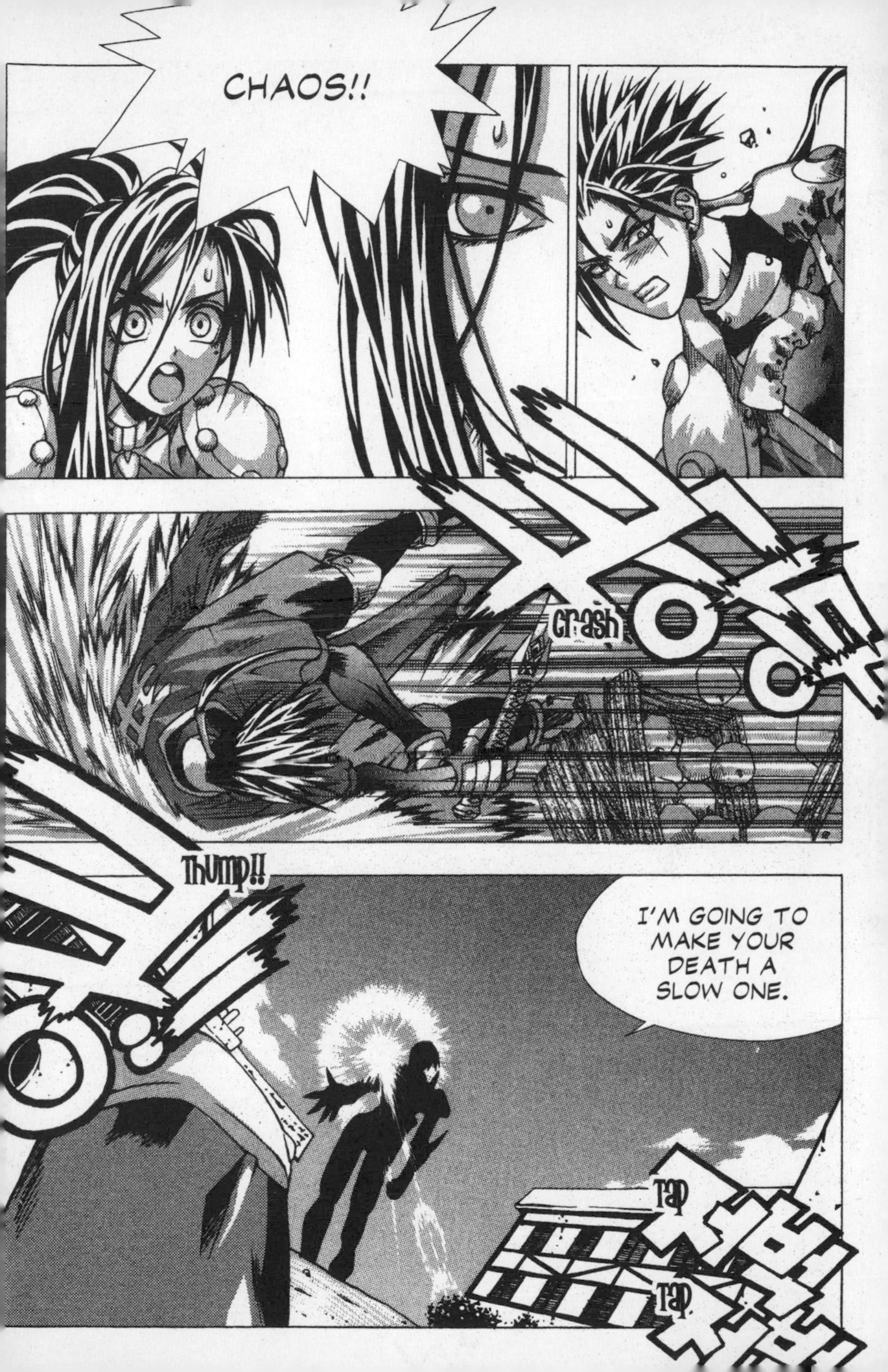
CHAOS!!
crash
THUMP!!
I'M GOING TO MAKE YOUR DEATH A SLOW ONE.
TAP
TAP

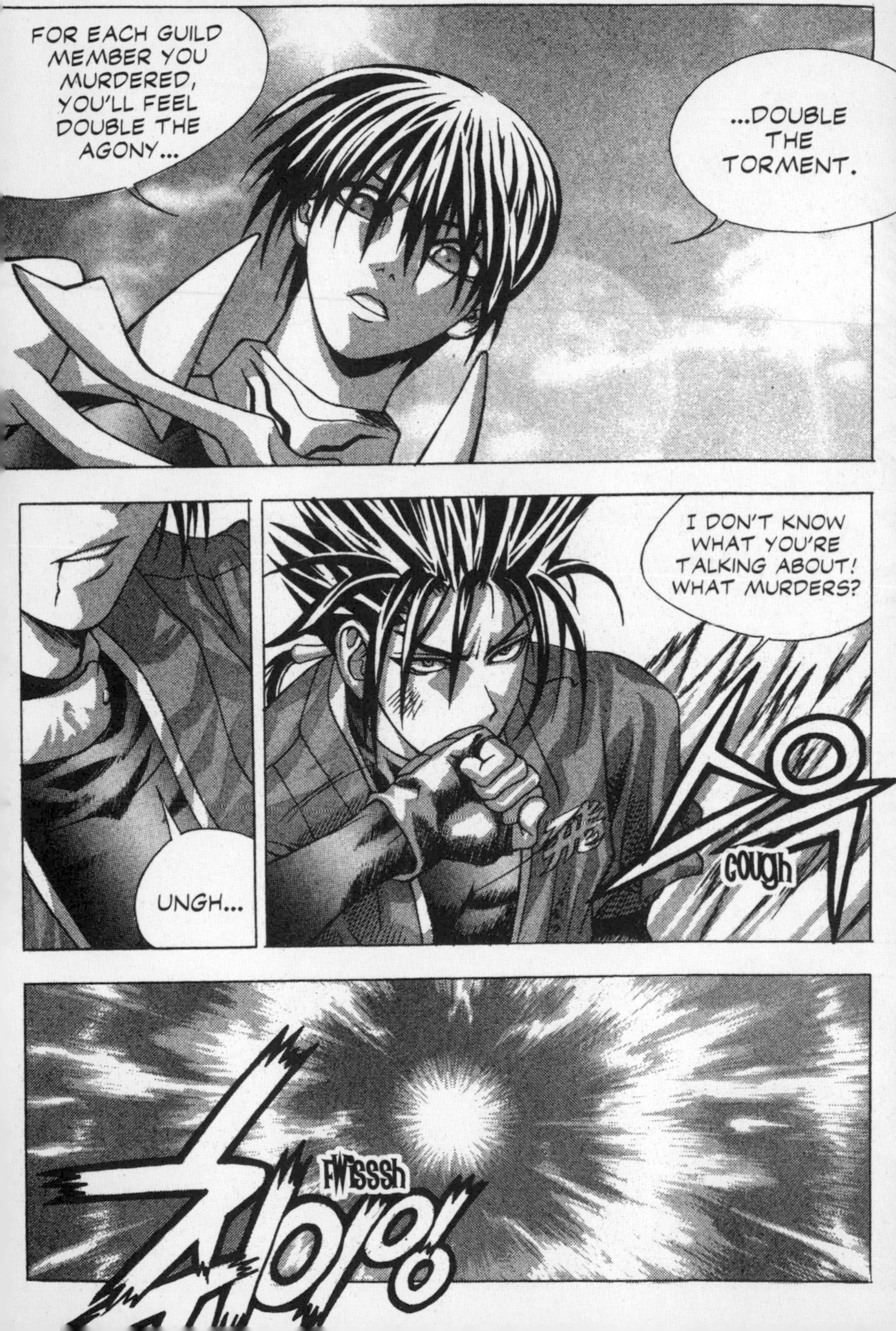
FOR EACH GUILD MEMBER YOU MURDERED, YOU'LL FEEL DOUBLE THE AGONY...
...DOUBLE THE TORMENT.
UNGH...
I DON'T KNOW WHAT YOU'RE TALKING ABOUT! WHAT MURDERS?
COUGH
FWISSSH

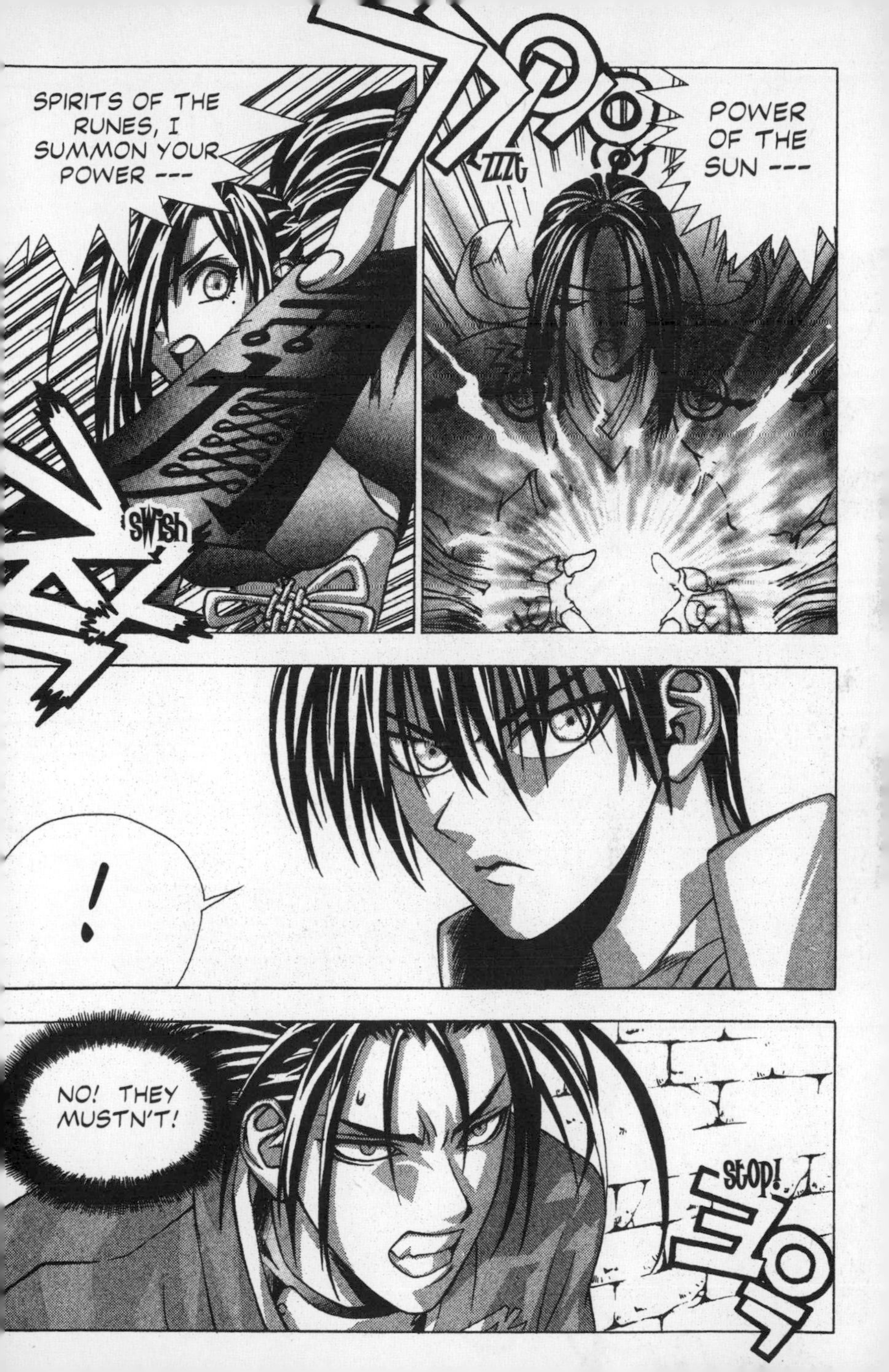
SPIRITS OF THE RUNES, I SUMMON YOUR POWER ---
SWISH
ZZZT
POWER OF THE SUN ---
!
NO! THEY MUSTN'T!
STOP!

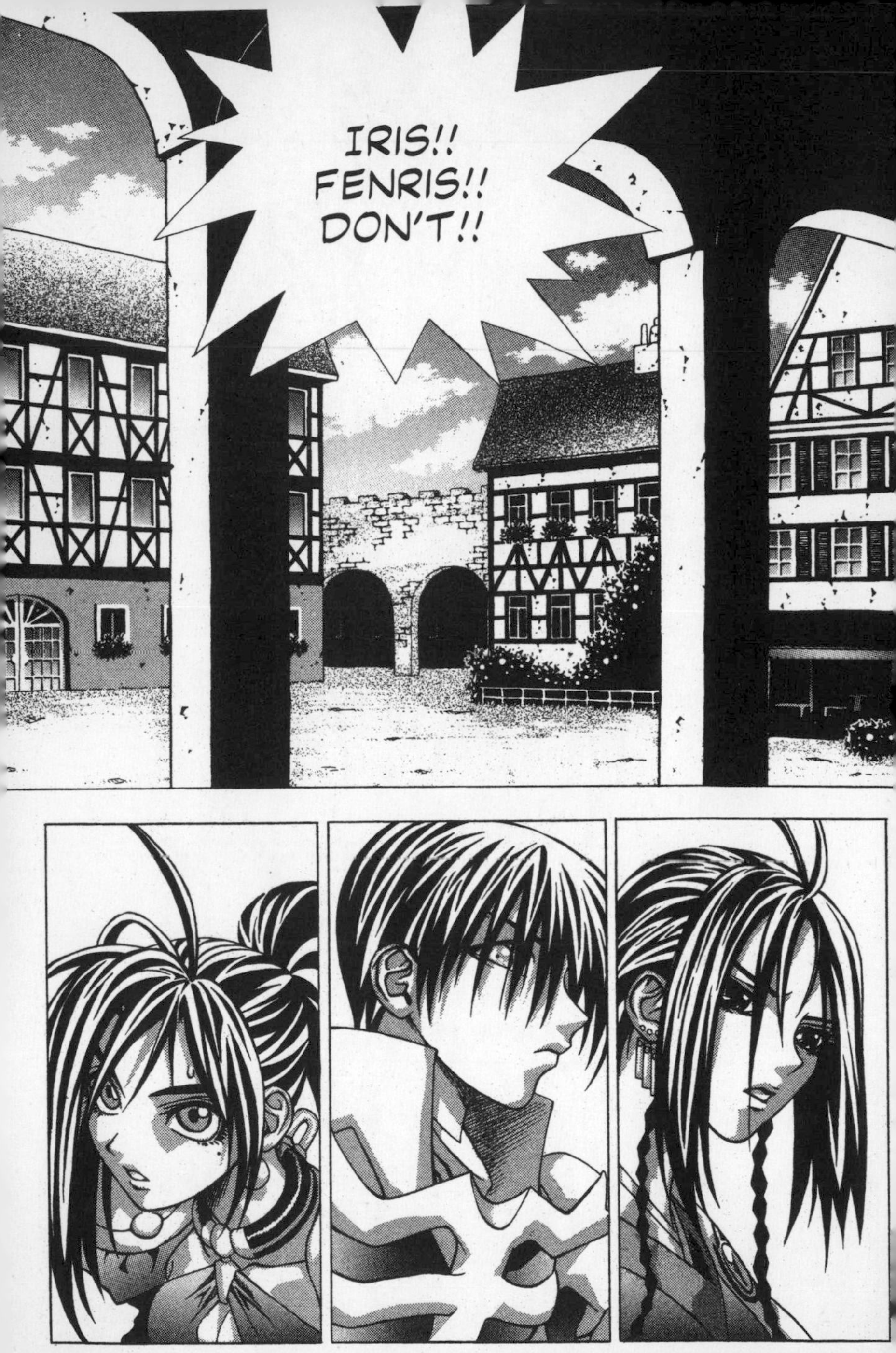
IRIS!!
FENRIS!!
DON'T!!

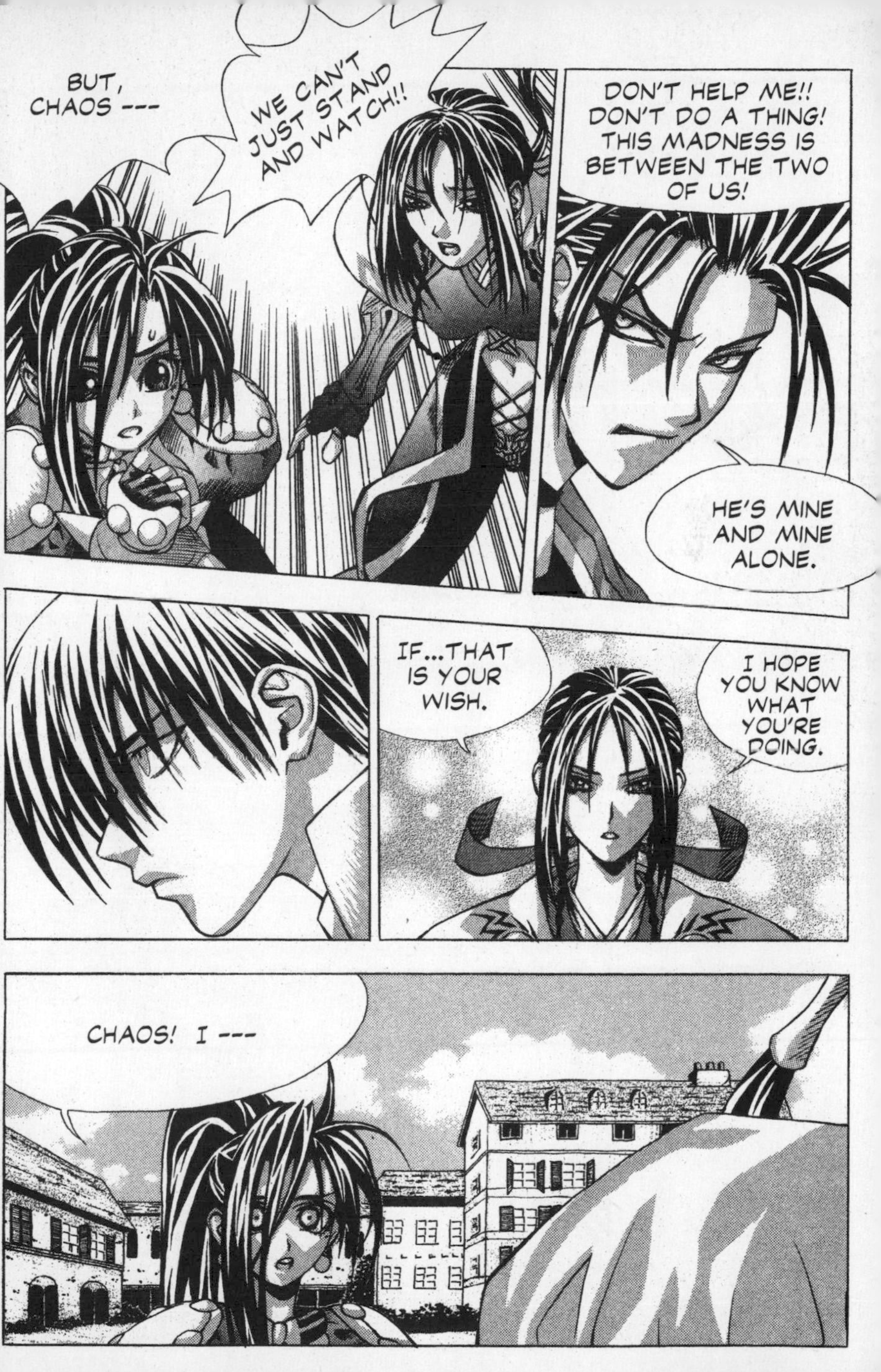
BUT, CHAOS ---
WE CAN'T JUST STAND AND WATCH!!
DON'T HELP ME!! DON'T DO A THING! THIS MADNESS IS BETWEEN THE TWO OF US!
HE'S MINE AND MINE ALONE.
IF...THAT IS YOUR WISH.
I HOPE YOU KNOW WHAT YOU'RE DOING.
CHAOS! I ---

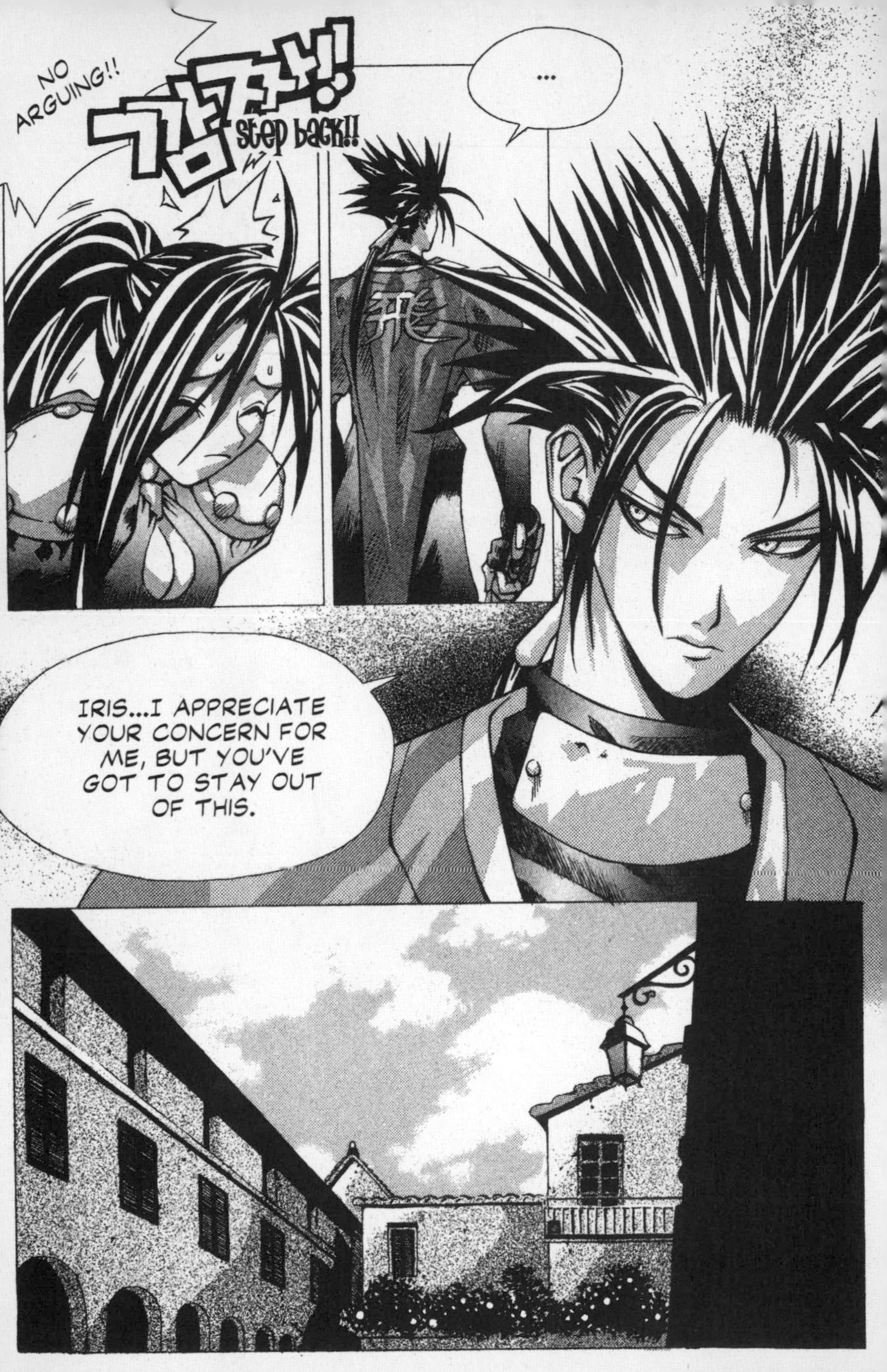
NO ARGUING!!
step back!!
...
IRIS...I APPRECIATE YOUR CONCERN FOR ME, BUT YOU'VE GOT TO STAY OUT OF THIS.

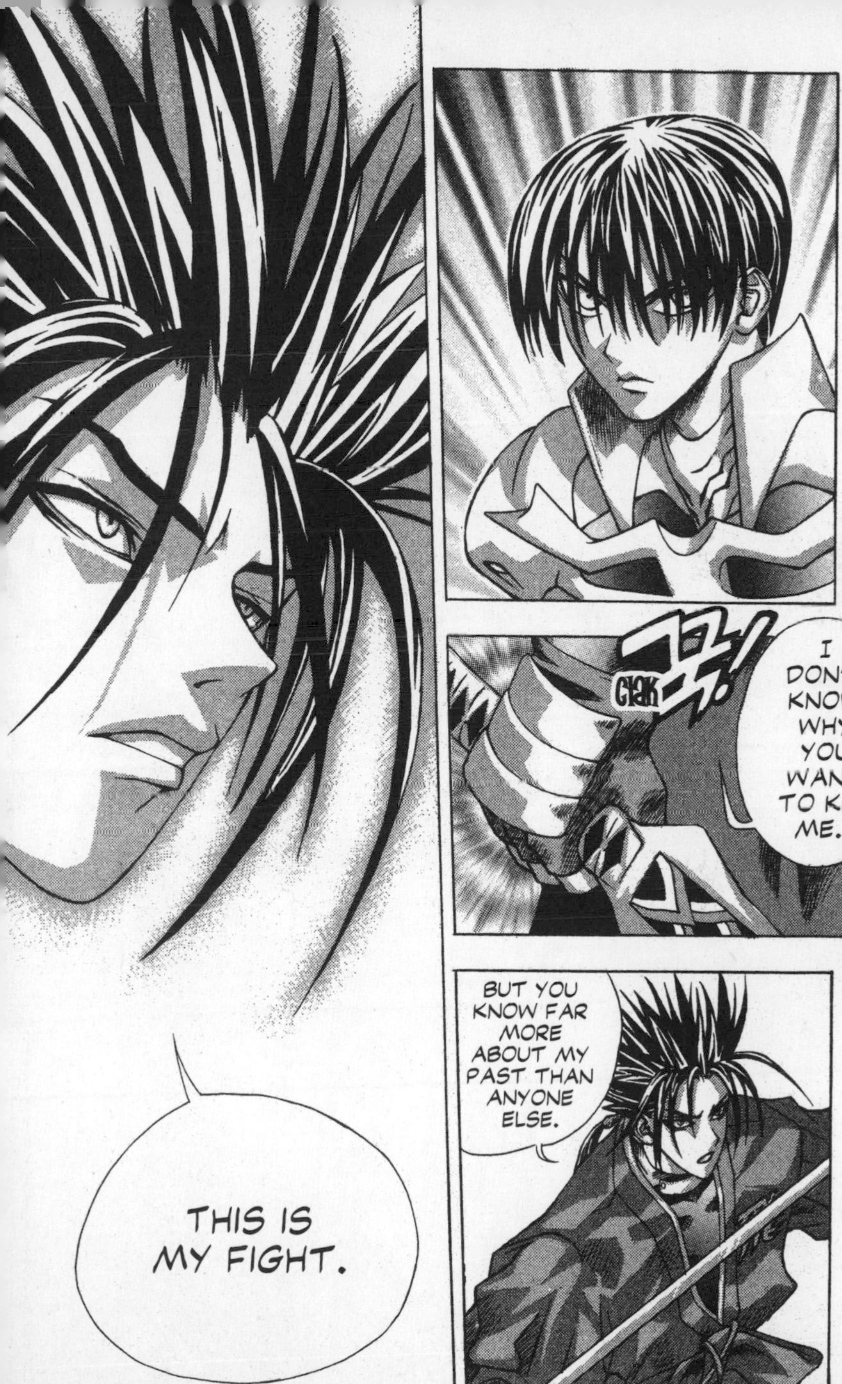
THIS IS MY FIGHT.
CLAK
I DON'T KNOW WHY YOU WANT TO KILL ME...
BUT YOU KNOW FAR MORE ABOUT MY PAST THAN ANYONE ELSE.

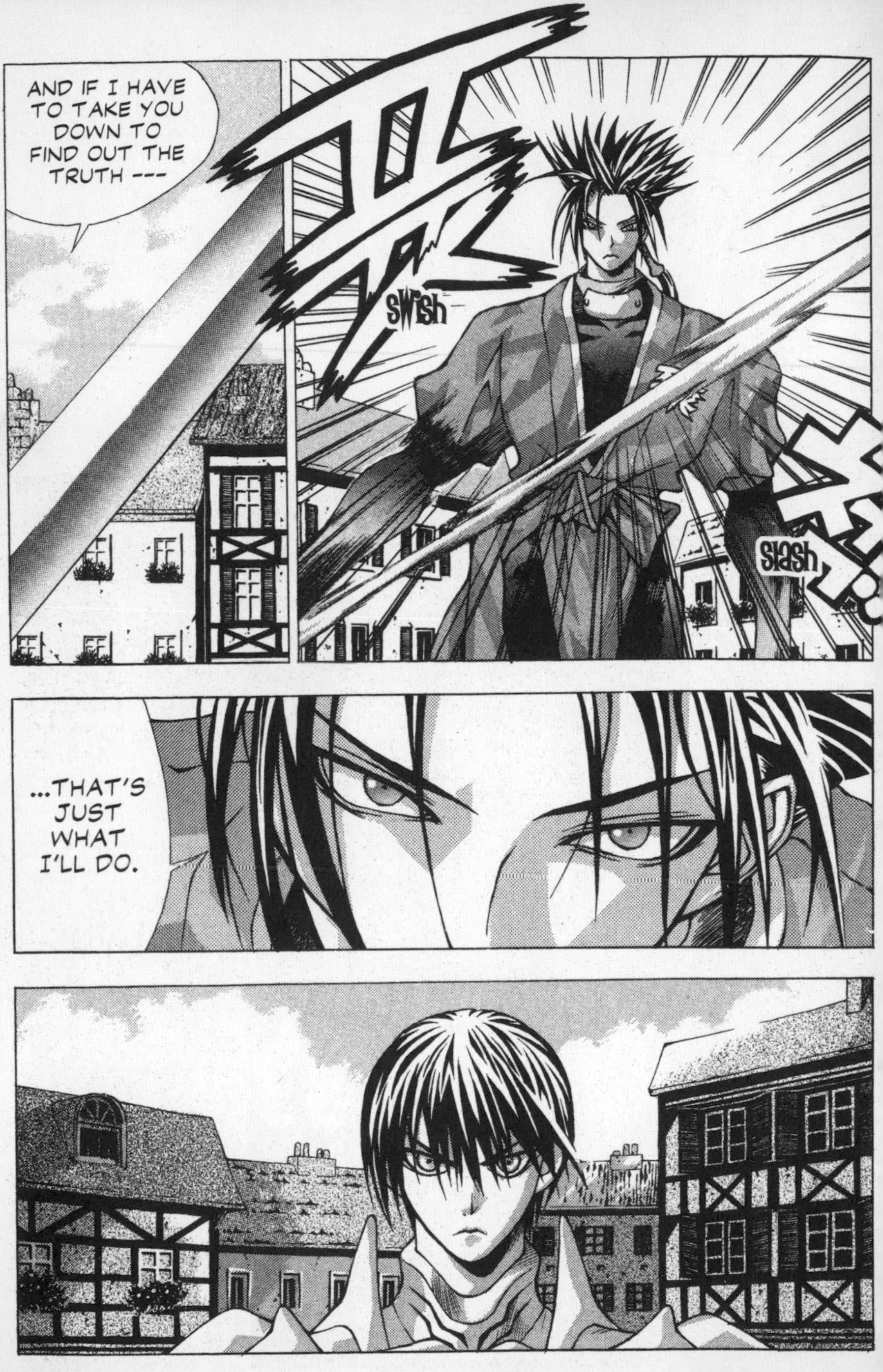
AND IF I HAVE TO TAKE YOU DOWN TO FIND OUT THE TRUTH ---
SWISH
SLASH
...THAT'S JUST WHAT I'LL DO.

RAGNAROK
라그나로크
IN TO THE ABYSS

HURRY-GO
-ROUND

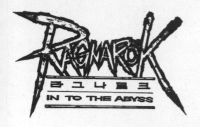

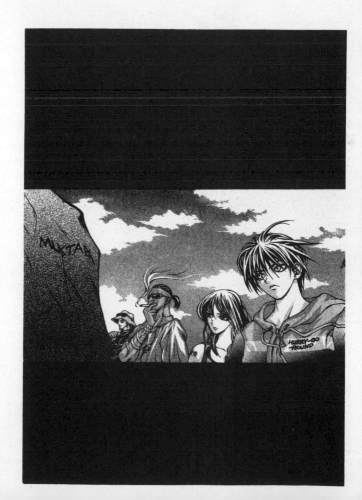

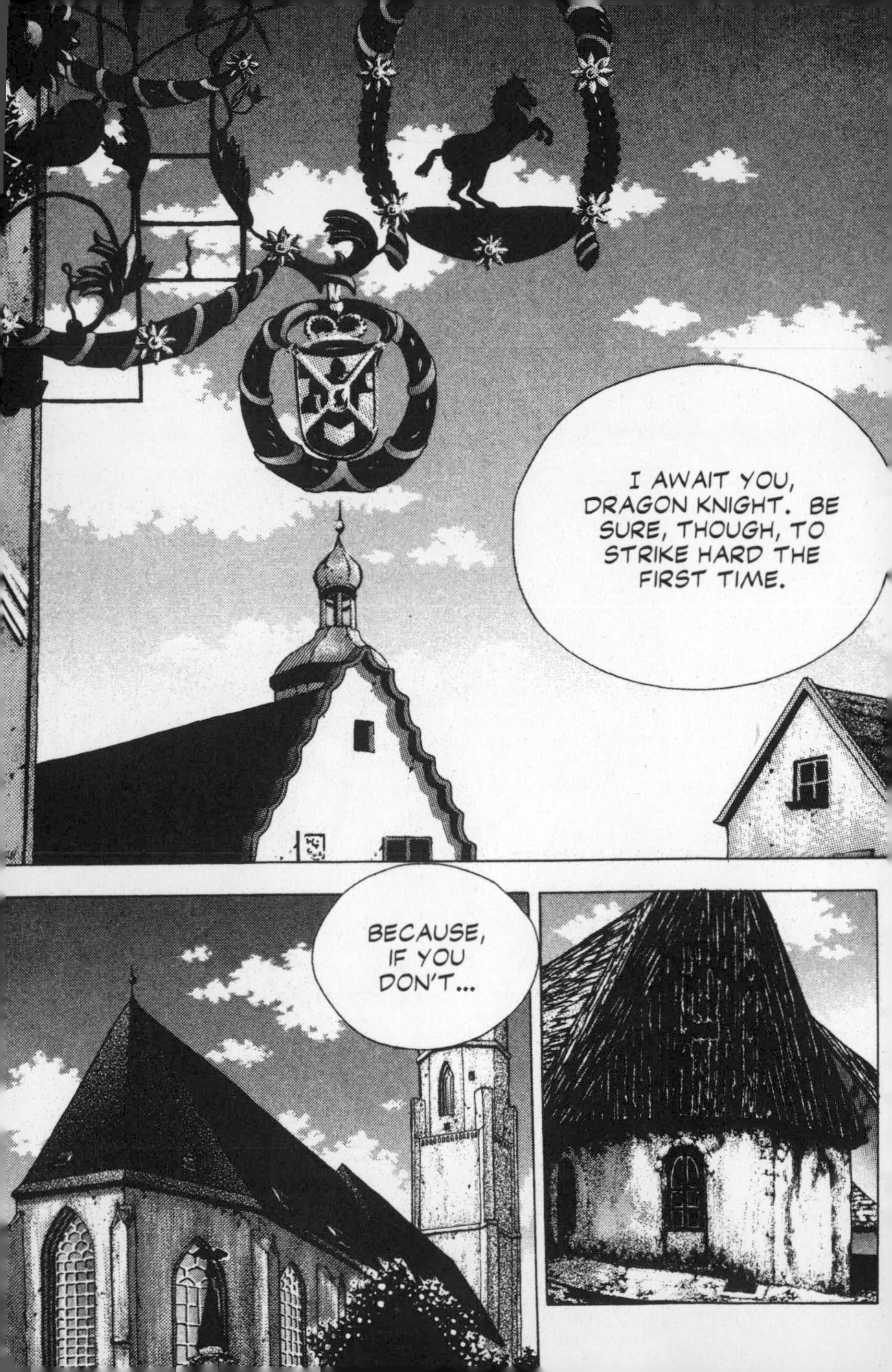
I AWAIT YOU, DRAGON KNIGHT. BE SURE, THOUGH, TO STRIKE HARD THE FIRST TIME.
BECAUSE, IF YOU DON'T...

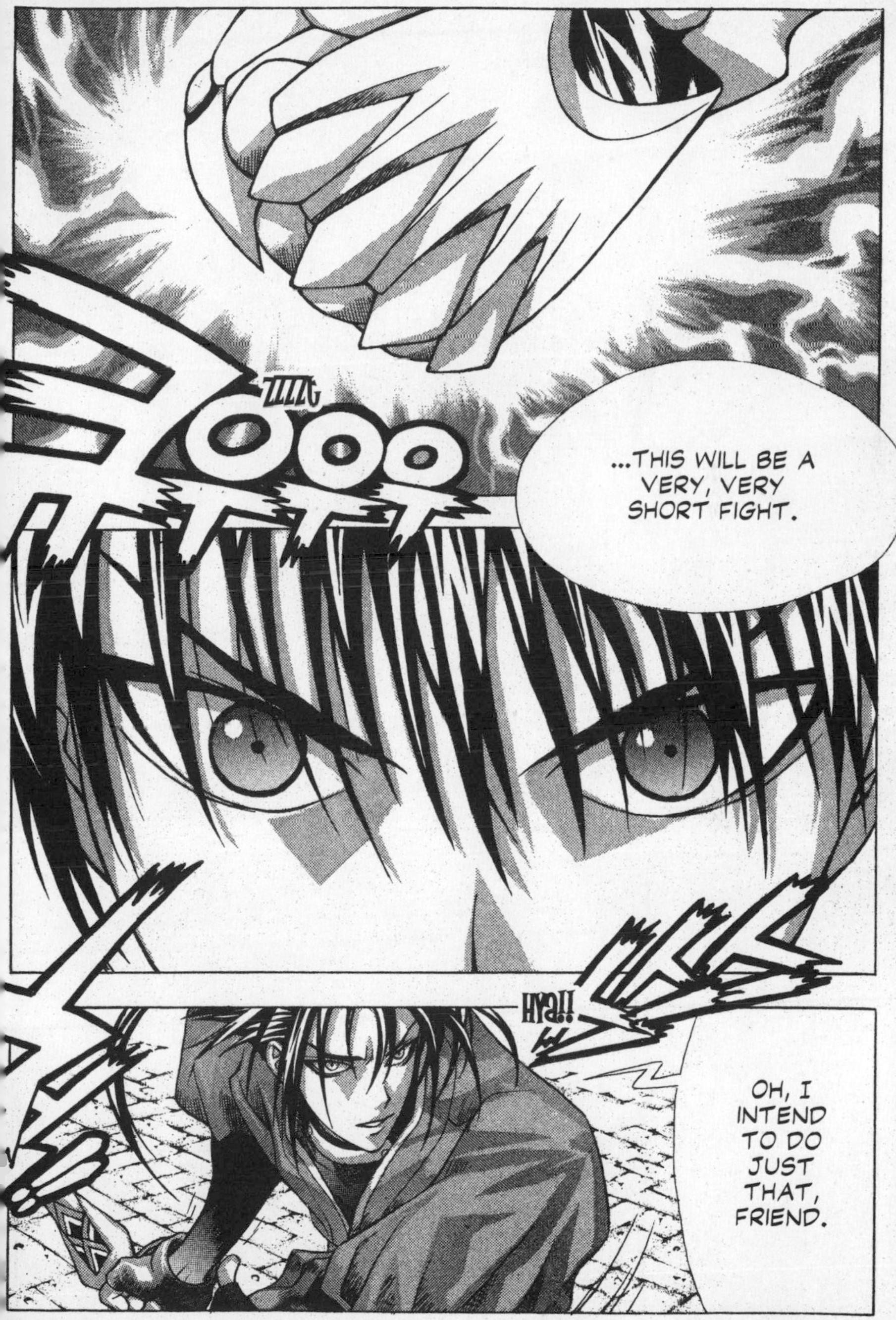
ZZZZt
...THIS WILL BE A VERY, VERY SHORT FIGHT.
HYa!!
OH, I INTEND TO DO JUST THAT, FRIEND.

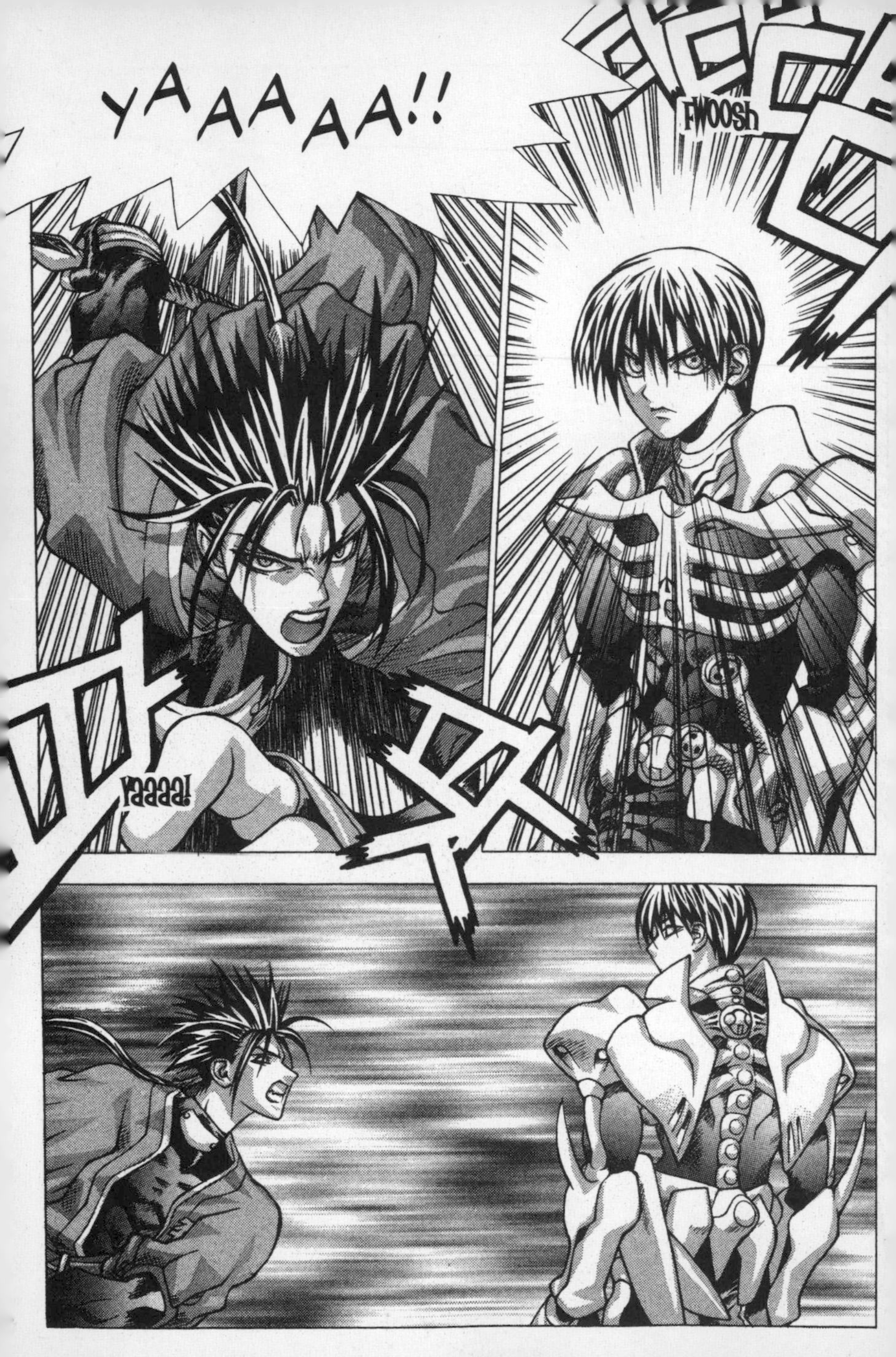
YAAAAAA!!
yaaaa!
FWOOSh

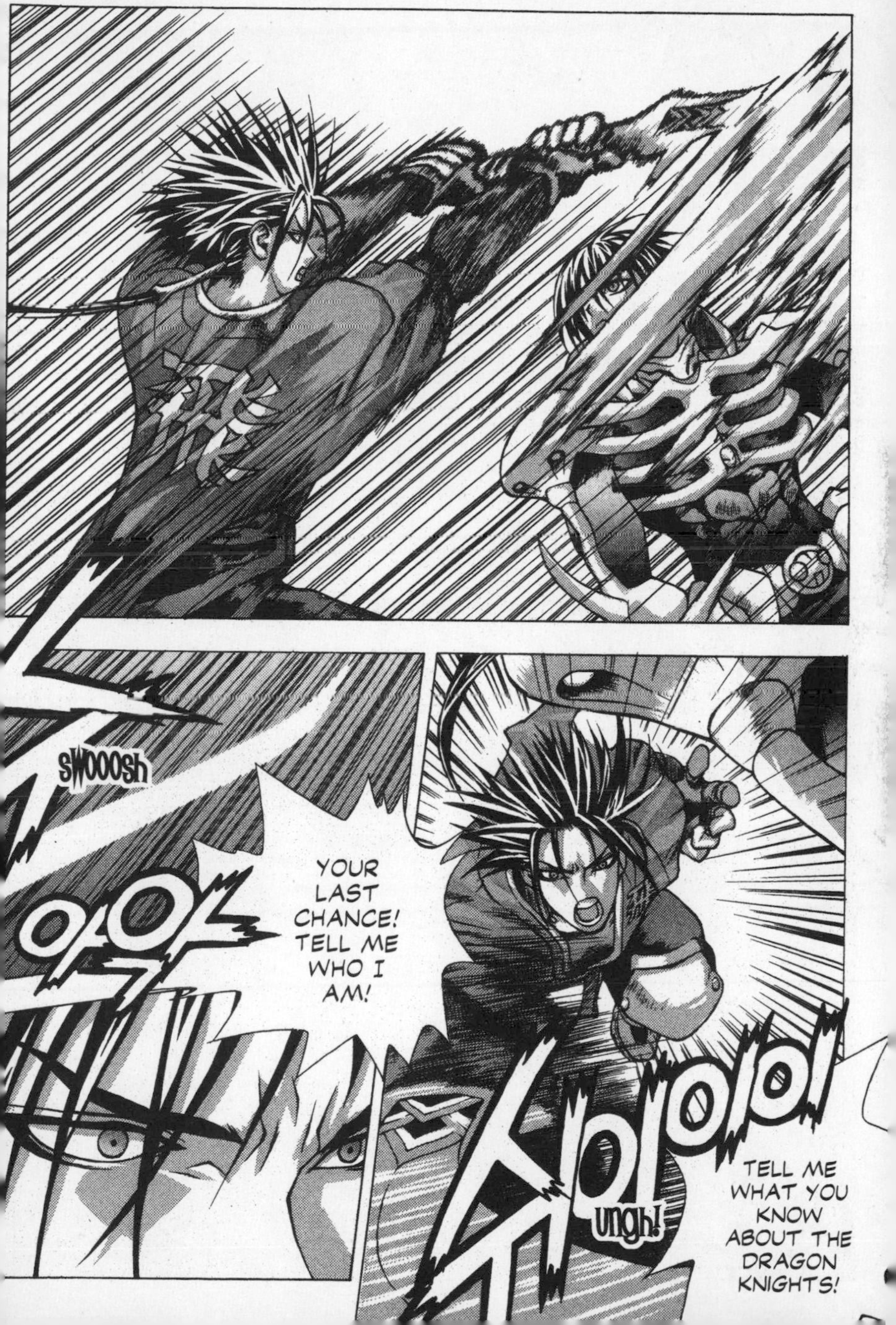
SWOOOSH
YOUR LAST CHANCE! TELL ME WHO I AM!
UNGH!
TELL ME WHAT YOU KNOW ABOUT THE DRAGON KNIGHTS!

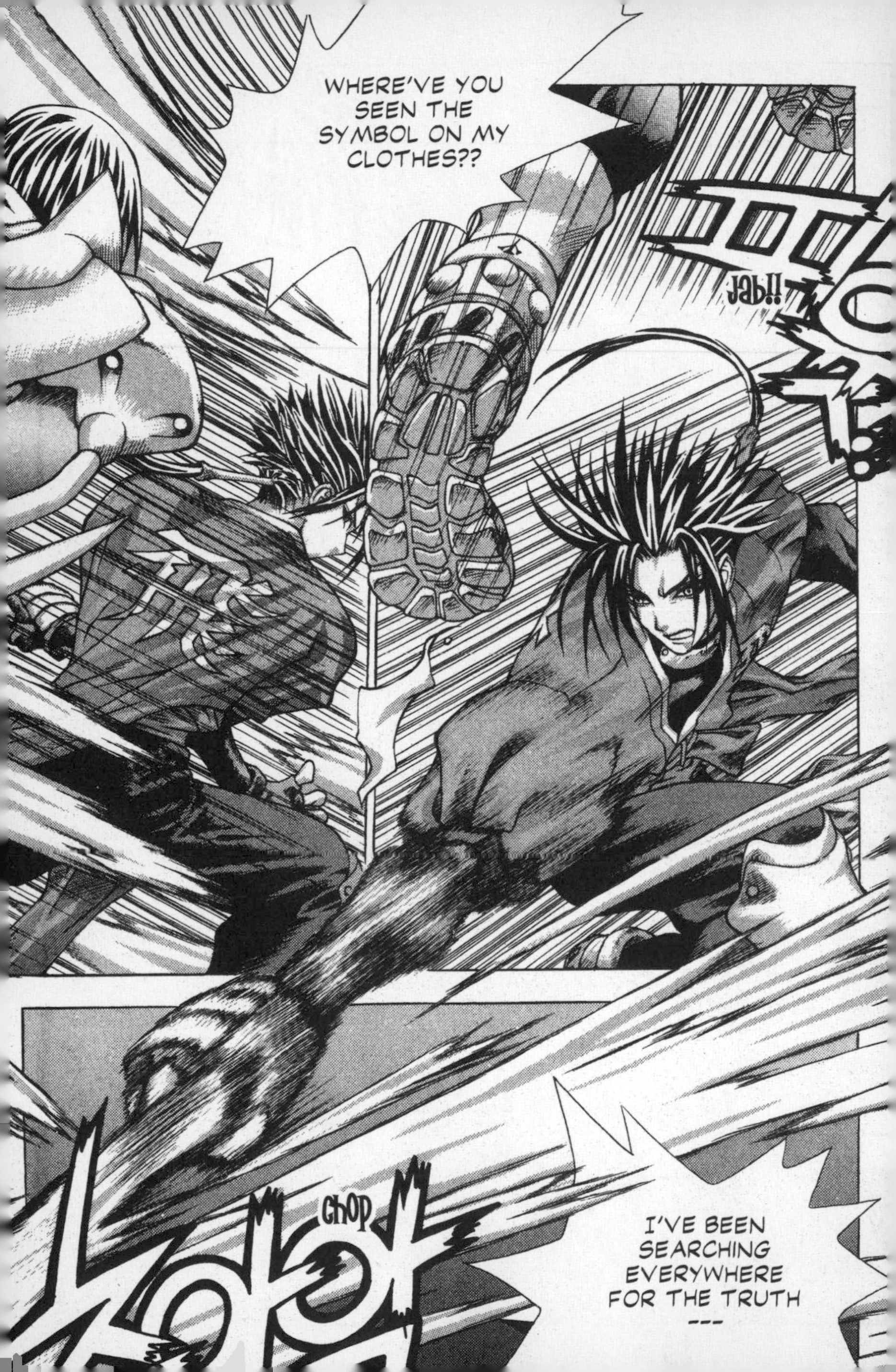
WHERE'VE YOU SEEN THE SYMBOL ON MY CLOTHES??
JAB!!
CHOP
I'VE BEEN SEARCHING EVERYWHERE FOR THE TRUTH

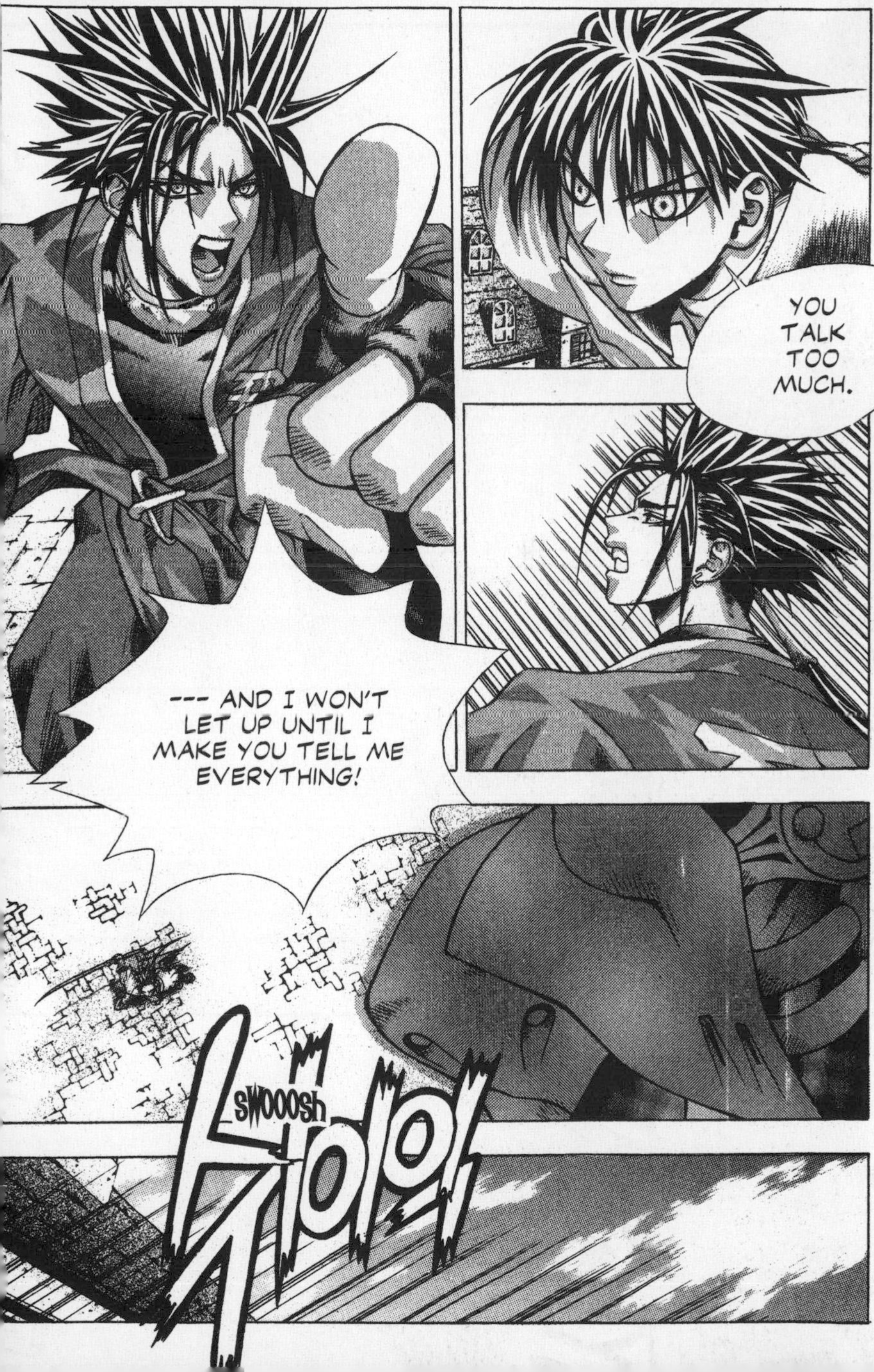
--- AND I WON'T LET UP UNTIL I MAKE YOU TELL ME EVERYTHING!
YOU TALK TOO MUCH.
SWOOOSH

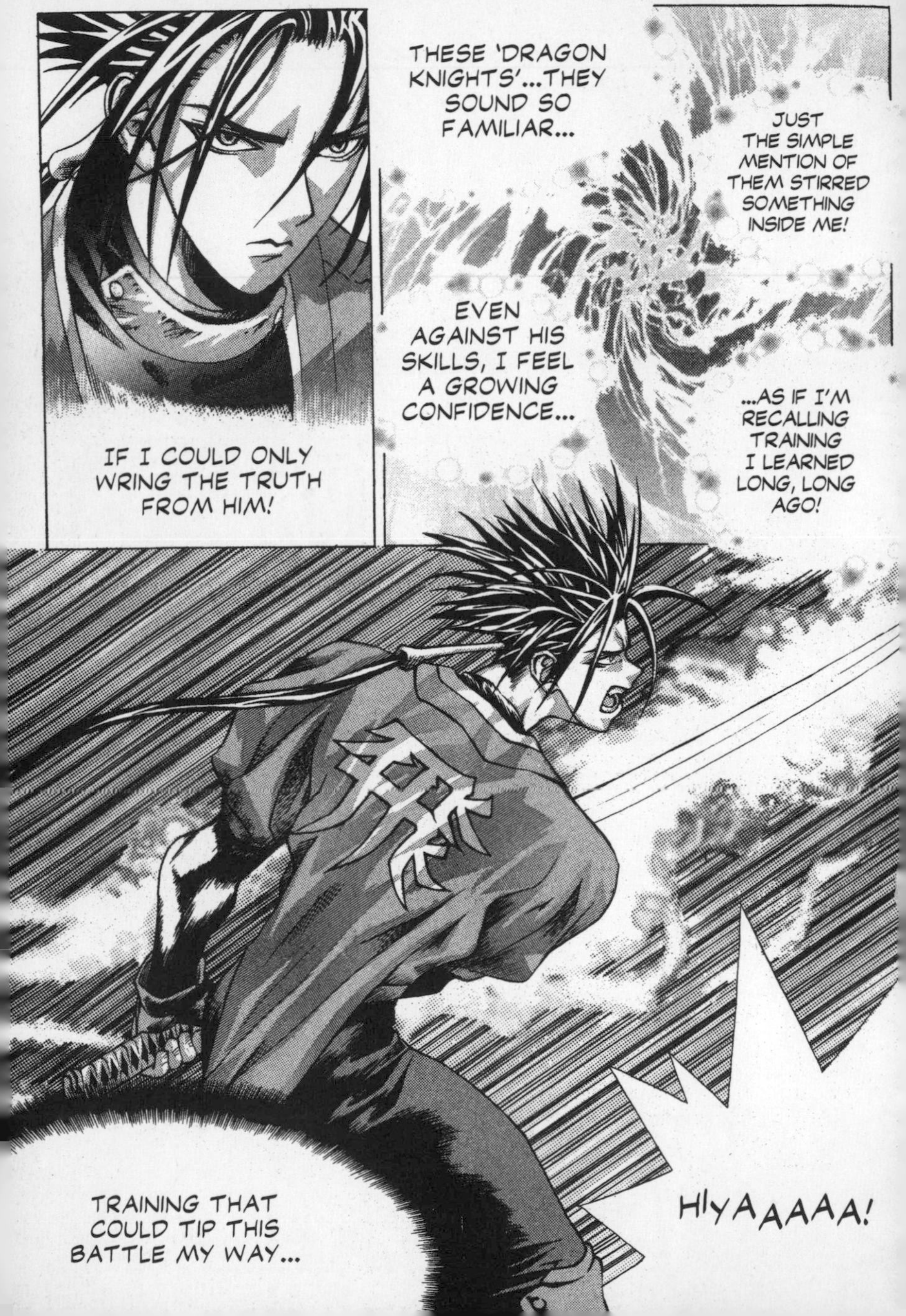
IF I COULD ONLY WRING THE TRUTH FROM HIM!
THESE 'DRAGON KNIGHTS'...THEY SOUND SO FAMILIAR...
JUST THE SIMPLE MENTION OF THEM STIRRED SOMETHING INSIDE ME!
EVEN AGAINST HIS SKILLS, I FEEL A GROWING CONFIDENCE...
...AS IF I'M RECALLING TRAINING I LEARNED LONG, LONG AGO!
TRAINING THAT COULD TIP THIS BATTLE MY WAY...
HIYAAAAA!

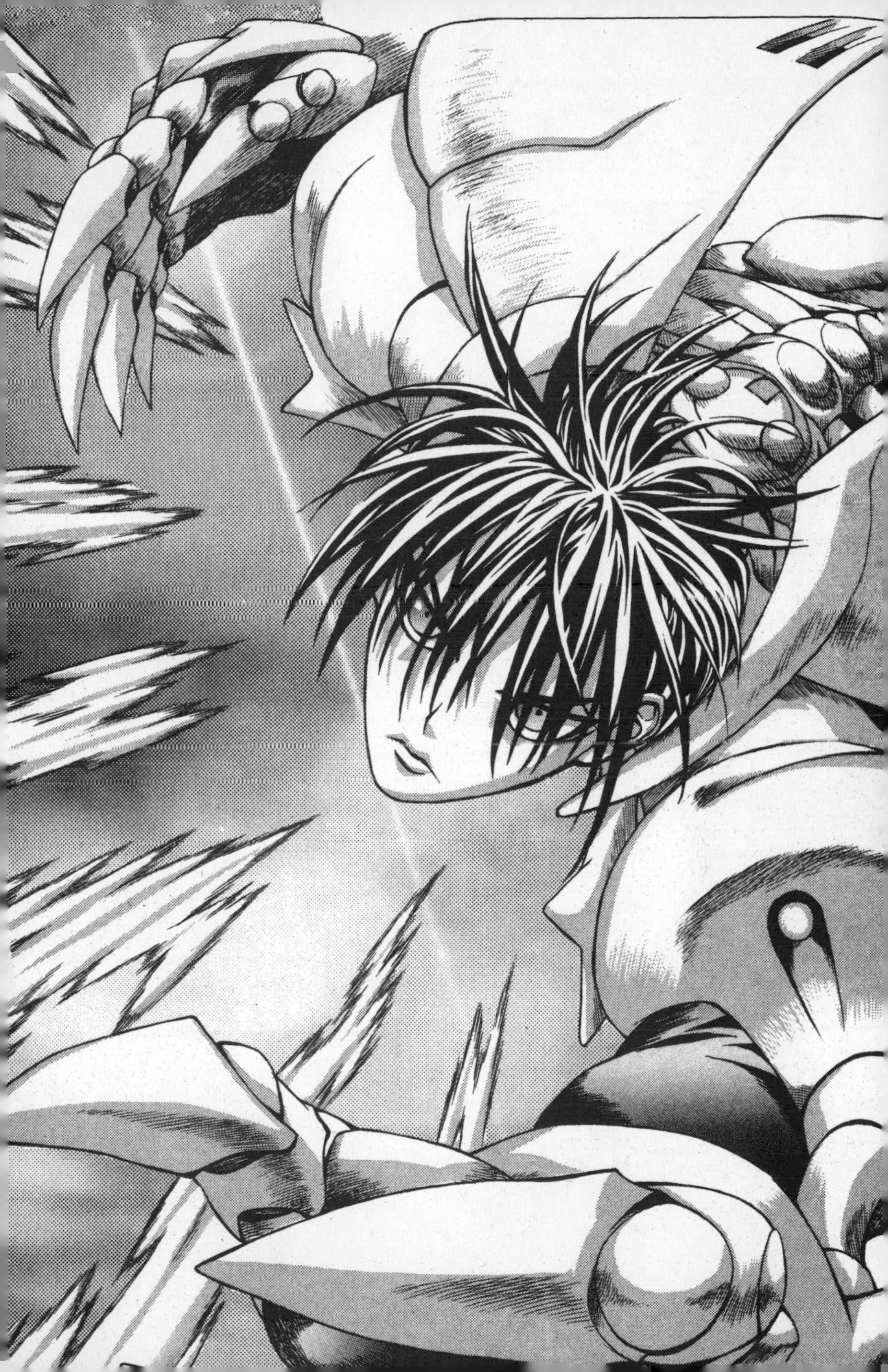

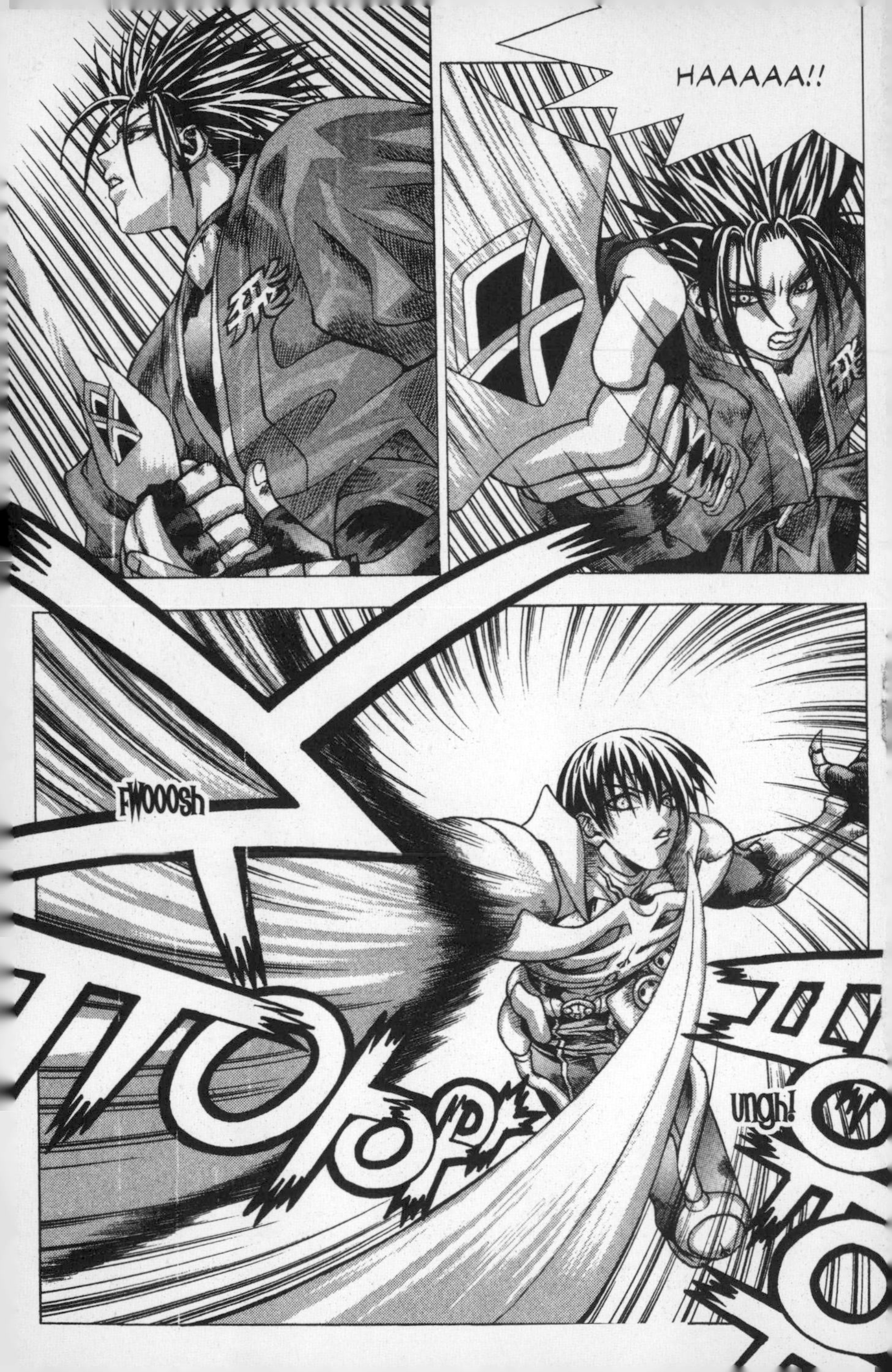
HAAAAA!!
FWOOOSh
ungh!

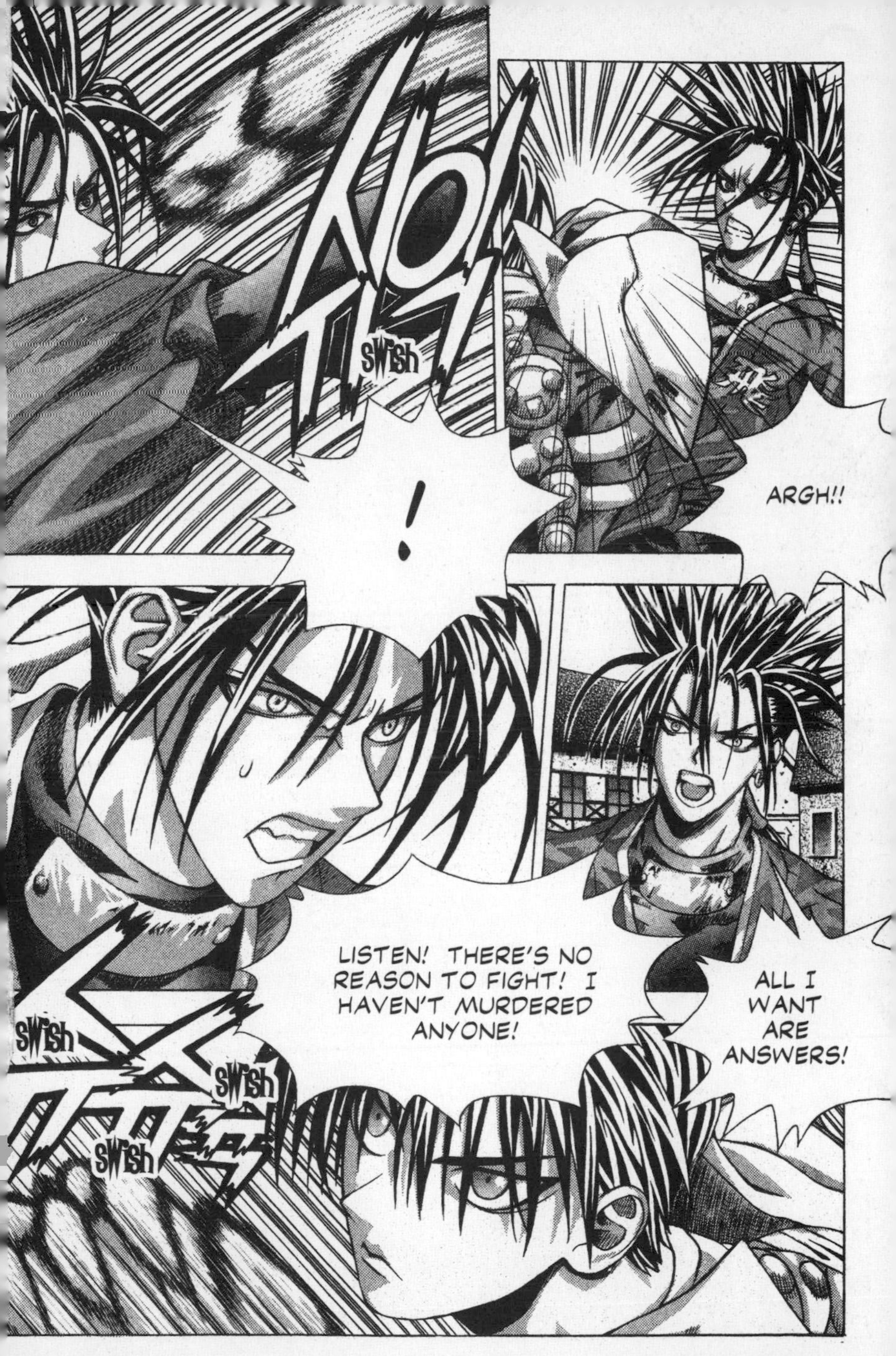
SWISH
!
ARGH!!
LISTEN! THERE'S NO REASON TO FIGHT! I HAVEN'T MURDERED ANYONE!
ALL I WANT ARE ANSWERS!
SWISH
SWISH
SWISH

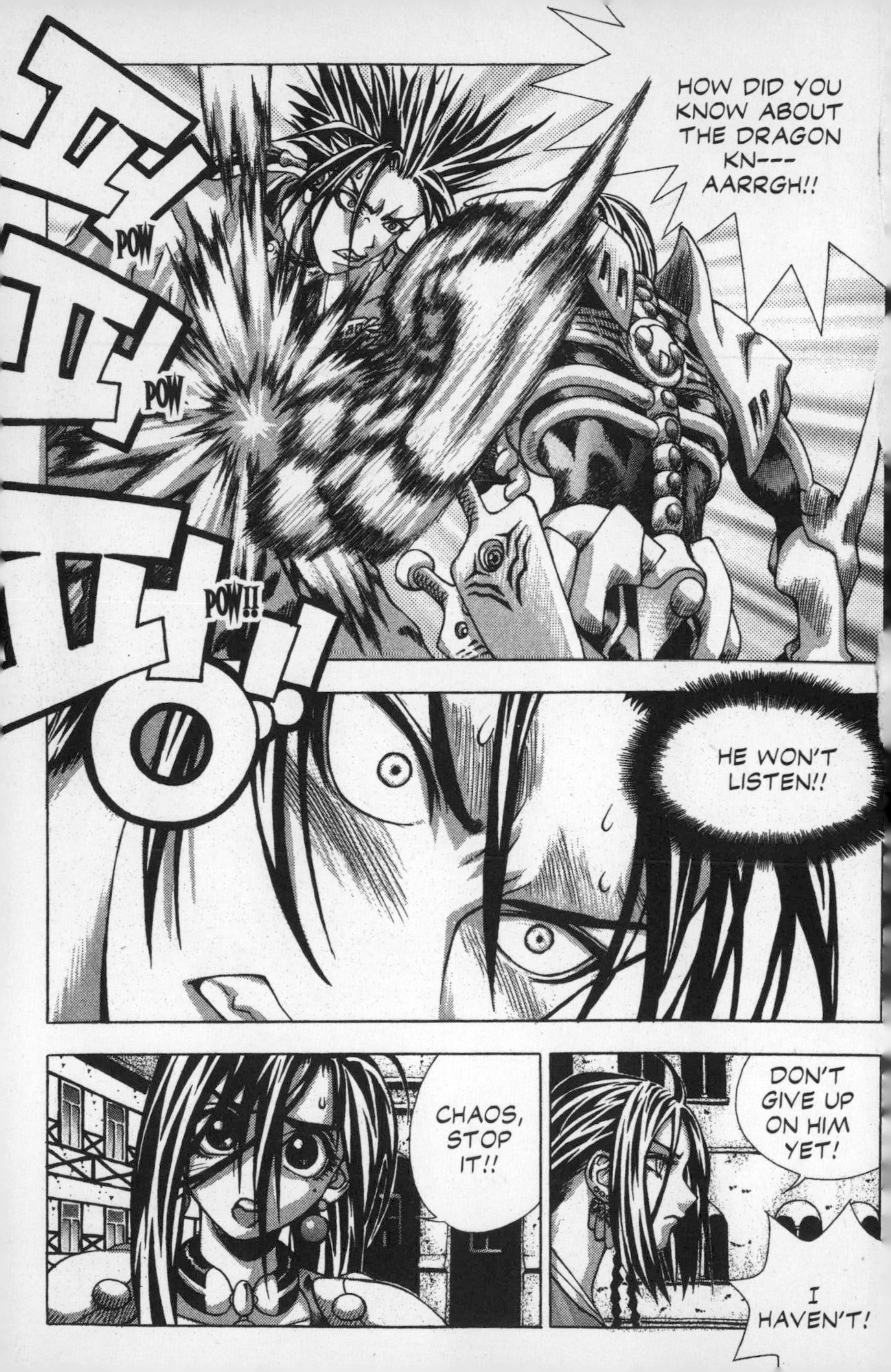
POW
POW
POW!!
HOW DID YOU KNOW ABOUT THE DRAGON KN--- AARRGH!!
HE WON'T LISTEN!!
CHAOS, STOP IT!!
DON'T GIVE UP ON HIM YET!
I HAVEN'T!

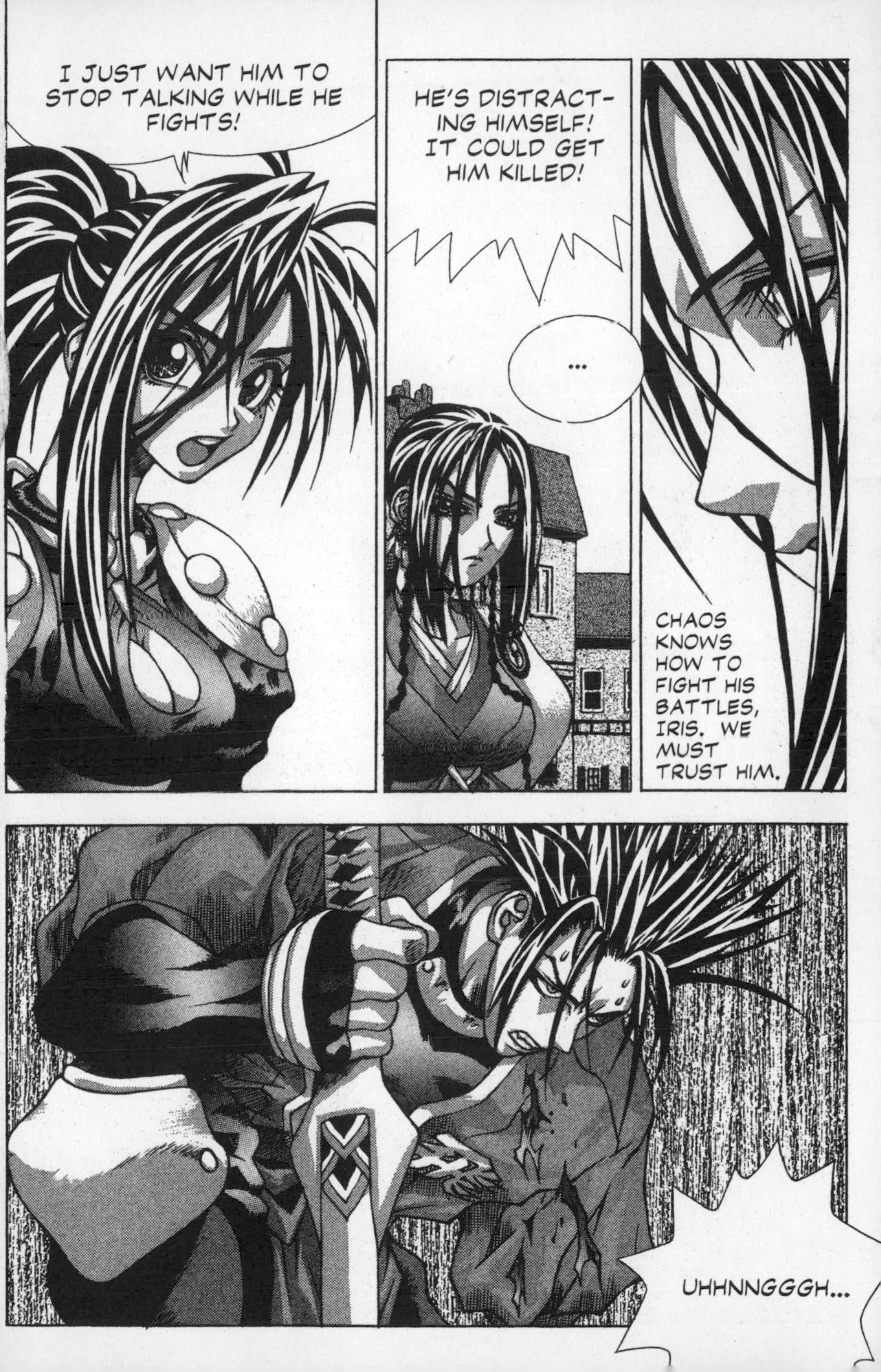
I JUST WANT HIM TO STOP TALKING WHILE HE FIGHTS!
HE'S DISTRACT-ING HIMSELF! IT COULD GET HIM KILLED!
...
CHAOS KNOWS HOW TO FIGHT HIS BATTLES, IRIS. WE MUST TRUST HIM.
UHHNNGGGH...

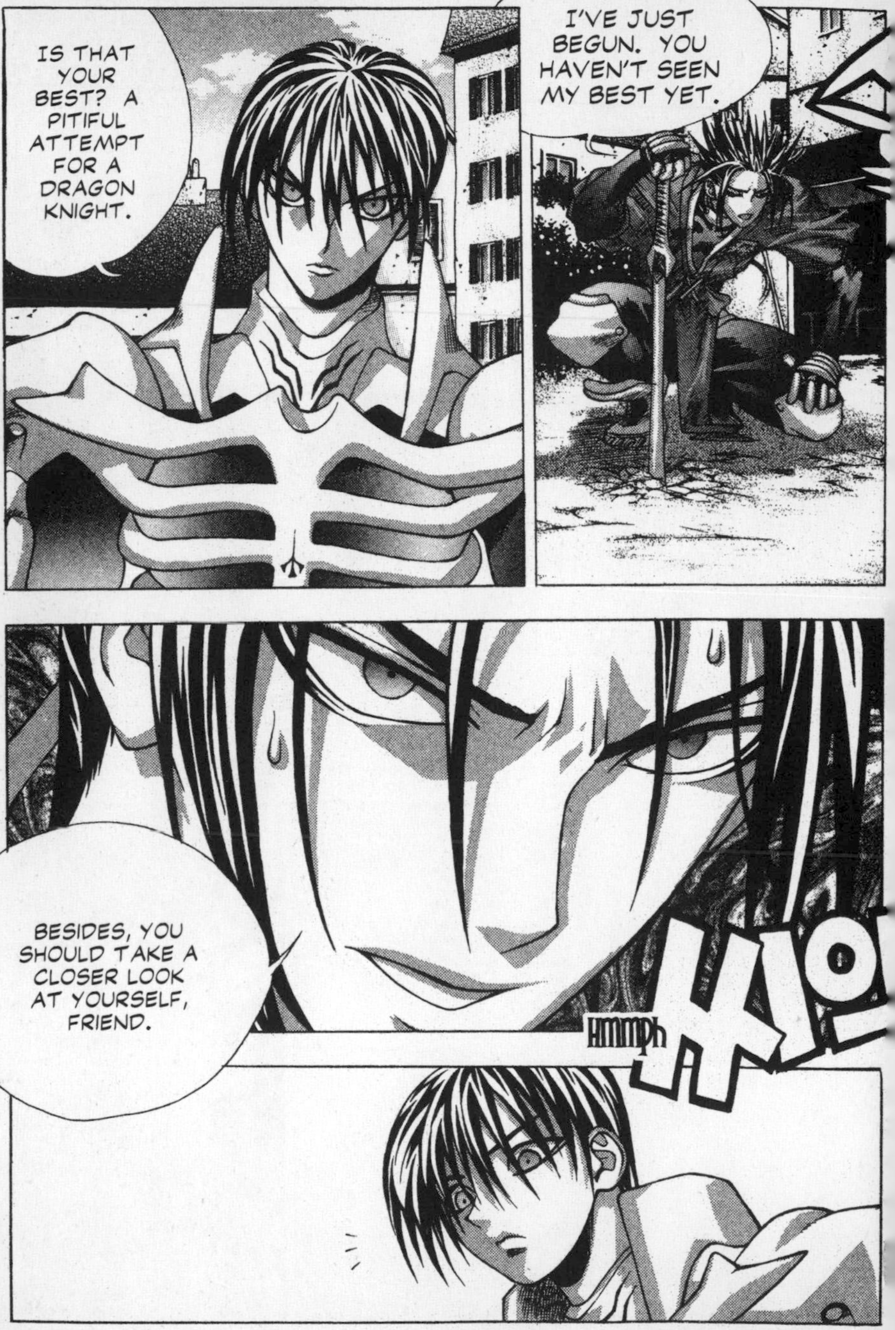
IS THAT YOUR BEST? A PITIFUL ATTEMPT FOR A DRAGON KNIGHT.
I'VE JUST BEGUN. YOU HAVEN'T SEEN MY BEST YET.
BESIDES, YOU SHOULD TAKE A CLOSER LOOK AT YOURSELF, FRIEND.
HMMPh

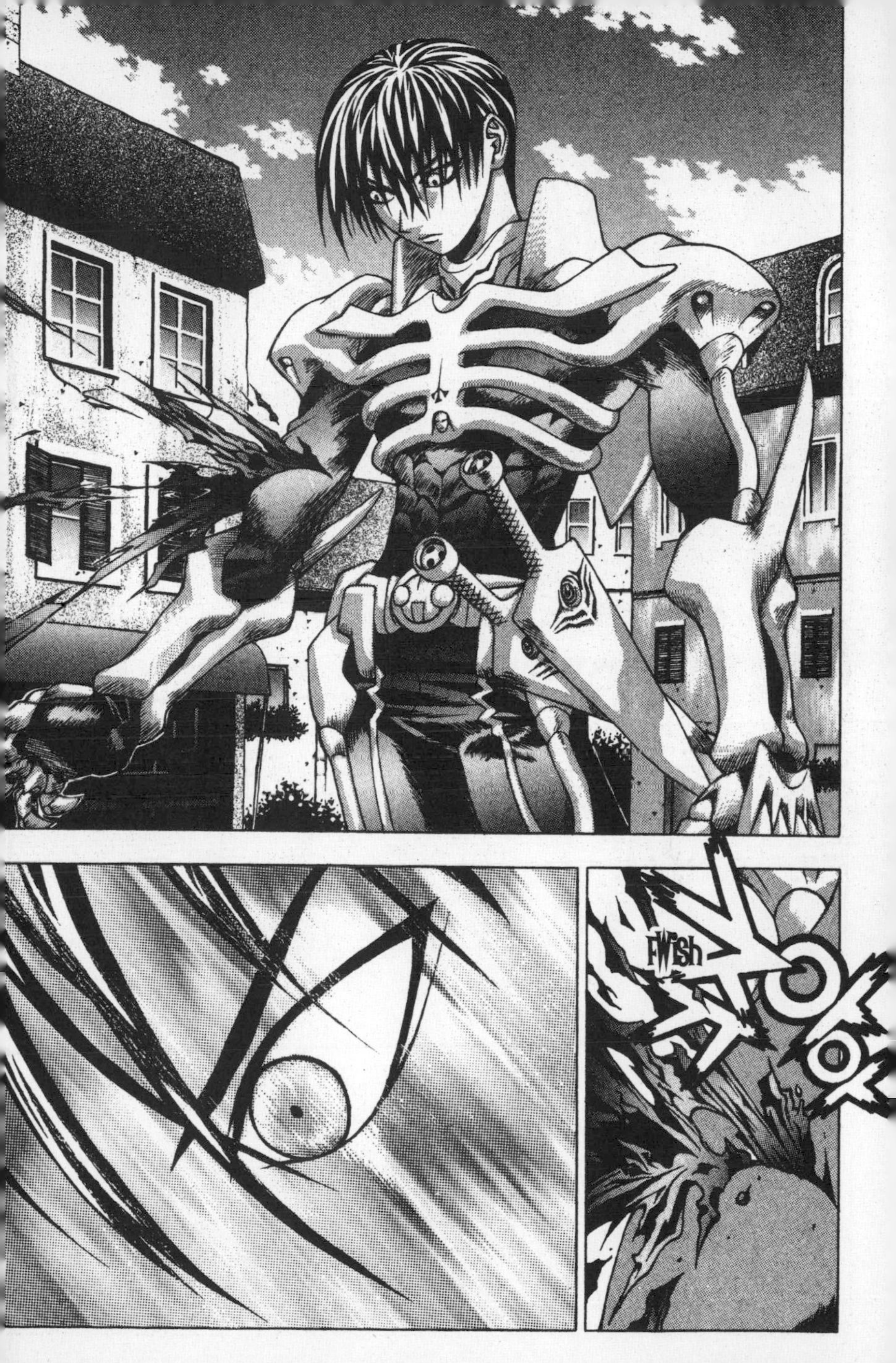
FWISH

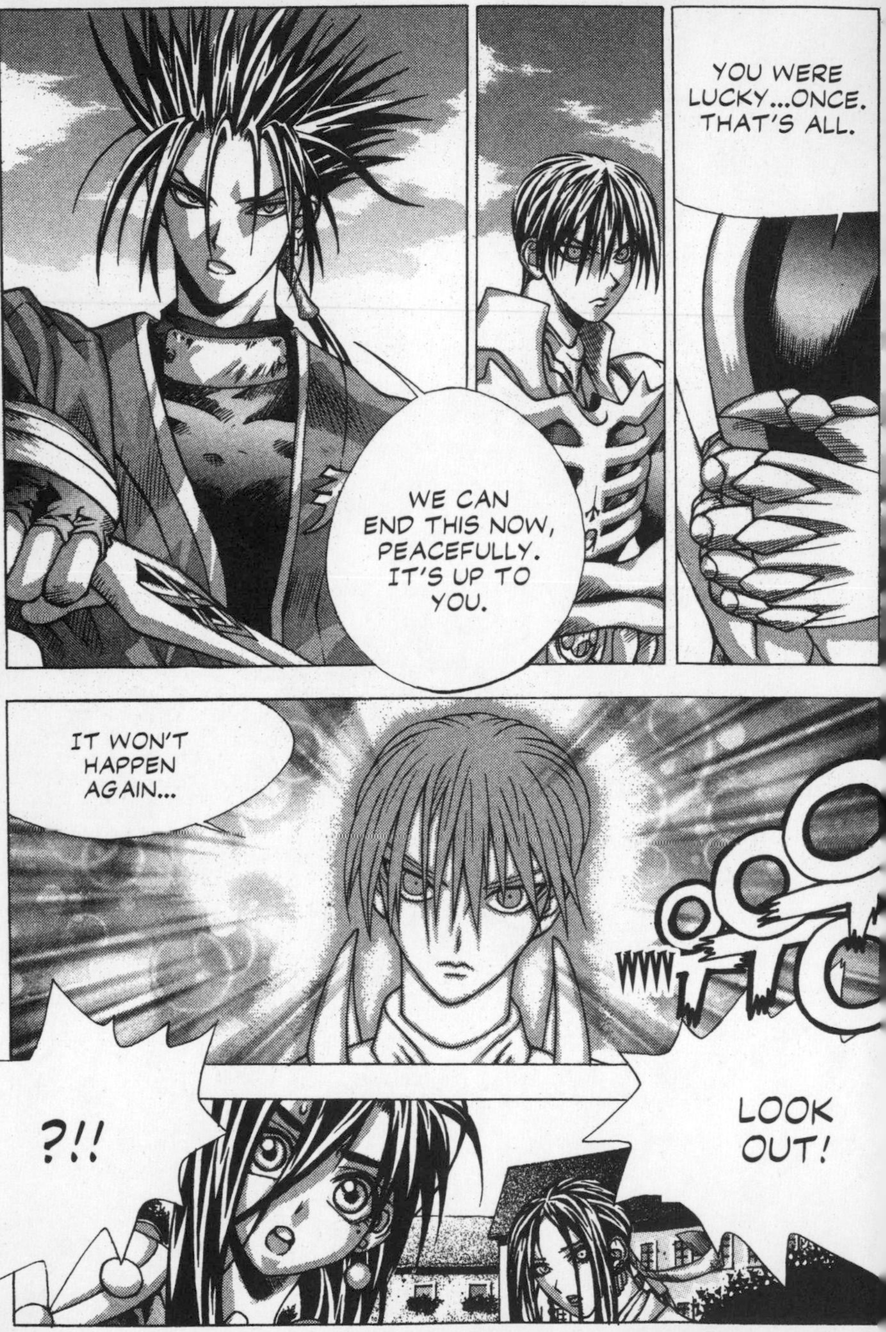
WE CAN END THIS NOW, PEACEFULLY. IT'S UP TO YOU.
YOU WERE LUCKY...ONCE. THAT'S ALL.
IT WON'T HAPPEN AGAIN...
?!!
LOOK OUT!

RAGNAROK
라그나로크
IN TO THE ABYSS

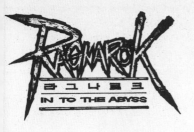

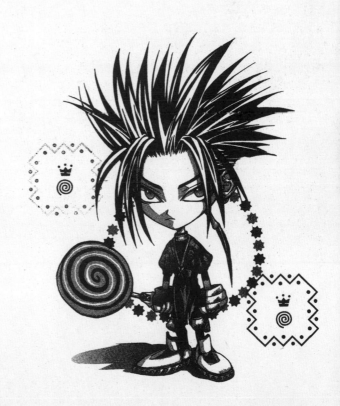

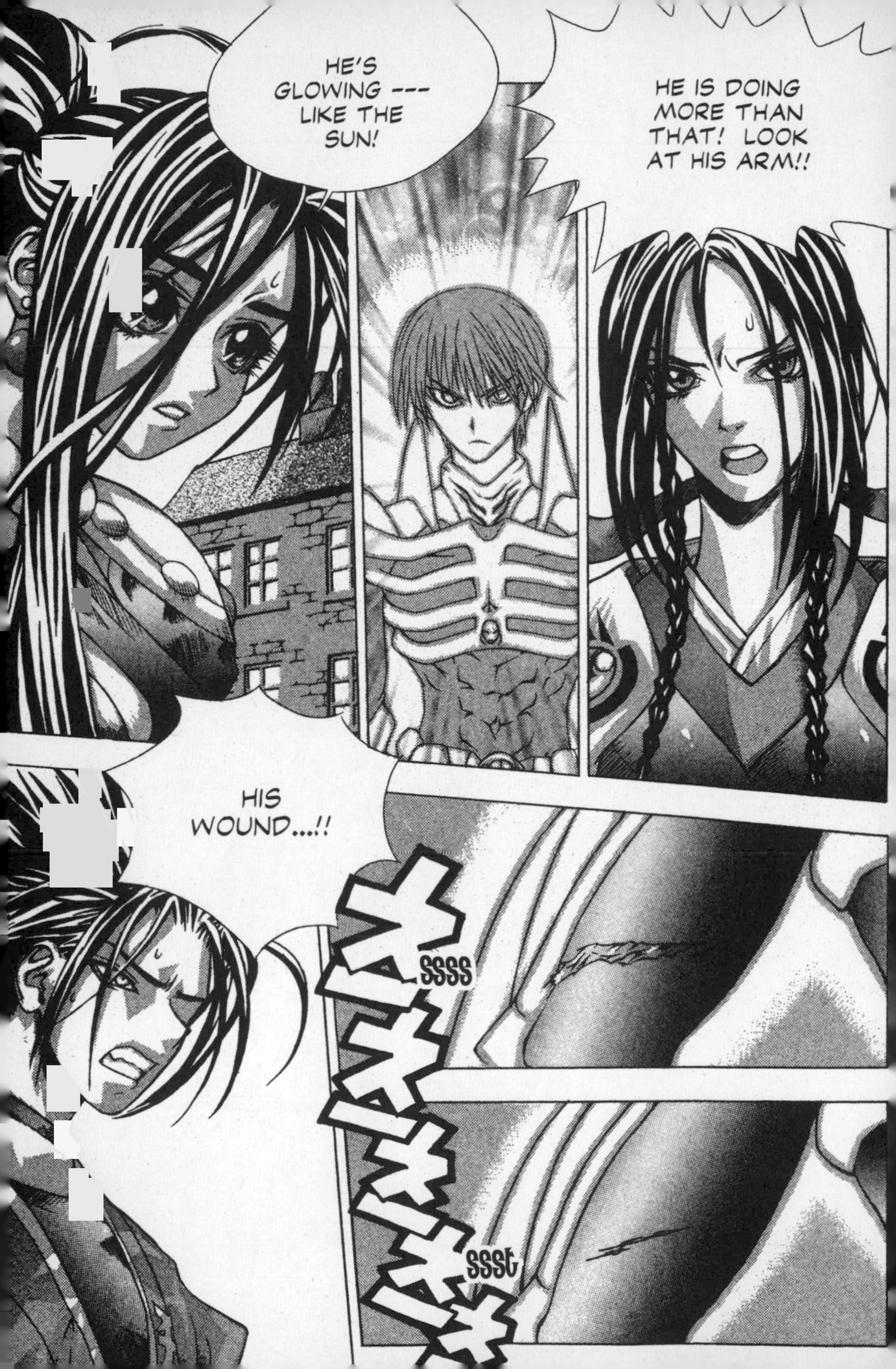
HE'S GLOWING --- LIKE THE SUN!
HE IS DOING MORE THAN THAT! LOOK AT HIS ARM!!
HIS WOUND...!!
SSSS
SSSt

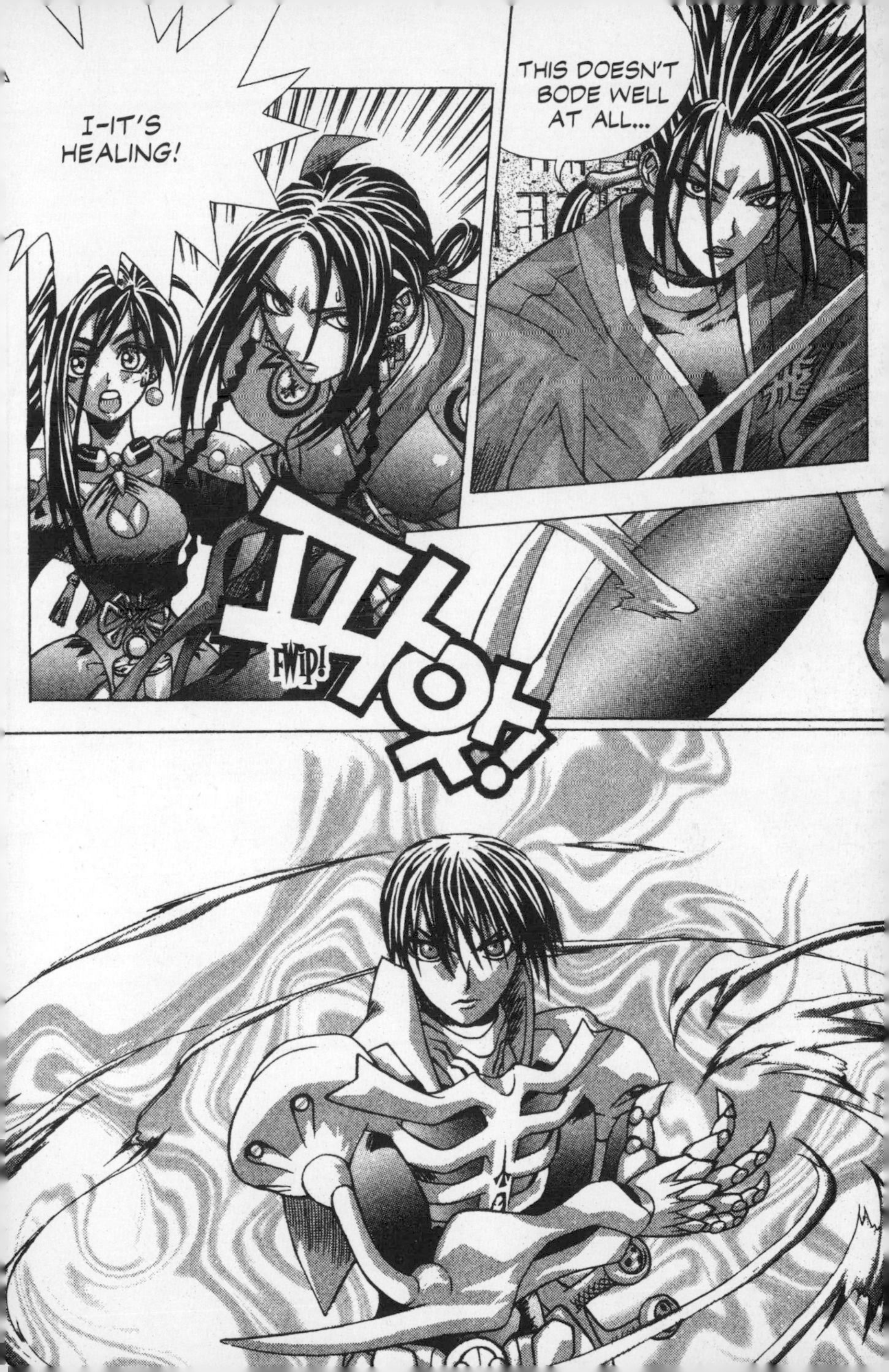
I-IT'S HEALING!
THIS DOESN'T BODE WELL AT ALL...
FWIP!

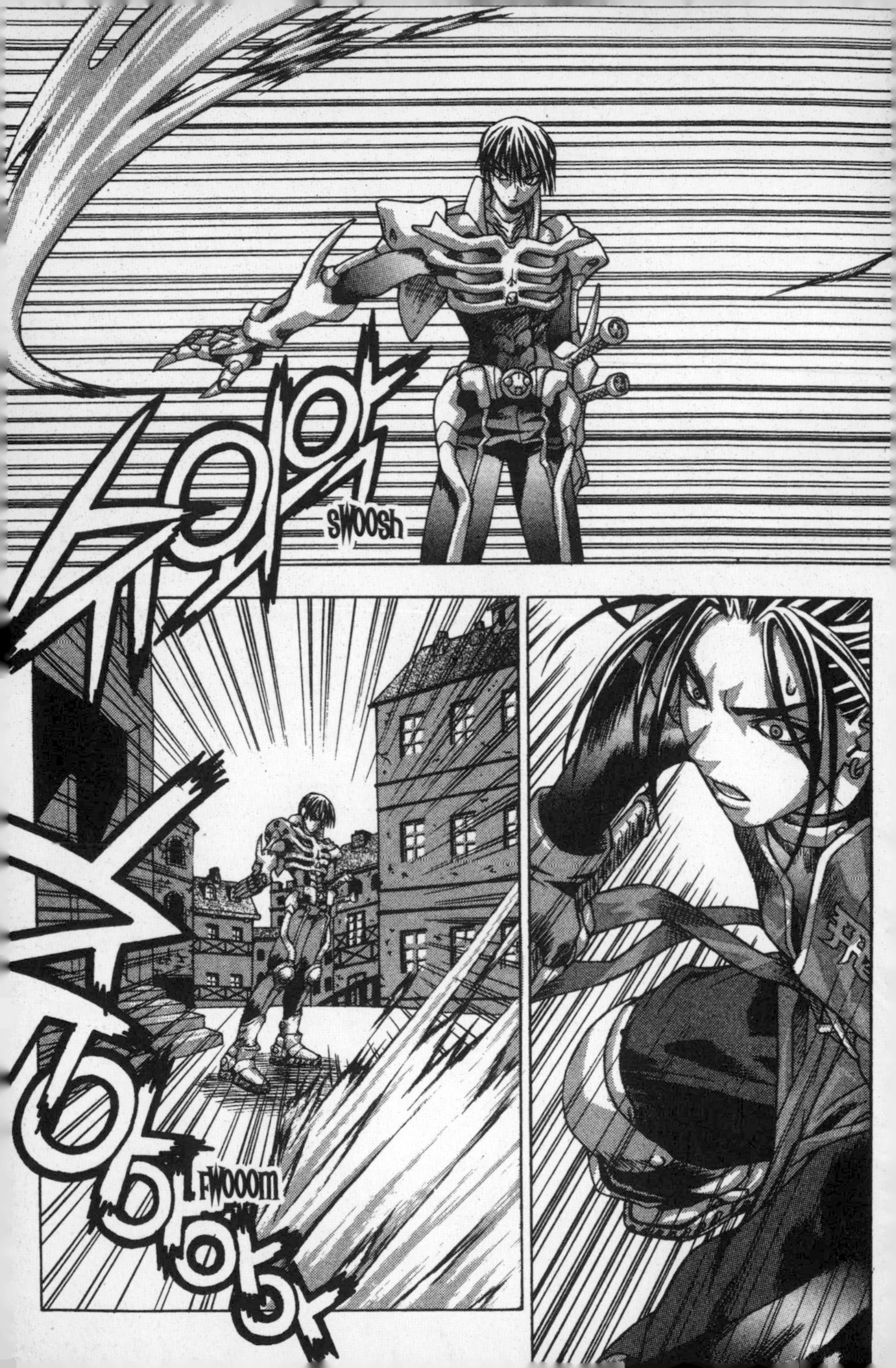
SWOOSH
FWOOOM

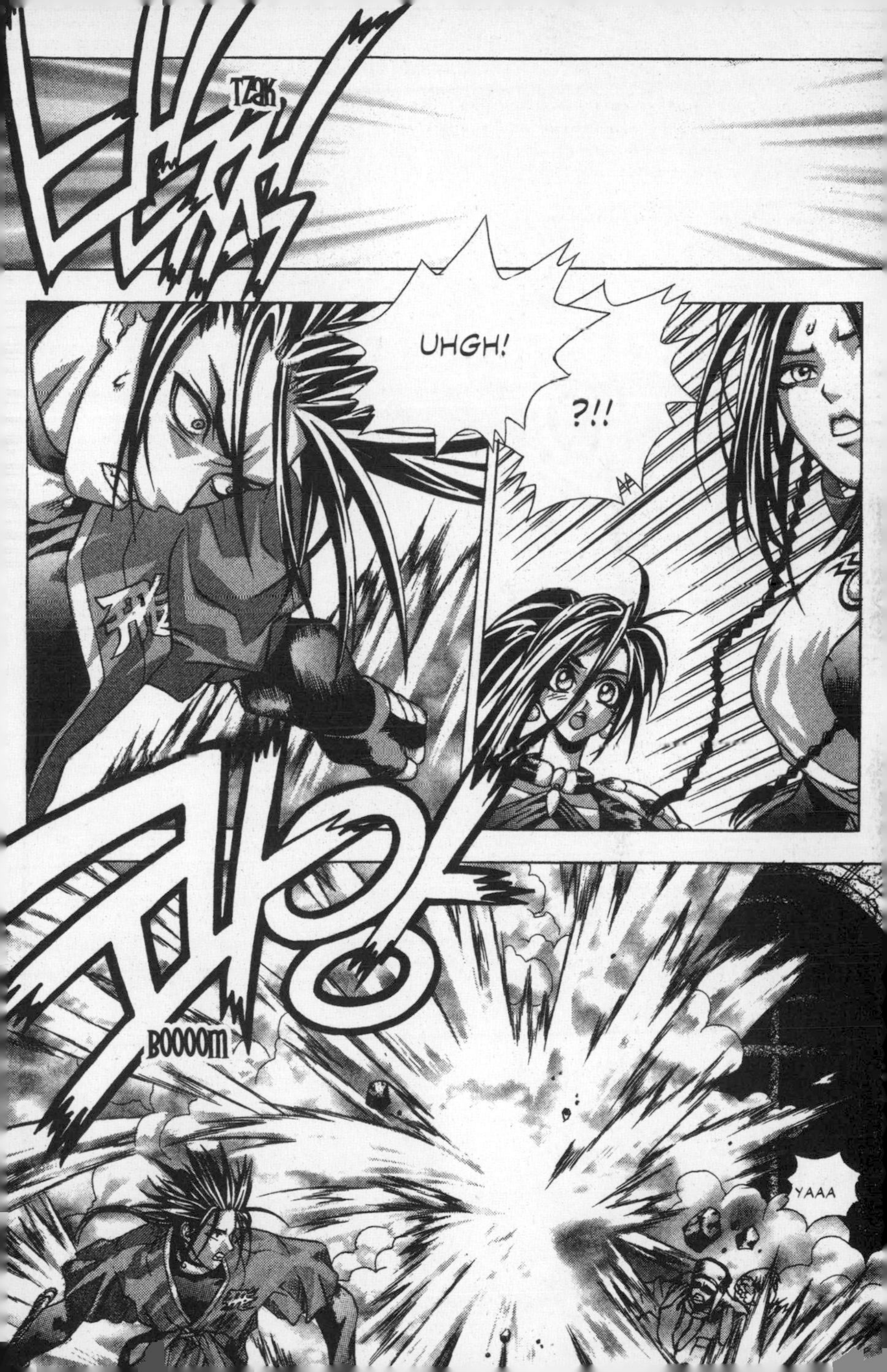
TZAK
UHGH!
?!!
BOOOOM
YAAA

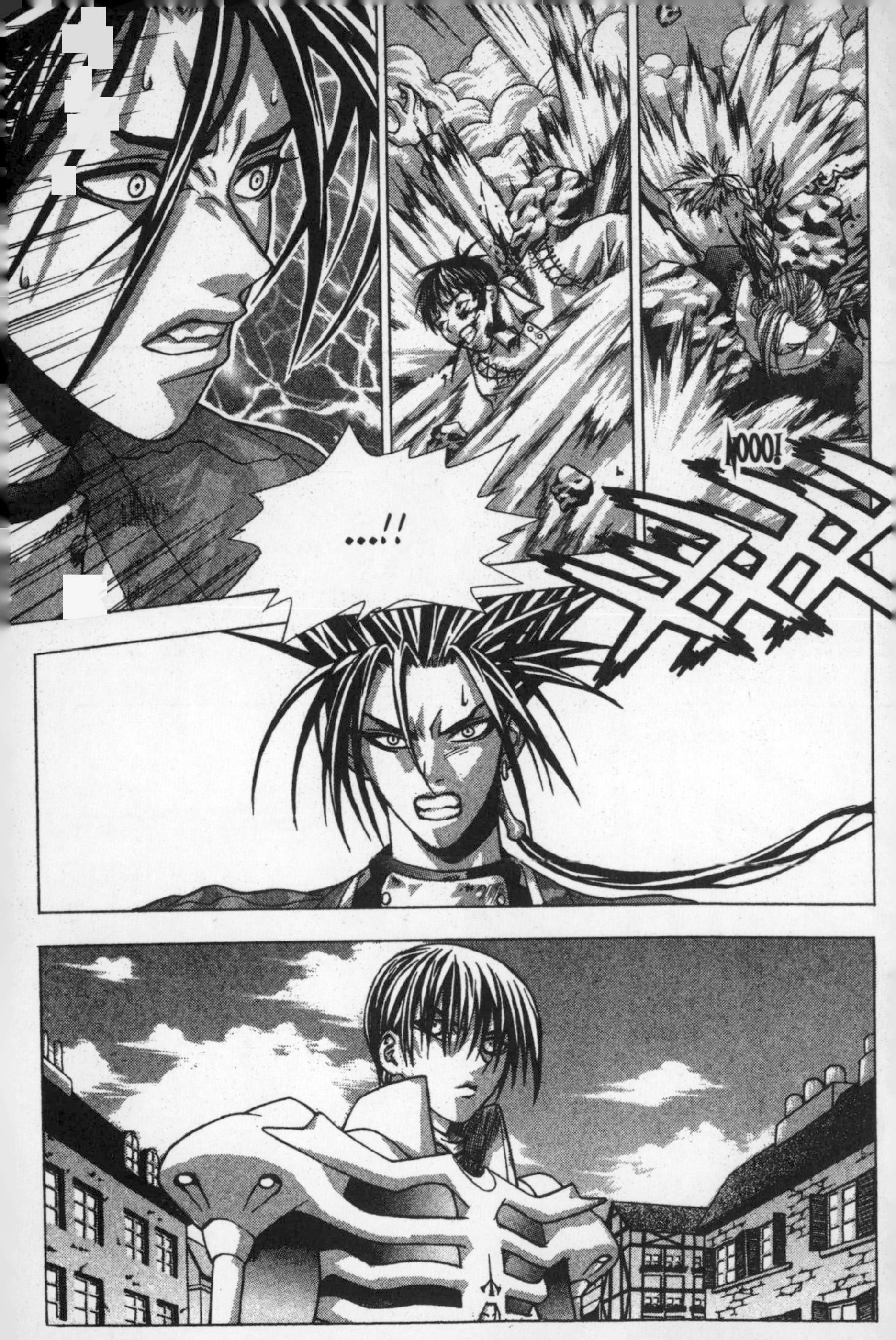

NOOO!
...!!

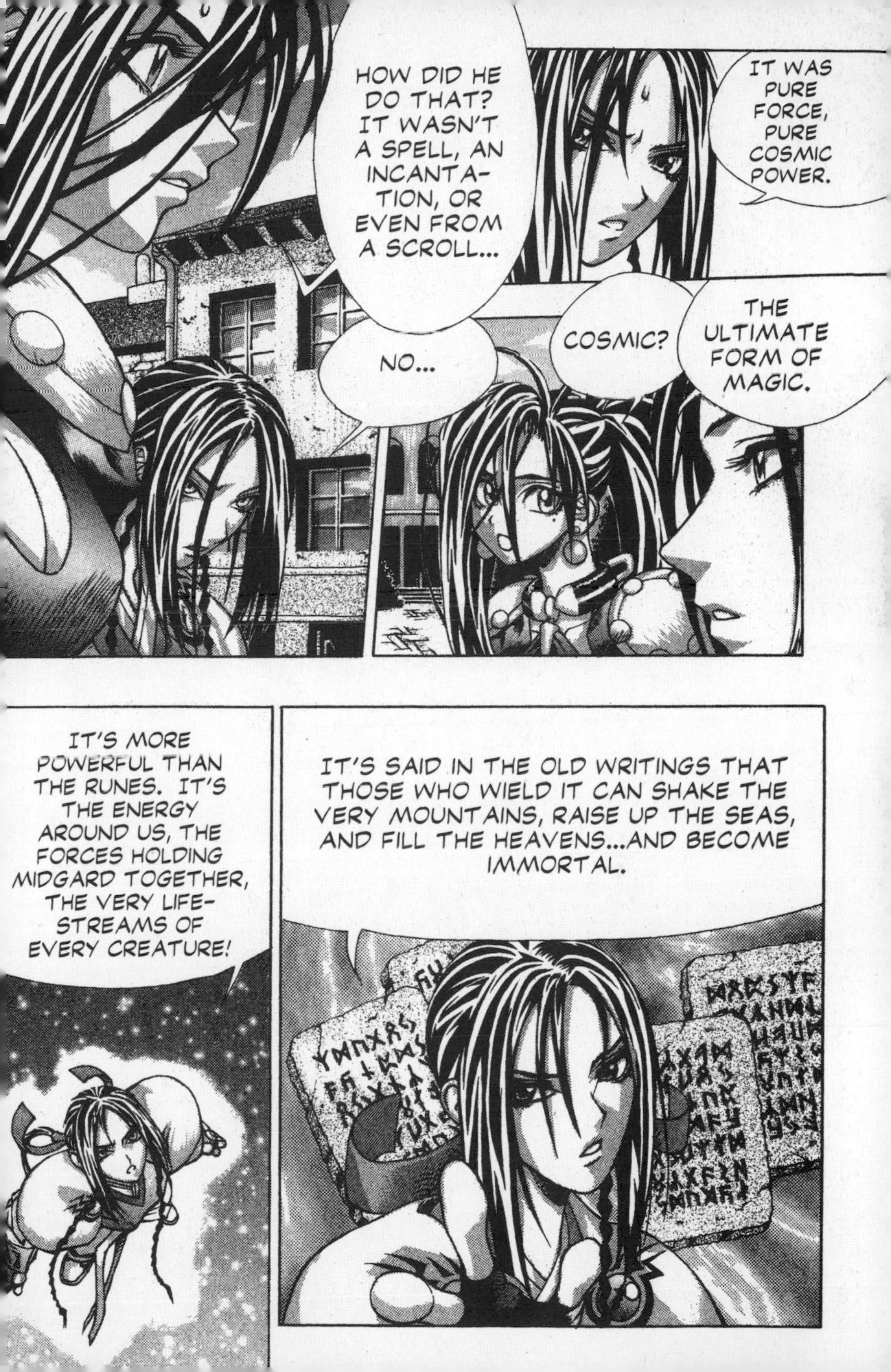
HOW DID HE DO THAT? IT WASN'T A SPELL, AN INCANTA-TION, OR EVEN FROM A SCROLL...
NO...
IT WAS PURE FORCE, PURE COSMIC POWER.
COSMIC?
THE ULTIMATE FORM OF MAGIC.
IT'S MORE POWERFUL THAN THE RUNES. IT'S THE ENERGY AROUND US, THE FORCES HOLDING MIDGARD TOGETHER, THE VERY LIFE-STREAMS OF EVERY CREATURE!
IT'S SAID IN THE OLD WRITINGS THAT THOSE WHO WIELD IT CAN SHAKE THE VERY MOUNTAINS, RAISE UP THE SEAS, AND FILL THE HEAVENS...AND BECOME IMMORTAL.

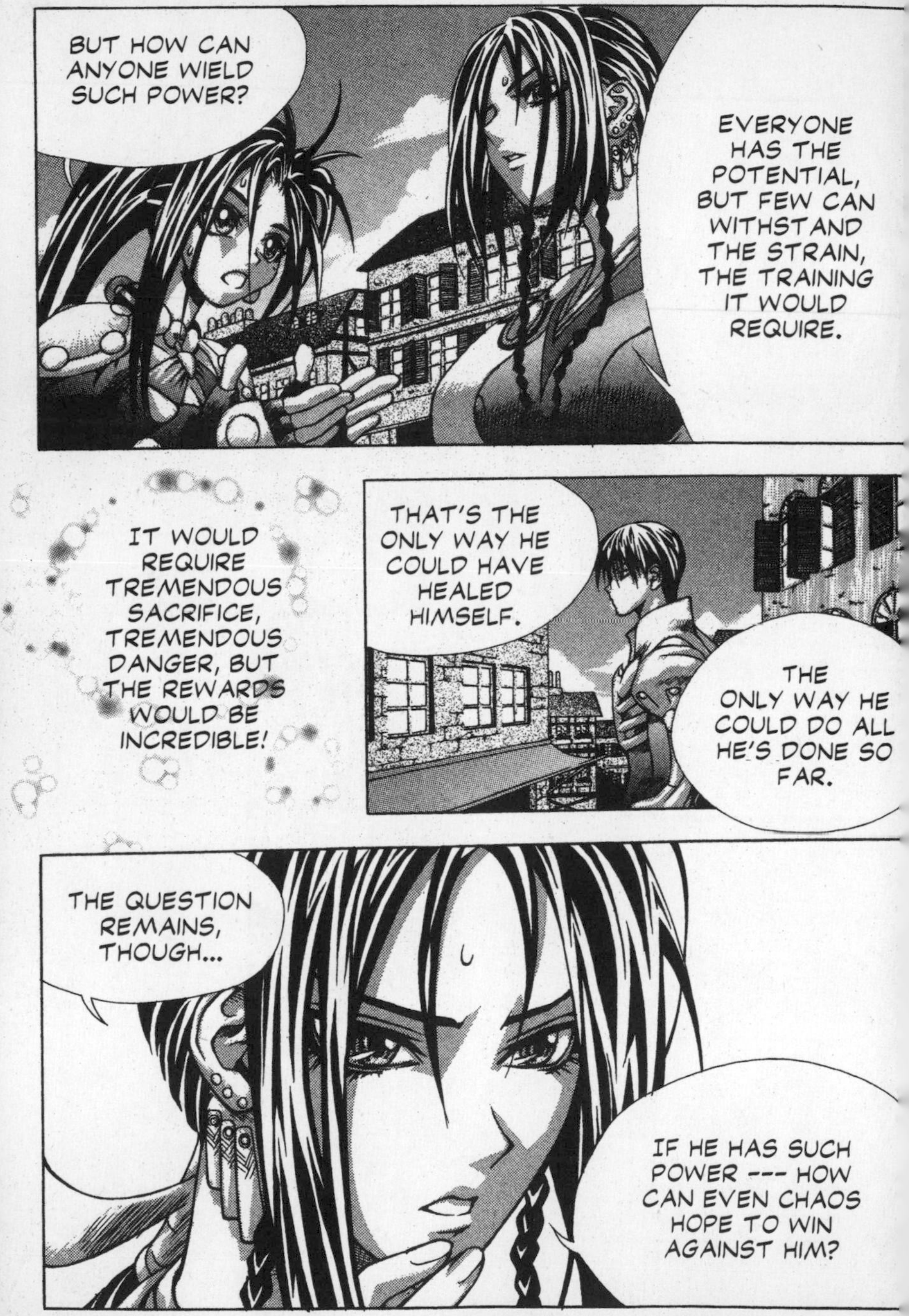
BUT HOW CAN ANYONE WIELD SUCH POWER?
EVERYONE HAS THE POTENTIAL, BUT FEW CAN WITHSTAND THE STRAIN, THE TRAINING IT WOULD REQUIRE.
IT WOULD REQUIRE TREMENDOUS SACRIFICE, TREMENDOUS DANGER, BUT THE REWARDS WOULD BE INCREDIBLE!
THAT'S THE ONLY WAY HE COULD HAVE HEALED HIMSELF.
THE ONLY WAY HE COULD DO ALL HE'S DONE SO FAR.
THE QUESTION REMAINS, THOUGH...
IF HE HAS SUCH POWER --- HOW CAN EVEN CHAOS HOPE TO WIN AGAINST HIM?

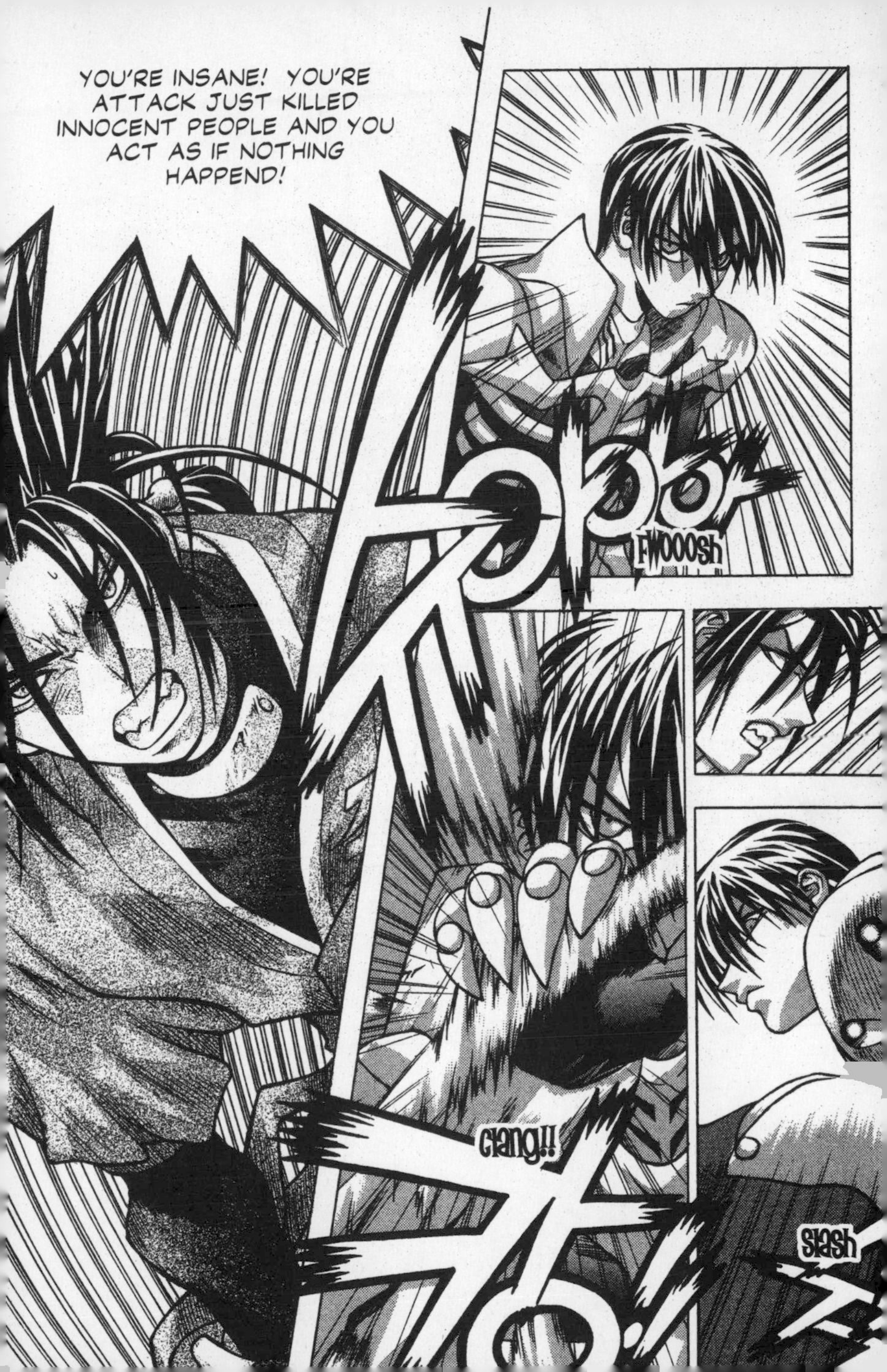
YOU'RE INSANE! YOU'RE ATTACK JUST KILLED INNOCENT PEOPLE AND YOU ACT AS IF NOTHING HAPPEND!
FWOOOSH
CLANG!!
SLASH

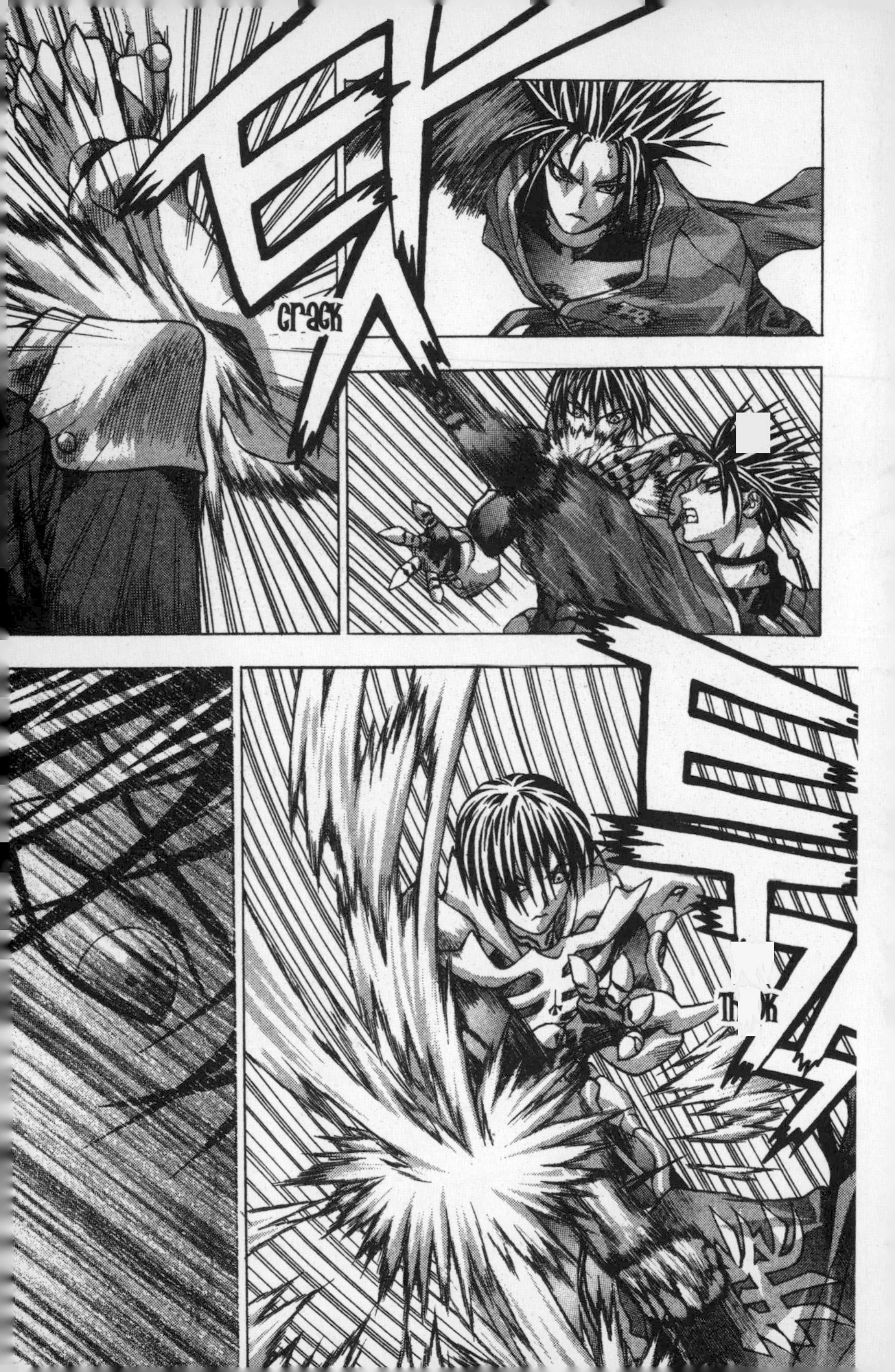
crack

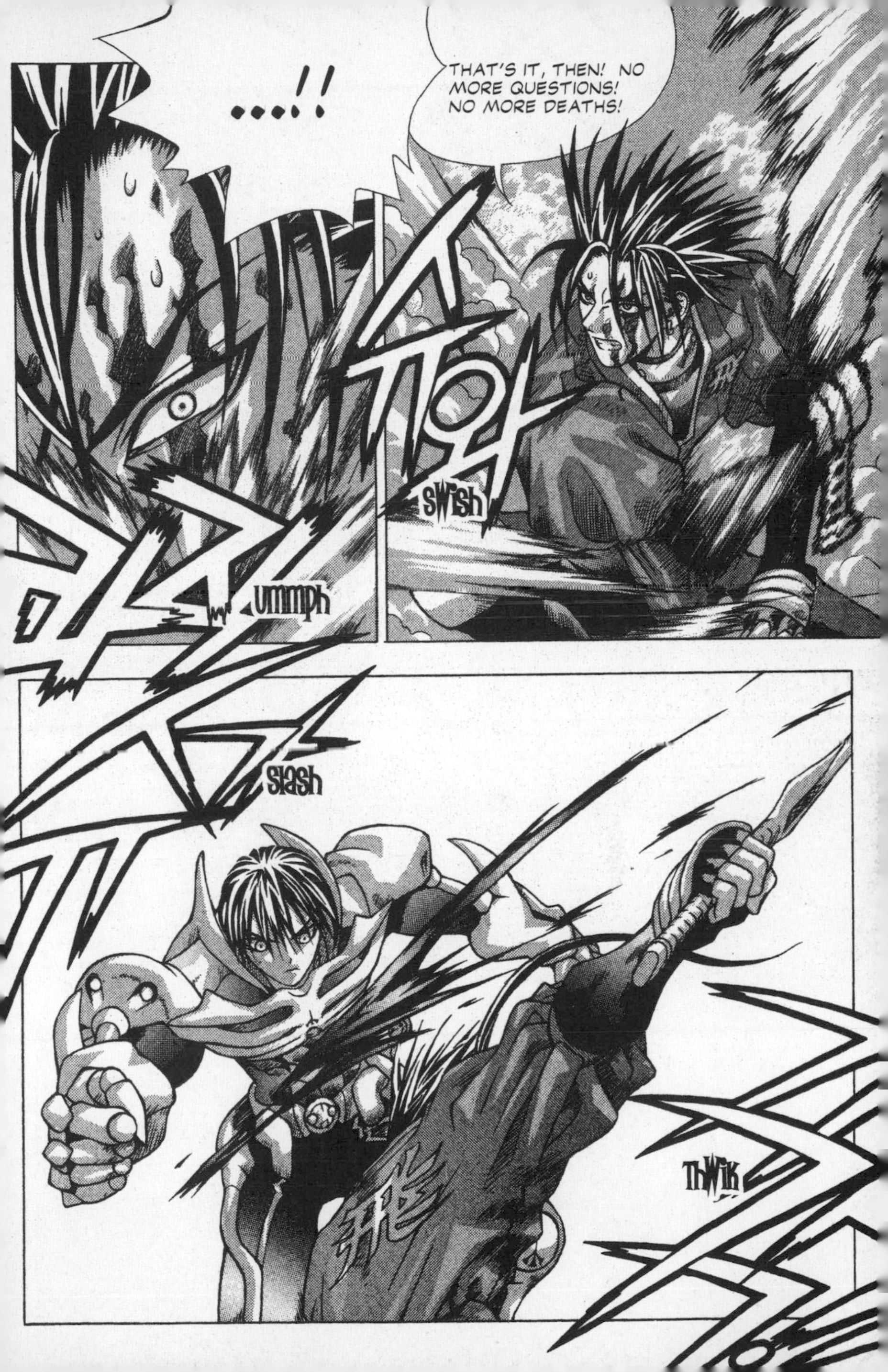
...!!
THAT'S IT, THEN! NO MORE QUESTIONS! NO MORE DEATHS!
SWISH
UMMMPH
SLASH
THWIK

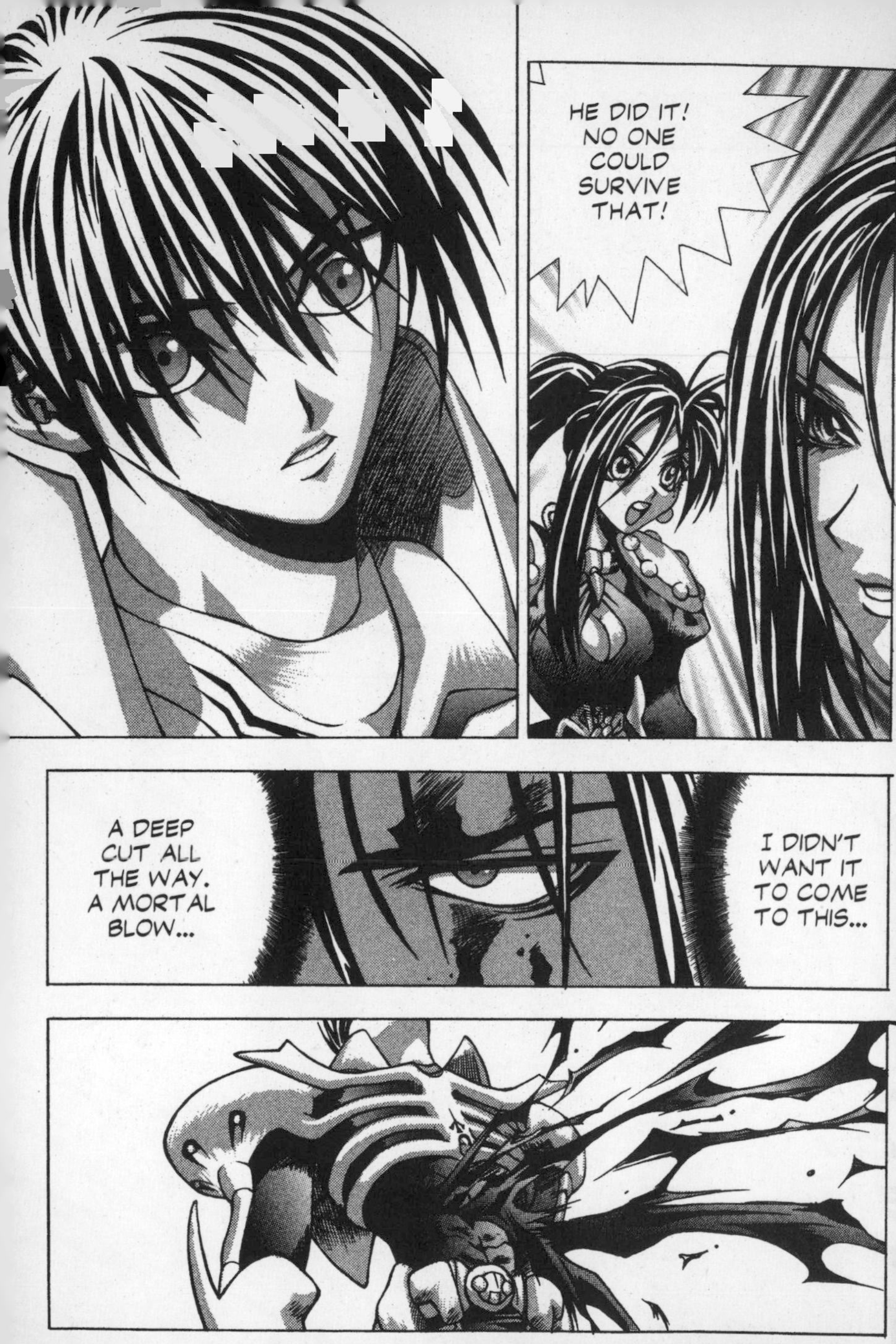
HE DID IT! NO ONE COULD SURVIVE THAT!
A DEEP CUT ALL THE WAY. A MORTAL BLOW...
I DIDN'T WANT IT TO COME TO THIS...

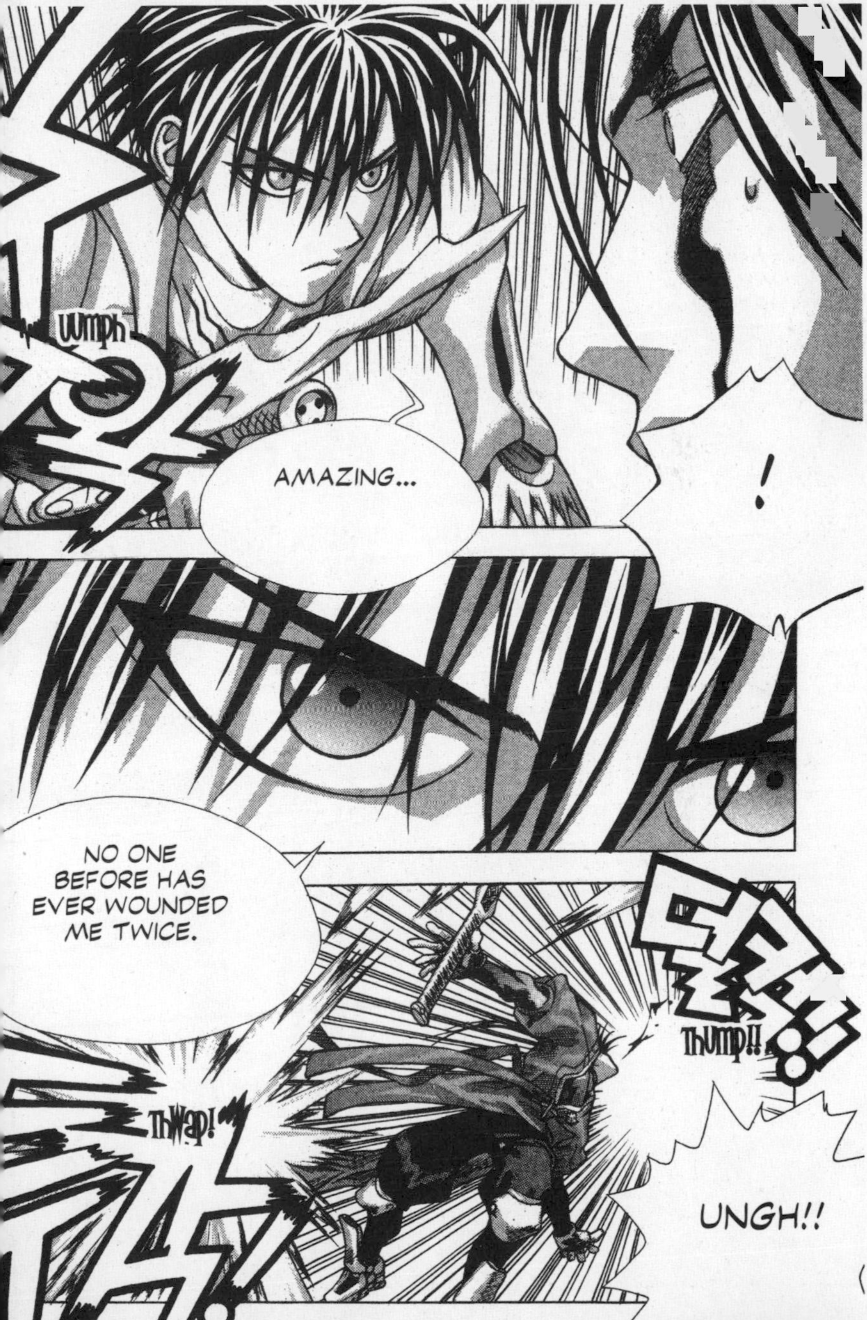
WUMPH
AMAZING...
!
NO ONE BEFORE HAS EVER WOUNDED ME TWICE.
THUMP!!
THWAP!
UNGH!!

BUT IT WAS A FATAL WOUND ---

HOW IS THAT POSSIBLE?

IT HAS TO BE. ONLY THAT WOULD EXPLAIN HOW HE COULD SURVIVE.

HE DIDN'T EVEN BLINK WHEN CHAOS STRUCK HIM, ALMOST AS IF HE WEREN'T HUMAN.

IT IS AS IF HE FELT NO PAIN, NO AGONY, NO SENSATIONS AT ALL.

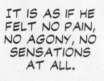

BUT SOMETHING DOESN'T SEEM RIGHT...

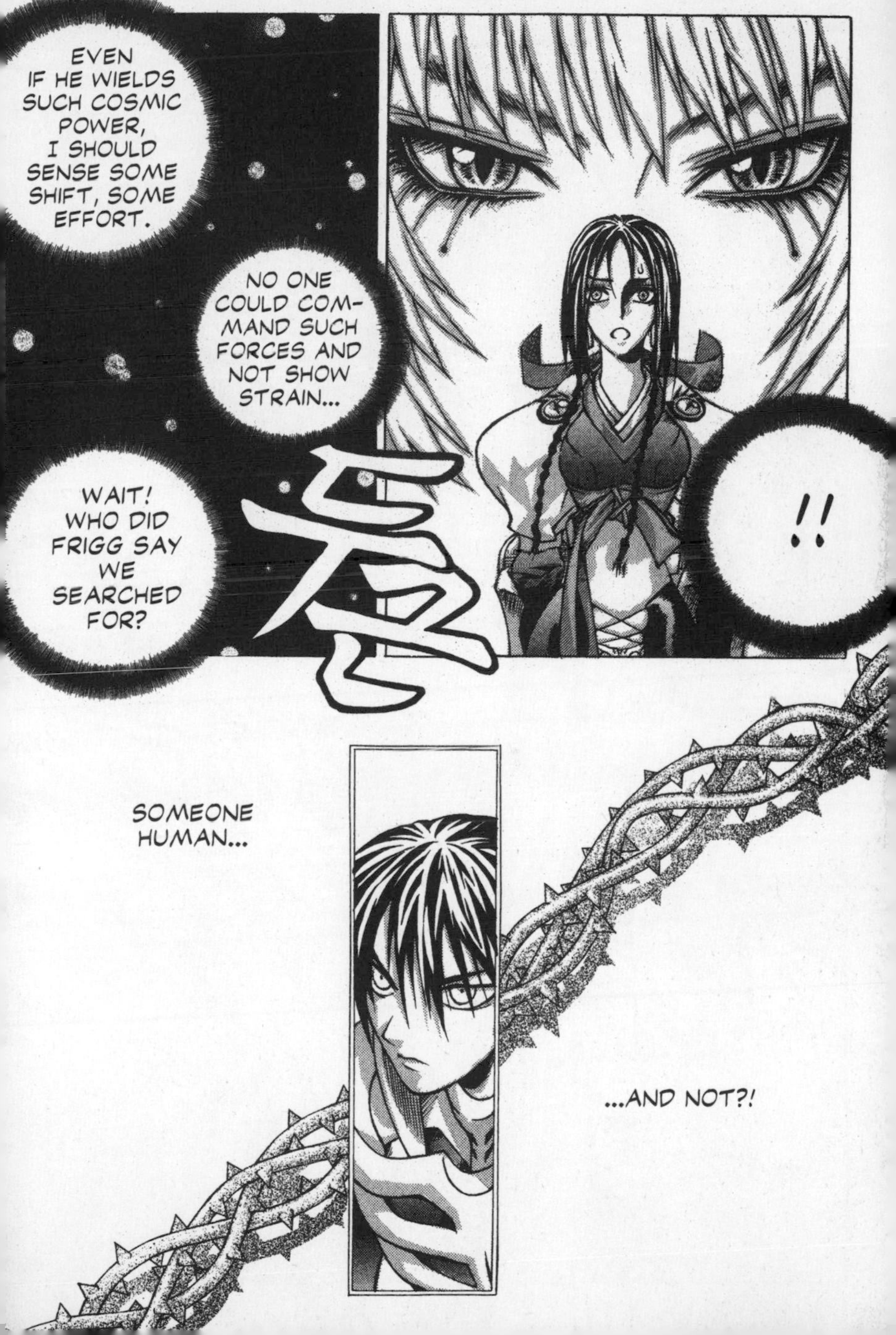
EVEN IF HE WIELDS SUCH COSMIC POWER, I SHOULD SENSE SOME SHIFT, SOME EFFORT.
NO ONE COULD COM-MAND SUCH FORCES AND NOT SHOW STRAIN...
WAIT! WHO DID FRIGG SAY WE SEARCHED FOR?
!!
SOMEONE HUMAN...
...AND NOT?!

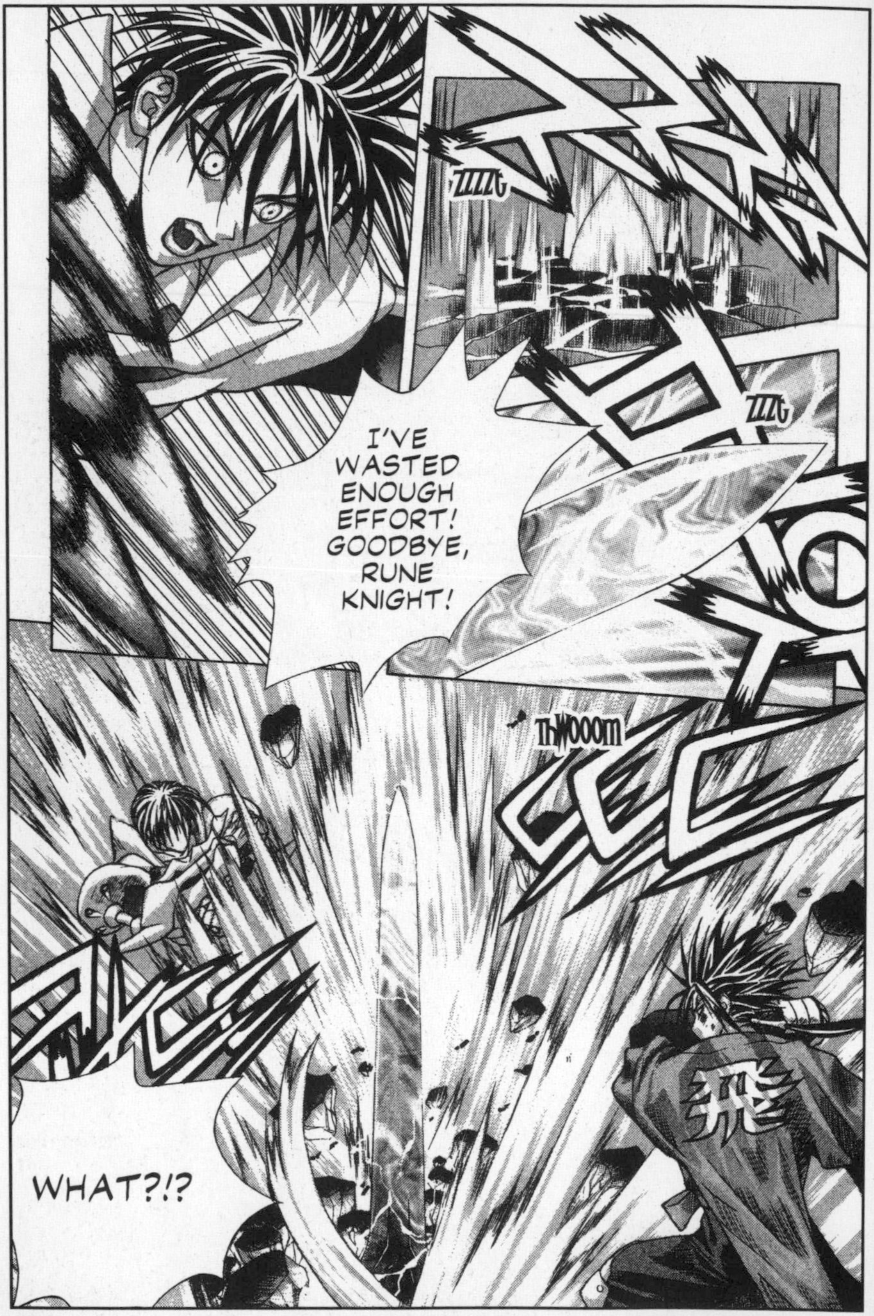

ZZZZT
ZZZT
I'VE WASTED ENOUGH EFFORT! GOODBYE, RUNE KNIGHT!
ThWOOOM
WHAT?!?

RAGNAROK
라그나로크
IN TO THE ABYSS

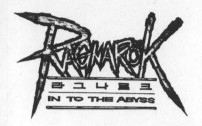

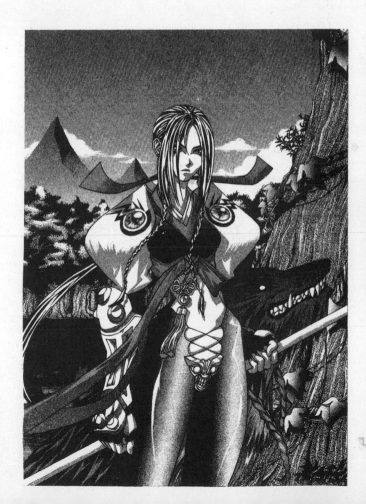

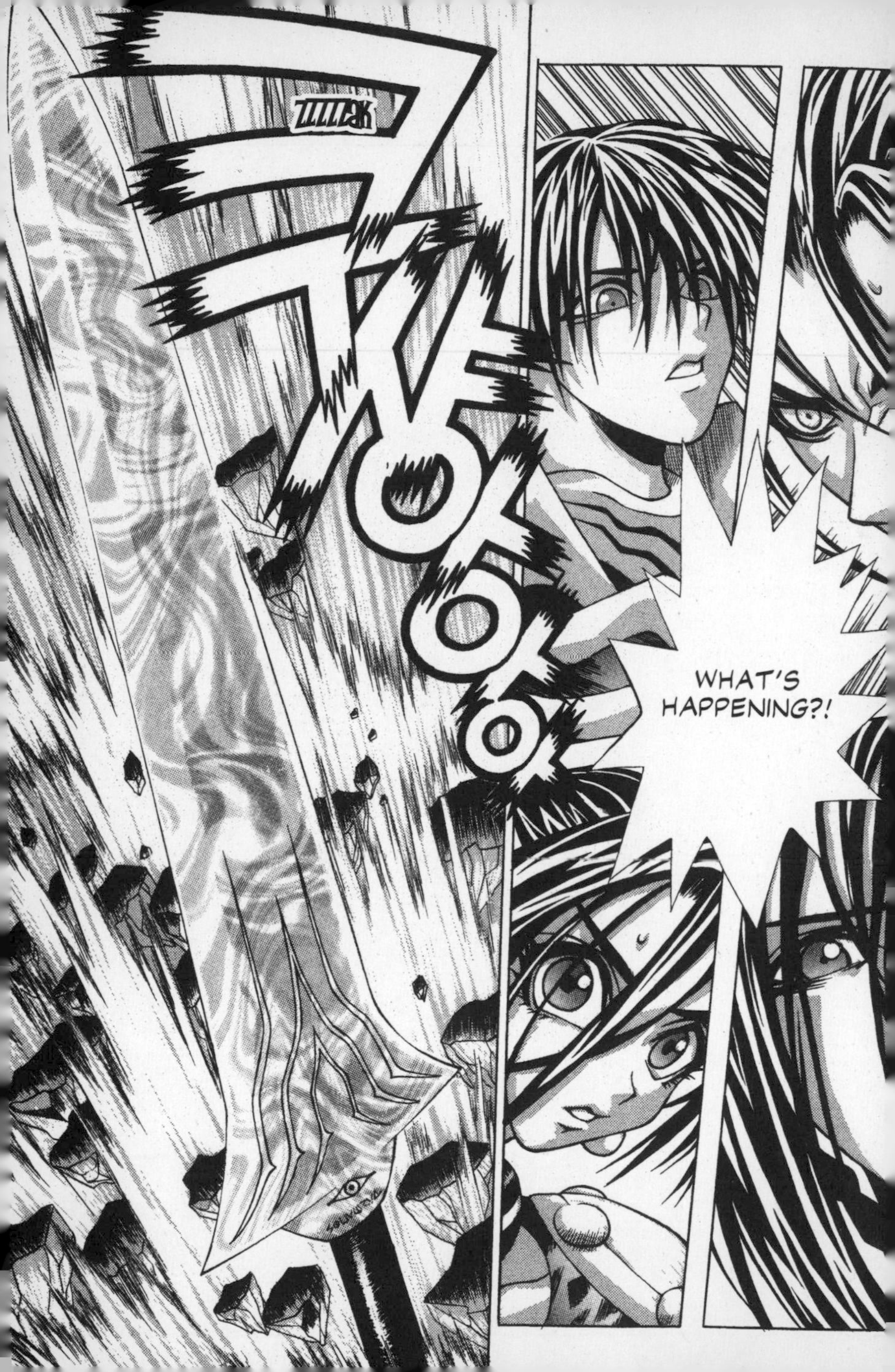
ZZZZAK
WHAT'S HAPPENING?!

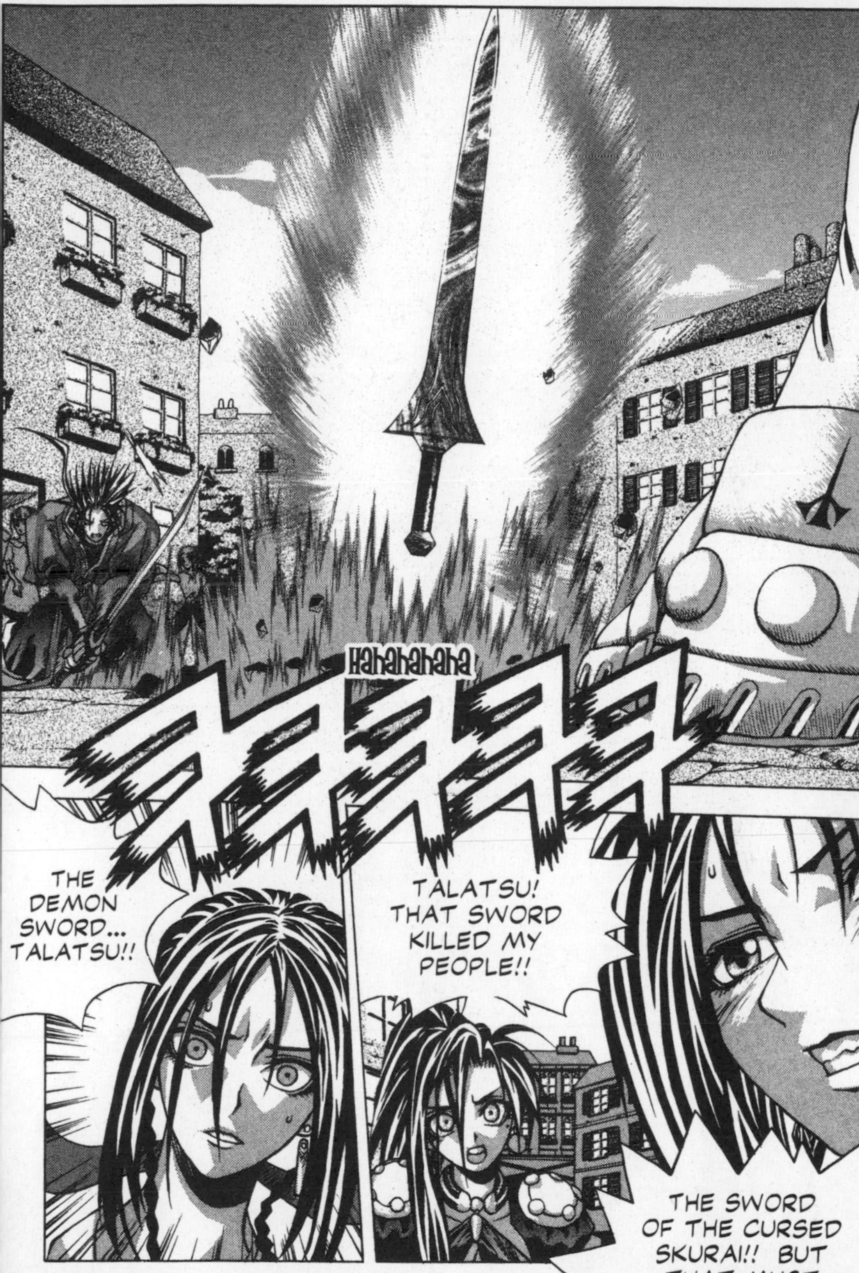
HAHAHAHAHAHA
THE DEMON SWORD... TALATSU!!
TALATSU! THAT SWORD KILLED MY PEOPLE!!
THE SWORD OF THE CURSED SKURAI!! BUT THAT MUST MEAN ---

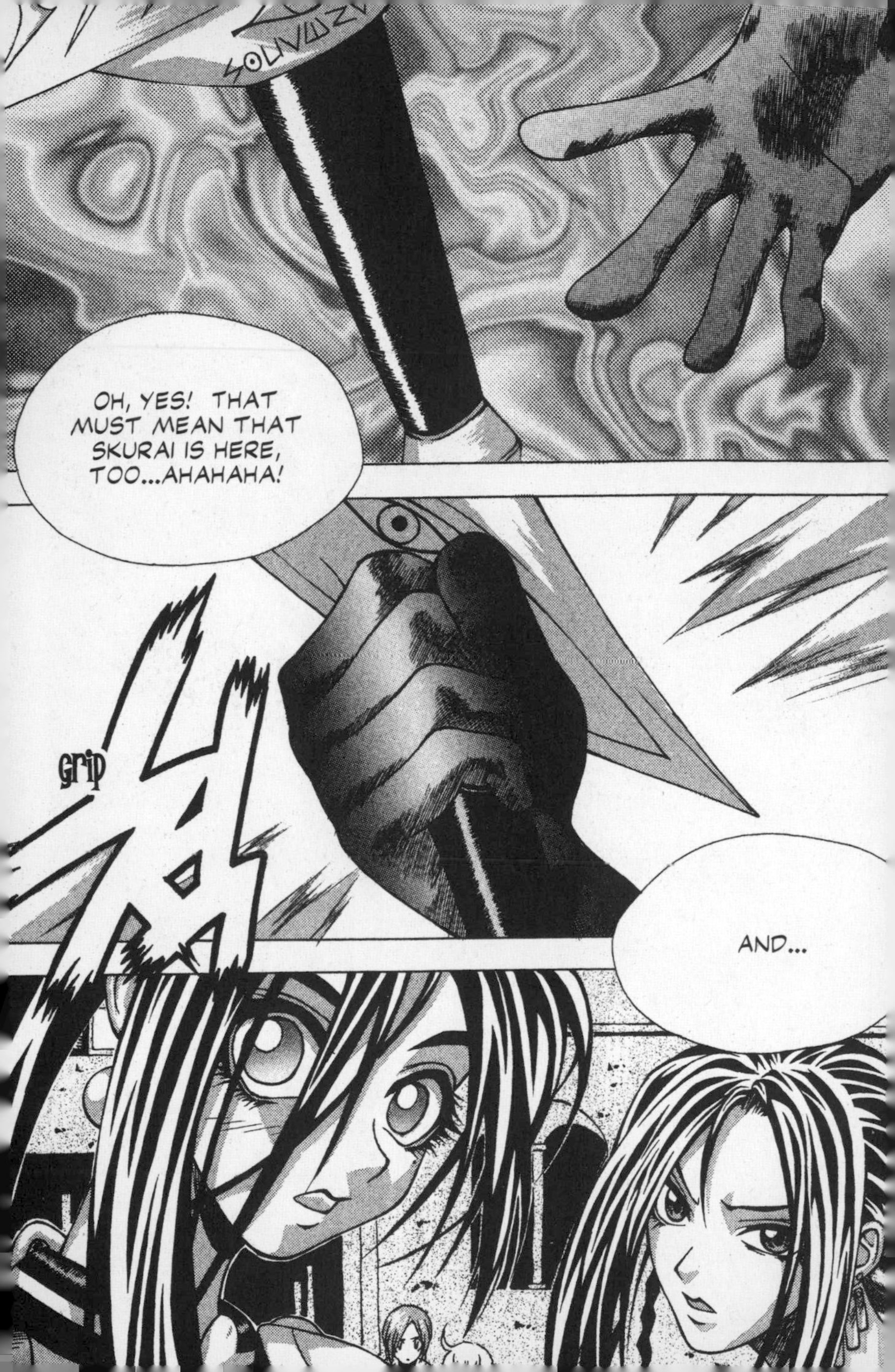

OH, YES! THAT MUST MEAN THAT SKURAI IS HERE, TOO...AHAHAHA!
GRIP
AND...

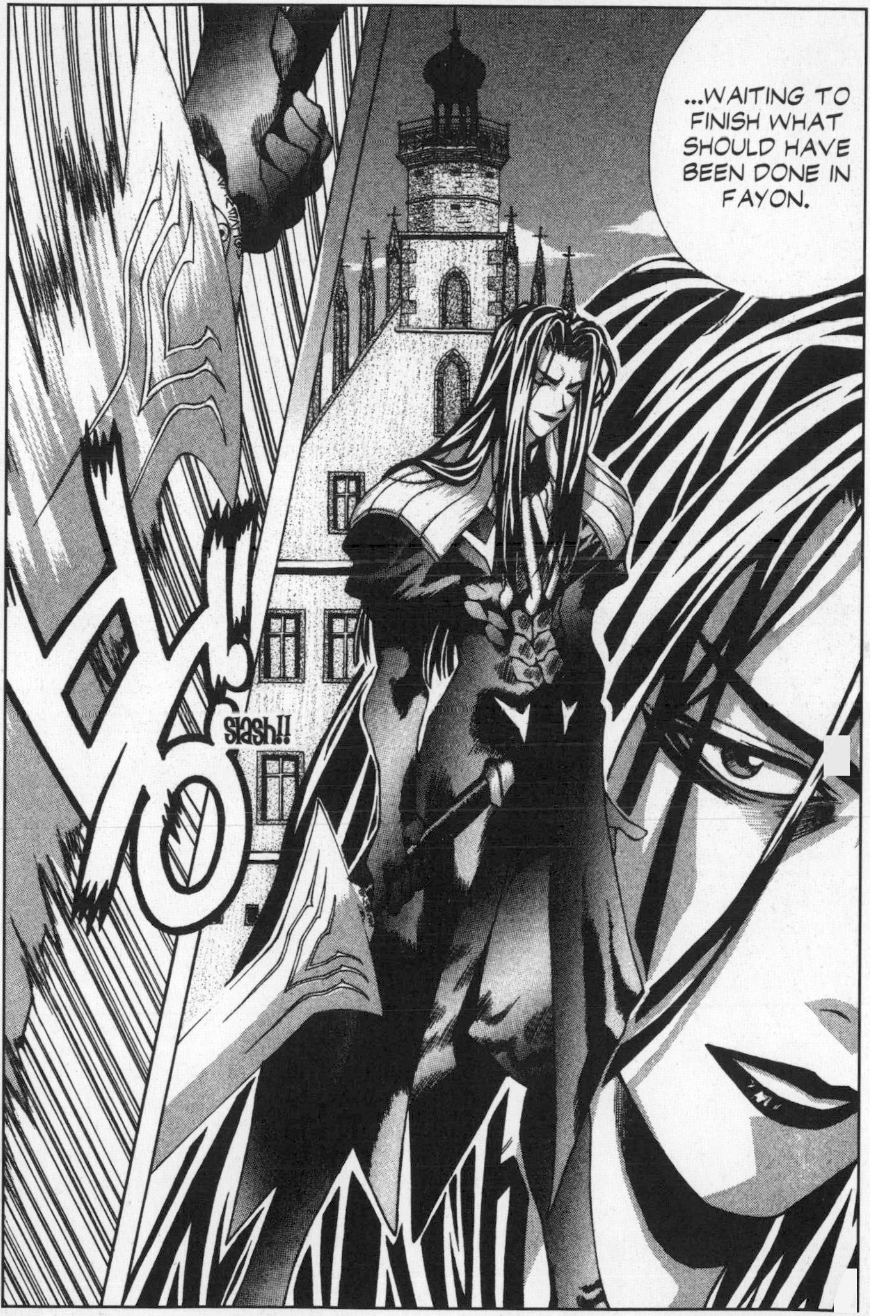
...WAITING TO FINISH WHAT SHOULD HAVE BEEN DONE IN FAYON.
SLASH!!

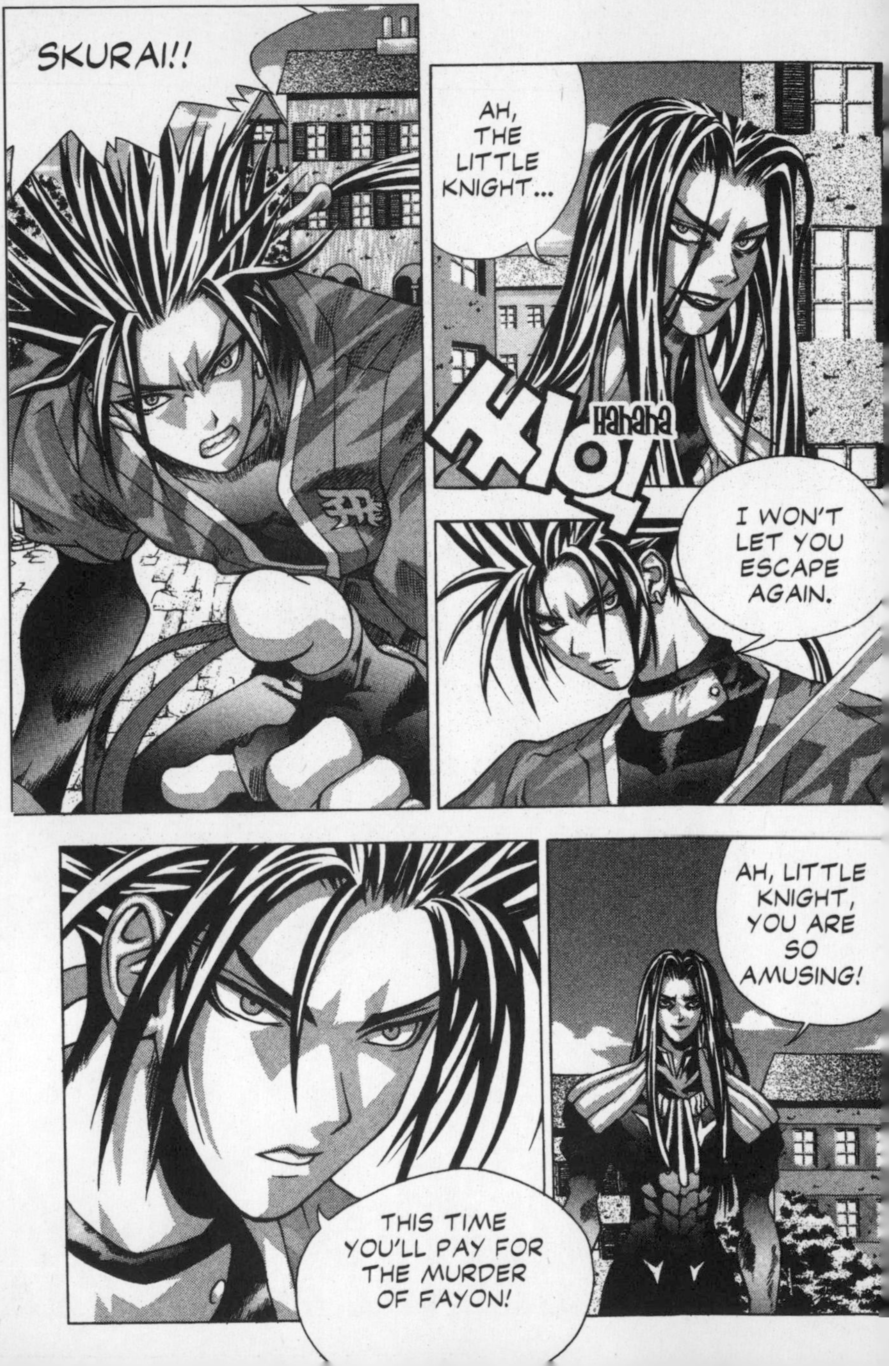
SKURAI!!
AH, THE LITTLE KNIGHT...
Hahaha
I WON'T LET YOU ESCAPE AGAIN.
THIS TIME YOU'LL PAY FOR THE MURDER OF FAYON!
AH, LITTLE KNIGHT, YOU ARE SO AMUSING!

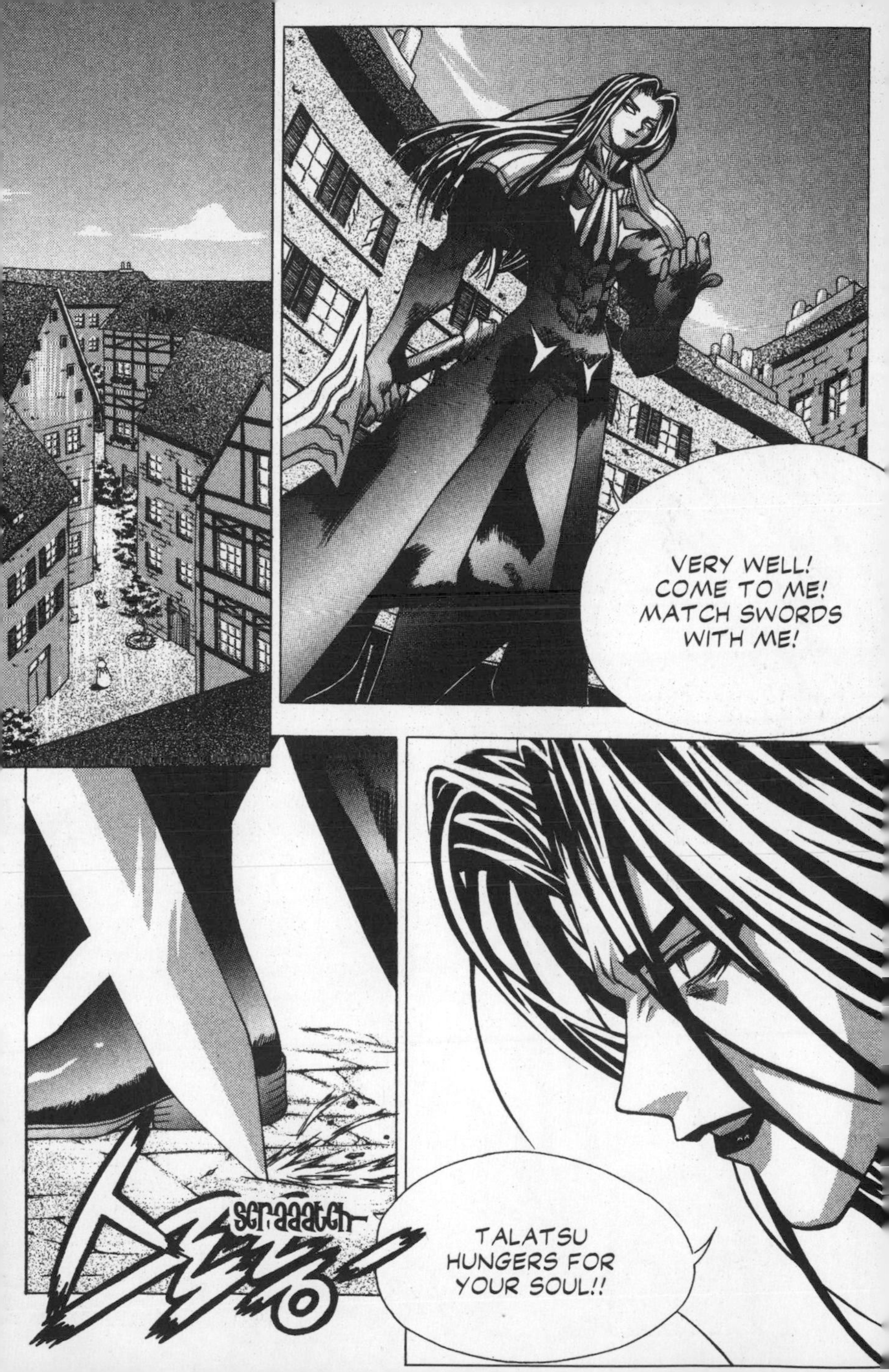
VERY WELL! COME TO ME! MATCH SWORDS WITH ME!
SCRAAATCH
TALATSU HUNGERS FOR YOUR SOUL!!

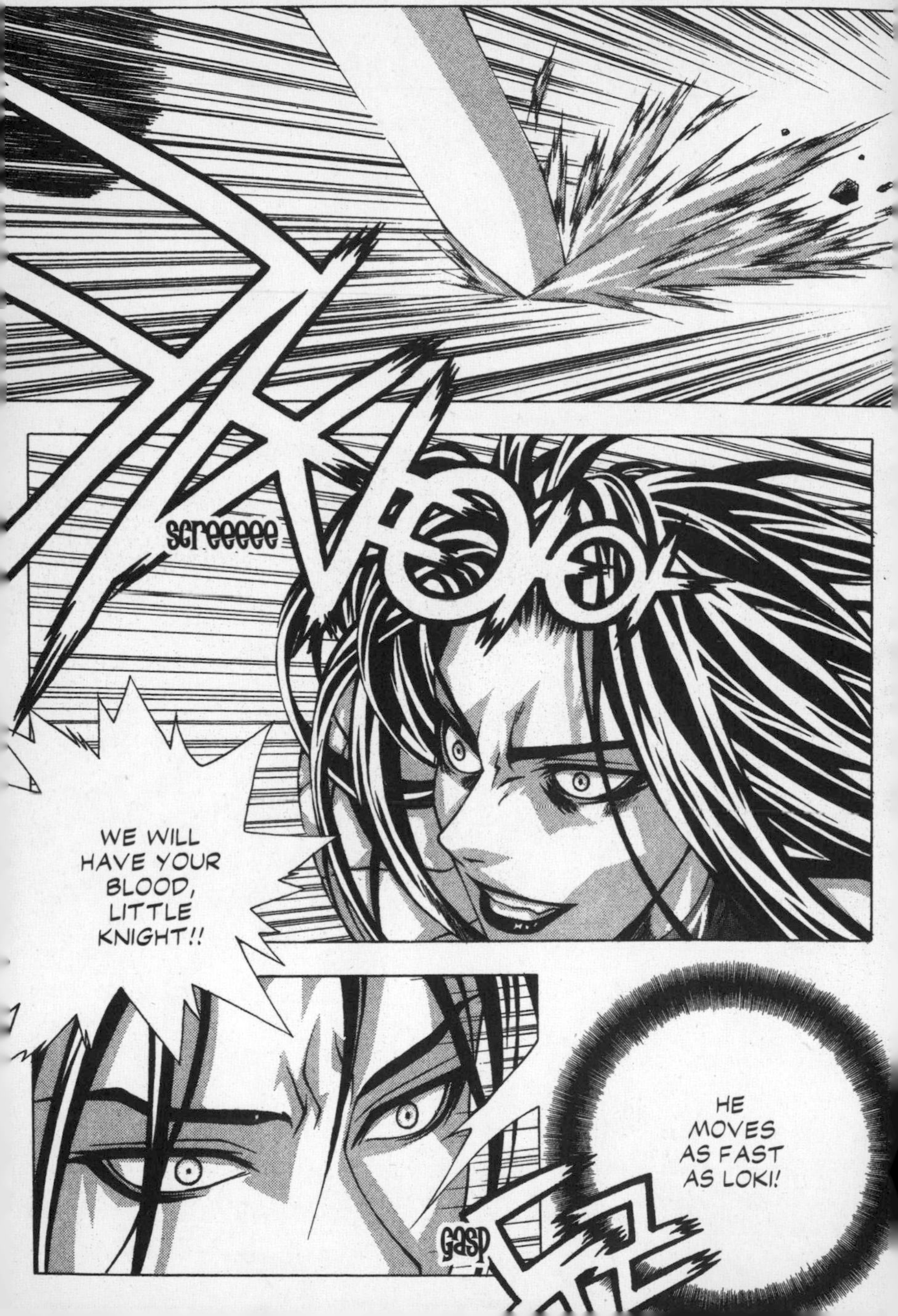

SCREEEEEE
WE WILL HAVE YOUR BLOOD, LITTLE KNIGHT!!
GASP
HE MOVES AS FAST AS LOKI!

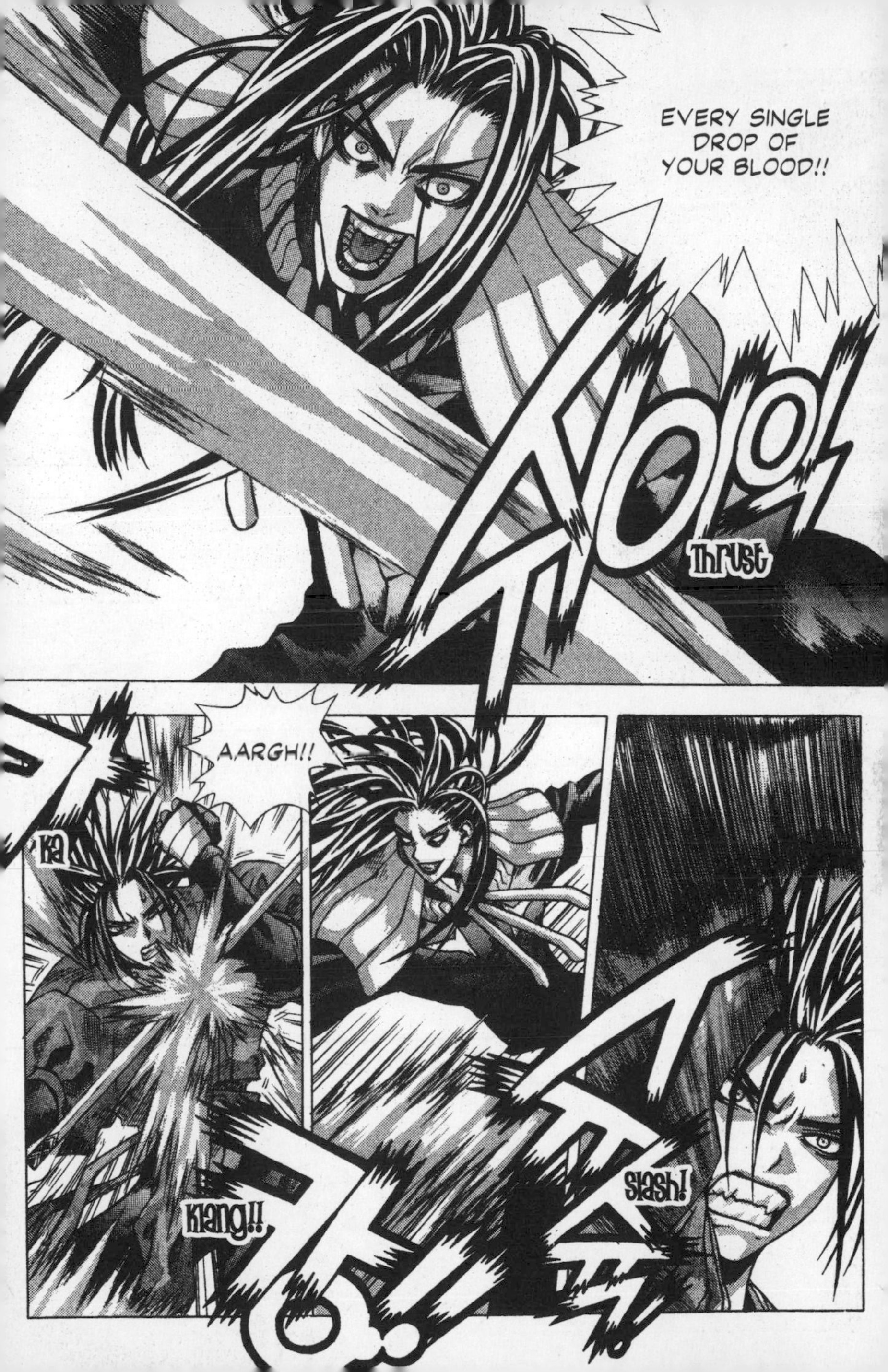
EVERY SINGLE DROP OF YOUR BLOOD!!
Thrust
AARGH!!
Ka
Klang!!
Slash!

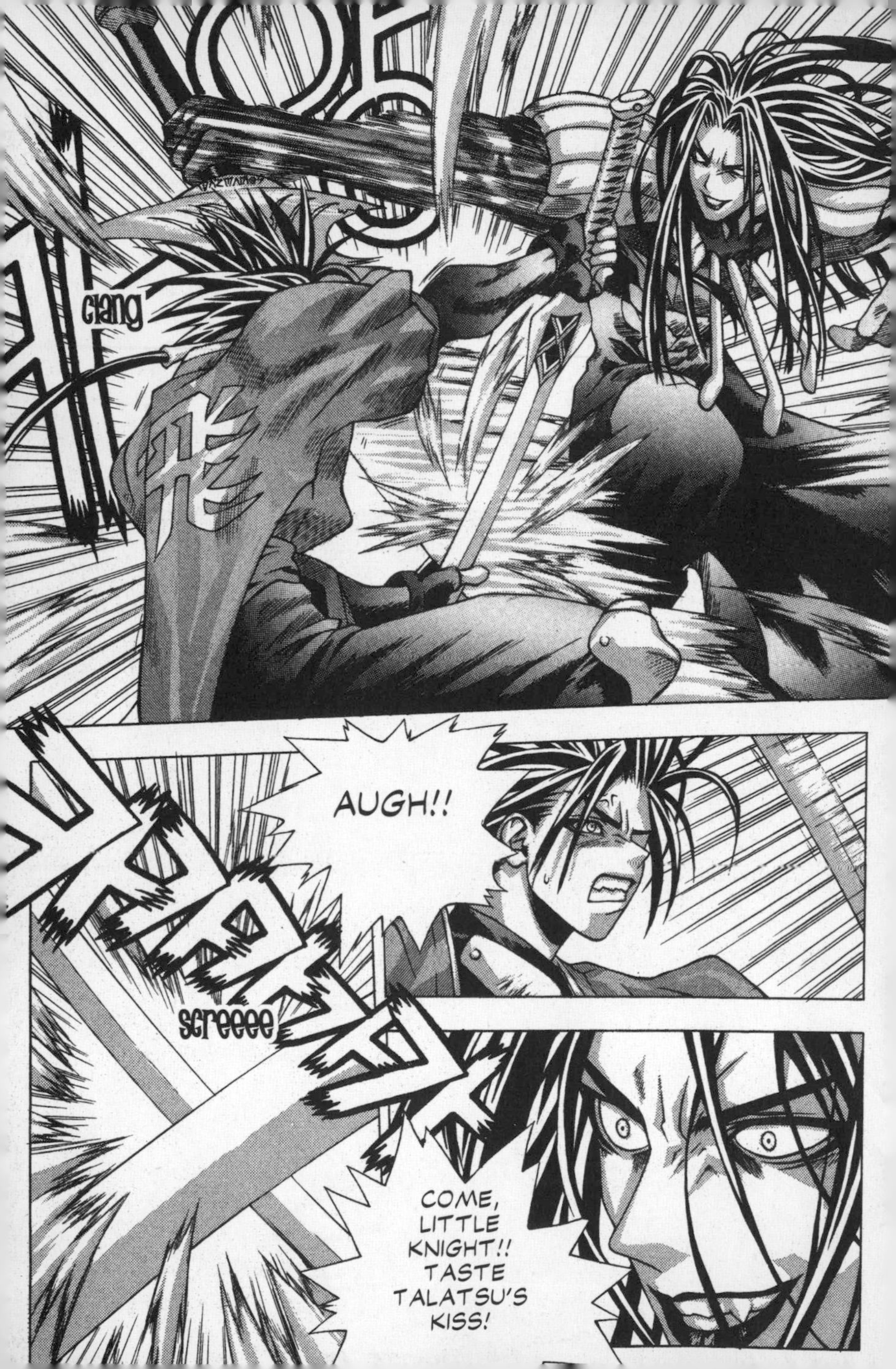
clang
AUGH!!
screeeee
COME, LITTLE KNIGHT!! TASTE TALATSU'S KISS!

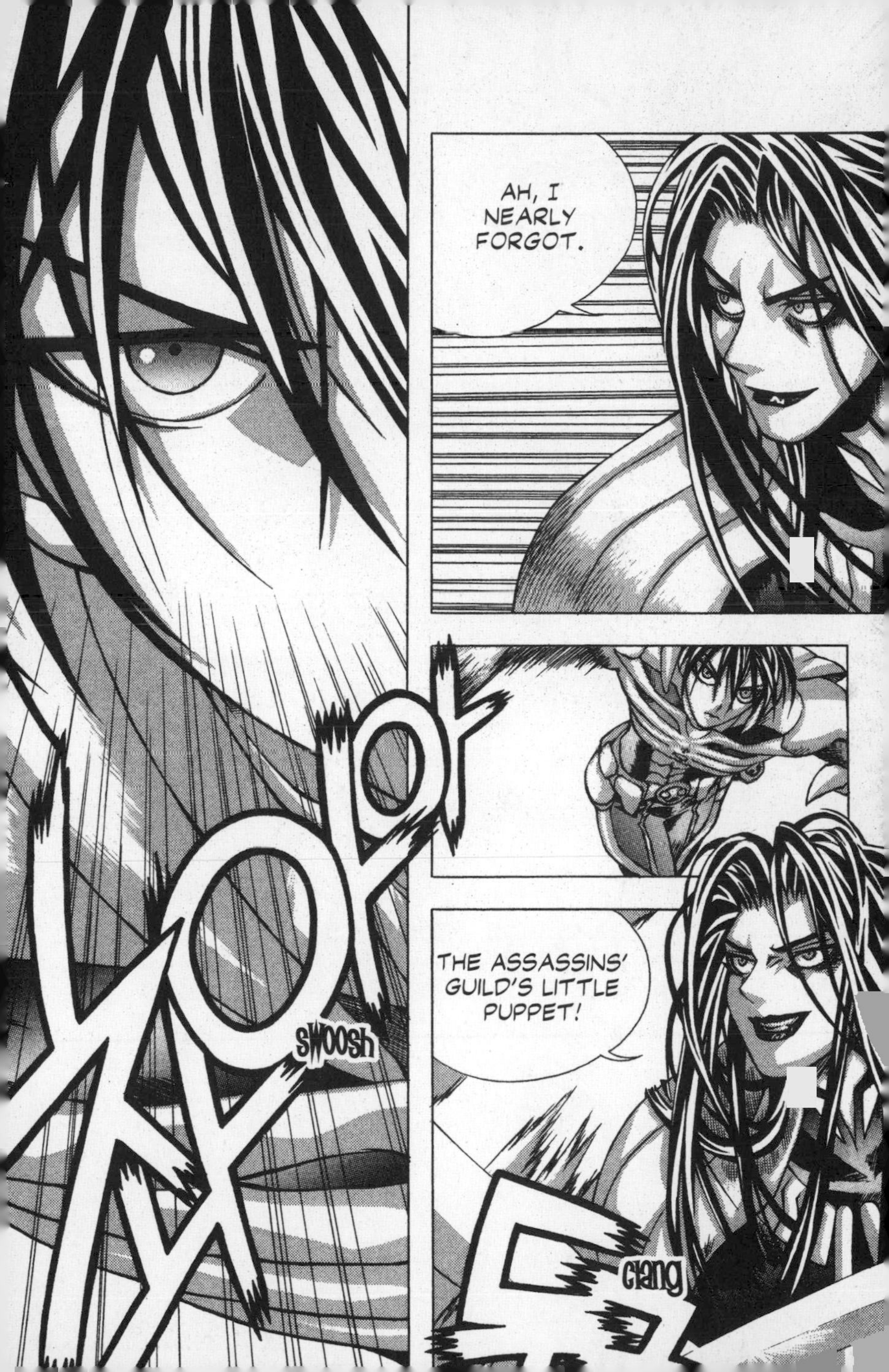
SWOOSH
AH, I NEARLY FORGOT.
THE ASSASSINS' GUILD'S LITTLE PUPPET!
CLANG

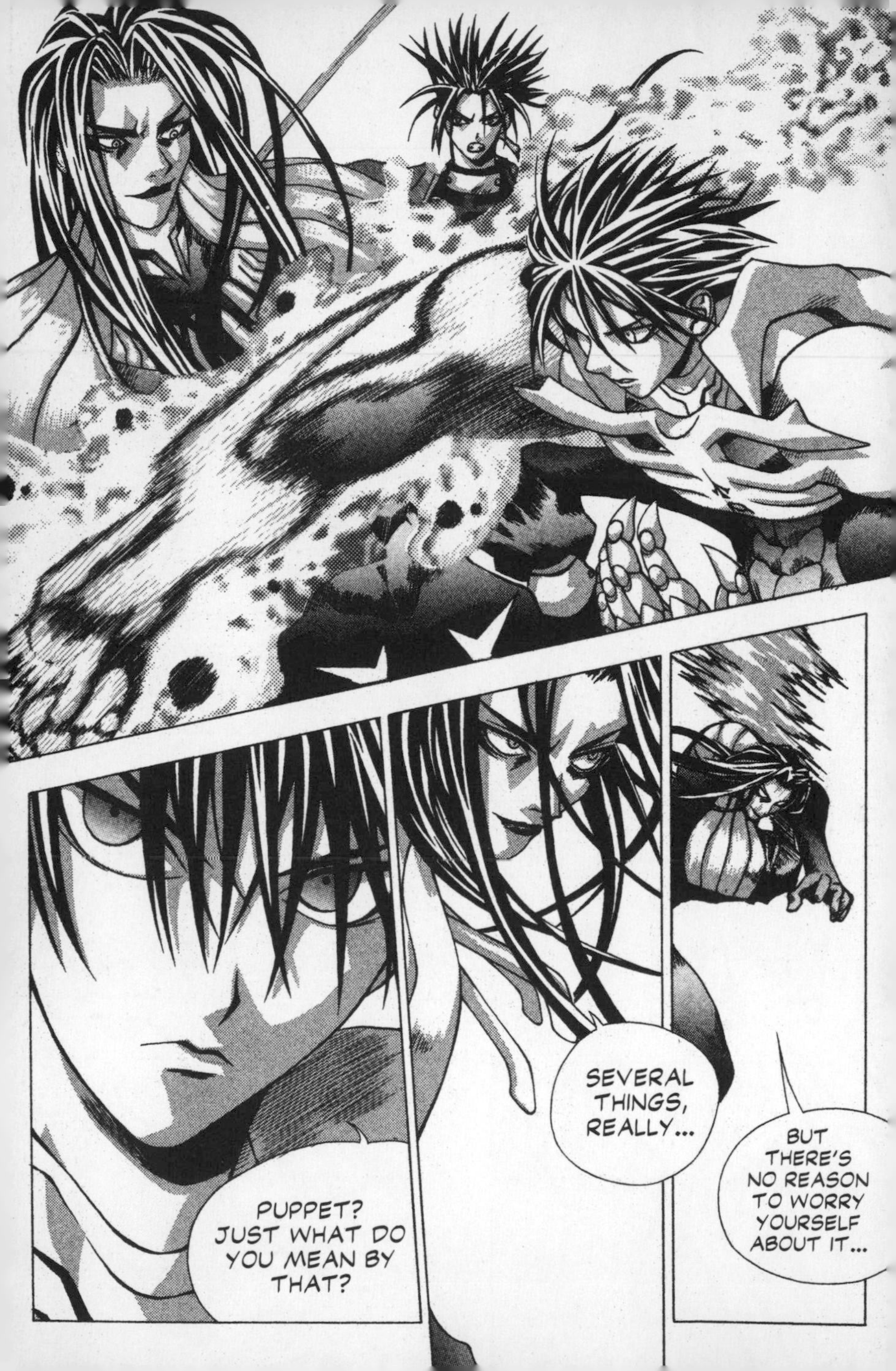
PUPPET? JUST WHAT DO YOU MEAN BY THAT?
SEVERAL THINGS, REALLY...
BUT THERE'S NO REASON TO WORRY YOURSELF ABOUT IT...

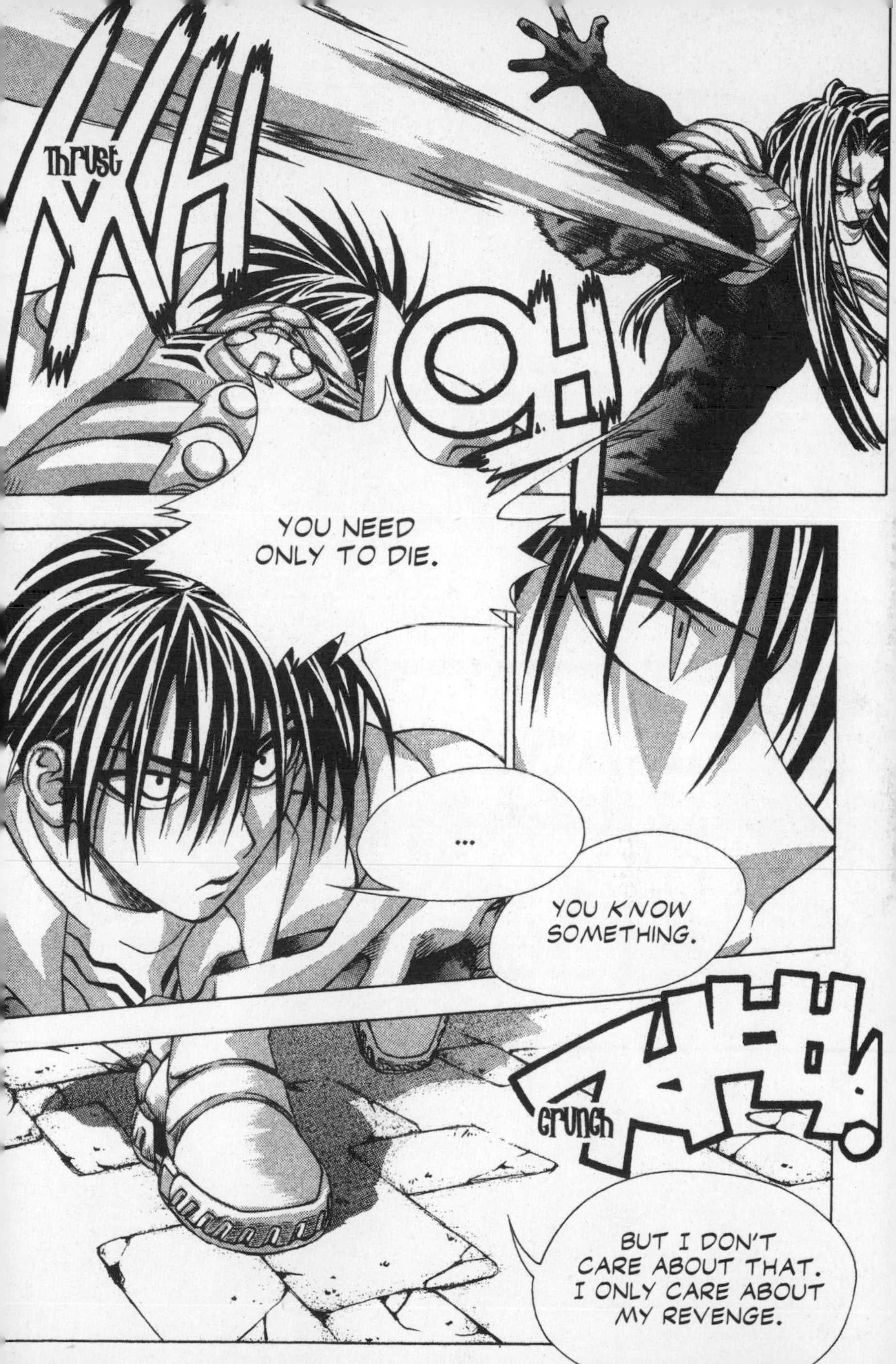
Thrust
YOU NEED ONLY TO DIE.
...
YOU KNOW SOMETHING.
Crunch
BUT I DON'T CARE ABOUT THAT. I ONLY CARE ABOUT MY REVENGE.

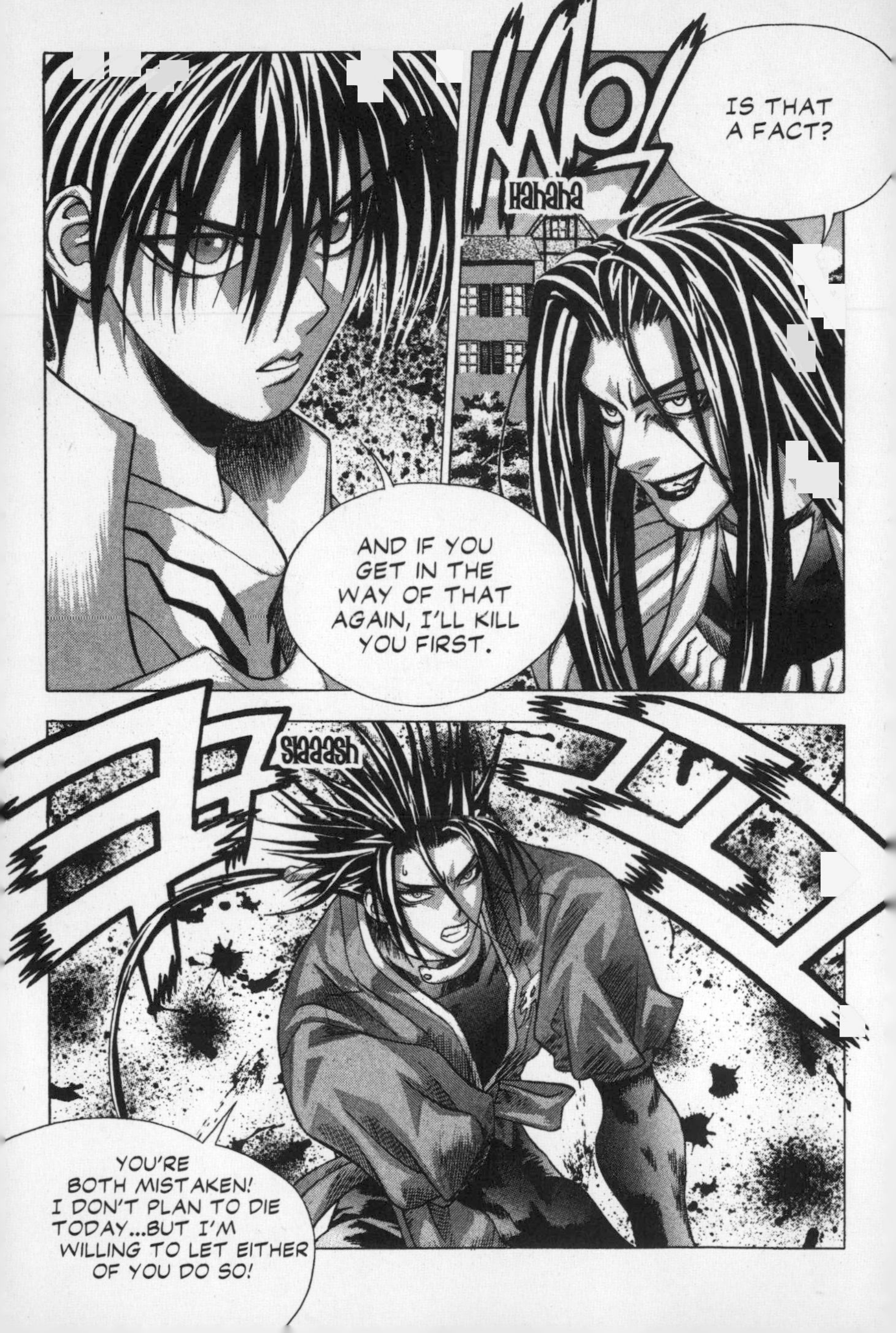
AND IF YOU GET IN THE WAY OF THAT AGAIN, I'LL KILL YOU FIRST.
Hahaha
IS THAT A FACT?
Slaaash
YOU'RE BOTH MISTAKEN! I DON'T PLAN TO DIE TODAY...BUT I'M WILLING TO LET EITHER OF YOU DO SO!

RAGNAROK

IN TO THE ABYSS

IRIS IRINE
THE CLERIC
STUDIO DIVE TO DREAM SEA
GO GO COMIC WORLD !!

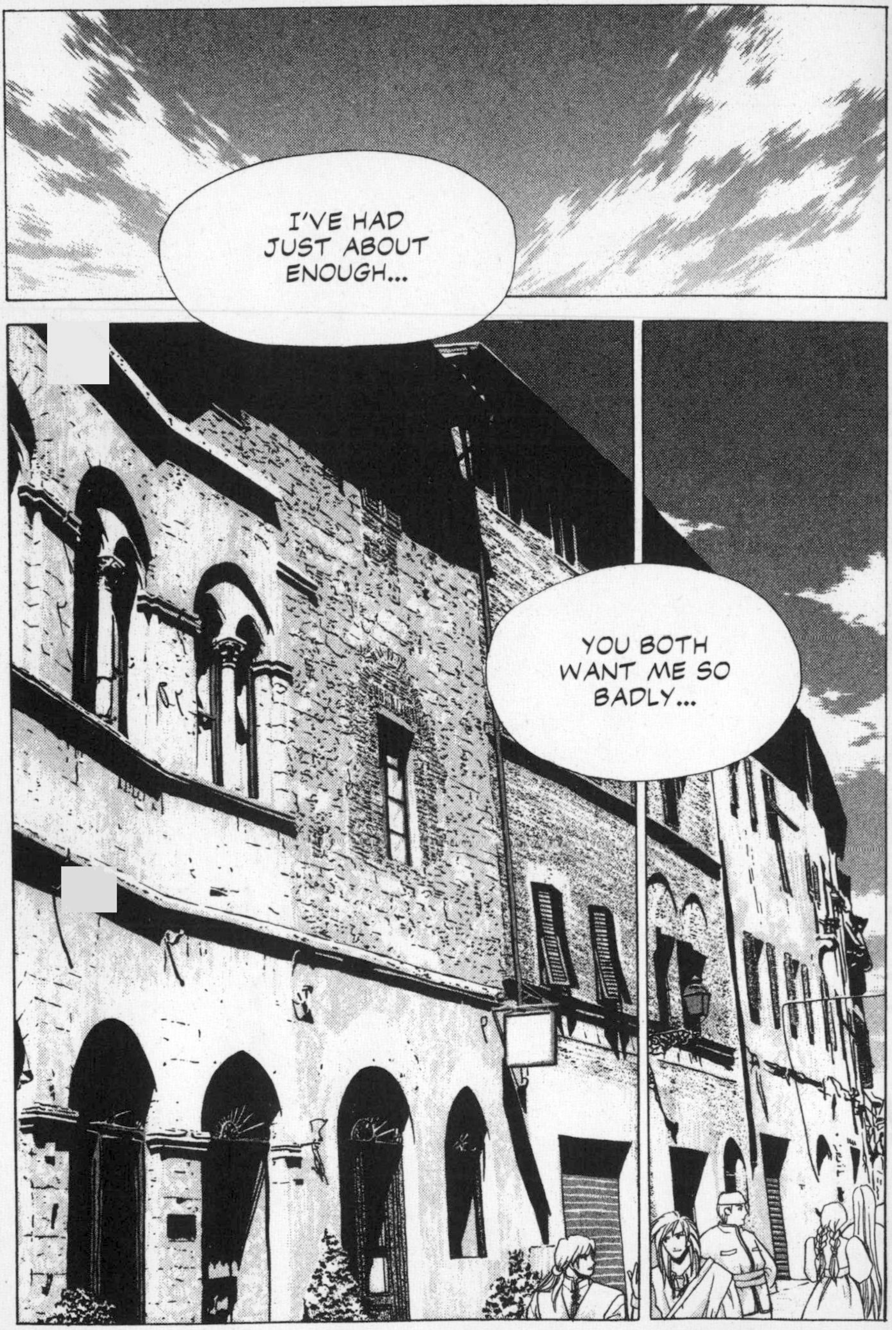
I'VE HAD JUST ABOUT ENOUGH...
YOU BOTH WANT ME SO BADLY...

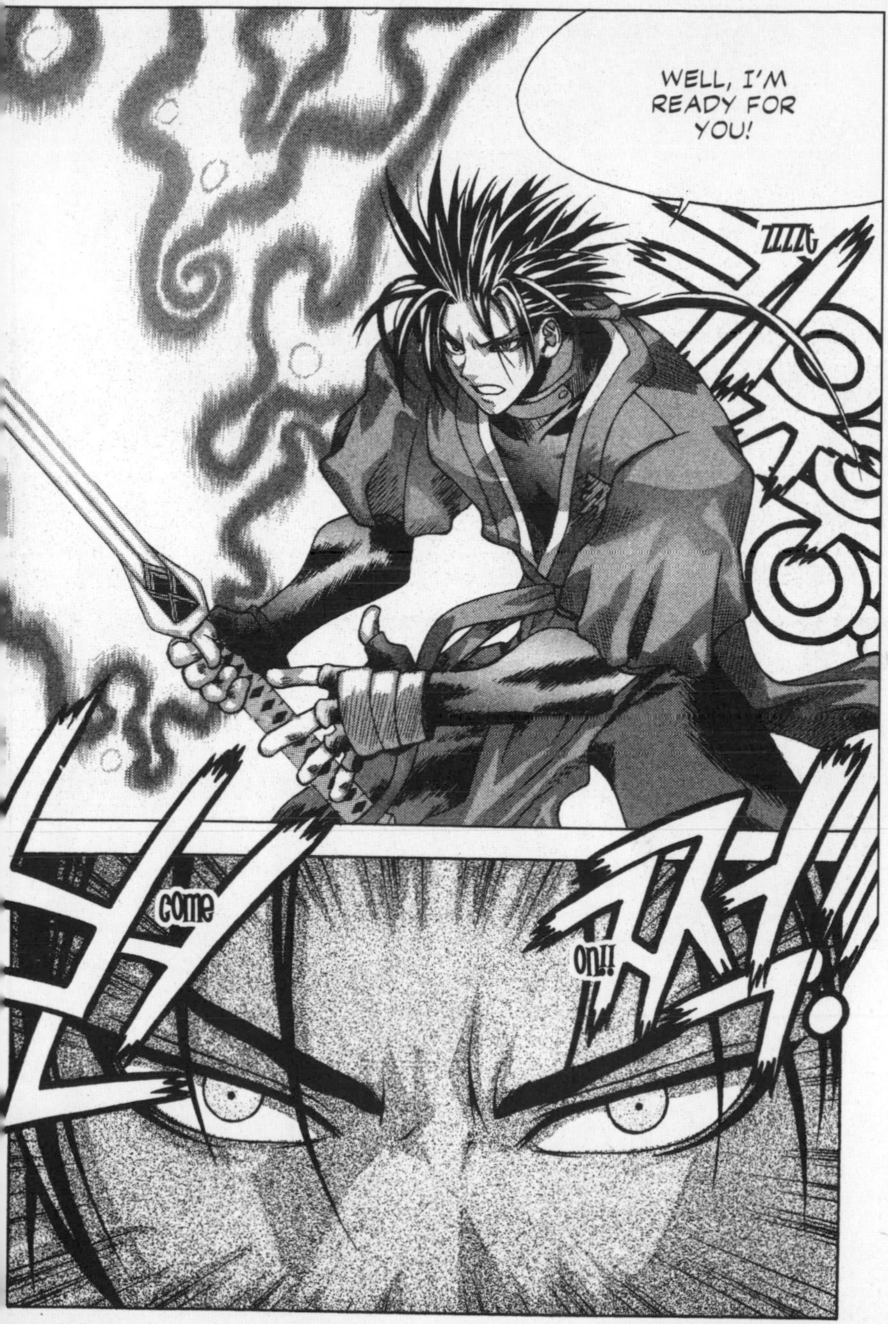
WELL, I'M READY FOR YOU!
ZZZZT
Come
on!!

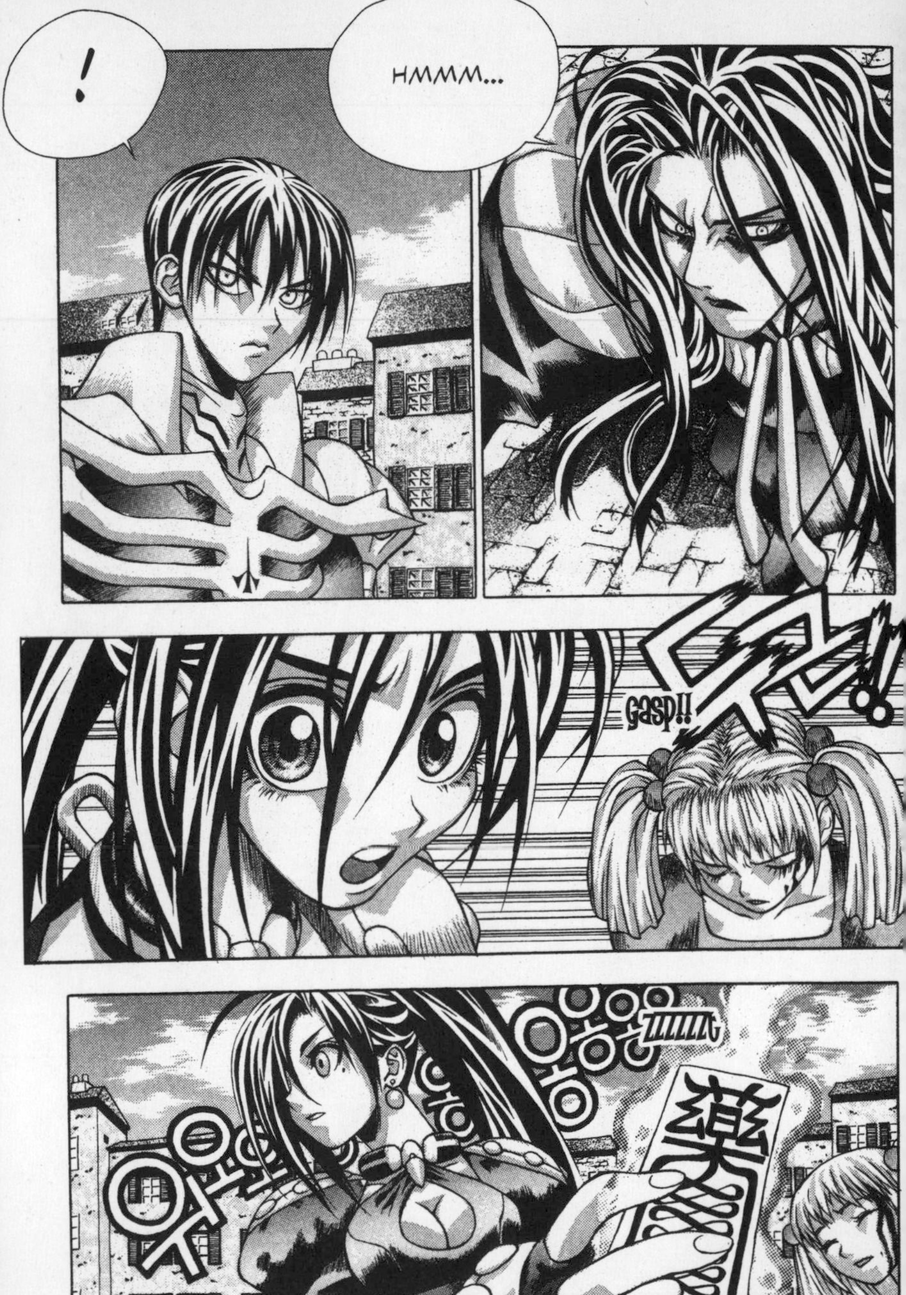
!
HMMM...
GASP!!
藥

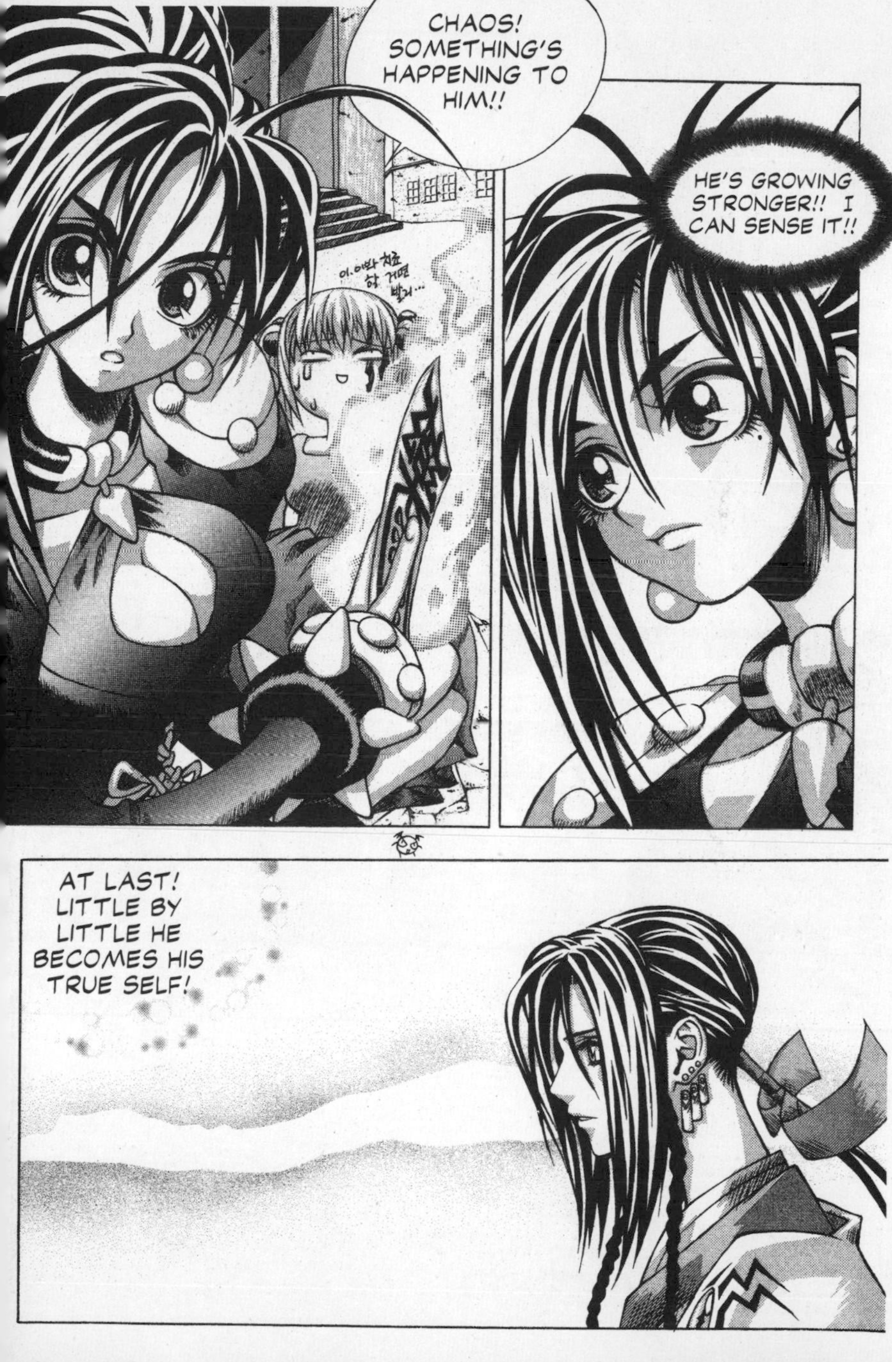
CHAOS! SOMETHING'S HAPPENING TO HIM!!
이.이봐 치료 할 거면 빨리...
HE'S GROWING STRONGER!! I CAN SENSE IT!!
AT LAST! LITTLE BY LITTLE HE BECOMES HIS TRUE SELF!

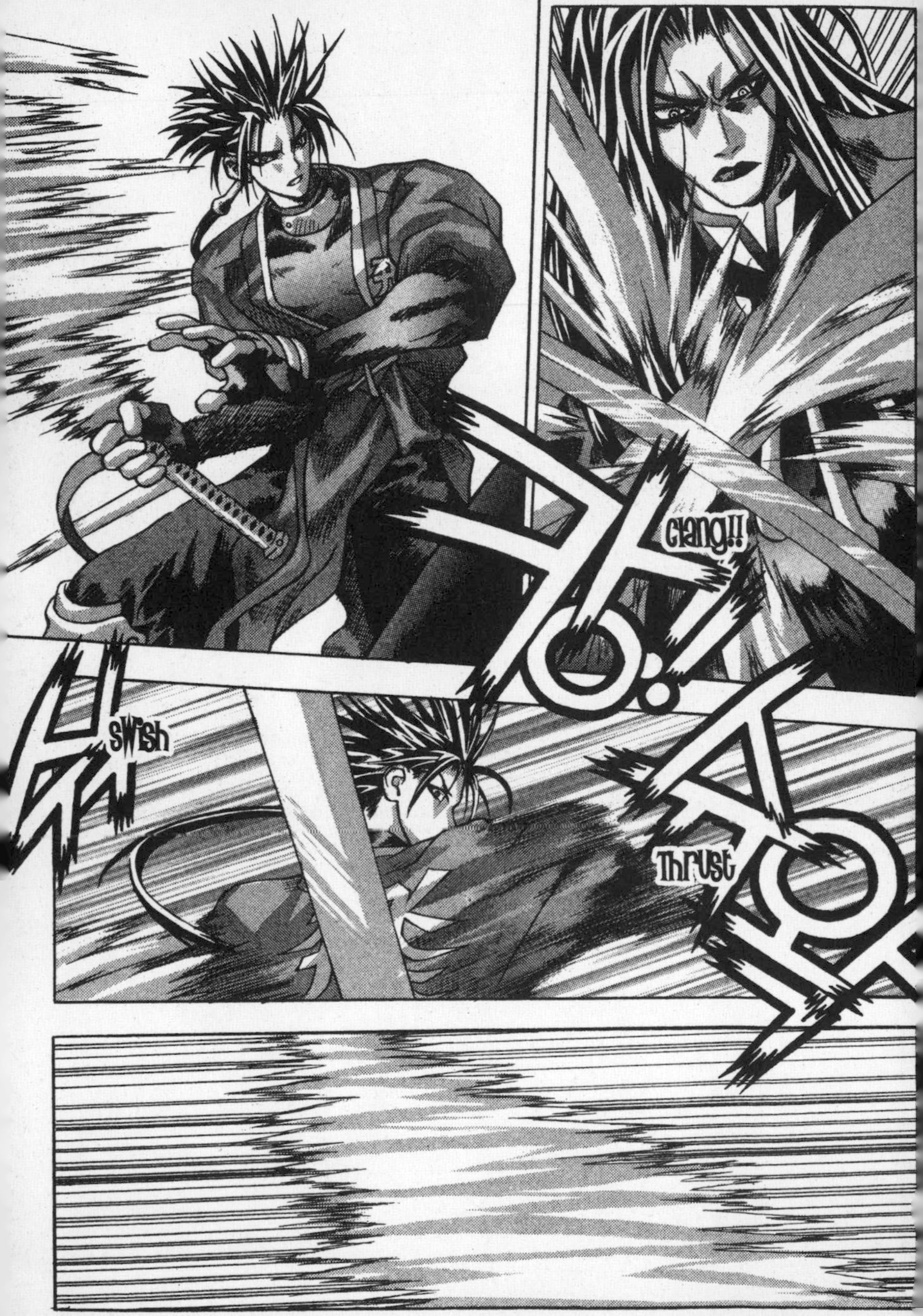
Clang!!
Swish
Thrust

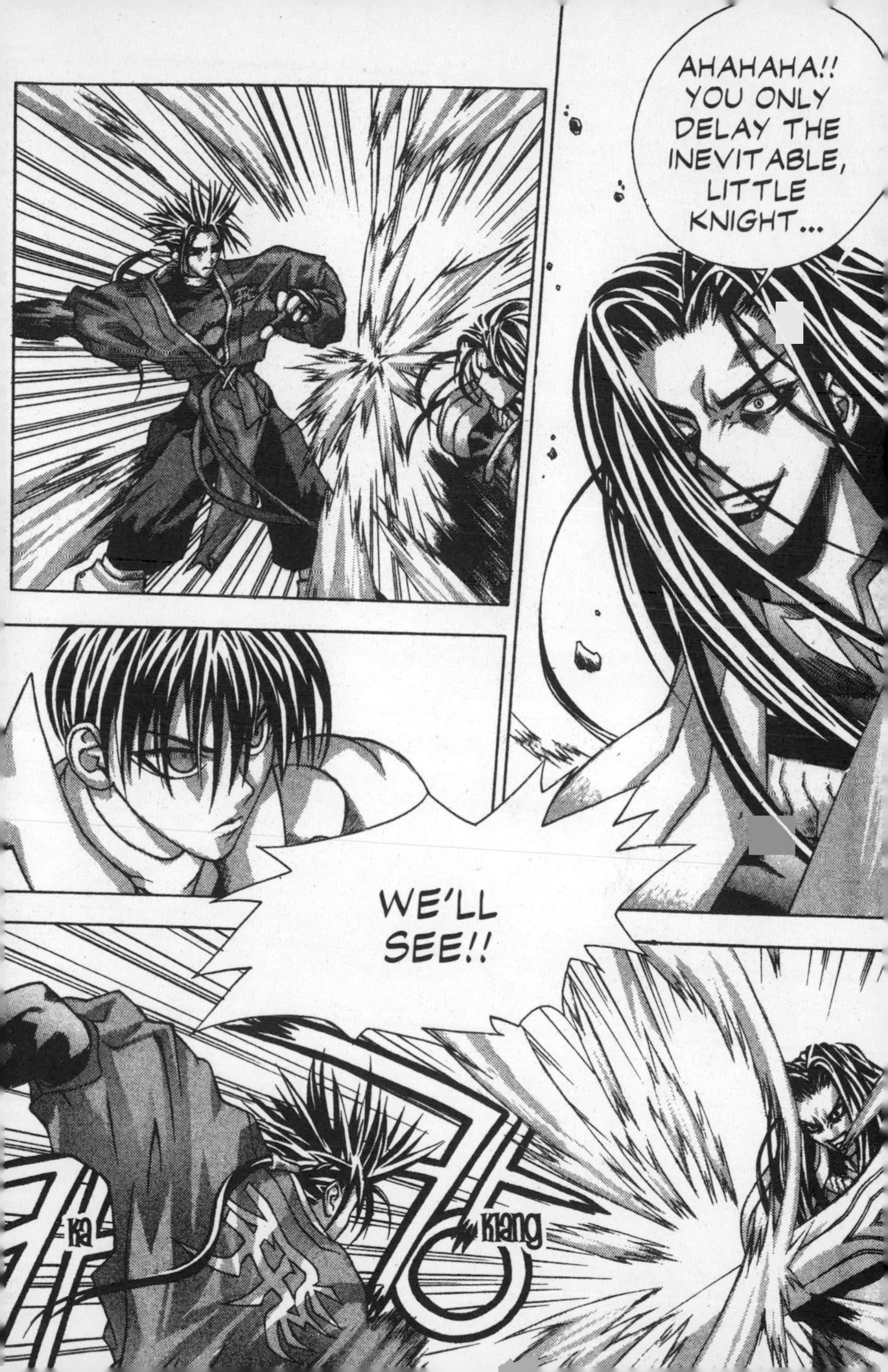
AHAHAHA!! YOU ONLY DELAY THE INEVITABLE, LITTLE KNIGHT...
WE'LL SEE!!
KA
KLANG

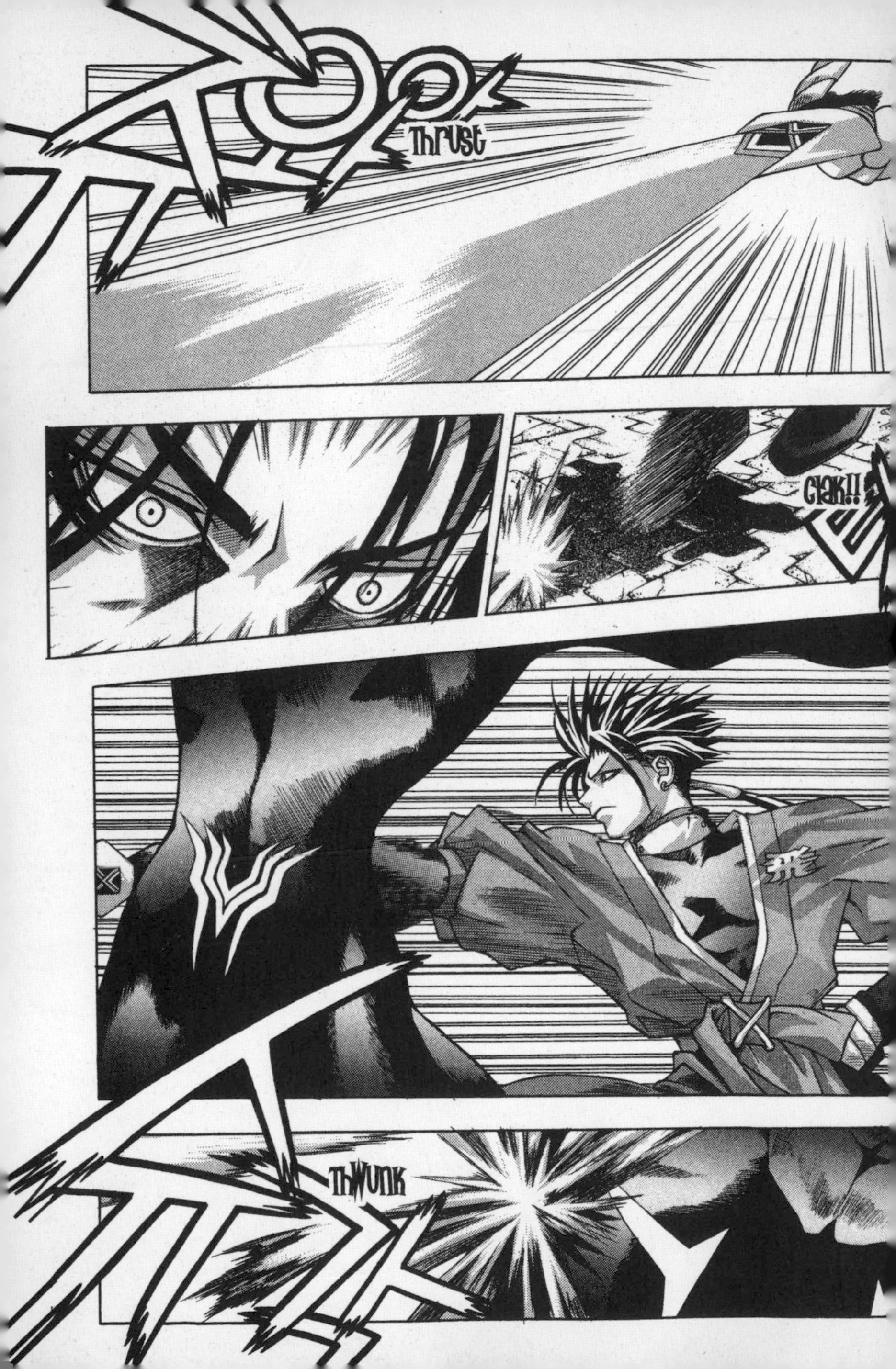
THRUST
CLAK!!
THWUNK

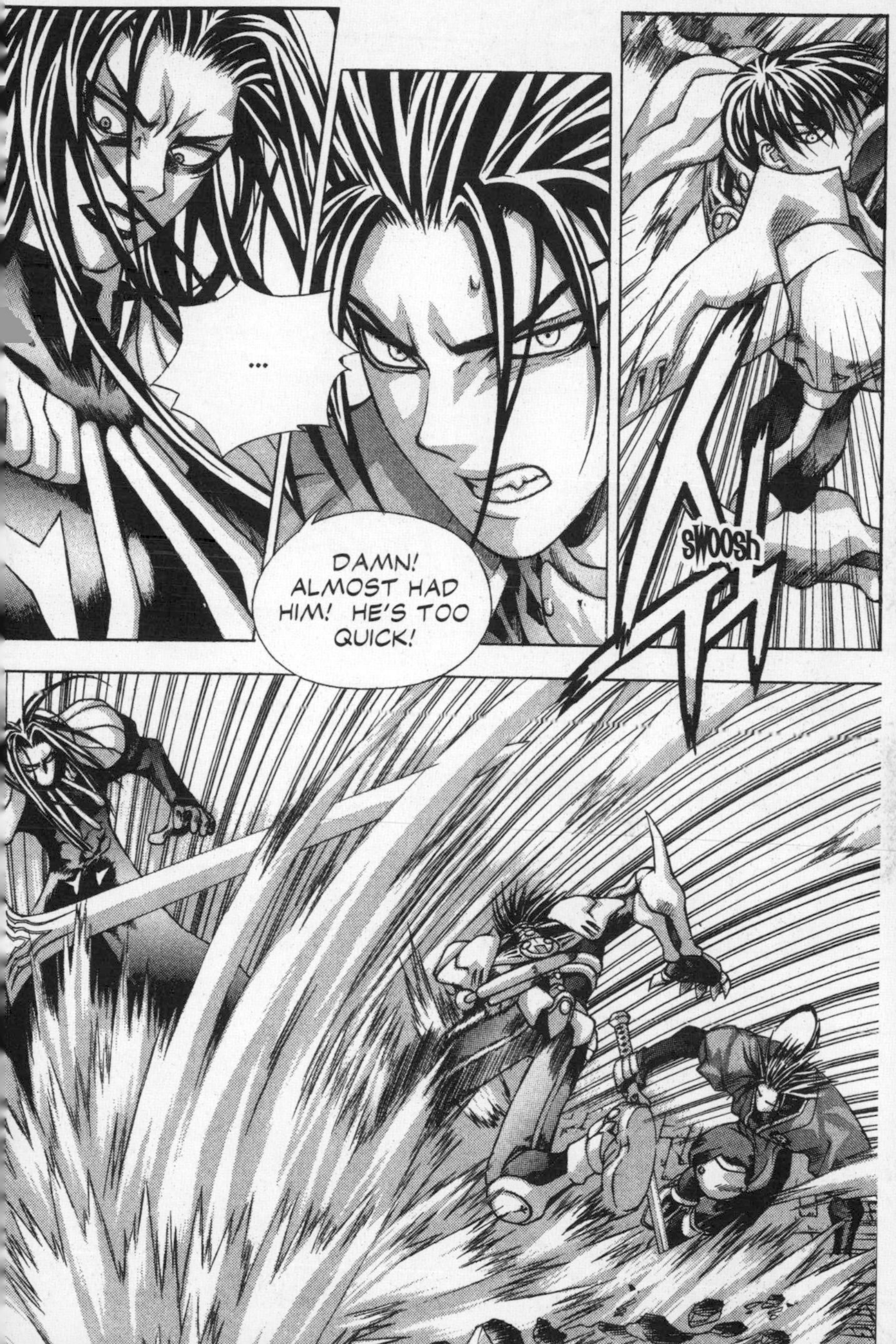
...
DAMN! ALMOST HAD HIM! HE'S TOO QUICK!
SWOOSH

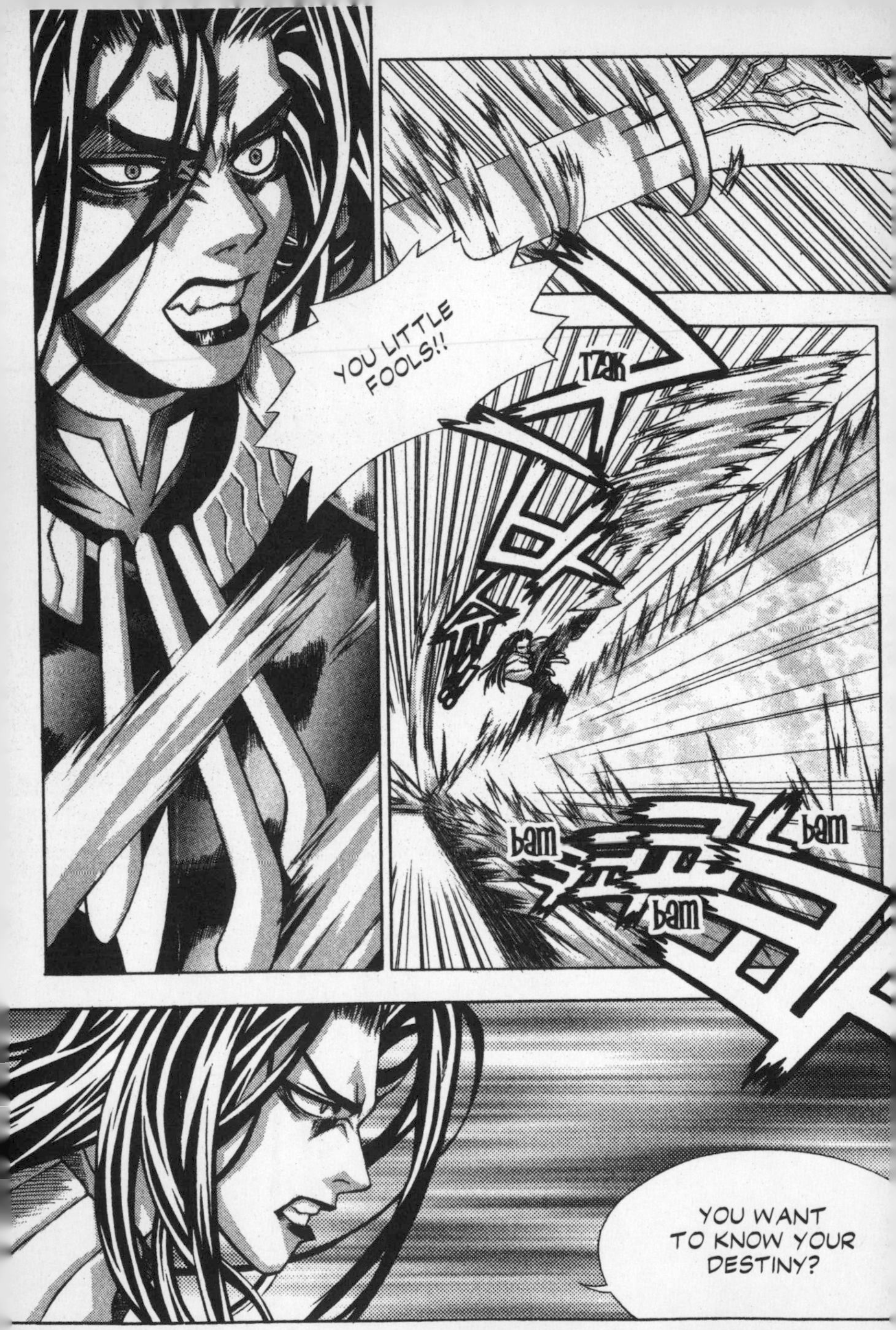
YOU LITTLE FOOLS!!
TZAK
BAM
BAM
BAM
YOU WANT TO KNOW YOUR DESTINY?

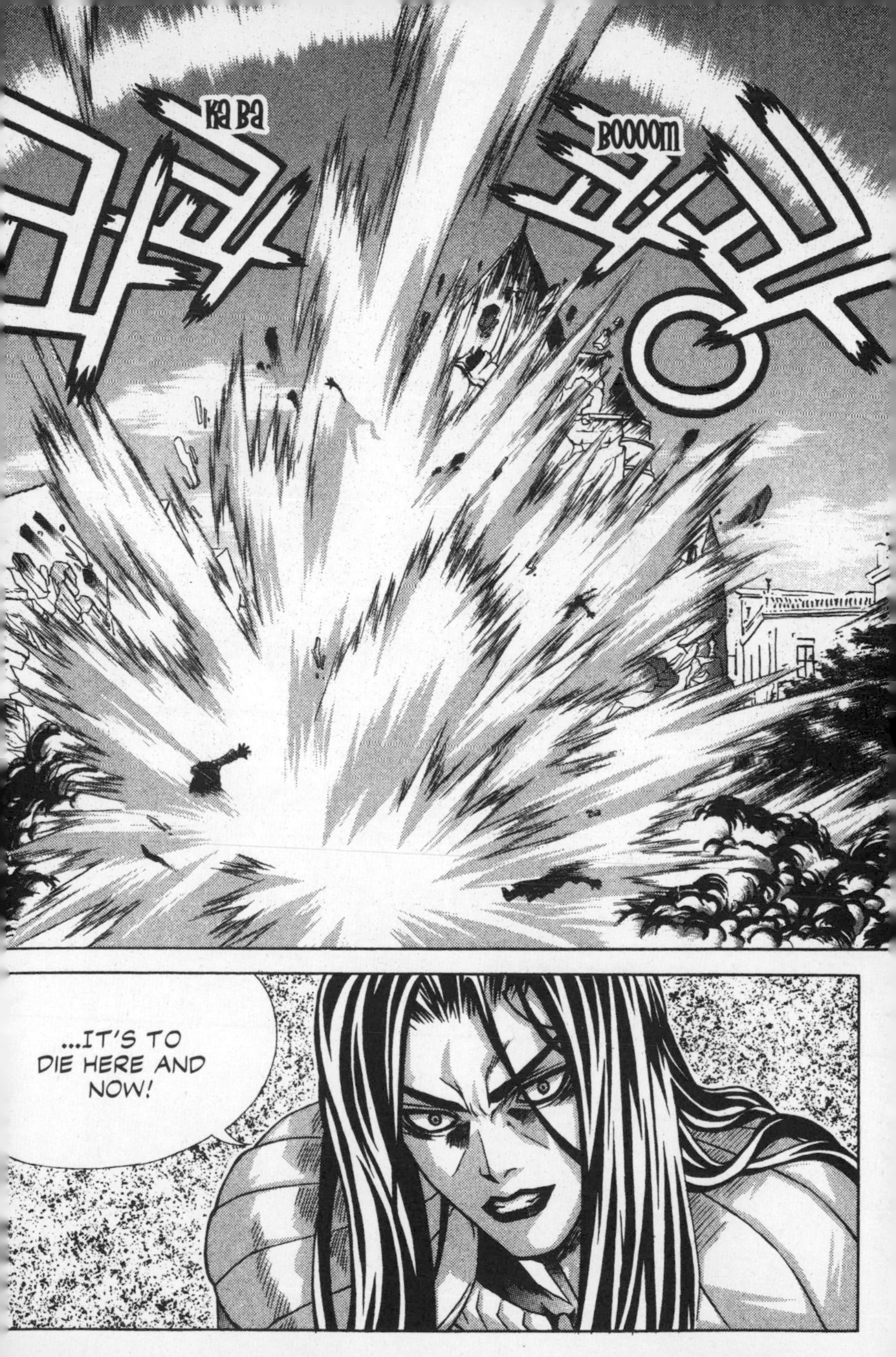
KA BA
BOOOOM
...IT'S TO DIE HERE AND NOW!

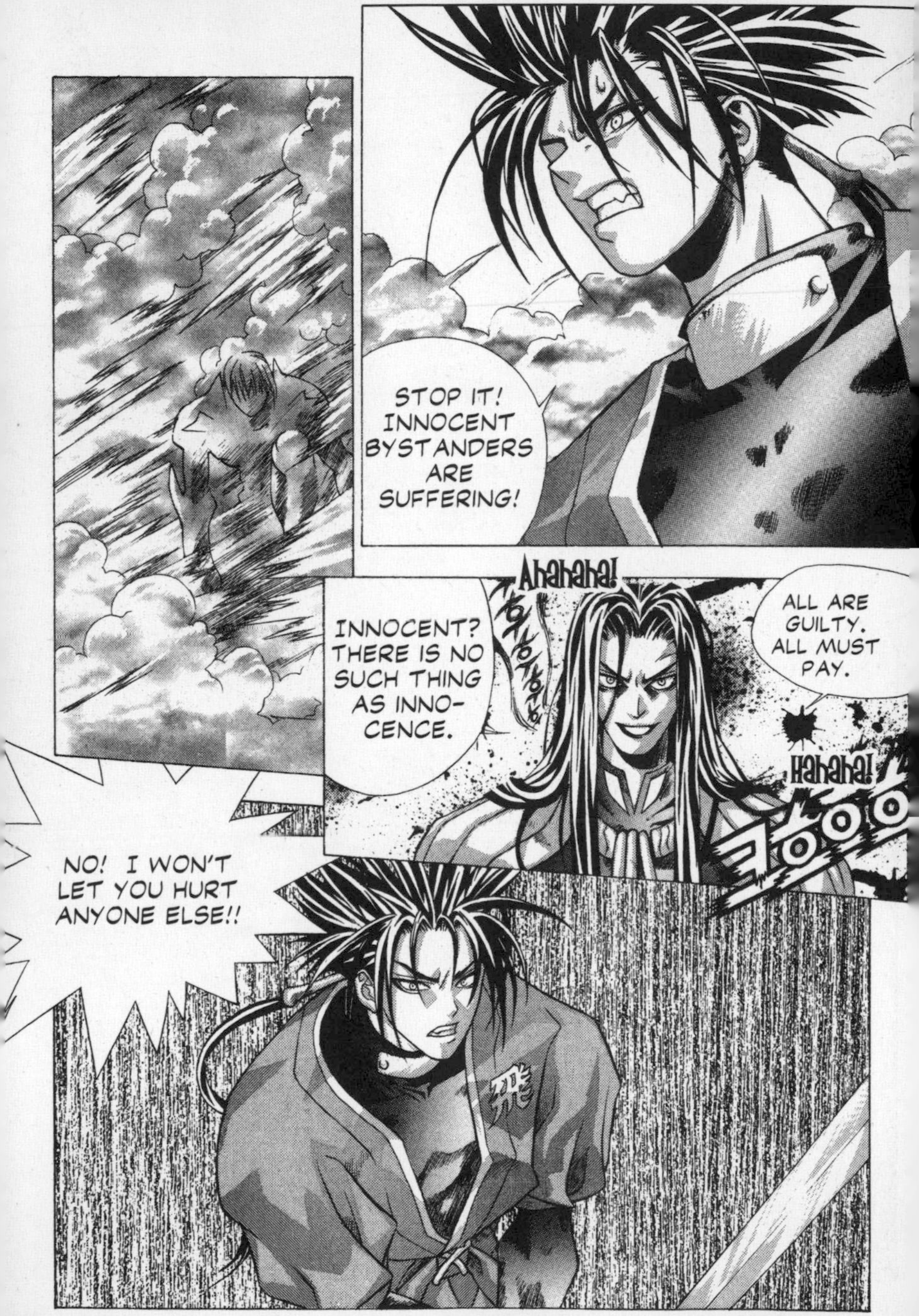
STOP IT! INNOCENT BYSTANDERS ARE SUFFERING!
Ahahaha!
INNOCENT? THERE IS NO SUCH THING AS INNO-CENCE.
ALL ARE GUILTY. ALL MUST PAY.
Hahaha!
NO! I WON'T LET YOU HURT ANYONE ELSE!!

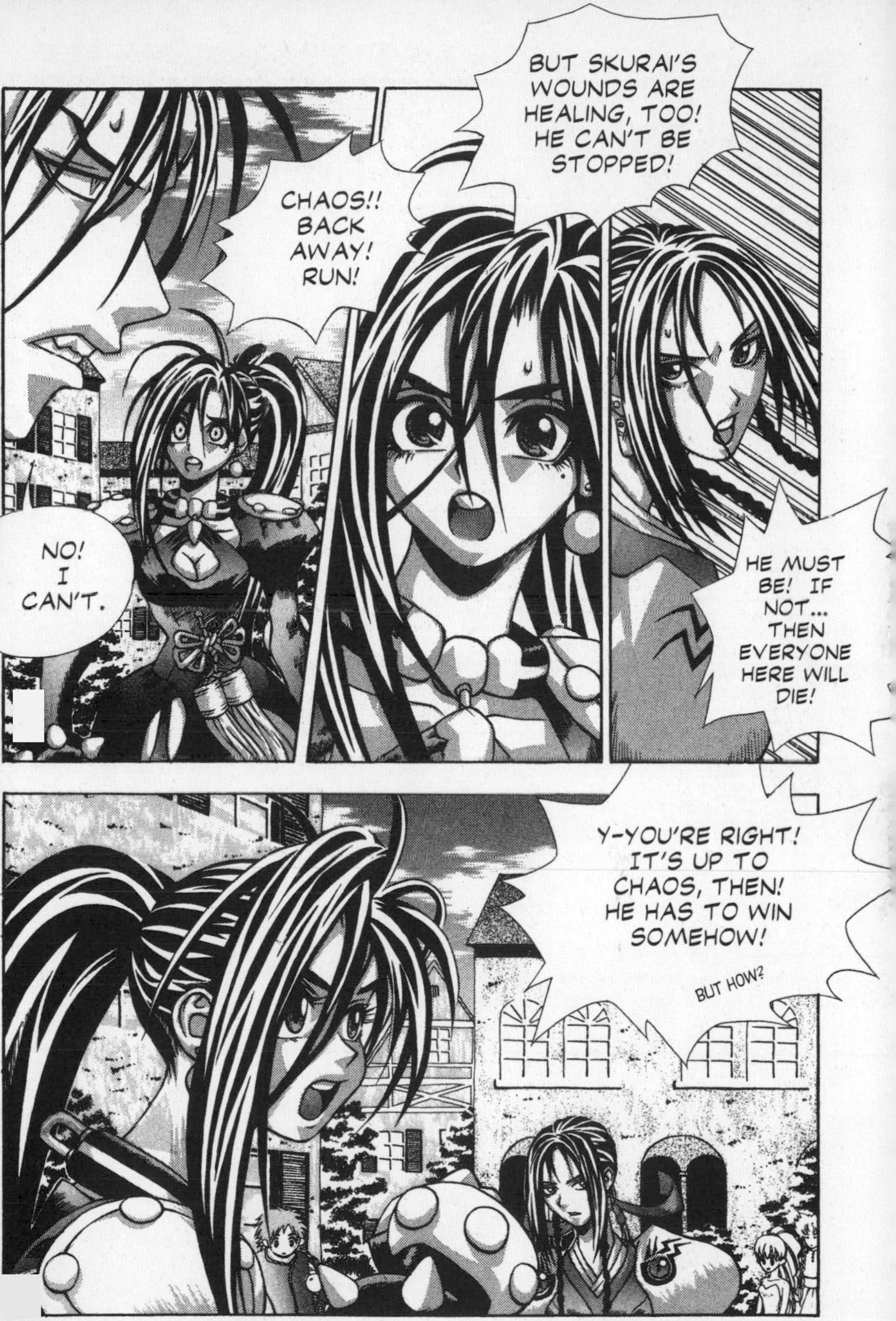
CHAOS!! BACK AWAY! RUN!
NO! I CAN'T.
BUT SKURAI'S WOUNDS ARE HEALING, TOO! HE CAN'T BE STOPPED!
HE MUST BE! IF NOT... THEN EVERYONE HERE WILL DIE!
Y-YOU'RE RIGHT! IT'S UP TO CHAOS, THEN! HE HAS TO WIN SOMEHOW!
BUT HOW?

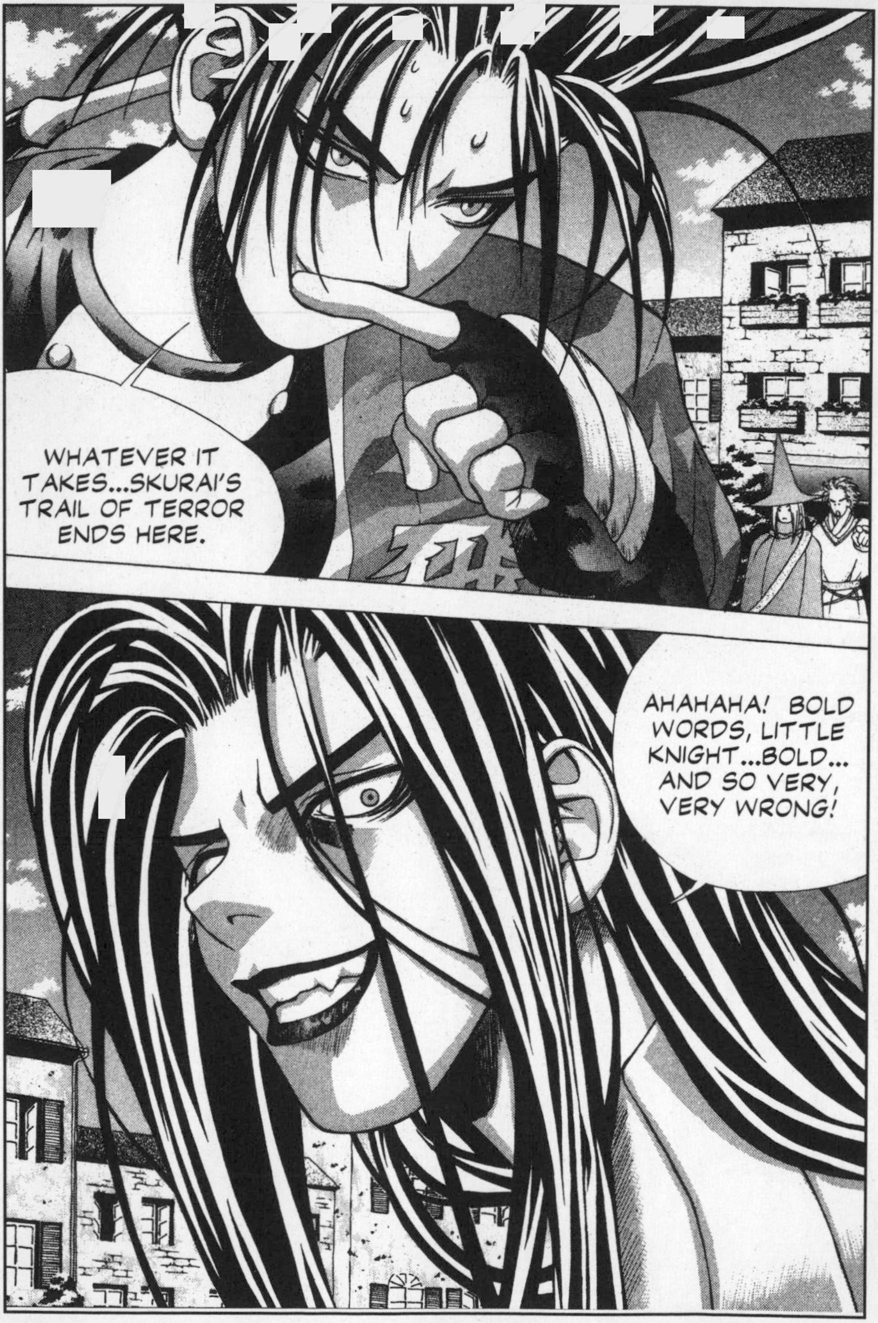
WHATEVER IT TAKES...SKURAI'S TRAIL OF TERROR ENDS HERE.
AHAHAHA! BOLD WORDS, LITTLE KNIGHT...BOLD... AND SO VERY, VERY WRONG!

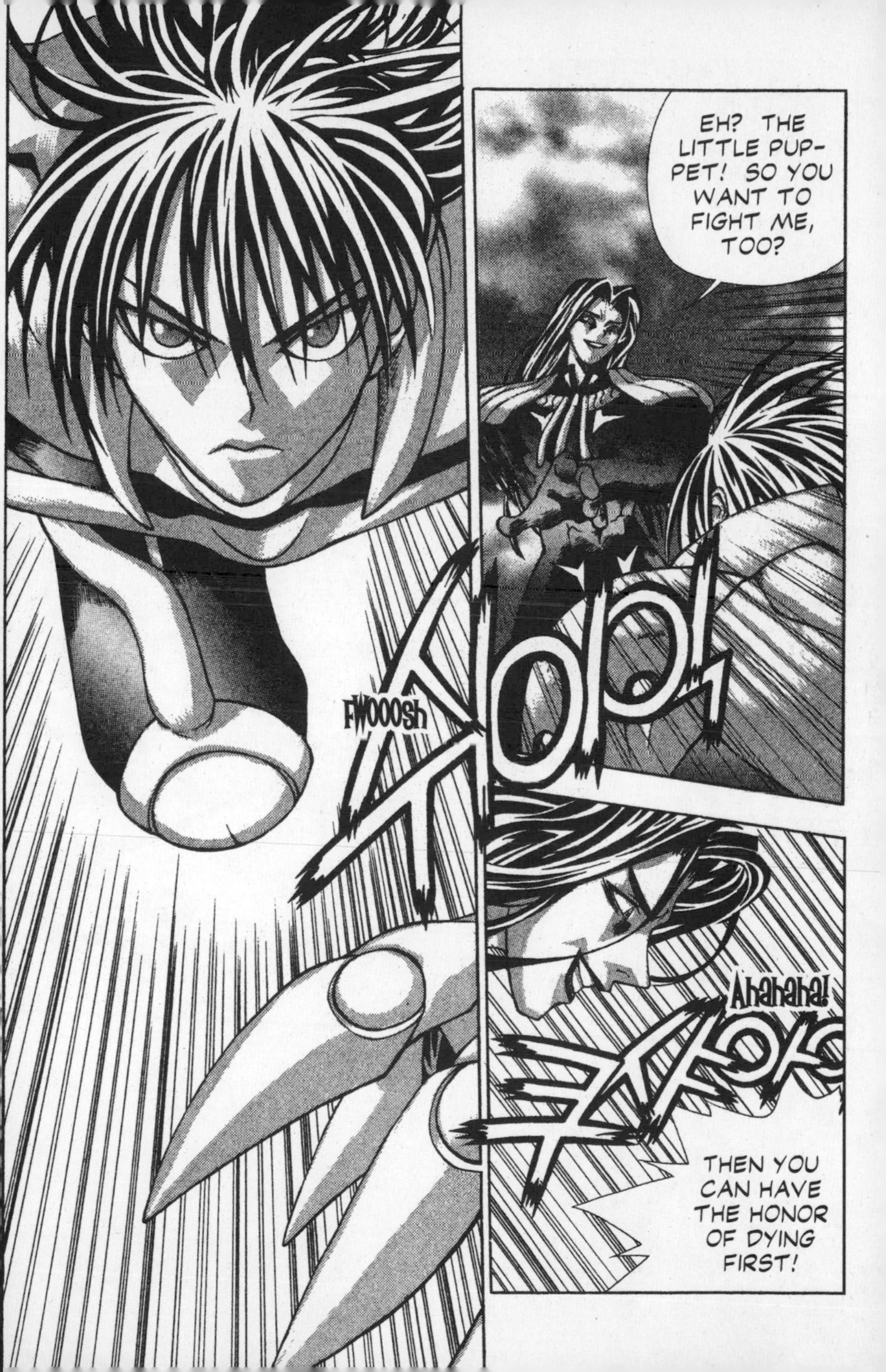
FWOOOsh
EH? THE LITTLE PUP-PET! SO YOU WANT TO FIGHT ME, TOO?
Ahahaha!
THEN YOU CAN HAVE THE HONOR OF DYING FIRST!

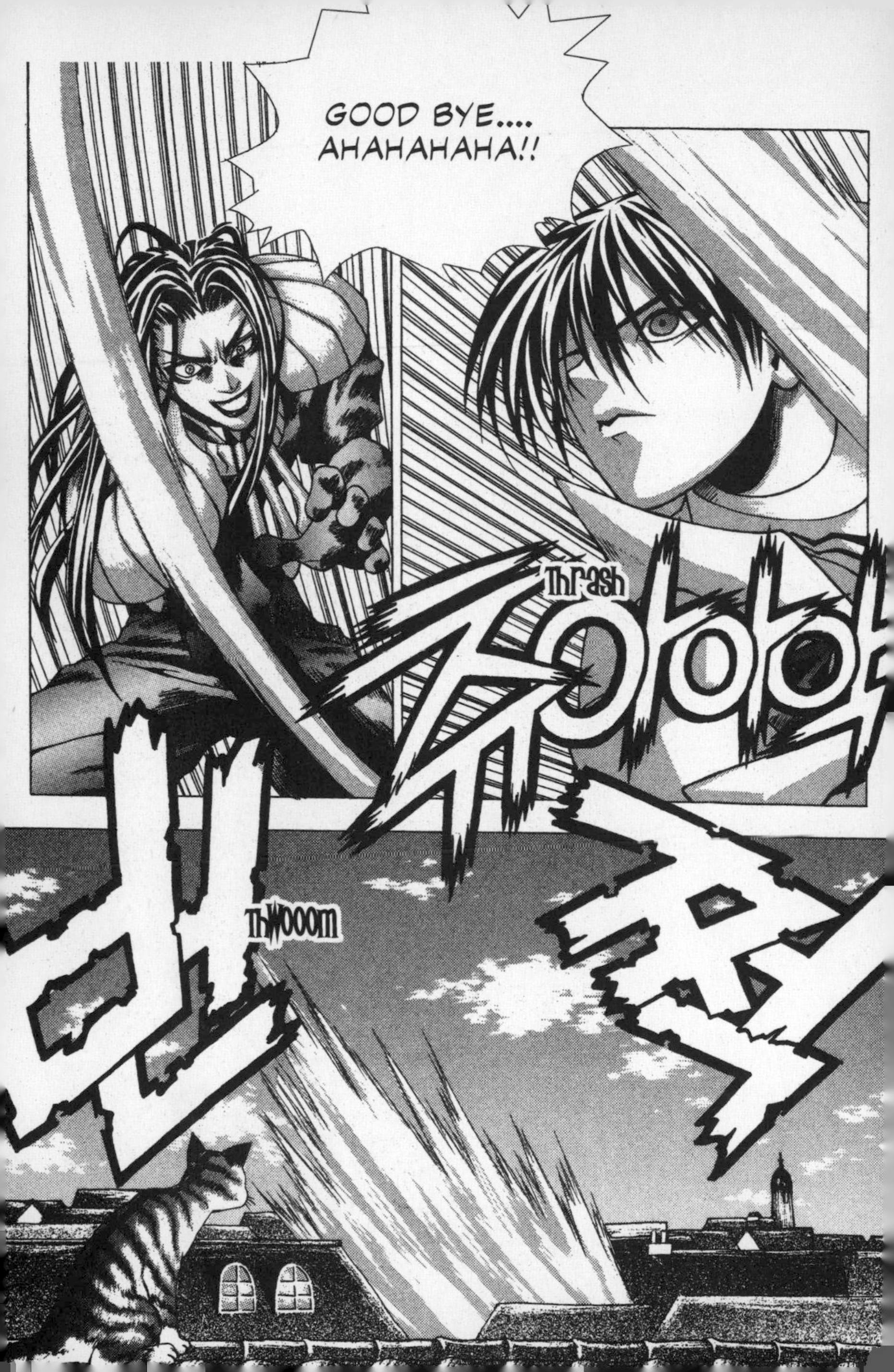

GOOD BYE....
AHAHAHAHA!!
ThRASH
ThWOOOM

RAGNAROK
라그나로크
IN TO THE ABYSS

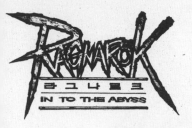

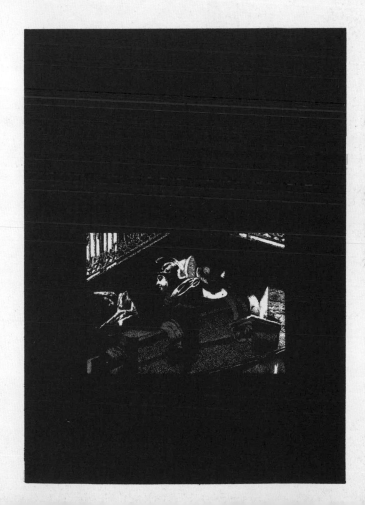

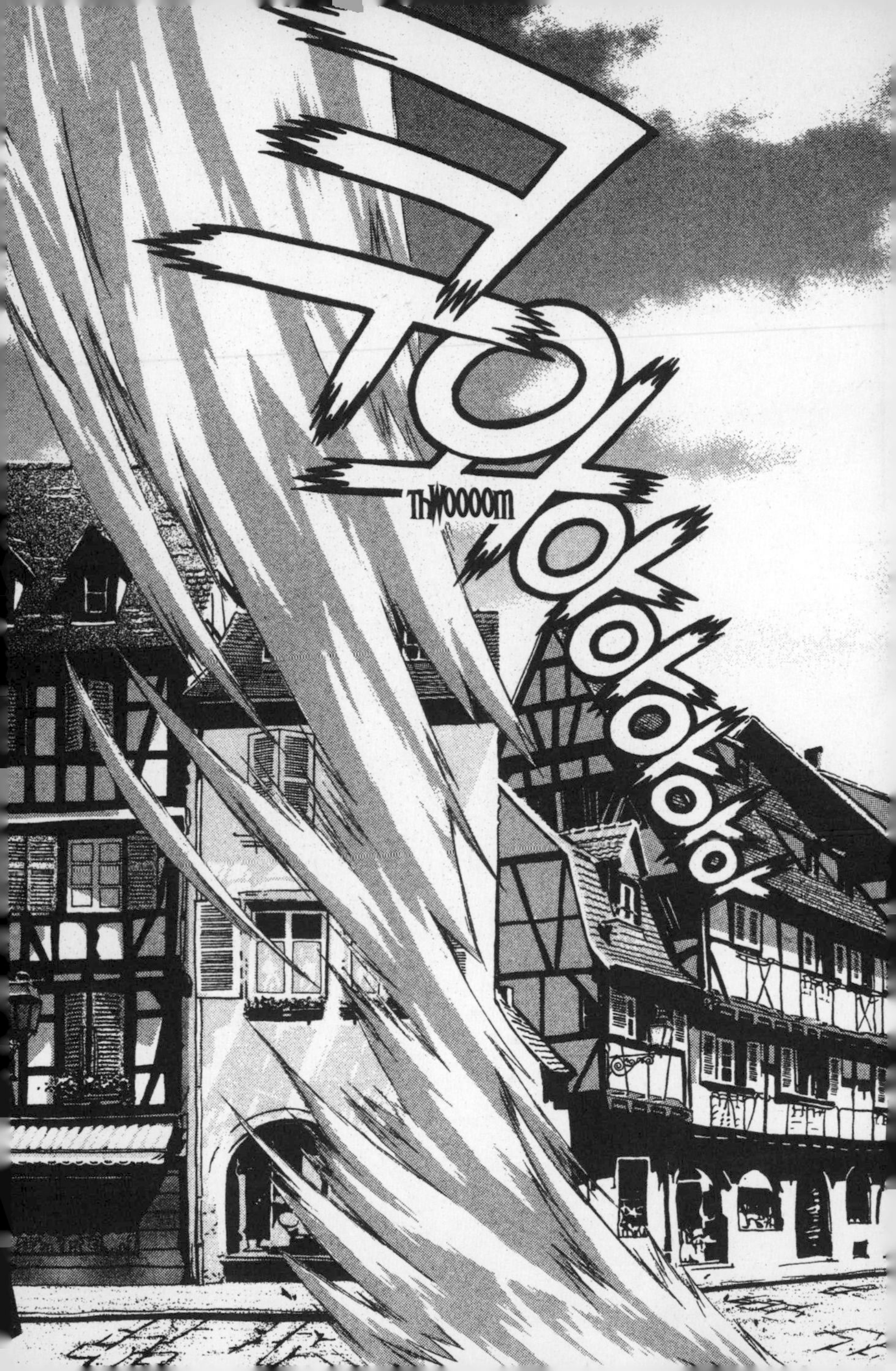
ThWOOOOM

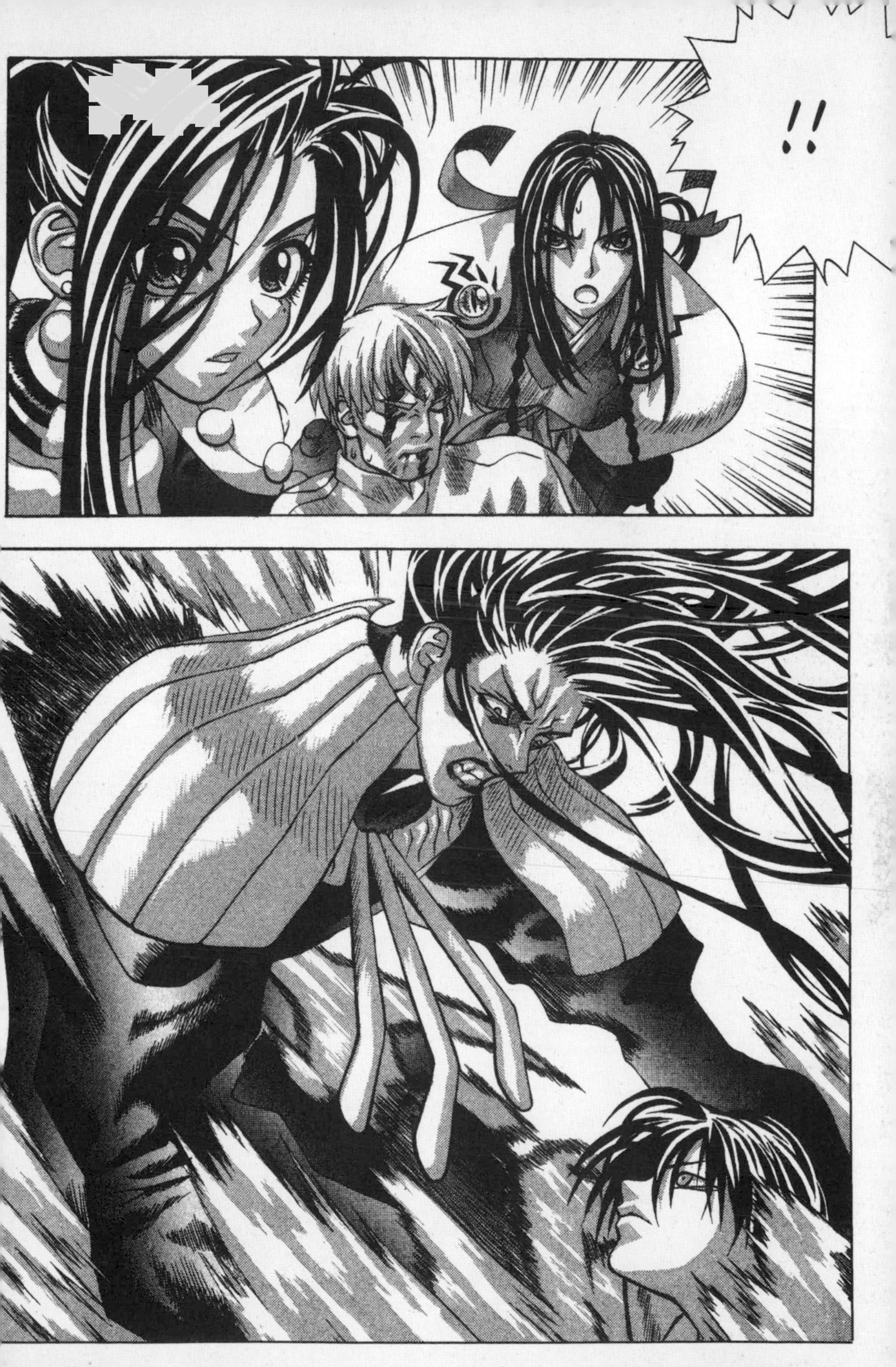
!!

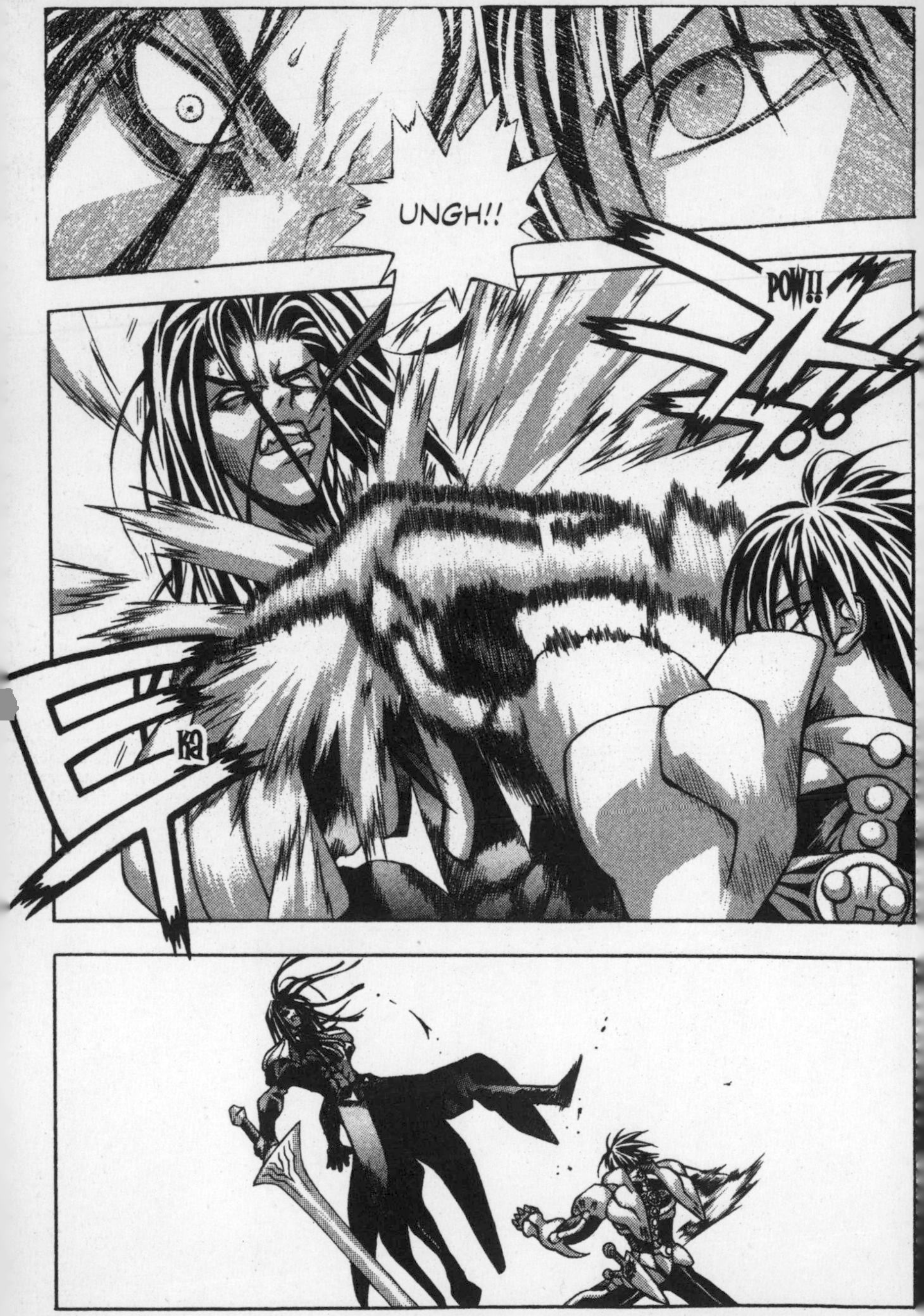
UNGH!!
POW!!
KA

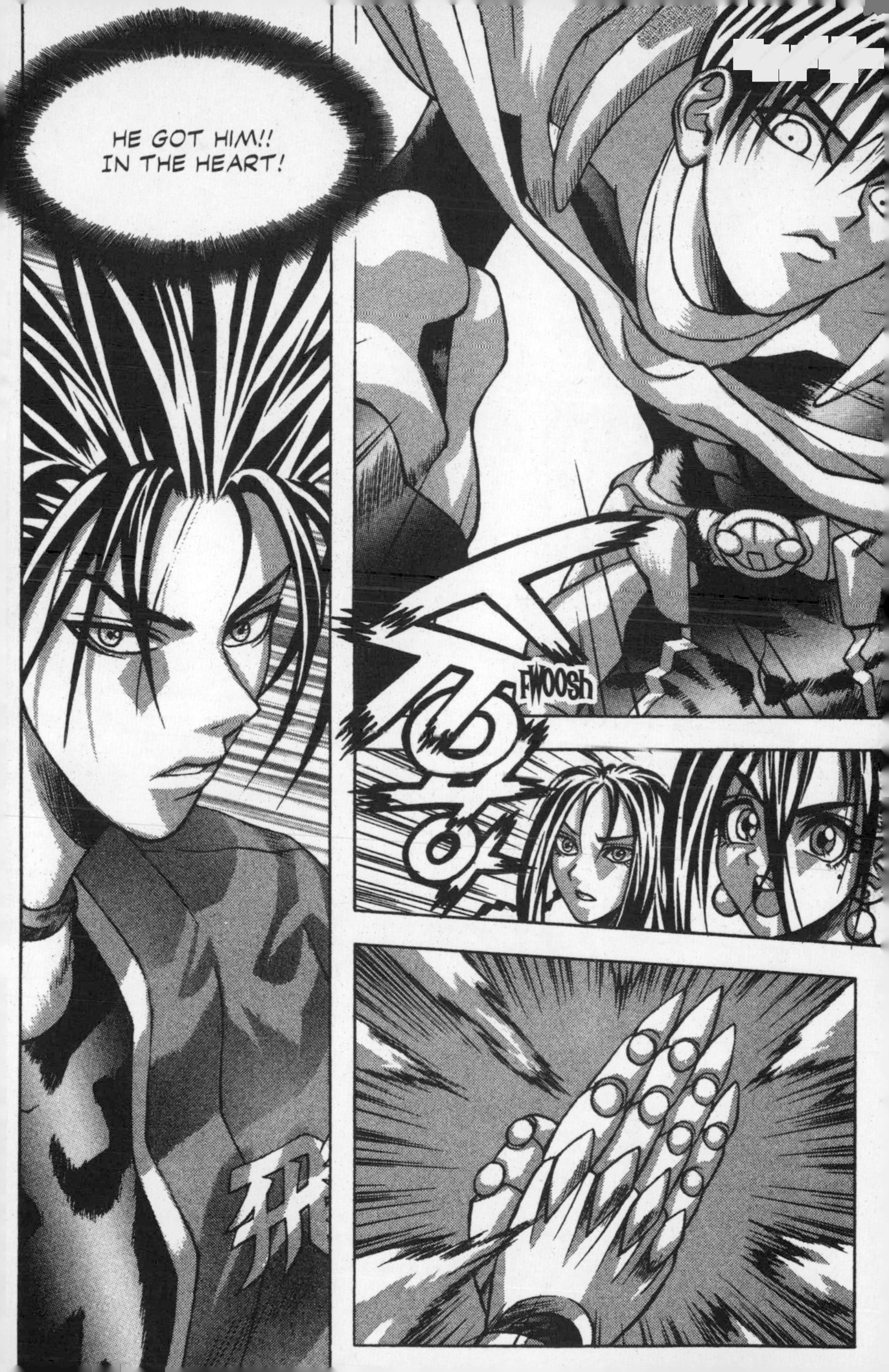
HE GOT HIM!!
IN THE HEART!
FWOOSh

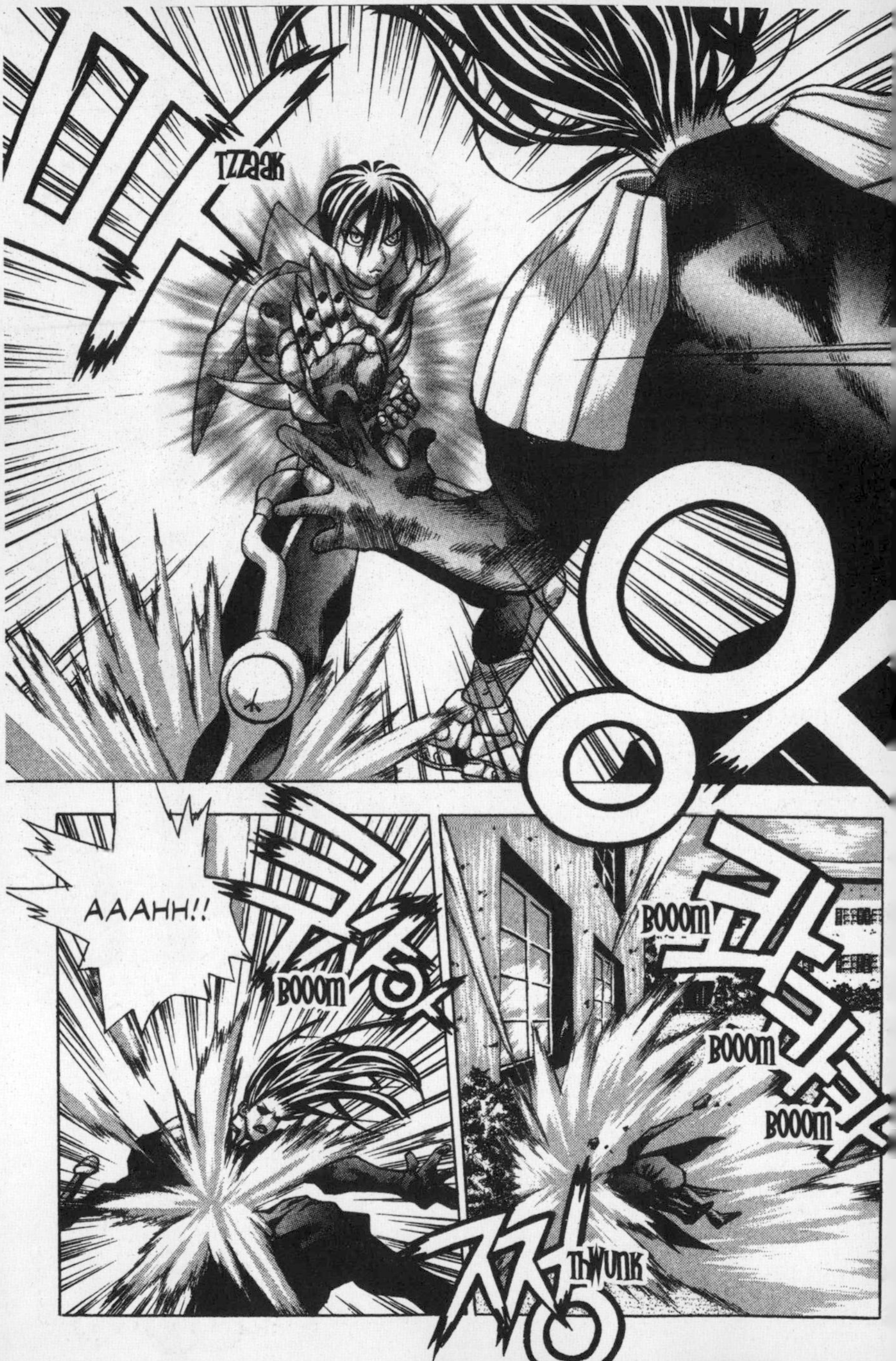
TZZAAK
AAAHH!!
BOOOM
BOOOM
BOOOM
BOOOM
THWUNK

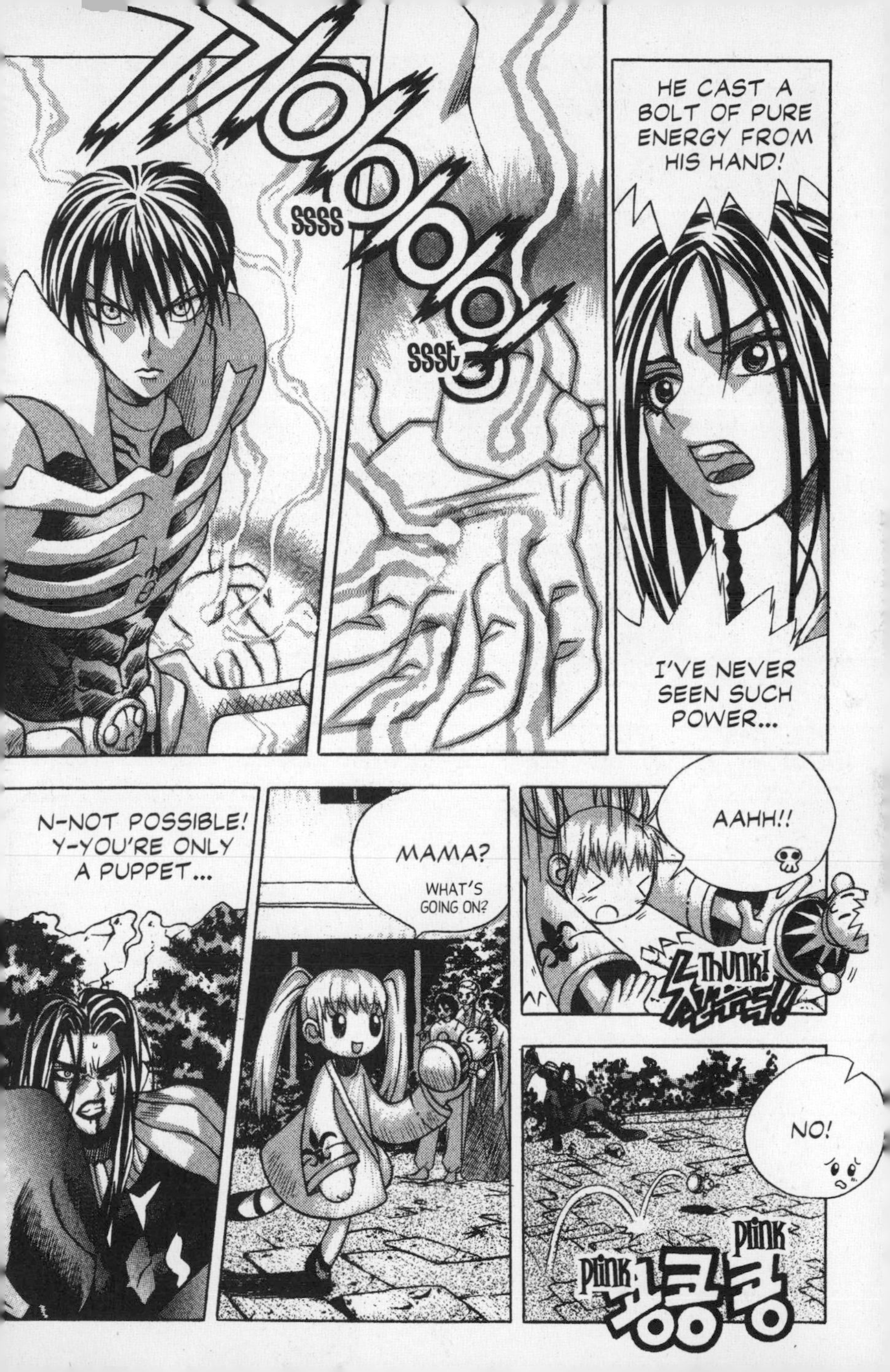
SSSS
SSSt
HE CAST A BOLT OF PURE ENERGY FROM HIS HAND!
I'VE NEVER SEEN SUCH POWER...
N-NOT POSSIBLE! Y-YOU'RE ONLY A PUPPET...
MAMA?
WHAT'S GOING ON?
AAHH!!
THUNK!
NO!
PLINK
PLINK

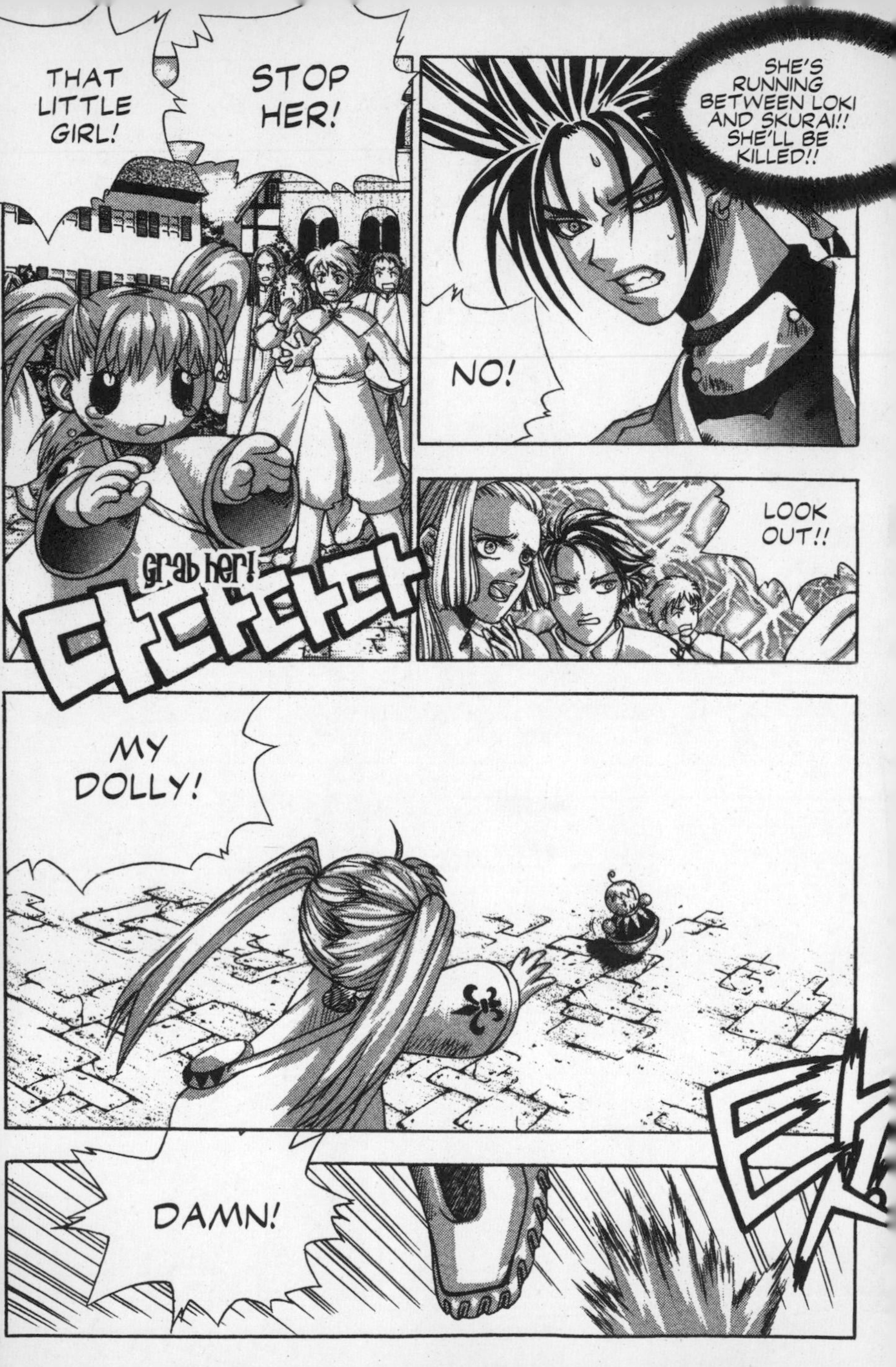
THAT LITTLE GIRL!
STOP HER!
Grab her!
SHE'S RUNNING BETWEEN LOKI AND SKURAI!! SHE'LL BE KILLED!!
NO!
LOOK OUT!!
MY DOLLY!
DAMN!

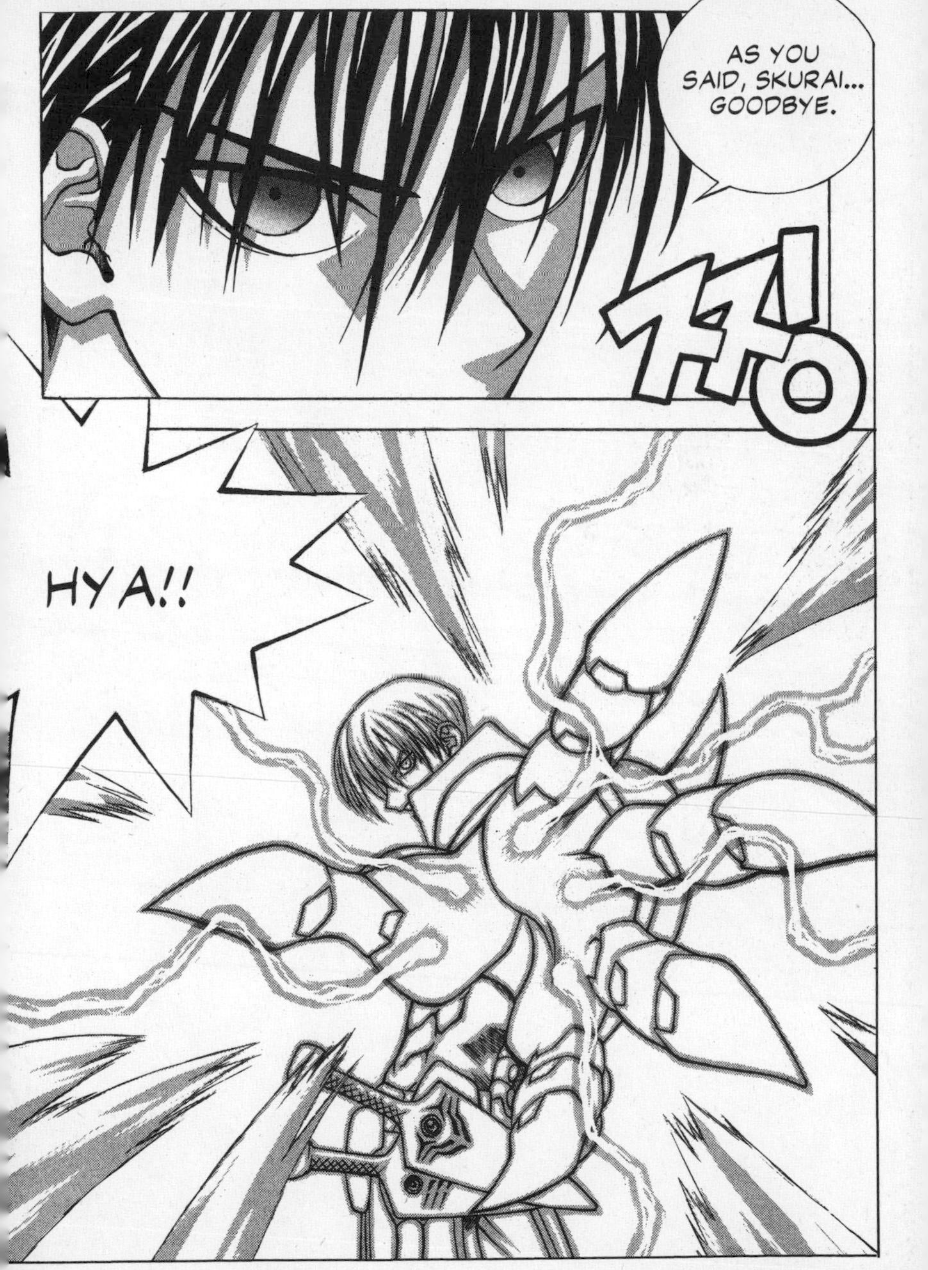
AS YOU SAID, SKURAI... GOODBYE.
HYA!!

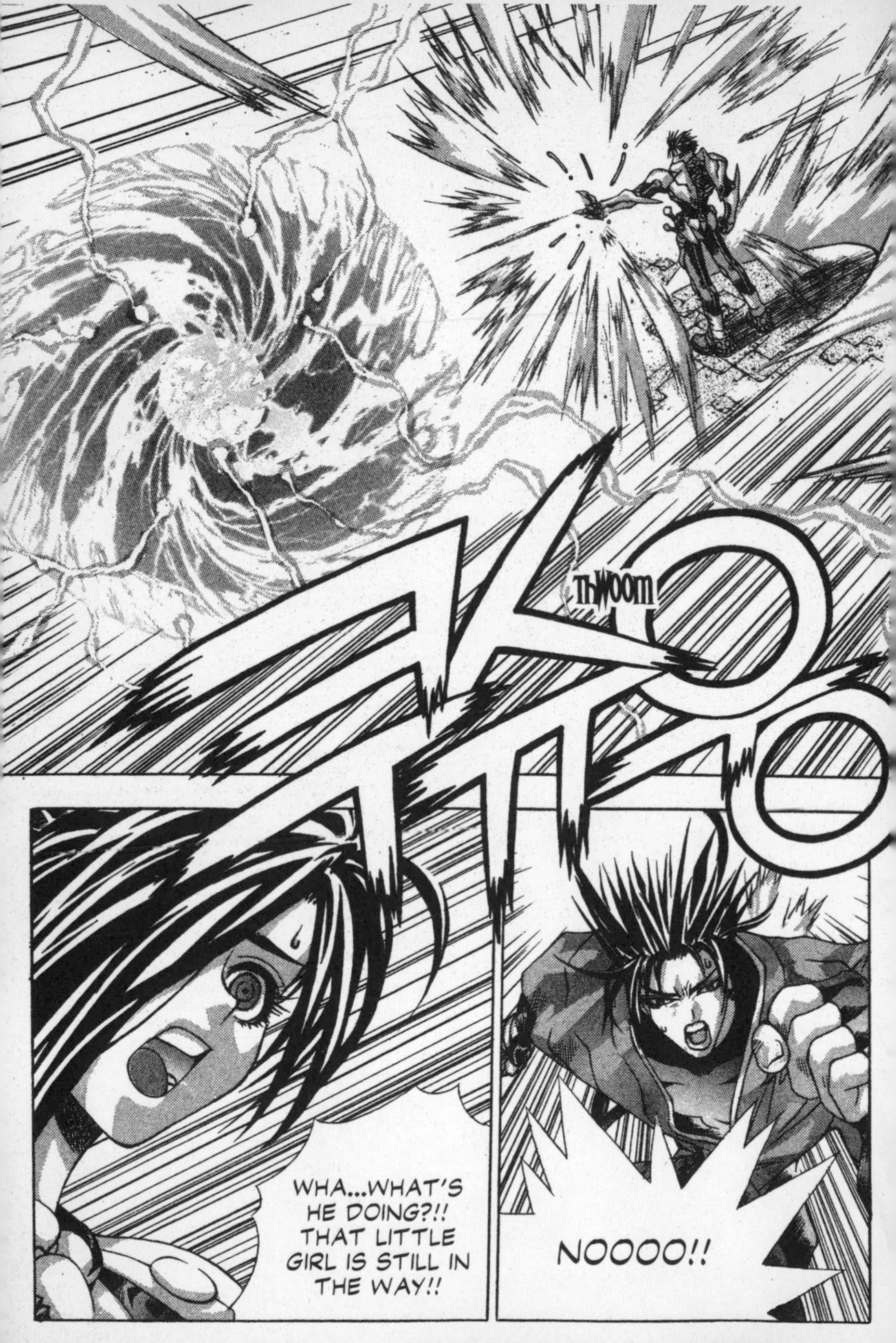
THWOOM
WHA...WHAT'S HE DOING?!! THAT LITTLE GIRL IS STILL IN THE WAY!!
NOOOO!!

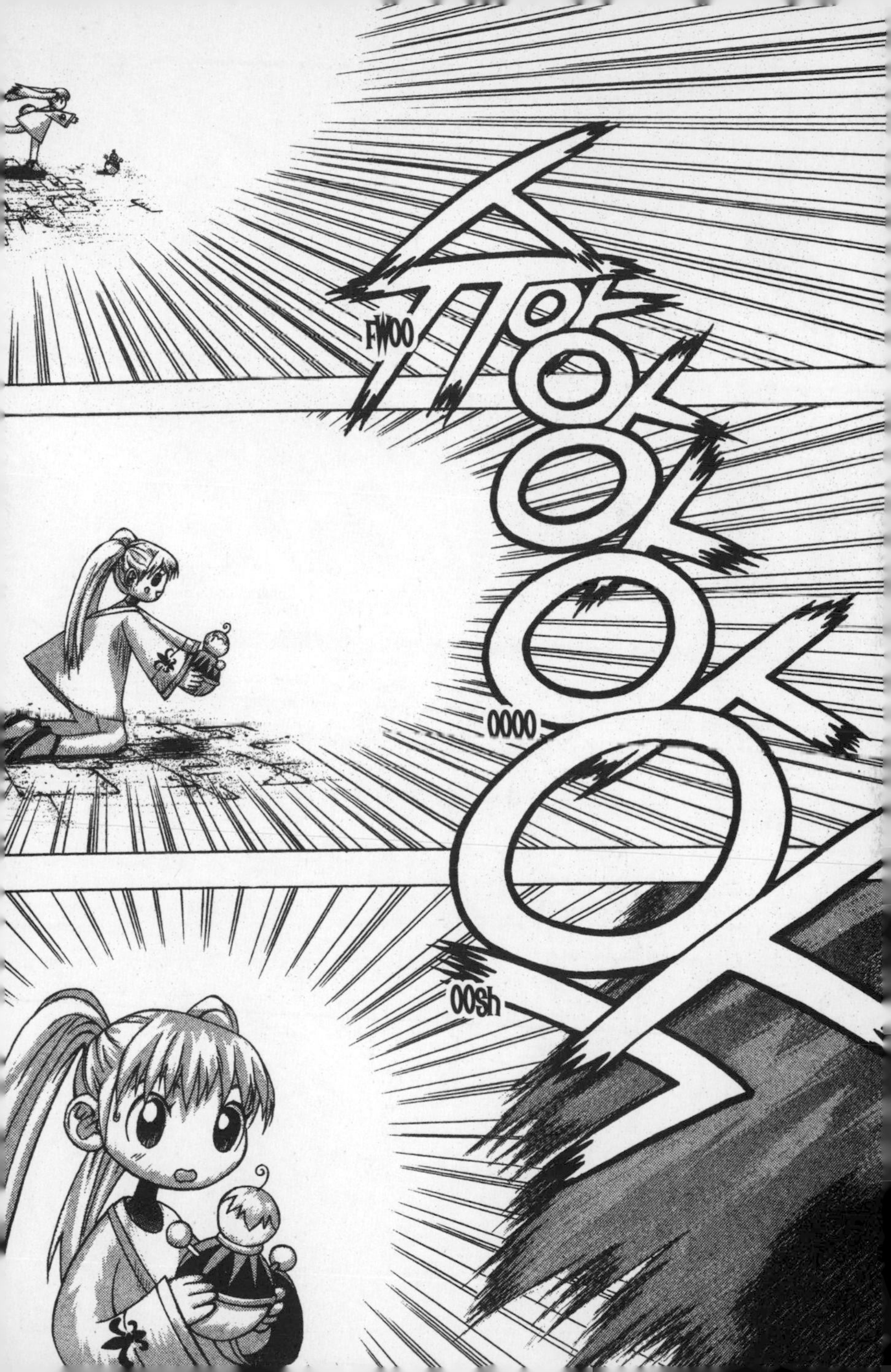
FWOO
OOOO
OOSH

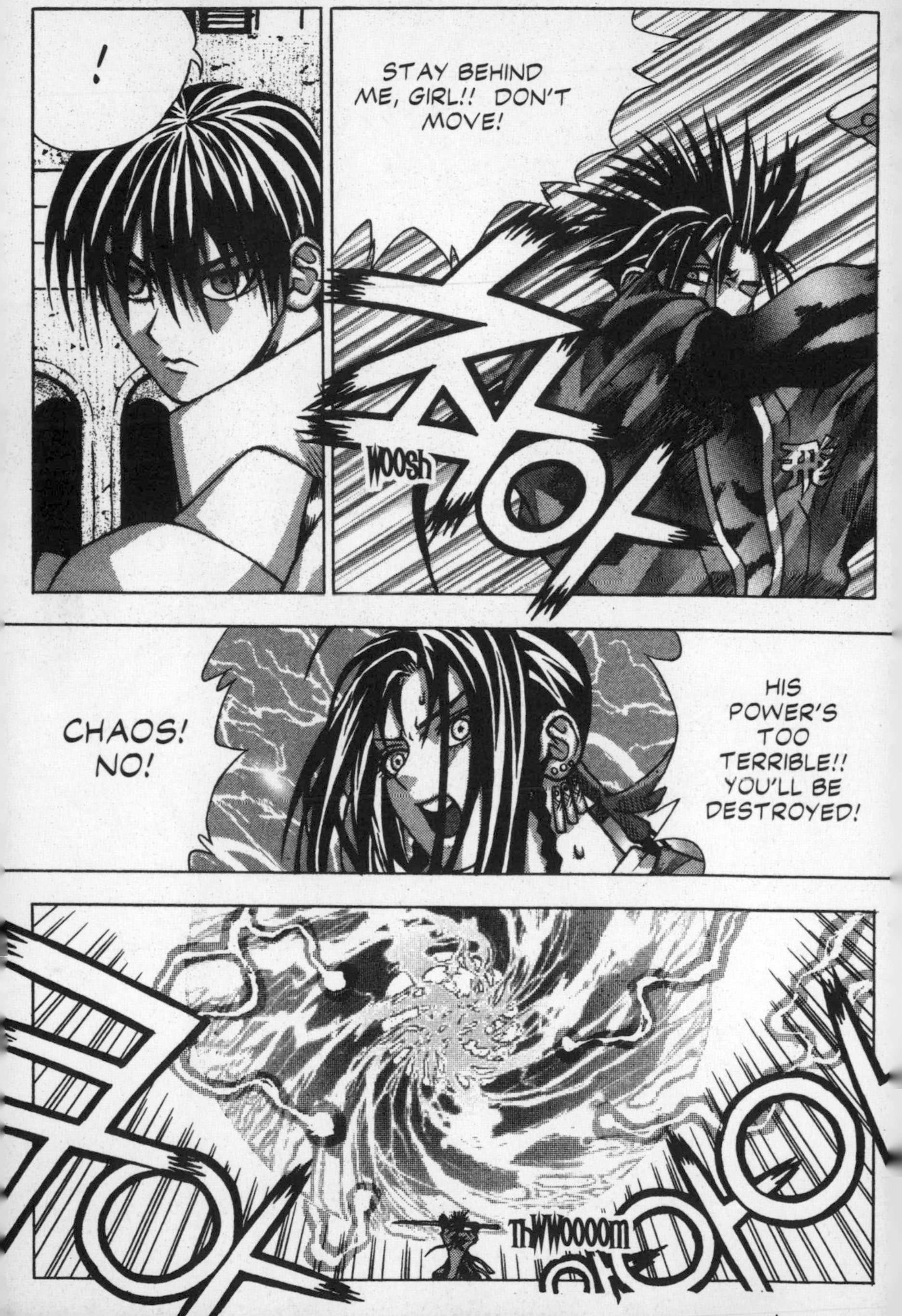
!
STAY BEHIND ME, GIRL!! DON'T MOVE!
WOOSH
CHAOS! NO!
HIS POWER'S TOO TERRIBLE!! YOU'LL BE DESTROYED!
ThWWOOOOm

The golden city of Prontera is under attack from Himmelmez, a Valkyrie and necromancer who commands the armies of Nilfheim. Her master, Freya, seeks the pieces of Ymir's heart, Midgard's lifeforce, in order to ensure that her reign will last another 1,000 years. Chaos and his companions enter Himmelmez's flying fortress to stop the Valkyrie, but they'll need the assistance of Loki if they hope to come out alive.

Chaos' quest takes a turn for the darker in *Ragnarok Volume 5: Twighlight of Terror*, coming January 2003.

By Myung-Jin Lee

MEET THE CREATOR OF RAGNAROK, MYUNG-JIN LEE!!

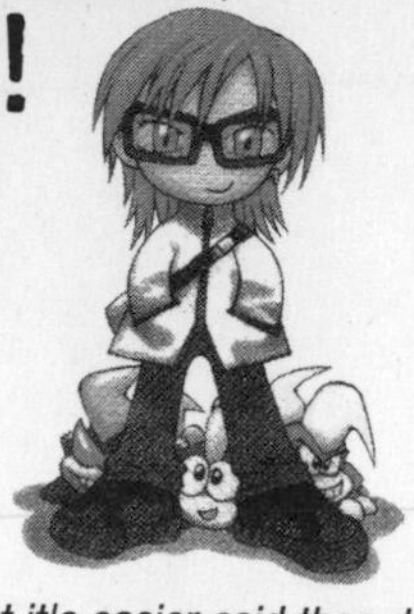

(interview originally appeared in *CHAMP Magazine*, where Ragnarok first ran in Korea).

CHAMP: Hello. How are you doing?
LEE: Fine, I'm doing well.

CHAMP: But your face is so pale, and your studio is chaotic.
LEE: Gasp...The truth is...I was working late last night.

CHAMP: As always, you're cutting it real close.
LEE: (With a guilty expression on his face) I try not to but it's easier said then done.

CHAMP: Relax. I'm not here because of the deadline. I'm here on behalf of "Go! Champ Reporter."
LEE: (Relieved expression) Ah, That's right.

CHAMP: First, let me ask you some questions from our *Ragnarok* readers. When did you first come up with this story?
LEE: Actually, from the very moment I started drawing manwhas, I was already conceptualizing Ragnarok. *It was probably when I was in Junior High. Although there was the project I ultimately wanted to work on. In a sense, although I met my readers for the first time through "I feel...night," Ragnarok was conceptualized first.*

CHAMP: I see. From what I understand, *Ragnarok* is an extremely long piece of work, exactly how long is it?
LEE: Just as you said, Ragnarok *is an extremely long piece of work. Currently, the time line for the series is almost 10 years, and it will encompass approximately 40-50 volumes. Of course, during the series there could be changes.*

CHAMP: Many of the readers complain that *Ragnarok* is too confusing and too difficult to understand, what is your take on that?
LEE: It's inevitable. Ragnarok *is a colossal story with many characters. Also, the story, currently being serialized, is 1000 years after the "war of the gods." Eventually, Chaos, our protagonist who was reincarnated with no memory of his previous life, will learn the secrets about his current self and his former life and the story of* Ragnarok *will unfold in it's entirety.*

CHAMP: Why didn't you make it simple for yourself and start the story from the "War of the Gods?" Then it would have been easier for the readers to understand, as well.
LEE: If I had started the story from the "war of the gods," Ragnarok would have been a predictable story. My hope is that the readers will bond with Chaos, our main character, and together discover the enormous secret and unexpected occurrences, and begin to comprehend the story little by little. This might sound grandiose but just like our future and fate is uncertain, amidst the questions within my manwha, I would like everyone to discover the facts slowly and understand it in little steps. With that in mind, I'm hoping the readers will say, as they read the manwha, "Ah, so that's what it was."...

CHAMP: I think you're asking for too much from our readers.

LEE: *(Laughing) Do you think so? Then I'll have to apologize.*

CHAMP: While we're on the topic, in order to facilitate our understanding of Ragnarok, please give us a succinct explanation of the entire work.

LEE: *Ragnarok is composed of 7 categories. 2, 3 and 4 are the main stories while 1, 5, 6 and 7 are the supplementary stories. Category 2 is about the war of the gods. Category 3 is the current "INTO THE ABYSS" sub-titled story, after the "war of the gods". In category 4, sub-titled "ESCAPE FROM THE ABYSS," a fierce battle will ensue heading toward an intense finale. The supplementary stories (1, 5, 6 and 7) will be comprised of stories about characters that were not developed in the main story, and a prequel to the main story.*

CHAMP: I see. Can you explain the meaning of the title Ragnarok, and the time and space of the setting?

LEE: *The term "Ragnarok" appears in Norse mythology and it means the "Ultimate war of the gods." In regards to the settings' time, since the concept is a mythological story, it's hard to pinpoint a time period. And the universe is divided into "Midgard" and "Asgard." 'Midgard' is where the mortals live, earth, this world. 'Asgard' is the world of the gods and it's a limitless world, thus it's not farfetched to assume they reside in space.*

CHAMP: How are the characters categorized, for example, in terms of good and evil?

LEE: *Gods, demons, giants, humans, dwarves, and new lifeforms of various kinds will be introduced. You mentioned the term good and evil, however, in mythology it's hard to distinguish between what is good and what is evil. What man sees as evil may be good to "others." Ragnarok is merely revealing to the readers, how man searches and finds his peace and freedom within the chaotic world of the gods.*

CHAMP: I see, that is what *Ragnarok* is trying to tell us.

LEE: *That's right. Through* Ragnarok, *it is revealed to the reader that a diminutive, weak and inconsistent race like man can be limitless, even more so than a race of gods. If the character Chaos, in* Ragnarok, *symbolizes freedom and chaos, then the goddess Freya symbolizes perfection and order, resulting in their antagonistic relationship.*

CHAMP: I think I understand but I'm not too sure.

LEE: *Honestly, although I'm the one talking it is somewhat difficult to explain. For a precise explanation, the readers will have to read* Ragnarok *and find out for themselves.*

CHAMP: Now let's change the subject and go on to a different question. What are some difficulties you have found in developing *Ragnarok*?

LEE: *I'm a little embarrassed to say this especially since* Ragnarok *is on a bi-weekly schedule but I most definitely need more help in production, this is where I find the most difficulty. It's especially so because of the longevity of the assistants (or lack thereof). I need assistance in writing the story, researching and especially drawing the scenery.*

CHAMP: There are many compliments as well as criticisms about *Ragnarok*, what are your thoughts on these?

LEE: I'm grateful for their comments. Whether it's compliments or criticisms, the mere fact that they are talking about my work is a reflection of their interest in it. I believe that you can't please everyone, and I'm merely writing for those readers who like my work.

CHAMP: Lastly, do you have a favorite motto and if so, what is it, and what would you like to tell the future manwha artists?

LEE: I'm a little embarrassed to say this, especially since I don't consider myself as a manwha-ka yet but this is something I've always liked saying, "Dreams come true!" It's a mere coincidence but it's also a title of a song. If you have a dream, pursue it and don't give up. Then someday it will become a reality. During difficult times, repeat to yourself" Dreams come true!"

CHAMP: Thank you for taking time away from your busy schedule to meet with us. Is there anything else you wish to tell our readers?

LEE: Readers! Thanks for all your interest in my work. Wishing all of you health and happiness.

ABOUT THE AUTHOR

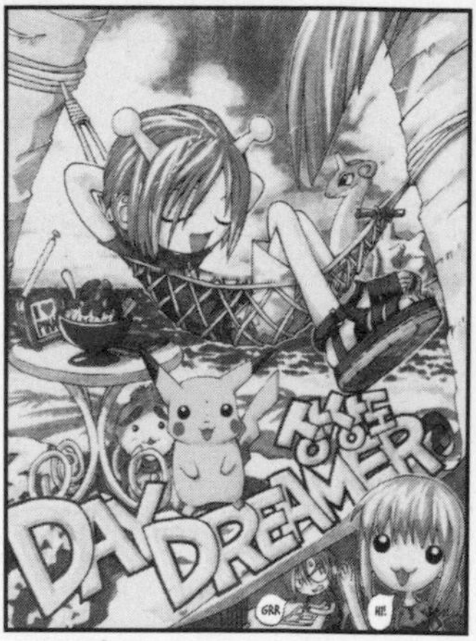
DAY DREAMER
GRR

* Born on 4-12-74
* Graduated from Northern Seoul Technical College in Yongsan Etaewon, Seoul. Majored in Visual Design.
* His manwha, *It's Going to be a Wonderful Night*, won distinction in the very first "Champ Super Manwha" contest in 1992.
* Work History:
  1) May 1992 - February 1995
  It's Going to be a Wonderful Night (9 vols)
  2) August 1995 - October 1997
  Served mandatory Korean military service
  3) January 1998-Present
  Ragnarok at Champ Comics
  4) *Genocide* (one volume manwha)

* LIKES: happiness, dreams, love, things that belong to me, things I can do at my own will, snow, eyes, wind, manwha, music, cats, laughter, tangerines, tomatoes (especially cherry tomatoes), faith, touch, freedom, thought, time (to spare),future

* DISLIKES: giving up, disappointments, betrayal, anything crooked (personality or otherwise), jealousy, bullies, mundane, simple things, indefiniteness, abuse, restrictions, thoughtlessness, uncertainty, all vermin starting with cockroaches, the concept of being a "salary-man".

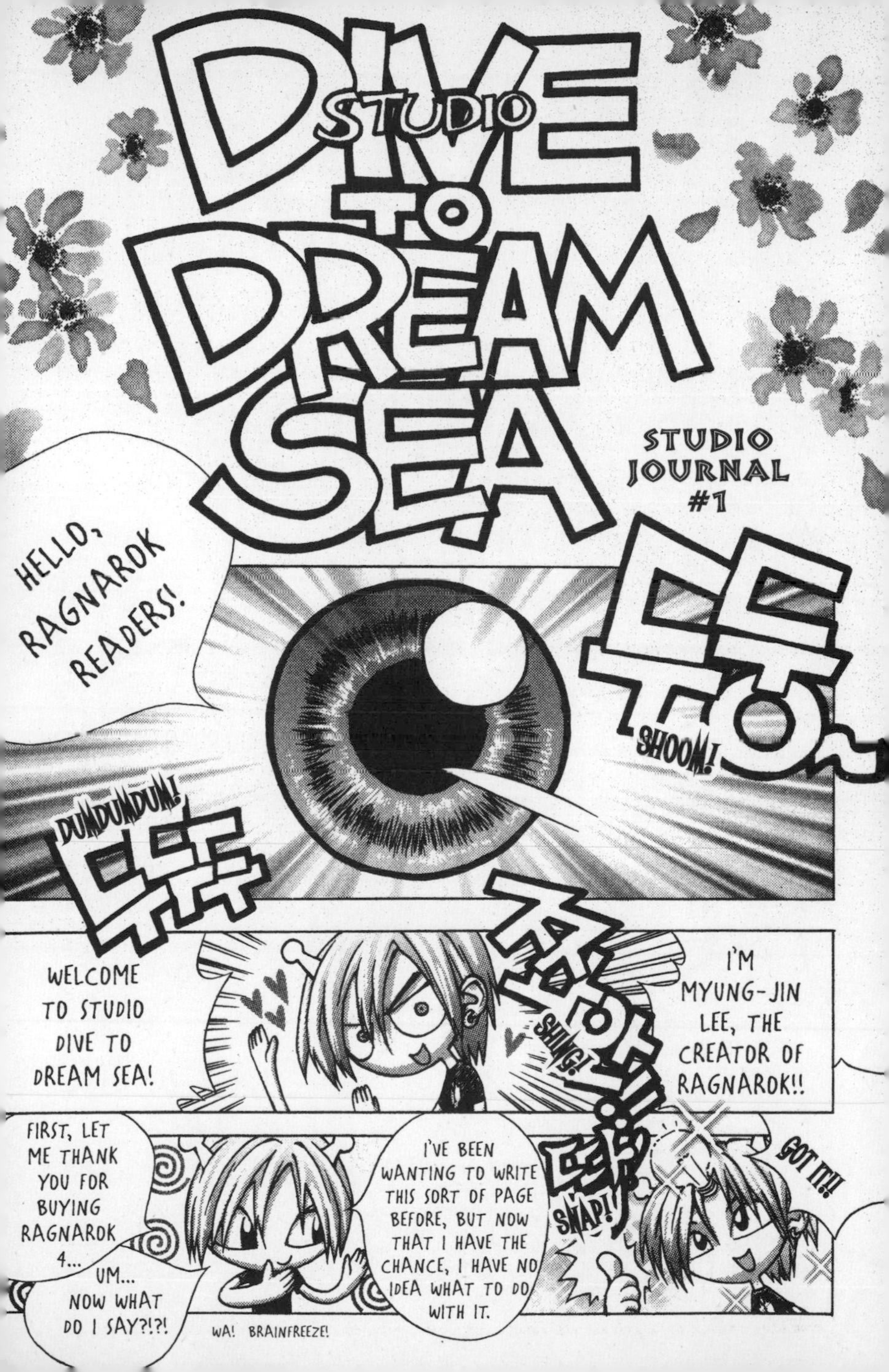

DIVE STUDIO TO DREAM SEA
STUDIO JOURNAL #1
HELLO, RAGNAROK READERS!
SHOOM!
DUMDUMDUM!
WELCOME TO STUDIO DIVE TO DREAM SEA!
SHING!
I'M MYUNG-JIN LEE, THE CREATOR OF RAGNAROK!!
FIRST, LET ME THANK YOU FOR BUYING RAGNAROK 4...
UM... NOW WHAT DO I SAY?!?!
WA! BRAINFREEZE!
I'VE BEEN WANTING TO WRITE THIS SORT OF PAGE BEFORE, BUT NOW THAT I HAVE THE CHANCE, I HAVE NO IDEA WHAT TO DO WITH IT.
SNAP!
GOT IT!!

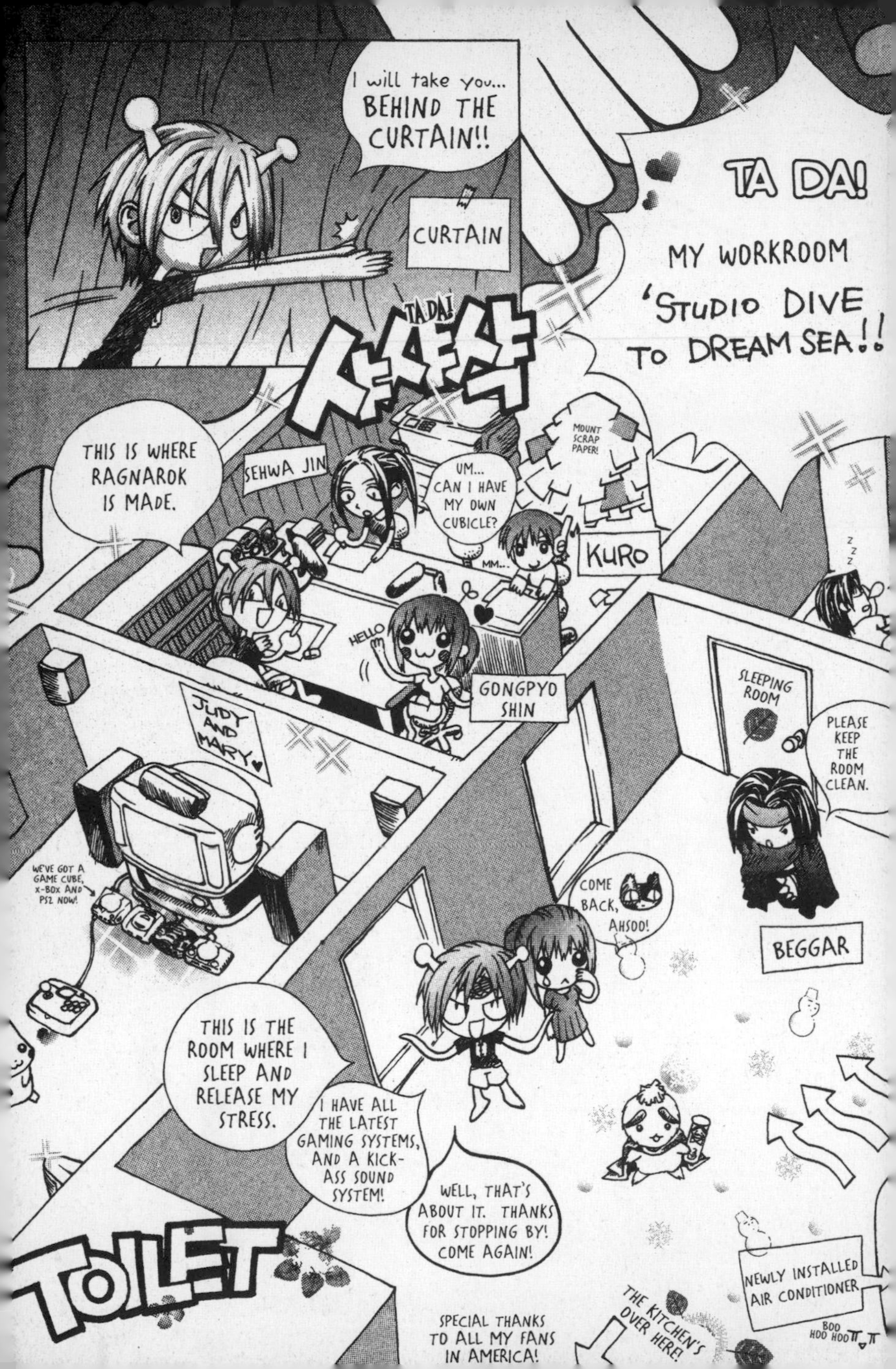
I will take you... BEHIND THE CURTAIN!!
CURTAIN
TA DA!
TA DA!
MY WORKROOM 'STUDIO DIVE TO DREAM SEA!!
THIS IS WHERE RAGNAROK IS MADE.
SEHWA JIN
UM... CAN I HAVE MY OWN CUBICLE?
MOUNT SCRAP PAPER!
KURO
MM...
ZZZ
HELLO
GONGPYO SHIN
JUDY AND MARY♥
SLEEPING ROOM
PLEASE KEEP THE ROOM CLEAN.
WE'VE GOT A GAME CUBE, X-BOX AND PS2 NOW!
COME BACK, AHSOO!
BEGGAR
THIS IS THE ROOM WHERE I SLEEP AND RELEASE MY STRESS.
I HAVE ALL THE LATEST GAMING SYSTEMS, AND A KICK-ASS SOUND SYSTEM!
WELL, THAT'S ABOUT IT. THANKS FOR STOPPING BY! COME AGAIN!
TOILET
NEWLY INSTALLED AIR CONDITIONER
THE KITCHEN'S OVER HERE!
SPECIAL THANKS TO ALL MY FANS IN AMERICA!
BOO HOO HOO